COUNSELING STRATEGIES AND INTERVENTIONS FOR PROFESSIONAL HELPERS

Ninth Edition

Sherry Cormier
West Virginia University

PEARSON

Boston   Columbus   Indianapolis   New York   San Francisco   Hoboken   Amsterdam
Cape Town   Dubai   London   Madrid   Milan   Munich   Paris   Montréal   Toronto
Delhi   Mexico City   São Paulo   Sydney   Hong Kong   Seoul   Singapore   Taipei   Tokyo

Vice President and Editorial Director:
  Jeffery W. Johnston
Vice President and Publisher: Kevin M. Davis
Editorial Assistant: Caitlin Griscom
Executive Field Marketing Manager: Krista Clark
Senior Product Marketing Manager:
  Christopher Barry
Project Manager: Lauren Carlson
Procurement Specialist: Deidra Skahill

Cover Designer: Studio Montage
Cover Art: Shutterstock/Oleksii Sagitov
Full-Service Project Management:
  Manvir Singh, Aptara®, Inc.
Composition: Aptara®, Inc.
Printer/Binder: LSC Communications, Inc.
Cover Printer: LSC Communications, Inc.
Text Font: ITC Garamond Std

Credits and acknowledgments for material borrowed from other sources and reproduced, with permission in this textbook appear on the appropriate page within the text.

Every effort has been made to provide accurate and current Internet information in this book. However, the Internet and information posted on it are constantly changing, so it is inevitable that some of the Internet addresses listed in this textbook will change.

Library of Congress Cataloging-in-Publication Data

Cormier, L. Sherilyn (Louise Sherilyn)
  Counseling strategies and interventions for professional helpers / Sherry Cormier,
    West Virginia University. — Ninth Edition
    pages cm.
  ISBN-13: 978-0-13-390522-9
  ISBN-10: 0-13-390522-5
  1. Counseling psychology—Textbooks.   I. Title.

BF636.6.C67 2014
158.3—dc23   2014029742

ISBN 10:   0-13-390522-5
ISBN 13: 978-0-13-390522-9

This book is lovingly dedicated to Sierra Elizabeth, Ian Jay, and Colin Frederick and to all those unnamed persons working to eradicate childhood famine around the globe.

ABOUT THE AUTHOR

Sherry Cormier is Professor Emerita of counseling, rehabilitation counseling, and counseling psychology at West Virginia University; a licensed psychologist in the state of West Virginia; and a long-standing member of the American Counseling Association. Her areas of expertise include counseling training, counseling skills and interventions, cognitive-behavioral therapy, clinical supervision, health and wellness, and grief and loss. Prior to her appointment at West Virginia University, she was a faculty member at the University of Tennessee.

BRIEF CONTENTS

CONTENTS

APPLICATION EXERCISES

PREFACE

Since the eighth edition of *Counseling Strategies and Interventions for Professional Helpers,* the helping professions have continued to expand and evolve. In writing the ninth edition, I have kept several well-grounded features from the previous editions. First, I have tried to blend comprehensiveness and conciseness. Second, the book has been written with upper-class undergraduates or beginning-level graduate students in mind in a variety of helping disciplines. Third, I have included a variety of learning exercises, called Application Exercises, to help students apply and review what they have learned. Fourth, the new edition includes a variety of recently published sources to present the most current information available to my readers.

For the first eight editions of this book, I have had the privilege and honor of collaborating with my major professor and mentor, Dr. Harold Hackney, known by Dick Hackney to most of us. Dick and I have worked together on several projects for a number of years. Dick has decided to pursue more leisure activities at this point in his life. I have missed his delightful presence and skilled writing in this edition and yet I feel grateful to be able to continue to build on his work.

NEW TO THIS EDITION

An overall goal in this new edition is the expansion of the section on basic helping skills. The ninth edition has three chapters that describe the sequence of basic helping skills, which includes attending skills (Chapter 4), listening skills (Chapter 5), and action skills (Chapter 6). Chapter 4 is an expanded version of the chapter in earlier editions, and Chapters 5 and 6 are new chapters for this edition. Also new to this edition is Chapter 10, "Considerations and Challenges for Beginning Helpers." This chapter was authored by Beth Robinson, PhD, Assistant Professor in the Master's of Education Counselling Program, at the School of Education, Acadia University, Wolfville, Nova Scotia.

A perusal of new content infused throughout the chapters includes the following topics:

- Counseling in military settings (Chapter 1)
- International multiculturalism (Chapter 1)
- Positive regard and the acceptance therapies (Chapter 2)
- Communication with lesbian, gay, bisexual, transgender, and questioning (LGBTQ) clients (Chapter 3)
- Communication with immigrant and refugee clients (Chapter 3)
- Verbal and nonverbal attending skills, Verbal following of cognitive and affective messages (Chapter 4)
- Paraphrase, reflection of feeling, summarization (Chapter 5)
- Open-ended and closed questions, reflection of meaning, and challenging responses (Chapter 6)
- Updates to informed consent, confidentiality, and privacy (Chapter 7)
- Assessment of key components of client issues (Chapter 8)
- SMART goals (Chapter 8)
- Mindfulness interventions (Chapter 9)
- Helping strategies for oppressed clients (Chapter 9)

• Family genograms (Chapter 9)
• The imposter phenomenon (Chapter 10)
• Professional development (Chapter 10)
• New and additional cases and application exercises focusing on ethical issues and cultural issues

In addition, at the end of each of the ten chapters are activities from MyCounselingLab, the online destination designed to help students make the transition from academic coursework to professional practice. This online content consists of video clips of authentic practitioner/client sessions with some well-known clinicians and of interviews with distinguished professionals in the field. Students can access MyCounselingLab by purchasing this directly from the website or by registering with the access code purchased with the text at: http://www.pearsonmylabandmastering.com/northamerica/mycounselinglab/students/.

OVERVIEW OF THE BOOK

Chapter 1 identifies the context of the helping professions—who the helping professional is; what kinds of activities he or she performs; and the qualities and skills of helpers, such as cultural competence, resilience, and mindfulness. In addition, Chapter 1 describes issues related to professionalism, such as identity, training, and credentialing of professional helpers. The context of helping includes a wide variety of roles and functions. It might even seem to the untrained eye that the differences among helpers are greater than the similarities. I attempt to dispel that impression in Chapter 2, which discusses the helping relationship. This helping relationship proves to be the unifying force for disparate roles and functions.

Although the helping relationship connotes a sense of shared purpose, there is an added expectation for the helper—the expectation that he or she be both responsible and responsive in exploring the client's needs and concerns. Chapters 3 through 9 identify the skills and interventions expected of a beginning professional helper. Some of these skills are rudimentary; others are more advanced and require coaching and practice. Chapter 3 defines the helper's responsibility to be aware of and attentive to the client's communication patterns, including patterns among diverse clients, and the usefulness of silence. Chapters 4, 5, and 6 describe the basic helping skills. These include attending skills (Chapter 4), listening skills (Chapter 5), and action skills (Chapter 6). These skills, which were introduced in the 1970s and have been refined since, are the building blocks by which helpers of all disciplines conduct helping sessions with clients. Chapter 7, which deals with session management, includes strategies for opening and terminating helping interviews as well as managing subsequent interviews. I also discuss ethical issues affecting initial sessions, such as confidentiality, informed consent, and privacy, and I also describe ethical and pragmatic issues in terminating the helping relationship.

Chapter 8 is a pivotal point in the book. It builds on the fundamentals of the early chapters and is the foundation for the remaining chapters of the book. Although the helper is instrumental in conceptualizing issues (usually with the assistance of a particular theoretical orientation), the goal-setting process inherently depends on mutual discussion and agreement between helper and client. Drawing on mutually accepted goals, the helper begins the most crucial portion of the relationship: the focus on overt change. This calls for more than relationship skills and more than active listening. Many helping interventions—derived both from theory and practice and supported by research—are synonymous with effective helping practices. Chapters 8 and 9 explain and suggest classroom activities that will help the helper understand and begin practicing these interventions. Chapter 9 offers a variety of different helping strategies that are integrative in focus and purpose and that reflect a host of theoretical orientations to helping, ranging from experiential and interpersonal to cognitive and behavioral; these theoretical orientation also include individual, systemic, and collective approaches.

Finally, Chapter 10 includes several areas pertinent to beginning helpers such as common concerns; preparing for ethical challenges such as confidentiality, informed consent, privacy, and multiple relationships; clinical supervision; and many aspects of professional development including professional identity, networking, professional affiliations, and discussion of self-care for helpers. This is a new chapter for this edition and was authored by Beth Robinson, PhD, Assistant Professor in the Master's of Education in Counselling at the School of Education, Acadia University, Wolfville, Nova Scotia.

INSTRUCTOR SUPPLEMENTS

This edition offers a revised online Instructor's Manual/Test Bank, authored by Melissa Brown, a graduate of the Master's of Education in Counselling program, Acadia University. The instructor's manual contains test questions, chapter summaries, recommended readings, and additional classroom and homework activities. To download the Instructor's Manual, go to the Pearson Instructor Resource Center at http://www.pearsonhighered.com/educator.

ACKNOWLEDGMENTS

I am grateful to a number of people who have helped make this ninth edition possible. I am most fortunate to have had the benefit of the wisdom and publishing acumen of my editor Kevin Davis. And without a doubt, the work of his team, consisting of Janelle Criner, Caitlin Griscom, Carrie Mollette, and Lauren Carlson, made my job so much easier, I gratefully acknowledge the reviewers of the manuscript for their insights and comments: I also am indebted to Dr. Beth Robinson for writing a new chapter for this edition that is full of instructive guidance for beginning helpers. And I greatly appreciate the work of Melissa Brown, who authored our Instructor's Manual.

Sherry Cormier

The Helping Professions

A woman goes into a beauty salon, and as she is getting her hair cut, she whispers to her hairdresser something about her marriage disintegrating.

A man goes into a sports bar and while watching a game, says something to the bartender about losing his job.

A couple seeks the counsel of a rabbi about the declining health of his and her elderly parents.

A child confides in a school counselor about the big bruise that shows up on his leg.

A young adult refers herself to a community mental health center because she thought about killing herself after disclosing to her parents that she is a lesbian. At the center, she is seen by a social worker and a case manager.

An older man seeks the services of a psychologist for sexual dysfunction issues following prostate surgery.

A person who has been hospitalized following an accident in which his back was broken decides to talk with a rehabilitation counselor.

It could be argued that helping occurs in all the above examples. Certainly, the woman whose hair is being cut probably feels helped by her hairdresser in much the same way that the man feels helped by telling the bartender about his job loss. And the couple that seeks the wisdom of a rabbi would not be doing so without some sort of implicit trust and respect for this person. The clients who are seen respectively by a counselor, social worker, case manager, psychologist, and so on, are also both seeking and, in all likelihood, receiving help. Yet there are differences—hopefully, positive ones. The hairdresser and the bartender—despite possibly providing help—would be referred to as nonprofessional helpers, whereas the rabbi, social worker, case manager, psychologist, and counselor would be called professional helpers. And even among these kinds of professional helpers, there are differences; the helping profession includes a broadly knit collection of professionals, each fitting a particular need or segment of society. Some are directly identified as helping professionals, such as psychiatrists, psychologists, professional helpers, marriage and family therapists, and social workers. Others are professionals from other disciplines who enter the helping network on a temporary basis. Most notable among these are ministers, physicians, nurses, and teachers.

Professional helpers can be distinguished from nonprofessional helpers by their identification with a professional organization, their use of an ethical code and standards of practice, and their acknowledgment of an accrediting body that governs training, credentialing, and licensing of practice (Gale & Austin, 2003, p. 3). These are important ways in which a professional helper develops a sense of professional identity. *Professional identity* is defined as the identity assumed by a practitioner of a particular discipline; it is reflected in the title, role, and intention of the profession and results from a cohesive decision of the members of the profession (Myers, Sweeney, & White, 2002; Moss, Gibson, & Dollarhide, 2014). As noted, one way that helping professionals achieve a sense of professional identity is by membership in a professional organization. As Vacc and Loesch (2000) point out, there are a number of relevant professional organizations for helping professionals, such as the American Counseling Association (ACA) for helpers, the American Psychological Association (APA) for psychologists, Canadian Association of Social Workers (CASW), Canadian Counselling and Psychotherapy Association (CCPA), Canadian Psychological Association (CPA), the National Association of Social Workers (NASW) for social workers, and the National Organization for Human Services (NOHS) for human service professionals. (See Appendix A for a list of websites for these and other organizations.)

Finally, professional helpers distinguish themselves from nonprofessional helpers by their sense of vocation and mission—the public promise (the meaning of the word *profess*) to act for the good of the public (Ponton & Duba, 2009, p. 117). Part of this mission involves affirming the public trust for the role and services offered by professional helpers. One of the ways that this public trust is upheld is through accountability: making sure that professionals deliver services and programs to clientele that are valuable, useful, affordable, and effective. Helping professions are increasingly ascertaining levels of accountability through what is known as evidence-based practice (EBP) and action research, both of which are methods for assessing effectiveness of individual and group counseling as well as programmatic efforts (Baker, 2012).

In this chapter, we examine the many facets of the helping professions. We also explore what constitutes differences among laypersons, such as the beautician who may help in the context of the job and professional helpers whose job is defined primarily by the focus of the helping process. Although our focus in this text is on counseling, we use the term *professional helpers* and other interchangeable terms, such as *practitioners* and *clinicians,* to emphasize that counseling occurs in many helping disciplines, even though the characteristics of each discipline may be different. We also focus on professional helpers because the counseling profession now specifically targets collaborative practice among various helping disciplines as a best practice strategy to address interrelated social issues with clients and the systems in which they live and work (Mellin, Hunt, & Nichols, 2011).

WHAT IS HELPING?

The process of helping has several dimensions, each of which contributes to the definition of *helping*. One dimension specifies the conditions under which helping occurs. Another dimension specifies the preconditions that lead one person to seek help and another to provide help. A third dimension relates to the results of the interaction between these two persons.

Helping Conditions

The conditions under which helping occurs are quite complex, but in their simplest terms, they may be described as involving four components: (1) someone seeking help and (2) someone willing to give help who is (3) capable of or trained to help (4) in a setting that permits help to be given and received. The first of these conditions is obvious; one cannot help without the presence of someone seeking help. If I do not want to be helped, nothing you can do will be helpful. If I am not sure I want to be helped, then perhaps you will be helpful, provided you can enjoin me to make a commitment to accept help. The second condition requires the willingness or intention to be helpful. Here, it would be good to differentiate between the intention to be helpful and the need to be helpful. Many would-be helpers are driven by the need to be helpful and use the helping relationship for their own needs. This is rarely a conscious act. Neediness has a way of camouflaging itself in more respectable attire. But when the relationship is dictated by the helper's needs, the possibilities for helping are minimal. The third condition reflects the helper's skills, either learned or natural. It is not enough to be well intentioned if your awareness and behaviors drive people away. Indeed, the primary purpose of pursuing training in the field of helping is to develop, expand, and refine your therapeutic skills. The fourth condition refers to the physical surroundings in which the helper and client meet. Privacy, comfort, aesthetic character of the room, and timing of the encounter all contribute to the setting in which helping transpires.

All four conditions occur within a cultural and environmental context in which individual clients may present with a variety of concerns and individual differences, including dimensions such as race, ethnicity, socioeconomic level, gender, religious and spiritual affiliation, ability status, sexual orientation, age, developmental stage of life, and so on. Naturally, such differences affect the help-giving and help-receiving processes in various ways. For example, some clients' cultural affiliations greatly affect even the decision to seek or not to seek help from a helping professional. Instead, they may turn to family or tribal elders, religious and spiritual advisors, or close family confidants for guidance. Cultural variables also affect the setting in which help giving occurs. For some clients, the idea of going to see a helper in a professional office is too foreign to consider as a viable option. These clients may prefer a more informal and less structured setting. Also, even your best intentions to be helpful are influenced by your own cultural affiliations and may affect the degree to which some clients perceive you as able and qualified to help. If you do not understand your clients' expressions, the subtle nuances of their communication patterns, their cultural values, or their culturally related views of their problems, your best intentions may not be enough.

What Do Professional Helpers Do?

Having discussed the process of helping, we now turn our attention to what professional helpers actually do. Perhaps this is best illustrated by a story such as the following:

> Irina came to see Sherry because, she said, "Even though I am 50 years old, I don't think for myself, and I have trouble making any decision." Earlier in her life, Irina had once seen a professional helper with her now ex-husband. Initially, Sherry educated Irina about the helping process and specifically about issues related to privacy and confidentiality. This educational process was followed by an exploration process in which Irina told her story while Sherry created a safe therapeutic environment for self-disclosure and listened carefully. At different times, Sherry gently probed to move Irina's narrative along, to obtain historical information about Irina's life, and to explore Irina's cultural background. As Irina continued to tell her story, with Sherry's help, it became clearer what Irina wanted from the helping process. She wanted to develop greater reliance on herself so she could trust herself and her decision-making process. Sherry helped Irina develop this goal for change more specifically and then initiated several intervention strategies for Irina to use in working toward this desired outcome, including problem-solving training, cultural genogram work, modeling, and role-playing and behavioral rehearsal (see Chapter 9 for descriptions of these strategies). As the sessions continued, Sherry helped Irina expand her story to include a newer version of herself—someone she saw as competent, confident, and capable. As Irina moved toward this point, Sherry helped her explore her readiness to terminate the helping process and continue the gains begun in counseling on her own.

As you read over this sample case, note how it generally illustrates the kinds of things that professional helpers do with clients:

- They help clients identify and explore life concerns and issues.
- They help clients identify and pursue culturally relevant expectations, wishes, or goals.
- They help clients identify, assess, and implement culturally relevant strategies for change.
- They help clients identify and assess results and plan for self-directed change in the client's own environment.

Professional helpers are trained in the general functions we just described of creating a helping relationship—communication, conceptualization, assessment, and intervention. In addition, some professionals—such as counselors, social workers, and psychologists—provide more specialized services based on their training and work setting. For example, some practitioners may work specifically with minority clients, whereas others may work primarily with children or adolescents or the elderly. Others may focus on couples and family systems or adults or even adults with particular kinds of issues, such as anxiety or depression or career counseling. Some clinicians may work primarily in group modalities; others may work in crisis intervention. And depending on the setting, professional helpers may focus on prevention, remediation, change, and/or life enhancement. Professional helpers use both theory and research to support best practices for working most effectively with particular kinds of clients in particular kinds of settings. Although differences exist within and between settings in which helping professionals work, they all honor the following principles:

- Professional helping involves responding to feelings, thoughts, actions, and social systems of clients.
- Professional helping is based on a stance or frame that involves a basic acceptance of clients.

- Professional helping is characterized by confidentiality and privacy.
- Professional helping is noncoercive.
- Professional helping focuses on the needs and disclosures of the client rather than the counselor.
- A skill underlying effective helping is communication.
- Professional helping is a multicultural experience (Hackney & Cormier, 2013, p. 5).

SETTINGS IN WHICH HELPERS WORK

As we mentioned at the beginning of this chapter, there are a variety of trained persons and specializations in the helping professions. It is estimated that in the years 2010 to 2020, the employment outlook for professional helpers is especially strong as emerging settings and needs continue to grow. Helpers in various disciplines are forging new paths all the time. Some helpers are working with persons with trauma; some are helping veterans; many others are working with older populations; and still others are working with residential youth schools and programs, parenting programs, and sports settings. The following discussion of representative settings and the services that helpers working in them provide will offer some sense of the helping spectrum.

School Settings

School counselors are found in elementary, middle or junior high, and high schools. Elementary school counselors do provide some individual counseling with children, but they are more likely to work with the total school environment. Much of the elementary school counselor's focus is on preventive and developmental guidance programs and activities, such as classroom guidance units, small-group counseling, and parent-teacher conferences (Baker, 2000). Middle school and junior high school counselors share this total school perspective but tend to spend more time with students—individually and in groups—and somewhat less time with teachers and parents. This slight shift in focus reflects the developmental changes that occur with preteens, who find themselves involved in self-exploration and identity crises. Two common programs in middle schools include peer facilitation and teacher-as-advisor programs (Vacc & Loesch, 2000). Counseling in the high school reflects a noticeable shift to the students as individuals. Career and college planning, interpersonal concerns, family matters, substance use, and personal identity issues tend to dominate the students' awareness, and the counseling process attempts to provide an environment in which to address these issues. The counselor's day is therefore much more task-oriented. Some students are referred by teachers, but many are self-referrals. The high school counselor often works with student groups on career and college issues, although counseling focuses on all types of secondary students, not just those who are college-bound. Secondary school counselors also engage in much consultation with teachers and administrators (Vacc & Loesch, 2000).

Regardless of the level of a school, school counselors work collaboratively with students, parents, teachers, administrators, and the community. Recent developments in school counseling focus on the use of school counseling programs that facilitate student achievement as well as student development. To help answer the question "How are students different as a result of what school helpers do?" the American School Counselor Association (ASCA; 2012) has developed the *ASCA National Model: A Framework for School Counseling Programs*. This document describes the competencies students obtain as a result of participating in school counseling programs and also defines both appropriate and inappropriate functions of school counselors. For example, ASCA recommends a school counselor to student ratio of 1:250 and also specifies that school counselors spend 80 percent or more of their time in direct and indirect services to students. It also describes the mission statement of school counselors as supporting all facets of the educational environment in three domains: personal/social, academic, and career development. (For more on this model, see schoolcounselor.org.) This national model highlights the dramatic transformation of school counseling in the last decade. While individual counseling, small-group work, and classroom guidance are still components of school counseling programs, the new initiatives in school counseling stress the importance of consultation and collaboration between school counselors and teachers, parents, and administrators, with the goal of promoting effective broad systemic change that offers access to opportunities and better achievement for all students (Clark & Breman, 2009, p. 7). A recent meta-analysis of school counseling interventions found some support for positive effects of certain school counseling interventions on students at the elementary, middle, and high school levels (Whiston, Tai, Rahardja, & Eder, 2011). At the same time, however, effectiveness data on students from diverse backgrounds are more limited (Whiston et al., 2011).

What will your future look like if you want to be a school counselor? First, you will need to be able and equipped to focus on the issues of the school as a system, in addition to the issues of individual students. An emerging role for school helpers is that of advocacy. This focus on systemic change and advocacy is central to the ASCA national model that we previously identified. This might mean speaking "with teachers who intentionally or unintentionally discriminate against students in marginalized or devalued groups or challenging administrators to address various forms of institutionalized educational inequities" (Bemak & Chung, 2008, p. 375). Or it might simply mean advocating for your roles and skills to be used effectively within your school setting because other school personnel or stakeholders may not be aware of what you do and how you are trained (Gysbers & Henderson, 2012; Shallcross, 2013c). Second, although responsive services to individuals will probably never "go out of style," there will be an increasing emphasis on developing programs that focus on prevention. In recent years, both advocacy and prevention programs have been targeted for school violence and bullying, including physical bullying, verbal bullying, cyberbullying, social aggression, and relational aggression because these forms of bullying are reaching epidemic proportions, often resulting in social isolation, depression, early suicides, and long-term effects into adulthood. (Shallcross, 2013a). Third, you will be heavily involved in the facilitation of groups, teams, or communities and on the achievement and educational needs of all students, making sure that minority students are as well served as other students (Colbert, Vernon-Jones, & Pransky, 2006). One new facet of this endeavor involves helping students and schools in 45 states as well as the District of Columbia meet what is called Common Core State Standards, which is what students are expected to learn to prepare them for college and future careers (see corestandards.org). Ways in which school counselors may be involved in helping to implement Common Core State Standards are described by perusing the following website: counseling.org/docs/resources. Fourth, there will be increasing emphasis on accountability in schools because both teachers and principals are now being evaluated on an annual basis to determine how well they are meeting student learning objectives (SLOs). School counselors are also demonstrating accountability through their use of the ASCA evidence-based counseling implementation plan, which delineates goals and collects data on how well the school counseling program meets the objectives in the three areas described by the ASCA model: personal/social, academic, and career development.

Higher Education Settings

Although much college counseling occurs in counseling centers or psychological services centers, some helpers in higher education settings also work in offices related to student affairs, such as residence halls, career services, academic advising, and so on. A wide variety of problems are addressed, including career counseling, personal adjustment counseling, crisis counseling, and substance abuse counseling. College counselors also see students with mild to severe pathological problems, such as anxiety, depression, suicidal gestures, eating disorders, and trauma. Boyd and colleagues (2003) observed that the recent past has seen a huge increase in the number of college counseling services and in the functions they provide. Emerging issues in college settings include financial issues, immigration status concerns, date rape, and domestic and relationship violence as well as physical and relational bullying and cyberbullying.

In addition to individual counseling, much reliance is placed on group counseling and on the needs of special student populations and student retention. For example, most college counseling centers have a special focus and staff person to engage in counseling-related services for students with disabilities. Also, many college campuses now employ counselors to work with students with substance abuse issues and also to provide wellness-oriented programs to students. Rollins (2005) described three special populations that are increasing on college campuses in the 21st century: domestic minorities and multiracial students, international students, and third-culture kids (TCK). Students who belong to these groups may be more reluctant than others to seek the services of a college counselor.

What does the future look like for you should you decide to become a college counselor? The answer to this is as diverse as the potential roles and functions that exist for college counselors. First, you will be heavily involved in working with students representing special populations. This work involves outreach programming and consultation with other student offices, such as the disability office, the international students office, and the multicultural affairs office, as well as with the residence halls. Second, you can expect to see clients who arrive on campus with more severe psychological issues. Some of these students may already be on psychotropic medications to manage conditions such as depression, anxiety, eating disorders, substance abuse, and even chronic mental illness. Unfortunately, some students who are severely distressed may be less likely to walk through the counseling center's doors (Faqrrell, 2005). In addition to reaching these students through psychological education, support groups, and outreach programming, you can also expect to become involved in technology because college counseling centers are adding online counseling resources to more traditional in-office services (Faqrrell, 2005). An excellent example of a recent technological advance in college counseling (as cited by Kennedy, 2004) is the *Career CyberGuide* offered by York University in Toronto, Canada (available online at yorku.ca/careers/cyberguide). As technological services grow, so do issues surrounding confidentiality and privacy. An ethical intention checklist surrounding online counseling services is available from Shaw and Shaw (2006). Also, in addition to providing psychological counseling, you may be very involved in wellness programming, which is designed to help college students reach their full potential on a number of levels, including physical, emotional, social, and spiritual.

Community Settings

Helpers working in community settings usually are social workers, mental health helpers, and other human service professionals, such as case managers, mental health aides, crisis intervention helpers, marriage and family practitioners, and community outreach workers.

Their places of employment are the most diverse of all helping settings. Family service agencies, youth service bureaus, satellite mental health centers, YWCA counseling services, homeless shelters, and substance abuse centers are examples of community settings. Much of what is done is psychotherapy, whether with individuals, couples, families, or groups. In addition, the community practitioner may become involved in community advocacy efforts and direct community intervention. The types of problems seen by community practitioners encompass the spectrum of mental health issues. Clients include children, adolescents, adults, couples, families, and the elderly. In other words, community-based helpers see an enormous variety of clients and problems in a typical month. The work demands are often heavy, with caseloads ranging from 20 to 40 clients per week.

Currently, mental health helpers are concerned with the delivery and implementation of services that are therapeutic, cost-effective, and evidence-based, and that reflect developmental notions as much as remediation. Couples and family practitioners as well as addiction specialists also offer services through a variety of community agencies.

What can you expect should you choose to work as a practitioner in some sort of a community setting? One issue you will have to grapple with is the effects of managed health care, created by the reimbursement system of third-party payees of health insurance. You may engage in brief and short-term counseling in these settings because managed care usually only covers the cost of a certain number of counseling sessions a year. You will also probably be required to provide a fair amount of written documentation and accountability, often in the form of client treatment plans to "justify" the sessions for a given client with a particular diagnosis. In conjunction with this activity, you can be expected to collect data to show that you are using best or evidence-based practices in your setting. Overall, you may be challenged to do more work with fewer available resources. Although at times this can be a test of your patience and resilience, working in a community setting provides the satisfaction of knowing that you are giving something back to the community in which you live.

Religious Settings

Vacc and Loesch (2000) note that "an interesting mixture of professions is evident in the growing number of clerics (e.g., rabbis, priests, ministers, sisters) who have completed counselor-in-preparation programs" (p. 344). Despite many similarities, helping in religious settings is different in some ways from that in other settings. The similarities include the range of individual and family problems seen, the types and quality of therapy provided, and the helpers' professional qualifications. The differences reflect the reasons that some religious groups establish their own counseling services. There is at least some acknowledgment of the role of religion or spirituality in the individual's life problems. Many religious helpers believe that human problems must be examined and changes introduced within a context of spiritual and religious beliefs and values. The religious counseling center is undeniably attractive for many clients who, because of their backgrounds, place greater trust in the helper who works within a religious affiliation. According to Vacc and Loesch (2000), the three major counseling activities engaged in by clerics are bereavement counseling, marriage and family counseling, and referrals to other professionals.

Helpers in religious settings are often ordained ministers who have obtained postgraduate training in counseling. However, increasing numbers of the laity are also entering religious counseling settings or are receiving training in pastoral counseling and working in nonreligious settings, such as private practice, hospitals, and hospices. The number of academic programs granting degrees in pastoral counseling has increased substantially in recent years, as has the number of helpers who integrate a faith-based worldview with their academic training and subsequent licensure. This is important because regulation and oversight of unlicensed religious helpers involve substantial ethical and legal issues.

What can you anticipate if you decide to work in a religious setting or offer faith-based counseling? You may end up seeing well-known people who prefer to deal with issues or lapses in judgment by seeing someone in a religious setting. You also may work with people who cannot afford counseling services in other kinds of settings. You will also probably see clients who want to incorporate their faith heritage, spiritual beliefs, or spiritual modalities such as prayer in the counseling sessions. You may also work fairly often with people in crisis, so brushing up on your crisis intervention skills is a good idea.

Industrial and Employment Settings

Many professionals consider the private sector to be the new frontier for helping services. Such services occur primarily in the form of employee assistance programs (EAPs) that are administered either within the employment setting or through a private contract with a counseling agency. These programs are occurring with increasing frequency in business, industry, governmental units, hospitals, and schools. Many EAPs focus on the treatment of substance abuse issues, whereas others have expanded services to include individual, couple, and family concerns. To make the workplace a psychologically healthy environment, EAPs also deal with counterproductive workplace behaviors and stress management issues. Some research has found a connection between work stress and infectious disease (Hewlett, 2001). An example of a counterproductive workplace behavior that you may see in employment settings has to do with workplace bullying or mistreatment such as verbal abuse or harassment, offensive conduct, or threatening or intimidating workplace sabotage. Because much of workplace bullying is insidious and often subtle, employers often do not have explicit policies to prevent or respond to such behaviors, and the employee takes his or her concerns to the clinician in the form of individual counseling.

Another type of counseling service that has appeared in industry settings is the outplacement counseling service. Outplacement refers to the process of facilitating the transition from employment to unemployment or from employment in one corporation to employment in another. The need for outplacement counseling has increased as corporations downsize their operations to cut costs or to address new goals and objectives. The client may be a top executive, middle manager, line supervisor, or laborer. Counseling takes the form of career counseling and includes the administration of career and personality inventories. The objectives for management clients are to provide data and counseling that will help employees assess their career options and develop plans for obtaining new positions as well as to support clients through that transition period. The objectives for employees who may be affected by plant closings are to identify career alternatives and to assist the company in designing retraining programs that will help unemployed workers obtain new jobs. The outplacement clinician has often worked in an industry setting and understands the characteristics of this clientele from firsthand experience. Practitioners in employment settings also focus on career issues and the interaction between the individuals and their work roles (Power & Rothausen, 2003).

What can you expect should you choose to work in industrial and employment settings? As job-related stress increases due to downsizing and outsourcing, you will see more clients who take advantage of employer-assisted counseling plans. Some clients may turn to substances such as prescription drugs and alcohol to self-medicate the anxiety and stress resulting from increased job demands. Having an excellent toolkit of substance abuse intervention skills is important. Also, as job stress increases, so too will the need and demand for employee wellness programs. Workplace violence and the prevention of it is also a focus area for helpers who serve in these settings.

Health Care and Rehabilitation Settings

An increasing number of practitioners are finding employment in health care settings such as hospitals, hospices, vocational rehabilitation centers, departments of behavioral medicine, rehabilitation clinics, and so on. Responsibilities of helpers in these settings are diverse and include tasks such as providing counseling to patients and/or patients' families; crisis management; grief work with the terminally ill; and the implementation of psychological and educational interventions for patients with chronic illnesses, people with physical challenges, and so on. More addictions specialists are also working in health care settings. Wellness programs are also increasing in these settings. It is believed that the number of helpers in health care and rehabilitation settings will continue to rise with increasing human services needs and advances in medicine. For example, the need for rehabilitation helpers now exceeds the supply by over 25 percent across the United States.

Your future as a helper in health care settings is constantly being defined and redefined. Generally, in these settings, you need a repertoire of skills to work effectively with both individuals and families and both illness and wellness. You are also likely to be functioning in a health care delivery setting that integrates both physical and behavioral/mental functioning because the two are so interrelated. You may become involved in teaching patients responsibility for medication compliance and pain management. And you will probably be heavily invested in prevention. For example, helpers currently provide informational and psycho-educational programs to patients whose disease processes are from unhealthy lifestyle factors, but the future looks more and more promising for the implementation of programs to prevent disease processes in the first place by teaching patients effective self-care—proper nutrition, exercise, and reduction of negative thoughts and feelings. An increasing number of health care settings are employing practitioners as health coaches to prevent illness and promote wellness. In recent years, there has been a proliferation of self-employed, independent health coaches marketing services designed to promote the potential and well-being of clients in a number of dimensions including mind, body, and spirit.

Military Settings

Counseling now is much more readily available for members of the armed services and for their families as well. Many military settings, both in the United States and on bases in other countries, employ both military and civilian counselors to deal with issues such as anxiety, depression, substance use, stress, and anger management, all through the lens of the military culture. Because of a dramatic increase in both suicide attempts and suicide completions by members of the armed forces, there is both a preventive and remedial focus on suicide prevention and response. Because suicide is associated with alcohol use for both former and current U.S. military personnel, a great deal of counseling in military settings also involves substance use, abuse, and addictions counseling. With cases of post-traumatic stress disorder (PTSD) at an all-time high, counseling services are available in both inpatient and outpatient settings for veterans who may return from combat with PTSD symptoms In addition, veterans can also obtain both vocational and educational counseling.

Practitioners in military settings work with families, including the armed service member, his or her spouse, and the children, concerning issues related to marriage, partnership, communication, and stress resulting from multiple deployments and absences by the armed service member. Counseling is available for families before a service member deploys, during the deployment, and after the deployment as well. This counseling may include family counseling, couples counseling, and child counseling. Researchers have identified military and veteran families as at risk for experiencing various forms of stress and distress (Walinski & Kirschner, 2013). Such distress is experienced not only for the military member and his or her spouse but also for the children in the military family.

What does your future look like if you are involved with military clients? Myers (2013) argues that to be an effective helper with military clients, you must be trustworthy, credible, and able to serve as an effective advocate. He maintains that this may involve linking these clients to other community resources or communicating with their other providers such as health care practitioners. And while you may be hired by a particular setting, such as a Veterans Administration (VA) hospital to work with the military, you also may work with military clients in private practice or other community settings. To build a private practice base of military clients, Myers (2013) recommends connecting with the local chapter of the Wounded Warrior Project and enrolling with your state's TRICARE panel (TRICARE is the insurance plan for the U.S. Department of Defense). Regardless of your setting, when your clientele involve military clients, you can expect to deal with a wide range of individual and family issues, including stress, communication, parenting, substance use, depression, loss, anger, and post-traumatic stress.

APPLICATION EXERCISE 1.1

Work Settings and Job Functions

Think about a helping setting that interests you. Interview a person employed as a helper in this setting. Explore the job responsibilities, types of clients served, unique aspects of the setting, and joys and frustrations of the helper. Your instructor may have you either present to your class an oral summary about your visit or write a summary of your interview. In writing this summary, note whether your findings about this setting are consistent with your expectations. Explain either way.

HELPER QUALITIES AND SKILLS

We have described seven settings in which helping and counseling occur. Of course, there are many others, including couples and family therapy, correctional institution counseling, geriatric counseling, and even sports counseling. In all these settings—and with the variety of presenting issues that are seen—there is a common core of characteristics and skills of effective helpers. Over the years, a number of writers have described this core. Qualities such as self-awareness and understanding, open-mindedness and flexibility, objectivity, trustworthiness, interpersonal sensitivity and emotional intelligence, curiosity, and caring are supported by the literature. We concur with all these. We also believe that these are general enough characteristics and skills that you can deduce what they mean on your own and decide if they describe you or not. In this section of the chapter, we want to focus on four qualities that are not as transparent in meaning and implication as the ones just mentioned but, in our opinion, have tremendous importance for practitioners in the 21st century: virtue, cultural competence, neural integration and mindful awareness, and resiliency.

Virtue

A simple definition of *virtue* has to do with goodness (Kleist & Bitter, 2014). Virtue addresses the character traits of the individual helper and asks the question "What kind of person are you?" (Kleist & Bitter, 2014). Aristotle spoke about virtue as a way of being in the world or a basic disposition toward the world. For example, are you a person who is kind? Are you someone with integrity? Part of being a virtuous helper involves the capacity to put the well-being of your clients at the top of your list of priorities. To do so, helpers in all fields are guided by various codes of ethical behavior (American Association for Marriage and Family Therapy, 2012; American Counseling Association, 2014b; American Psychological Association, 2010; Canadian Association of Social Workers, 1994; Canadian Counselling and Psychotherapy Association, 2007; Canadian Psychological Association, 2007; National Association of Social Workers, 2008; National Organization for Human Services, 2000). A major guiding principle of these ethical codes is the recognition of the importance of being committed to the client's well-being. We think virtue is important today because much of our world seems to be morally compromised and fractured. Ethical codes of conduct do not just convey information; they also help inform a particular way of being in the world. Sullivan (2004)—who has designed an undergraduate mentorship for developing wise and effective habits of character—describes ethics as a particular worldview that incorporates virtue and aspiration. This ethical model assists us in learning to discern what helps persons and communities flourish and what does not (p. 69). For example, when it comes to choosing between the well-being of your client and your own pocketbook, how do you make this decision by using the ethical codes to guide you? What kind of character underlies this decision? What kind of "self" are you bringing to the ethical decisions you will inevitably need to make about clients? Some of you undoubtedly are reading this text while holding views that may label you as leaning toward the political left, while other readers hold views characterized as leaning toward the political right. Despite differing views and values, both liberals and conservatives can share the characteristic of virtue. You may hold opposing views on politics or religion yet share something virtuous about your way of being in the world and the goodness that you bring to the ethical decisions you make about your clients. Virtue is also an important foundational quality in being a culturally competent helper.

Cultural Competence

Helping professionals are seeing an increasingly diverse group of clients. It is expected that such increasing diversity will continue in the 21st century and beyond. As the dimensions of client diversity expand, the competence of helpers to deal with complex cultural issues must also grow. As Robinson (1997) points out, diversity and multiculturalism are not synonymous. *Diversity* describes clients who are different across dimensions such as age, gender, race, religion, ethnicity, sexual orientation, health status, social class, country of origin, geographic region, and so on. *Multiculturalism* involves an awareness and understanding of the principles of power and privilege. Power and privilege can be defined in many ways, but we especially like the definitions that Lott (2002, p. 101) has offered: *Power* is "access to resources" and *privilege* is "unearned advantage" and, thereby, "dominance." As you can see from these definitions, power and privilege are linked together in important ways. Those who have unearned privilege often use or abuse their power to dominate and subordinate (or oppress) those who do not have privilege and power. Multiculturalism is "willingly sharing power with those who have less power" and using "unearned privilege to empower others" (Robinson, 1997, p. 6). People who hold unearned privilege and power often seek to maintain their power by labeling, judging, and discriminating against those who do not. This discrimination usually occurs on the basis of various dimensions of diversity, such as race, social class, religion, age, gender, sexual orientation, health status, and so on. Those who are discriminated against on the basis of these dimensions not only feel excluded and disempowered but they also have, in reality, fewer resources. For example, people living in poverty have less access to employment, decent housing, health care, pay and benefits, and even resources such as technology. Privilege can also occur with respect to countries as well as to individuals. Lowman (2013) argues that advanced "Northern" countries are largely privileged compared to non-Western "Southern" countries, meaning that Western countries are more likely to have laws and policies in place to respond to issues of oppression and discrimination even though individuals within Western countries still, of course, often suffer from oppression and discrimination.

Another unfortunate result of power and privilege is the possibility that someone could have a professional commitment to diversity without a corresponding commitment to multiculturalism. As an example, consider the client who comes to see you after a particularly volatile staff meeting at her worksite. Her colleagues are primarily White men, with the exception of one African-American woman. Your client reports that during the meeting, one of the men (not the boss) publicly shamed her female colleague in front of the group for a particular way that this woman had handled a situation. Your client has also been publicly criticized by this same man. The man who has done this also publicly professes a strong commitment to diversity, yet his behavior suggests he has no commitment to multiculturalism. Similarly, a clinician may be committed to multiculturalism but not committed to or knowledgeable about internationalism. Consider the case of an immigrant and his spouse who have moved here from another country and put their first-born child in the public school setting. After several months, the school counselor was contacted by the child's teacher because of the child's disruptive behavior in the classroom. The school counselor initiates a meeting with the parents and suggests some cognitive-behavioral parenting strategies to implement at home with the child. The parents rejected the counselor's suggestions at the outset and said that they preferred to seek the advice of a physician who is also a member of their native country and could better understand their family and their religious beliefs. In this case, the counselor may have had some understanding of multicultural issues but clearly did not understand the international issues posed by the non-American clients.

In 1992, Sue, Arredondo, and McDavis developed a set of multicultural competencies that focused on attitudes, knowledge, and skill areas for the development of culturally sensitive practitioners. These competencies were updated in a 2002 guidebook (Roysircar, Arredondo, Fuertes, Ponterotto, Coleman, Israel, & Toporek, 2002) and more recently summarized by Arredondo and Perez (2006). There are many other ideas of what it means to be a culturally competent helper. The most recent literature on this subject expands multiculturalism to include internationalism. Because we live in a global world, essentially without borders, what happens in one country affects what goes on in the remainder of the world in so many arenas: health care, finance, psychological-emotional issues, politics, and so on. Lowman (2013) argues that "current challenges of multiculturalism are not confined to any one country or region . . . [D]iscrimination on the basis of nonchosen human characteristic (e.g., race, age, sexual orientation, gender) is a near-universal societal phenomenon" (p. 8). Lowman (2013) further asserts that international multiculturalism involves an approach that suggests attention both to what is happening within one's own culture and also across the context of at least two or more countries. A practitioner must be skilled to work with international clients within one's own country, such as immigrants, as well as with international clients residing in a different country. Both Hurley and Gerstein (2013) and Wedding (2013) have described competencies for multicultural and international fluency for mental health professionals. These represent particular competencies designed to help practitioners provide culturally appropriate services to clients whose primary country of identification differs from that of the practitioner.

Despite all of the recent discussion about diversity and multiculturalism, there is still no universal agreement about what constitutes cultural competence (Sanchez-Hucles & Jones, 2005). However, there is general agreement that counseling/clinical competence is not the same as multicultural counseling competence (Sue & Sue, 2013). From the perspective of these authors, many helping professionals "have difficulty functioning in a culturally competent manner" (p. 39).

How do helpers develop cultural competence and skills? The answers to this question are not always simple, and developing cultural competence does not happen overnight. Indeed, it is most likely a lifelong process. However, we can make the following recommendations:

- Become aware of your own cultural heritage and affiliations and of the impact that your culture has on the counseling relationship. Remember that culture affects both you and your clients. No one—regardless of race or ethnicity or country of origin—is devoid of culture.
- Become immersed in the cultures of people who differ from you (Sue & Sue, 2013). Seek opportunities to interact with people who represent different cultural dimensions, and be open to what they have to say. Create opportunities rather than waiting for them to come to you. Hansen and colleagues (2006) suggest seizing opportunities such as getting culture-specific case consultation and learning about indigenous resources (p. 72). Wedding (2013) recommends "doing homework" to gain information about other countries as well as your own (p. 297).
- Be realistic and honest about your own range of experiences as well as issues of power, privilege, and poverty. Become aware of the great impact of poverty. Think about the positions you have or hold that contribute to oppression, power, and privilege. In the United States or European countries, being White, able-bodied, young, intelligent, male, Christian, heterosexual, middle or upper class, and English-speaking all convey aspects of privilege. Individuals who do not share these privileged attributes are disempowered in significant ways, and the inequities between privileged and nonprivileged persons contribute to much injustice and oppression, *especially when privilege is ignored by those who hold it* (Crethar, Rivera, & Nash, 2008).
- Remember that, as a helper, you, not your clients, are responsible for educating yourself about various dimensions of culture. For example, if you feel uninformed about the background and cultural and religious heritage of your new client who is Muslim and you ask your client to inform you, this essentially constitutes a role reversal, and the client is likely to feel frustrated. A similar misuse of culture would be to tell your Latino client about your new Latino and/or Latina friends. A facet of cultural competence that emerges consistently from the literature is how important it is for helpers to demonstrate an interest in a client's culture and to seek out opportunities to educate yourself about cultures and countries different from your own. At the same

time, being a false know-it-all and pretending to have all the knowledge and answers about a client's varying dimensions of culture is also misguided.

• Become aware of your own biases and prejudices, of which racism is the most problematic (although not the only *-ism* that affects practice). Remember that racism is not restricted to overt behaviors but also includes everyday opinions, attitudes, and ideologies (Casas, 2005, p. 502). Recent literature has attested to covert racism in the form of what is known as racial microaggressions (Sue et al., 2007). Racial microaggressions are more insidious forms of racism, often committed by a well-intentioned person but still deeply wounding, that are subtle insults (whether verbal, nonverbal, and/or visual) that communicate denigrating messages to people of color (Sue, 2010). Data indicate that higher frequencies of racial microggressions are associated with depression and poorer mental health for clients of color (Nadal et al., 2014).

As an example of a microaggression, consider the way that language is used. Watts-Jones (2004) points out the power conveyed by words and phrases such as "black sheep," "black mark," "white lie," and "Indian giver" and suggests that from a social justice perspective, practitioners need to pause and query when such language is used in the counseling room. Too often, we do not recognize such language, let alone challenge it. For example, in working with persons with disabilities, the use of first-person language is empowering. Group designations such as "the disabled" or "the blind" are inappropriate because they do not convey respect and equality. First-person language such as "persons with disabilities" or "individuals with visual impairments" is preferred (Daughtry, Abels, & Gibson, 2009, p. 204).

All helpers need to be aware of potential racist origins and implications of their actions and also to be sensitive to potential racist origins and implications of the actions of colleagues. Saying to a client of color "you are so light-skinned that you really don't look Black" or telling a client of color not to worry about getting racially profiled because "it happens to a lot of people all the time" are examples of very wounding racial microaggressions that drive clients away from the helping process. Sue (2010) has recently written a groundbreaking book—suitable for both helpers and clients on the insidious effects of microaggressions—that is based on 5 years of research he and his students have conducted. We list this book in the Recommended Readings at the end of the chapter, and we consider it to be essential reading for all helping professionals because many microaggressions are committed by people like you and me—well-meaning, well-intended, decent folks who lapse into states of unawareness that produce various categories of microaggressions that are devastating to the recipients of such slurs, insults, or invalidations.

• It is the responsibility of the helper, not the client, to get issues related to culture "out on the counseling table," so to speak. This responsibility has been defined by Day-Vines et al. (2007) as *broaching*—that is, the helper's "ability to consider the relationship of racial and cultural factors to the client's presenting problem, especially because these issues might otherwise remain unexamined during the counseling process" (p. 401). Broaching is important because the acknowledgment of cultural factors enhances the credibility of the helper, establishes trust, fosters greater client satisfaction, and influences the clients' decisions about returning for further sessions. Broaching behaviors essentially refer "to a consistent and ongoing attitude of openness with a genuine commitment by the counselor to continually invite the client to explore issues of diversity" (Day-Vines et al., 2007, p. 402). An example of a broaching behavior would be for the practitioner to say at the beginning of an initial counseling session something like the following: "I notice that we are from different ethnic backgrounds. I am wondering how you are feeling about working with someone like me who is a White European American woman . . ." (Day-Vines et al., 2007, p. 402).

In recent years, all major professional organizations for helping professionals have offered descriptions of various multicultural competencies required for helpers. (These are usually available from the organization's website, many of which we list in Appendix A.) We strongly encourage you to familiarize yourself with these competencies and to identify areas in which you need to develop greater awareness, sensitivity, and proficiency.

Neural Integration and Mindful Awareness

Earlier, we said that virtue was important in the development of cultural effectiveness. It is also likely that the development of cultural competence is affected by the therapist's own level of neural integration. *Neural integration,* although complicated as a process, can be simply stated as describing what occurs when separate parts of the brain (hence the word *neural*) are connected together into a functional whole (hence the word *integration*; Siegel, 2007). What does the counselor's level of neural integration have to do with being an effective helper? The recently emerging field of interpersonal neurobiology (Siegel, 1999, 2010) asserts that neural integration allows clinicians to enter a state of mind in which their ability to think clearly and maintain an emotional connection with clients is enhanced. When helpers do not have it "together," their capacity to think clearly during counseling and develop effective connections with clients is diminished. Siegel and Hartzell (2003) made the following analogies: having neural integration is like taking as the "high road" and not having it is like taking the "low road" (p. 154). When taking the "high road," neurally integrated practitioners are able to process information with clients that involves rational and reflective thought processes, mindfulness, and self-awareness. These neural processes occur in the prefrontal cortex of the brain, located in the front part of the brain behind the forehead. When the opposite occurs—taking the "low road," or being in a nonintegrated brain state—helpers are governed more by emotions, impulsive reactions, and rigid rather than thoughtful responses to clients. In this nonintegrated state, the prefrontal cortex shuts down and disconnects from other parts of the brain that need its signals to function well.

Why is it so important for helping professionals to be neurally integrated? We now know from a decade or so of brain research that neural integration aids practitioners in developing empathy as well as having reflective conversations with clients that help them process information and regulate emotions. The helper's own level of neural integration helps to foster new neural connections in the brains of clients, a process referred to as neural or brain plasticity. It is now believed that neural plasticity may be the path by which psychotherapy alters the brain (Siegel, 2010).

At this point, perhaps you are thinking, "How in the world can I integrate myself 'neurally'? What is the process? What does it mean? How does it happen?" One major way that neural integration occurs for helpers is through mindful awareness. Siegel (2006) stated that mindful awareness invokes receptivity to what arises within the mind's eye on a moment-to-moment basis. In other words, being mindful is simply paying attention to what is happening as it is happening. It is being aware of what we are doing *while* we are doing it. This morning, when I watered the outdoor plants, I caught myself doing it mindlessly—on automatic pilot, so to speak—until I noticed a hummingbird and a beautiful coral-colored zinnia popping its head up through the yellow black-eyed Susan patch. Immediately, I became mindful (or aware) and stopped to notice and to appreciate. One way to develop mindful awareness is through a daily practice of some form of meditation. Meditation involves the focusing of our nonjudgmental attention on our own internal states—intentions, thoughts, feelings, and bodily functions (Siegel, 2006, p. 15). Although meditation comes in many forms, in its most elemental form, meditation simply means becoming still and quiet for a period of time, in which you sit with yourself and focus on a mantra (such as "I am peaceful") or on your breath.

Two noted clinicians—Marsha Linehan and Carl Thoresen—have provided some tips for cultivating mindfulness (Reiser, 2008; Harris, 2009):

- Cultivate the practice of mindfulness on a daily basis. One way to do so is to take mindful breaks during the day. For example, set a timer or use a clock that chimes on the quarter hour. Each time the timer goes off or the clock chimes, stop, turn your attention to your breath, and observe your in-breath and out-breath for three cycles (more if feeling stressed). You can even install a bell of mindfulness on your computer; download it at mindfulnessdc.org/mindfulclock.html.
- Develop one or more of what Thoresen (in Harris, 2009) refers to as the "mindfulness-based spiritual practices," which include the following:
  - *Passage meditation:* Use a memorized passage or prayer from any religious or spiritual tradition and repeat it silently—once daily, preferably in the morning—to set a positive intention for the day.
  - *Mantra meditation:* Use a mantra or sacred word or phrase from any tradition you prefer—basically, a word or phrase that is meaningful to you, such as *peace* or *love*.
  - *Slowing down:* Make conscious efforts to slow down your pace of daily life; drive more slowly, eat more slowly, type on the computer more slowly, talk more slowly.
  - *One-pointed attention:* Become more focused on one thing and less preoccupied with trying to cram everything you can do into a short period of time. One-pointed attention is the opposite of multitasking, which is extremely stress-inducing.
  - *Train the senses:* With the acceleration of technology, we are bombarded with an onslaught of nonstop sensory information. Designate a time during the day in which you turn off the cell phone, the landline phone, the computer, and so on.

Research has discovered that having clinicians who meditated prior to counseling sessions resulted in better treatment outcomes for clients (Grepmair et al., 2007). Mediation also promotes integration of various parts of the brain that are associated with a secure and safe attachment relationship between helper and client. This in turn helps to promote resiliency in clients and helpers.

Resiliency

As important as resiliency is for clients, it is equally important for practitioners. *Resiliency* is defined as the capacity to bounce back from challenges or adversity. Resiliency is derived from the emerging strengths perspective. Always a cornerstone of human services and social work practice, this perspective is also becoming stronger in both psychology and counseling. The strengths perspective also has important implications for virtue and cultural competence. Smith (2006) noted that the *strengths-based perspective* is important because "it represents a dramatic paradigm shift" from focusing on pathology to developing assets (p. 16). She asserts that a strengths perspective seeks to understand human virtue and to answer the question of what strengths a person has used and continues to use to deal effectively with life. As you can see, this issue affects both clients and helpers alike. Smith (2006) also observed the connection between a strengths perspective and cultural competence, noting that "a core component of the strength-based theory is that culture has a major impact on how people view and evaluate human strengths" (p. 17).

Why do a strengths perspective and resiliency matter for helpers? Today, helpers are expected to do more with less and to cope with different global challenges such as terrorism and natural disasters as well as everyday stressors and hassles. As clinicians share their sense of hope and optimism with clients, this perspective begins to be transferred to clients and informs the helping relationship (Smith, 2006, p. 42). How do we as helpers hold up during the stressful work that we do while offering support and help to our clients? The answers to this question come from the strengths-based perspective and the resiliency literature, which has found that resiliency is most closely related to both self-efficacy and positive emotions (Lee, Nam, Kim, Kim, Lee, & Lee, 2013). Resiliency means that helpers are able to:

- Use an active, positive, proactive approach to challenges and issues.
- Perceive pain and frustration constructively, seeing a glass as half full rather than half empty.
- Make decisions based on their own strengths of character, such as virtue, integrity, and courage.
- Identify and use the protective factors present in their own cultural and ethnic group as well as their environment (Smith, 2006).

In general, clinicians develop resiliency by replenishing the well that gets drained in doing therapeutic work with clients (Wicks, 2007). This is accomplished by acute care and sensitivity to one's own ongoing reflective process, such as daily journaling, and by strengthening one's own self-care protocol with tools such as exercise, solitude, and mindfulness.

An interesting extension of the resiliency literature is provided by Osborn (2004), who describes helper resiliency as stamina—the endurance and capacity to withstand or hold up under challenging conditions. Osborn gave seven suggestions for both off-the-job and on-the-job activities as well as ways of thinking to enhance our resilience and stamina. Based on the acronym of STAMINA (selectivity, temporal sensitivity, accountability, measurement and management, inquisitiveness, negotiation, acknowledgment of agency), these ways of being in the world and with our work are setting limits, honoring the rhythms and cycles of time, respecting our ethical standards and employing virtue to make ethical decisions, conserving and protecting our resources, looking for the uniqueness of our clients, engaging in a give and take, and attending to the life force within ourselves. Note that this last skill in particular involves neural integration; when we are in a state of mindful awareness, we engage our energy and our life force in a way that flows and plays. On especially stressful days, can you imagine yourself dancing into your work setting?

APPLICATION EXERCISE 1.2

Skills of Helpers

Observe the day-to-day work of helping professionals or even the helper you observed for Application Exercise 1.1. What do you conclude about their skills? Were you aware of particular personal qualities that stood out for you? What did you notice about the way they interacted with other people in their work setting? Did anything about the interventions they used seem especially useful? From your observations, could you draw any conclusions about their cultural competence and commitment to social justice? What kinds of diverse clients do they serve? How many clients do they see from other countries? Did you obtain any information that would provide you with conclusions about their virtue? How did they promote the well-being of their clients? What challenges did they face in their work? Did they appear to be resilient in the face of such challenges or not? In their interactions with others, did they seem mindful and centered or were they frazzled and responding rigidly and/or emotionally?

TRAINING AND CREDENTIALING OF PROFESSIONAL HELPERS

Credentialing of professional helpers usually involves three activities:

1. Graduation from an accredited program
2. Certification
3. Licensure (Vacc & Loesch, 2000, p. 304)

The first activity reflects the training that occurs for professional helpers, while the second and third activities represent the credentialing process that occurs for practitioners.

Training

Professional helpers are trained in programs that are based on specific competencies and standards. By and large, professional helpers trained at the undergraduate level are found in human services programs and social work programs, and U.S. programs are based on national standards developed by the Council in Human Service Education and the Council on Social Work Education. Many social work students also go on to obtain their master's degree in social work; this advanced degree is required in some states for licensure as a social worker. Professional counselors in the United States are trained in master and doctoral degree programs designed to meet professional criteria established by the Council for Accreditation of Counseling and Related Education Programs (CACREP). Psychology programs are accredited by the American Psychological Association Commission on Accreditation (APA-CoA), marriage and family therapy programs are accredited by the Commission on Accreditation for Marriage and Family Therapy Education (COAMFTE), and rehabilitation counseling programs are accredited by the Council on Rehabilitation Education (CORE). Accreditation for professional helper training programs "is a quality assurance and enhancement mechanism" using self-study and external peer review based on a "public set of standards of quality, policies, and procedures developed by an accrediting body through consultation with its respective higher education and professional communities" (Urofsky, 2013, p. 6). There appear to be a number of distinct advantages to accreditation, including better performance on national examinations, more employment opportunities, greater ease in becoming credentialed, and development of a more consolidated professional identity.

Several countries outside the United States also now have graduate degree programs in counseling and other helping specialty areas. A special issue of the *Journal of Counseling and Development* in 2010 and several special issues of the *Journal of Counseling and Development* in 2012 described the role of counseling programs in many different countries throughout the world. Some countries such as Canada and Britain have very clear accreditation standards and practices, while other countries such as Cuba and Bhutan have neither standards nor accreditation systems (Stanard, 2013).

All accrediting bodies of professional helper training programs have published standards, also known as criteria or performance indicators. Such standards address issues related to the institution as well as to the specific training program. For professional counselors in the United States, CACREP adopted the 2009 standards, which, among other things, included a shift to outcome-based standards. Most CACREP accredited training programs for professional counselors begin with a series of courses that introduce the helping professions, settings, client populations, and professional ethics. Early in most programs, a counseling techniques laboratory or practice course introduces students to communication skills and entry-level counseling interventions and provides opportunities to try these skills in an observable setting (either through a two-way mirror or a closed-circuit video). Such a course includes content that is presented in this text. Also, usually in conjunction with or concurrent with this pre-practicum, students receive training in content referred to as counseling theories. Counseling theories represent various models and approaches to conceptualizing and helping clients. The helping and counseling strategies that we describe in Chapter 9 are representative of various counseling theories or approaches, and many of these theories are described in greater detail in our other text, *The Professional Counselor* (Hackney & Cormier, 2013). Typically, these courses are followed by a field-based practicum in which students work with real clients under the supervision of a skilled practitioner who serves as the student's supervisor. That supervision may include live observation, video-recorded review, or audio-recorded review. Whatever the medium, sessions are reviewed by the supervisor, and feedback is provided to the trainee for assessment and professional growth (see also Chapter 10).

Along with other coursework, most students take courses in group counseling (sometimes including a group practicum), educational and psychological testing, career counseling and development, research, human development, multicultural counseling, and substance abuse. Toward the end of the program, most trainees are required to complete an internship in a counseling setting related to their program. This may be in school counseling, agency counseling, college counseling, or another related setting. Programs in rehabilitation counseling, social work, human services, and marriage and family therapy differ in some of the didactic content, but the experiential portions are similar. Training programs and professional associations alike are also concerned with research, particularly practice research. This kind of research provides information about the efficacy of particular counseling approaches and interventions that—when supported by research—are called evidence-based interventions or best practices. The impetus for this kind of research, as Bradley, Sexton, and Smith (2005) noted, is that "on a daily basis, the practitioner is faced with the decision of how to take a counseling theory and implement it into counseling practice" (p. 491). Collecting data about client outcomes helps practitioners to "substantiate the treatment that is most effective or ineffective with a particular mental health disorder" (p. 491).

Credentialing

In addition to receiving a degree in counseling or a related field, most counselors and other help-giving professionals also seek to become a credentialed counselor following their training and degree. Credentialing has become an important issue in recent years because of health care reforms (i.e., managed care) in which the credentials of the counselor are important for obtaining third-party reimbursement. Sweeney (1995) defined credentialing as "a method of identifying individuals by occupational group" (p. 120). It involves either certification and/or licensing. Although certification and licensing are similar processes, they differ in several important ways. *Certification,* unlike licensure, is established through independent, nonlegislative organizations that help regulate the use of a particular title. Vacc and Loesch (2000) noted that "application of this title is more than self-anointment by those who refer to themselves as counselors" (p. 228). Counselors in the United States can be certified through the National Board of Certified Counselors (NBCC), rehabilitation counselors are certified through the Commission for Rehabilitation Counselor Certification (CRCC), and social workers are certified through the National Association of Social Workers (NASW). School counselors are also credentialed by the state in which they work (Myers, Sweeney, & White, 2002). Human services professionals can be credentialed as a human services board-certified practitioner by the National Organization of Human Services (NOHS) and the Council for Standards in Human Service Education (CSHSE).

Licensure is a legislatively established basis of credentialing that is considered even more desirable than certification because it regulates not only the title but also the practice of the profession. All states have passed legislation to license professional counselors. Social workers can also obtain social work licenses through state legislation, and some states have passed legislation to license marriage and family therapists. It is important to note that licensing laws, in particular, vary among different states, and "only by examining a specific law and the rules by which it is administered can one determine the full implications of the law in a given state" (Sweeney, 1995, p. 121). It is important to note, however, that credentialing also differs in other countries. There is no current credentialing in some countries for counselors, and in other countries it is limited or perhaps even more expanded than in the United States. In Malaysia, for instance, counselors have licensure, whereas psychologists and social workers do not.

Myers, Sweeney, and White (2002) summarized a number of advantages to the credentialing process. First, it invokes a sense of pride that is important both for advocacy and job satisfaction. Second, credentialing increases a feeling of competence. Such competence helps professionals and should also be reassuring to the public or clients who see credentialed practitioners. Finally, credentialing promotes accountability within a profession by its members.

APPLICATION EXERCISE 1.3

Credentialing and Professional Identity

Continue with the interview you began in Application Exercise 1.1. Ask the helper you interviewed about his or her sense of professional identity. How was this person trained? What certification and/or license does this person have? What information did you gather about the code of ethics this person uses? With what professional organizations does this person affiliate? Present an oral summary of your findings to your class or write your findings in a written report.

Summary

This chapter has examined the meaning of helping in the context of human concerns and who the helpers are. Professional helpers are found in many settings and encounter a wide variety of human issues. Professional helpers can be distinguished from nonprofessional helpers by their identification with a professional organization; their use of an ethical code and standards of practice; and acknowledgment of an accrediting body that regulates their training, certification, and licensing of their practice. The effective helper brings to the setting certain personal qualities, without which the client would not likely enter into the alliance in which help occurs. These personal qualities include character traits such as virtue and ethical decision making, mindful awareness or neural integration, resilience and stamina, and cultural knowledge and sensitivity. The effective helper is committed to the sharing of resources, power, and privilege across diverse clients in a world essentially without borders. Although the exact parameters of these skills may be defined by the helper's theoretical orientation, there is no denying that the effective helper has them and the ineffective helper does not. Increasingly, professional helpers are entering new employment settings and encountering more diverse groups of clients, including many from various countries around the globe.

In the chapters that follow, we shall examine these skills and provide you with exercises and discussion questions to help in your integration of the material.

Chapter 2 will look at the helping relationship and conditions that enable it to develop in positive directions to facilitate the client's progress. Chapter 3 examines a number of communication patterns that show up in the helping process, both within an interview and also across diverse kinds of clients. Chapters 4, 5, and 6 comprise a series of chapters devoted to basic helping skills. We explore attending skills in Chapter 4, listening skills in Chapter 5, and action skills in Chapter 6. Chapter 7 describes some strategies to manage helping sessions, with particular attention to beginning and ending an interview. Chapters 8 and 9 address the helper's skills in conceptualizing issues and selecting and implementing strategies and interventions. Finally, Chapter 10 explores common challenges for helpers. It is important to note that all the skills and processes we describe in the following chapters are affected by both the social milieu and the cultural context of the practitioner and client.

Reflective Questions

1. In a small group of three to five class members, identify a preferred setting in which you would choose to be a professional helper (do the same for all members of the group). Discuss among yourselves why you chose the particular setting. Does it have to do with your personal qualities? Your perception of the demands of the setting? Your perception of the rewards of working in that setting?

2. Now choose a second-most-preferred setting (other than your first choice). Continue the discussion as directed in Reflective Question 1. How did you find your reactions to be different in this second discussion? What might you learn from these differences? Did you perceive the other group members as having similar or different reactions to

the second choice? What did you learn about them as a result? Share your reactions candidly.

3. Identify a person you have known who was, in your opinion, an exceptional helper. What qualities did this person possess that contributed to his or her helping nature? How do you think these qualities were acquired? Do you have any of these qualities?

4. In your opinion, what does it mean to help? To give help? To receive help? How are these processes related?

5. What has had an impact on your decision to become a helper? Consider the following sources of influence: your family of origin (the one in which you grew up), life experiences, role models, personal qualities, needs, motivations, pragmatic concerns, culture, country, and environment.

MyCounselingLab

For each exercise, log on to MyCounselingLab and then click the Video Library under Video Resources to watch the following two video clips.

1. Select the Intro/Orientation to Counseling collection. Watch the video "Cultural Considerations in Counseling." (Note that video clips will always appear in alphabetical order within each collection.) Describe how you think the helpers' understanding

of the clients' culture helped them work more effectively with this couple.

2. Click the Ethical, Legal, and Professional Issues in Counseling collection for the following selection: "A Cross-Cultural Miscommunication." How would you assess the cultural competence of the helping professional you saw in this video clip?

Recommended Readings

Capuzzi, D., & Gross, P. (2013). *Introduction to the counseling profession,* 6th ed. New York, NY: Taylor & Francis.

Corey, M. S., & Corey, G. (2016). *Becoming a helper,* 8th ed. Belmont, CA: Brooks/Cole, Cengage.

Day-Vines, N. L., Wood, S. M., Grothaus, T., Craigen, L., Holman, A., Dotson-Blake, K., & Douglass, M. J. (2007). Broaching the subjects of race, ethnicity, and culture during the counseling process. *Journal of Counseling and Development, 85,* 401–409.

Gibelman, M., & Furman, R. (2008). *Navigating human service organizations.* Chicago, IL: Lyceum Books.

Hepworth, D., Rooney, R., Rooney, D. G., & Strom-Gottfried, K. (2013). *Direct social work practice,* 9th ed. Belmont, CA: Brooks/Cole, Cengage.

Hohenshil, T. H., Amundson, N. E., & Niles, S. G. (2013). *Counseling around the world: An international handbook.* Washington DC: American Counseling Association.

Lee, J. H., Nam, S. K., Kim, A.-R., Kim, B., Lee, M. Y., & Lee, S. M. (2013). Resilience: A meta-analytic approach. *Journal of Counseling and Development, 91,* 269–279.

Mellin, E. A., Hunt, B., & Nichols, L. (2011). Counselor professional identity: Findings and implications for counseling and interprofessional collaboration. *Journal of Counseling and Development, 89,* 140–147.

Nadal, K. L., Griffin, K. E., Wong, Y., Hamit, S., & Rasmus, M. (2014). The impact of racial microaggressions on mental health: Counseling implications for clients of color. *Journal of Counseling and Development, 92:* 557–566. doi:10.1002/j.1556-6676 .2014.00130.x

Ponton, R. F., & Duba, J. D. (2009). The ACA Code of Ethics: Articulating counseling's professional covenant. *Journal of Counseling and Development, 87,* 117–121.

Roysircar, G., Sandhu, D. S., & Bibbins, V. (2003). *Multicultural competencies: A guidebook of practices.* Washington, DC: American Counseling Association.

Sales, A. (2007). *Rehabilitation counseling: An empowerment perspective.* Washington DC: American Counseling Association.

Siegel, D. (2010). *The mindful therapist.* New York: W. W. Norton.

Smith, E. (2006). The strength-based counseling model. *The Counseling Psychologist, 34,* 13–79.

Sue, D. W. (2010). *Microaggressions in everyday life: Race, gender and sexual orientation.* Hoboken, NJ: John Wiley & Sons.

Welfel, E. (2013). *Ethics in counseling and psychotherapy,* 5th ed. Belmont, CA: Brooks/Cole, Cengage.

Whiston, S. C., Rahardja, D., & Eder, K. (2011). School counseling outcome: A meta-analytic examination of interventions. *Journal of Counseling and Development, 89,* 37–55.

Wicks, R. J. (2007). *The resilient clinician.* New York: Oxford University Press.

Woodside, M., & McClam, T. (2011). *An introduction to human services,* 7th ed. Belmont, CA: Brooks /Cole, Cengage.

The Helping Relationship

Much of what is accomplished in counseling depends on the quality of the relationship between the helper and the client. The helping relationship is a different kind of relationship than one that occurs between close friends, family members, or even between nonprofessionals. It is a relationship characterized by security, safety, privacy, and healing. The roots of this particular kind of helping relationship lie in a theoretical approach to counseling called the person-centered approach. The *person-centered approach* derives principally from the work of one individual: Carl Rogers. Rogers emerged on the scene at a time when two psychological approaches—psychoanalysis and behaviorism—were dominant. Through his influence, the focus began to shift to the relationship between therapist and client, as opposed to the existing emphasis on the client's intrapsychic experience or patterns of behavior. In one of his early writings, Rogers (1957) defined what he believed to be the "necessary and sufficient conditions" for positive personality change to occur, including accurate empathy, unconditional positive regard, and congruence. These concepts have evolved over the years, and today they are generally acknowledged by most theoretical approaches as *core conditions* in the therapeutic process. Exploration by a task force on empirically supported relationship variables has reemphasized the contributions of these core conditions and the helping relationship to effective therapy processes and outcomes (Norcross, 2001). In other words, the therapeutic relationship makes specific contributions to the outcomes of counseling regardless of the theoretical approach, treatment type, or intervention strategies that the practitioner uses (Norcross, 2011).

THE IMPORTANCE OF THE RELATIONSHIP TO CLIENTS

The quality of the therapeutic relationship has the potential to be helpful and healing or hurtful and even damaging to clients. Many—if not most—clients who come to see us have missed out on the caring communication and healthy attachment to a caregiver in early life that is necessary for good health (physical and mental) and well-being. Instead of having experiences and expressions of themselves received and validated, clients may have had their experiences and expressions of self denied or judged. As a result, they develop narratives (or stories) and conclusions about themselves that are either too rigid or too chaotic, with not enough brain integration for them to regulate themselves effectively, particularly their emotions (Siegel, 2006). The therapeutic relationship has the potential to help repair some of these denied and judged experiences through collaborative communication and emotional processing of the dyadic experience between helper and client (Fosha, 2005). As a result, clients who feel cut off from themselves and their experiences have an opportunity to regain wholeness. Clients will be able to regain important connections with themselves and with other people, and the relationship with the helper is the first step in this process.

Perhaps you can see from this why we discussed the importance of neural integration and mindful awareness as a positive quality for counselors in Chapter 1. If the helper brings a lot of leftover issues and unresolved personal "baggage" into the counseling session, it will be "in the room" with the client and will impede the quality of communication and the process of change. A recent study found that clients are very sensitive to helpers' negative emotional states, more so than helpers' positive emotional states (Nissen-Lie, Havik, Hoglend, Monsen, & Ronnestad, 2013).

When helpers' unresolved issues get projected onto clients, we call this *countertransference*. And when clients' unresolved issues get projected onto helpers, we call this *transference*. Both helpers and clients can regulate unfinished business by learning to become aware of themselves and mindful of their feelings and emotions—what they are experiencing at any given moment in time. Indeed, some theoretical orientations view this as a primary goal of counseling and therapy (Fosha, 2002). This involves being aware of our own feelings as helpers and also being attuned to the feelings and experiences of our clients through the core or facilitative conditions previously mentioned. In the following sections of this chapter, we describe these core conditions in depth.

ACCURATE EMPATHY

There are numerous definitions of empathy in the counseling literature. The definition that we like is the following: the ability to understand the client's experience and feel with or emotionally resonate to the client's experience as if it were your own but without losing the "as if" quality (Rogers, 1957; Bozarth, 1997). Clark (2007) noted that empathy is a complex process and is often used in different ways and for different purposes in the helping relationship. When used effectively, empathy increases clients' sense of safety, their feelings of being understood, and their satisfaction with the helping process. Effective use of this core condition also decreases premature termination and promotes client exploration (Elliott, Bohart, Watson, & Greenberg, 2011). Empathic understanding involves two primary steps:

1. "Empathic rapport": Accurately sensing the client's world and being able to see things the way he or she does

2. "Communicative attunement": Verbally sharing your understanding with the client (Bohart & Greenberg, 1997, pp. 13–14)

How do you know when the client feels you have understood? Client responses such as "Yes, that's it" or "That's exactly right" indicate some sort of recognition by the client of the level of your understanding. When your clients say something like that after one of your responses, you are assured that they feel you are following and understanding what is occurring.

Learning to understand is not an easy process. It involves skillful listening, so you can hear not only the obvious but also the subtle shadings of which the client is perhaps not yet aware. Empathy also involves having good internal boundaries for yourself. An internal boundary helps to separate personal thoughts, feelings, and behavior from the thoughts, feelings, and behaviors of others (Mellody, 1989, p. 11). Rogers (1957) asserted that empathy is being sensitive to a client's experiencing a feeling. This is sometimes called resonant empathy (Buie, 1981). You can feel with the client without taking on the client's feelings and actually feeling them yourself. This is an area that occasionally poses problems, especially for beginning counselors. In your eagerness to be helpful, you may find yourself becoming so involved with the client that you get disconnected from yourself and what you are feeling. Instead, you take on the client's feelings and perhaps even find yourself obsessing about the client long after the session is over. Such immersion is not helpful because you lose your capacity to be objective about the client's experience. As a result, you may avoid seeing, hearing, or saying important things in the session. If you feel this is happening to you, you can talk it over with a supervisor. You can also get reconnected to yourself during a session by taking a minute to focus internally and privately on what you are feeling and by taking some deep breaths.

Understanding clients' perspectives alone is not sufficient. You also must verbally express to clients your sense of understanding about them. This kind of communication is, in effect, a kind of mirror—feeding back clients' feelings to them, without agreeing or disagreeing, reassuring or denying. For a client to know that the practitioner is empathic, it must be expressed or made visible to the client (Clark, 2007). For example, suppose your client, Precious, tells you that she is having a hard time in school since losing her pet, which is a result of being moved into a shelter after her dad lost his job. In making empathy visible to Precious, the helper might say something like the following: "Precious, I imagine you are pretty upset now about losing your pet and your home too."

Accurate empathy involves not only mirroring your clients' feelings but also some parts of the immediate process. For example, if clients continually ask many questions rather than discuss the issues that brought them to counseling, it would be appropriate to reflect on the obvious with statements such as:

- "You have a lot of questions to ask right now."
- "You seem to want a lot of information about this."
- "You are asking a lot of questions. I wonder if you are uncertain about what to expect."

Learning to develop accurate empathy with your client and with other people takes time and practice, in part because empathy is not only an understanding of the client's feelings but also an understanding of the client's experiences. As Elliott and colleagues (2011) observed, empathic therapists do not simply parrot clients' words back or reflect only the content of those words; they also validate the moment-to-moment experiences, meanings, and implications of the words. Effectively used, empathy helps clients to "symbolize, organize, and make sense" of their experiences (Bohart & Greenberg, 1997, p. 15). In the above example, the helper goes beyond simply mirroring the feelings of the client Precious and also reflects empathically on her experiences, as in the following example: "Precious, it sounds like you are going through a lot of changes right now in your life and everything feels turned upside down at this time."

Several caveats about the effective use of empathy are worth noting. First, the effects of empathy are most useful when the other two core conditions of positive regard and congruence are also present. Second, empathy is not the same as sympathy. Empathy is about communicating your understanding of the client and her or his experience. Sympathy is about feeling sorry for or sad about the client. Finally, not all clients will perceive empathic understanding as useful; some may experience empathy as intrusive, directive, or foreign to them (Elliott et al., 2011).

The Brain Connection and Empathy

In 1996, in Italy, a team of neuroscientists discovered neurons that fire in our brains called "mirror" neurons. These neurons are specifically tailored to mirror the emotions and bodily responses of another person and are located in various cortical regions of the brain, such as the frontal and parietal lobes. These mirror neurons link perception and motor action and interact with an area of the brain called the insula that makes a neural circuit in which behavioral imitation, emotional or felt resonance, and attunement of intentional states occur (Siegel, 2006). As a result, when you perceive the expressions of another person, the brain is able to create within the body an internal state that is thought to "resonate" with that of the other person. The implications of the mirror neuron system in the brain and the resulting potential for empathic attunement with our clients are profound. Siegel asserted that being empathic with clients extends beyond helping them feel better (p. 13). This empathic mirroring helps clients feel "felt" and ultimately leads to brain changes in clients through the establishment of new neural firing patterns and increased neural integration. (For further information about this, see also the UCLA Center for Culture, Brain, and Development at www.cbd.ucla.edu.) Elliott and colleagues (2011) indicate that this emergence of research on the brain-based view of empathy has been the most significant development in the construct of empathy in the last two decades!

Empathy and Mindfulness

In Chapter 1, we discussed the importance of mindful awareness as an integral quality of helpers. We now know that mindful awareness, or mindfulness, is not only useful for helpers but is also an important link to empathy. When we as helpers are mindful, we are more attuned to our own internal states by using our "sixth sense." In turn, being attuned to our own internal states helps us be attuned to the internal states of others, such as (but not limited to) our clients. In other words, mindfulness and empathy overlap to such a degree that being mindful augments our capacity to be empathic (Siegel, 2007). Stated another way, when we become frenetic or frazzled and lose our connection to ourselves, we are more likely to lose the relational connection and understanding with our clients too. Bein (2008) has written a remarkable book on Zen and mindfulness in helping and asserts that "ethical and skillful behavior flows from mindfulness" (p. 50). Siegel's recent book *The Mindful Therapist* (2010) demonstrates how therapist mindfulness helps us stay open to possibilities with clients and to appreciate present moments without making debilitating judgments. Siegel (2010) states: "As a mindful therapist, I must bring the curiosity, openness, acceptance, and loving-kindness to my own states of mind in order to be mindfully attentive to the states in my patient" (p. 212). Mindfulness helps us be present with clients, and presence is an important ingredient in the relationship qualities that promote healing.

Cultural and Relational Empathy

Empathy also involves understanding the client's gender and cultural backgrounds. Chung and Bemak (2002) noted that in North America, the concept of empathy is derived largely from Western Eurocentric values. They believe there is a need for culturally sensitive empathy. Cultural empathy is inclusive and reaches for understanding both among and between diverse groups. When used in the helping process, cultural empathy helps practitioners understand not just the individual sitting in front of them but also something about the client's worldview and context in which the client lives (Pedersen, Crethar, & Carlson, 2008). A major way in which a helper's cultural empathy may be blocked is by one's state of *privilege*. Recall from Chapter 1 that privilege is an unearned advantage, such as being White, being able bodied, being heterosexual, or having economic resources. Because such privileges are unearned, it is easy to take them for granted and to underestimate the impact that lack of privilege has on others. For example, consider the kind of cultural empathy that would be conveyed if helpers could really understand the discrimination, oppression, and losses experienced by clients who may be of another race, ethnic origin, or religion or by clients who may be experiencing loss of health status or income.

Cultural empathy is also affected by the mirror neurons we talked about earlier. The Italian researchers who discovered the mirror neuron system are also exploring the role of mirror neurons in communicating information about emotions and social life across cultures. The brain is undoubtedly behind our capacity to create and maintain cultural and relational empathy. Cultural empathy includes consideration of context and society in which both the counselor and the client live. When context is ignored and attempts to understand are made solely from an individualistic frame of reference, "blaming the victim" can result. Ignoring social context overlooks the relational world in which clients live—the dyads; families; racial, ethnic, and/or religious groups; social classes; occupational groups; and genders to which clients belong. Theorists have coined the term *relational empathy* to describe this process (Jordan, 1997). Relational empathy involves empathy for oneself, other people, and the healing relationship. In empathic interactions with the therapist, the client develops self-empathy as well as an increase in empathic attunement to others. This leads to "enhanced relational capacity and to an increase in self-esteem" (p. 345). For therapists to work effectively with clients from cultures different from their own, they must be able to step back from usual ways of knowing and be open to different ways of seeing things (Jenkins, 1997).

Chung and Bemak (2002) offered three specific ways that counselors can foster cultural and relational empathy:

1. Have a genuine interest in learning more about the client's cultural affiliations.
2. Have a genuine appreciation for cultural differences between the counselor and the client.
3. Incorporate culturally appropriate help-seeking behaviors and treatment outcomes and expectations into the helping process as needed. (p. 157)

APPLICATION EXERCISE 2.1

Accurate Empathy and Cultural Empathy

A. Hearing and Verbalizing Client Concerns

Using triads with one person as speaker, a second as respondent, and the third as observer, complete the following tasks. Then rotate the roles until each person has had an opportunity to react in all three ways.

1. The speaker should begin by sharing a concern or issue with the listener.
2. The respondent should
   a. listen to the speaker and
   b. verbalize to the speaker what he or she heard.
3. The observer should note the extent to which the others accomplished their tasks and whether any understanding or misunderstanding occurred.

Following a brief (five-minute) interaction, respond verbally to the following questions:

SPEAKER: Do you think the respondent heard what you had to say? Did you think he or she understood you? Did the listener seem to understand your culture? Discuss this with the respondent.

RESPONDENT: Did you let the speaker know you understood or attempted to understand? How did you do this? What blocks within you interfered with doing so? Did you struggle with the person's cultural affiliations?

OBSERVER: Discuss what you saw taking place between the speaker and the respondent.

Now rotate roles, and complete the same process.

B. Understanding Client Concerns

This exercise should be completed with a group of three to ten people sitting in a circle.

1. Each participant is given a piece of paper and a pencil.
2. Each participant should complete—in writing and anonymously—the following sentence: My primary concern about becoming a helper is

_____

_____

3. Papers are folded and placed in the center of the circle.
4. Each participant draws a paper. (If one person receives his or her own paper, all should draw again.)
5. Each participant reads aloud the concern listed and then talks for several minutes about what it would be like to have this concern. Other participants can then add to this.

This process continues until each participant has read and discussed a concern. When discussing the concern, attempt to reflect only your understanding of the world of the person with this concern. Do not attempt to give a solution or advice.

After the exercise, members should give each other feedback about the level of empathic understanding that was displayed during the discussion. Feedback should be specific so participants can use it for behavior change.

(Continued)

C. Cultural and Relational Empathy

Consider your capacity to relate to clients who are both similar to and different from yourself along cultural dimensions. Explore and discuss the following four areas:

1. What are your family's beliefs and feelings about the group(s) that comprise your culture of origin? What parts of the group(s) do they embrace or reject? How has this influenced your feelings about your cultural identity?
2. What aspects of your culture of origin do you have the most comfort "owning"? The most difficulty "owning"?
3. What groups will you have the easiest time understanding and relating to? The most difficult?
4. What privileges do you have as a function of being you? As a function of how and where you grew up and how and where you live now? Consider dimensions such as race, ethnic origin, gender, socioeconomic status, health status, age, sexual orientation, and so on. How might such a privilege(s) impede your understanding of a client and the client's context?

Shame and the Empathy Bond

Another factor that is increasingly recognized as having a substantial impact on the helping relationship is shame. *Shame* is viewed as a central component or main regulator of a person's affective life. Normal shame is about values and limits; it is recognized, spoken about, and acknowledged. The shame that is considered problematic and a primary contributor to aggression, addictions, obsessions, narcissism, and depression is hidden shame—shame that is unacknowledged, repressed, or defended against—that seems to result in either an attack on others or an incredible self-loathing (Karen, 1992).

According to Lewis (1971), shame is inescapable in the counselor-client relationship and has major implications for the empathic bonding of the counselor to the client. Karen (1992) quoted Lewis as follows: "However good your reasons for going into treatment, so long as you are an adult speaking to another adult to whom you are telling the most intimate things, there is an undercurrent of shame in every session" (p. 50). Lewis (1971) asserted that not only do counselors overlook shame in clients and bypass dealing with it but they also inadvertently add to a client's "shame tank" through judgmental interpretations. Value judgments about the client's culture can also contribute to a sense of shame. Lewis stated that, when this happens, the client becomes enraged at the counselor, but because he or she cannot accept feeling angry toward someone who is a "helper," it is turned inward and becomes depression and self-denigration. Lewis cautions counselors to be alert to client states of shame so they can help clients work through and discharge the feeling. In this way, clients can move ahead. Otherwise, they are likely to continue to move in and out of shame attacks or shame spirals, both within and outside the counseling sessions.

A major precursor to shame appears to be the lack of parental empathy. According to S. Miller (1985), a child's sense of self-esteem comes largely from the parents' capacity to tune in empathetically with the child—to mirror and reflect the child as she or he develops. As Karen (1992) pointed out, in therapy, "the same phenomenon requires a special sensitivity on the part of the therapist. The patient is hypersensitive about acceptance and abandonment and uncertain of whether he can trust the therapist with his wound—a wound that, he no doubt senses, the therapy session has great potential to exacerbate. The therapist must win over the hiding, shameful side of the personality and gradually help it to heal" (p. 65).

In many situations, creating an empathy bond with clients can help heal shame, but in some situations, empathy can also evoke client shame. As Cowan, Presbury, and Echterling

(2013) point out, "the client's increasing contact with 'forbidden' thoughts and feelings through the counselor's empathic efforts can also evoke an anxious sense of vulnerability. The counselor is becoming important to the client as a new attachment figure, and the client fears that the counselor will in some way reject, punish or abandon the client as others have done in the past." (pp. 57–58). When this happens, instead of responding affirmatively to the helper's offerings of empathy, the client may "test" the helper and become critical and rejecting, leading the helper to conclude that the client is being "resistant" when, in fact, the client is simply reexperiencing shame (p. 58). It is important for helpers to navigate this potentially tricky passage by staying the course and walking the middle ground, so to speak. Overidentifying with clients' distress may make clients feel too powerful, as if they or their feelings can harm the therapist, while underreacting to clients' distress may make clients feel as if the therapist is invalidating or discounting their distress in the same way that their original caregivers did.

As Cowan and colleagues (2013) point out, when empathy activates the client's shame, staying inside what Siegel (2010) refers to as the client's "window of tolerance" (pp. 50–53) is a helpful therapeutic stance. Siegel (2010) describes a window of tolerance as a "band of arousal" in which each of us functions well and is flexible and adaptable. Outside this window of tolerance, we become dysfunctional and rigid or feel out of balance. We are all unique because we have had different attachment histories with caregivers and varying exposure to traumatic situations. Siegel (2010) states, "Our job with clients is to feel the movement toward the window's boundaries and work at this 'safe but not too safe' zone of treatment where change becomes possible" (p. 58).

Shame can also be culture-bound. Hardy and Laszloffy (1995) pointed out that every cultural group has pride and shame issues—that is, "aspects of a culture that are sanctioned as distinctively negative or positive" (p. 229). These are important issues to identify about a client's cultural group because they help to define appropriate and inappropriate behavior within a cultural context. In his new book, *The Empathic Civilization*, author Jeremy Rifkin (2009) asserts that globally, we need to develop empathic connections in order to avoid disaster on a worldwide basis.

POSITIVE REGARD

In his early writings, Carl Rogers (1957) described positive regard as unconditional. More recent writers have relabeled positive regard as nonpossessive warmth. The effectiveness of positive regard appears to lie in its ability to facilitate a long-term working relationship and is so powerful that these authors argue it should not be withheld from any client (Farber & Doolin, 2011, p. 183). Positive regard is associated with clients' perceptions of improvement on issues, and it sets the stage for the use of various helping strategies and interventions (such as those we describe in later chapters). Lack of positive regard often produces and contributes to ruptures in the helping relationship (Farber & Doolin, 2011).

Positive regard or nonpossessive warmth seems to be conveyed by helpers to clients through the dimensions of friendliness, helpfulness, and trustworthiness (Williams & Bargh, 2008). Neurobiological research has found an area of the brain (the insular cortex) that is related to the processing of interpersonal warmth information; this area of the brain appears to be linked to early attachment in infancy with warm, physical contact with caregivers (Williams & Bargh, 2008).

Positive regard—or nonpossessive warmth—is often misconstrued as agreement or lack of disagreement with the client. Instead, it is an attitude of valuing the client. To show positive regard is to express appreciation of the client as a unique and worthwhile person. It is also involves being noncritical—providing an "overall sense of protection, support, or acceptance, no matter what is divulged" (Karasu, 1992, p. 36). In this context, it is important for counselors not only to feel positively about clients but also to convey these positive feelings to clients.

Consider the following scenario:

> Lettia, the counselor, tells her supervisor that she has seen her client, Pedro, for three sessions. She says she feels annoyed and frustrated with him because he comes in every session and "whines about his low grades," which she believes are bad because of his constant partying.

Can you find any regard in Lettia's attitude toward Pedro? Instead of experiencing Pedro as a unique person of value and worth, Lettia feels "put off" and frustrated by her client. It is hard to work effectively with clients if you do not like, respect, and value them for who they are. In this situation, Lettia's lack of regard may not only be for this individual client but may also extend to aspects of his culture. Sometimes, issues in positive regard are exacerbated in cross-cultural counseling, making progress and change even more difficult.

Contrast this with the way Lettia speaks about her other client, Maria. Maria is a young woman who has a chronic health condition that limits her functioning in several ways. While Maria's progress in counseling is also slow, Lettia notes how much she looks forward to each session with Maria and how supportive she feels toward her. As you can see, regard for clients is closely related to empathy and also to the other core relationship condition of congruence, or genuineness, which we consider later in this chapter.

Positive Regard and the Acceptance Therapies

Although the concept of positive regard originated with Rogers, in recent years this construct has been expanded through the emergence of what we now call the acceptance therapies. These therapies represent approaches in which validation and acceptance of the client are seen as key precursors to change. Notable among these approaches are motivational interviewing (MI), acceptance and commitment therapy (ACT), and dialectical behavior therapy (DBT). Although the space and scope of this text does not permit us to overview these three approaches in great detail, we will highlight for you the ways in which each of these approaches contributes to positive regard by focusing on and promoting acceptance.

MOTIVATIONAL INTERVIEWING Motivational interviewing was developed by Miller and Rollnick (2012) and is an offshoot of person-centered therapy. It has been described as a collaborative, client-centered, empathic, and supportive helping style that supports the client's conditions for change through acceptance rather than persuasion. This approach stresses that it is the role of acceptance rather than pressure that ultimately empowers clients to change. MI is an approach that is nonjudgmental, nonconfrontational, and nonadversarial. Core interviewing skills in MI are referred to as OARS:

Open-ended questions—inviting clients to tell their story without leading them in a particular direction.

Affirmations—using statements that affirm some strength shown by the client, such as "I am so glad you have really taken some time to think this over."

Reflective statements—acknowledging what you have observed and heard from the client, such as "I can see and hear that you feel really distressed and upset about what has been happening to your mother."

Summaries—tying together significant aspects of a discussion such as a theme. For example, "Let me try to summarize everything I have heard you say about the situation with your job. Essentially it feels like a situation where you think there is no room for your input. Is that about right?"

Essential characteristics of the MI approach include the following:

Avoid arguing with clients.

Listen to clients with respect.

Encourage and empower clients' capacity to change in directions they desire for themselves.

Work in a collaborative manner.

Be a supportive presence.

Listen rather than tell.

ACCEPTANCE AND COMMITMENT THERAPY   Acceptance and commitment therapy, also described in greater detail in Chapter 9, is an approach developed by Hayes (Hayes, Strosahl, & Wilson, 2012). As the name of this approach suggests, the goals of ACT are twofold: (1) to help the client accept and transform "symptoms" or difficult private, internal events, and (2) to help the client commit to meaningful action based on the client's core values. In this respect, ACT differs from many other psychotherapeutic approaches in that it does not focus on symptom reduction as a therapeutic goal. In fact, its focus is quite the opposite. ACT posits that trying to get rid of a symptom actually creates a clinical problem! Instead, clients learn methods to accept symptoms and thereby render them harmless and transient, even if such symptoms feel temporarily uncomfortable. This approach stresses that it is the process of trying to get rid of or avoid unwanted private experiences that creates psychological suffering, particularly over the long-term. Harris (2006) describes the mantra of ACT as follows: *"Embrace your demons and Follow your heart!"* (p. 8).

In ACT, practitioners ask clients to identify ways in which they have tried to get rid of or avoid the symptoms and to describe the results. Through acceptance, the therapist tries to increase clients' awareness that trying to control or fix their symptoms is actually doing more harm than good. ACT suggests to clients that the more they try to fight off a negative feeling, the more likely they are to feel overwhelmed by it because this "fight" produces a secondary level of distress about the primary distress, compounding the initial discomfort in myriad ways.

ACT uses six methods to promote acceptance within clients: defusion, acceptance without struggle, contact with the present moment, the observing self, values, and committed action.

Defusion is a method designed to help clients separate from disturbing thoughts that they have become identified with or fused to. It teaches clients how to step back and observe thoughts so thoughts are regarded as impermanent and have much less power to affect them adversely.

Acceptance without struggle teaches clients how to make space for intrusive thoughts and emotions without giving them improper or undue attention.

Contact with the present moment helps clients develop mindfulness skills and practices so they can bring their full attention and awareness to their here-and-now experience.

The observing self teaches clients how to view their internal experiences as if they were a spectator, an observer. This activity is designed to decrease emotional reactivity and to prevent overidentification with thoughts, feelings, images, memories, and so on.

Values is a clarification process in which clients are asked to reflect on what is most meaningful and important to them and whether they can pursue their values in spite of their distress over symptoms.

Committed action helps clients to set goals based on their self-identified values and then to commit to taking action steps that support such goals and values.

DIALECTICAL BEHAVIOR THERAPY   Dialectical behavior therapy, developed by Linehan (Linehan, 1993; Linehan & Dexter-Mazza, 2008; Koerner & Linehan, 2012), a Zen student herself, was created in part by her recognition that an unrelenting focus on behavior change was so invalidating to clients that it, in and of itself, evoked client resistance. She developed DBT to include concepts she refers to as *radical acceptance* and *validation*. For her, validation of the client and the client's experiences and feelings are at the heart of radical acceptance. She states:

> The essence of validation is this: The therapist communicates to the client that her responses make sense and are understandable within her *current* life context or situation. The therapist actively accepts the client and communicates the acceptance to the client. The therapist takes the client's responses seriously and does not discount or trivialize them. (p. 222).

Essentially, validation in DBT is both the recognition *and* acceptance of the client's experiences as being valid. Note that validation does not mean that the therapist agrees or disagrees with the client's subjective reality and experience but is able to understand the client's world as experienced by the client. Linehan describes six levels of therapeutic validation. As summarized by Linehan and Dexter-Mazza (2008), these six levels of validation are as follows:

Level 1: *Listening and Observing*
The helper listens and observes not only the client's words but also the client's body language and nonverbal behavior. In level 1, the helper shows interest in the client.

Level 2: *Accurate Reflection*
The helper builds on the observations gathered in level 1 and feeds back to the client what has been observed and understood.

Level 3: *Articulating the Unverbalized*
In essence, in level 3, the helper is able to communicate understanding about things that have not been expressed directly by the client but are implied or inferred by the client. Typically this is done by perspective taking—how someone in the client's situation could and would feel.

Level 4: *Understanding the Client's Behavior in Terms of History and Biology*
In this level, the helper validates the client's behavior in terms of its causes. The helper might say something like "Given what happened to you on that night, I completely understand why you might not want to be around that person again."

Level 5: *Normalizing the Emotional Reactions*
In level 5, the helper validates that the client's emotional reactions are typical or reasonable given the current context. The helper might say something like "It's true that most people would be pissed off and upset when their boss never honors their requests for time off."

Level 6: *Radical Genuineness*
Level 6 is really a compilation of all the prior levels of validation and is essentially an attitudinal stance that the helper takes toward the client, recognizing that the client is a person of worth just as the helper is a person of worth. It is a level of validation based on the idea of seeing the client as an equal to the helper.

To be effective, validation has to be true. Validation of clients is not about lying to them or making up strengths for them that do not exist, nor is it about agreeing with them. It is simply about accepting the client's experiences as real and understandable. It is also useful for helpers to recognize typical ways in which we invalidate clients. These include judging, denying, minimizing, and blaming. Invalidation can also be communicated to clients in nonverbal ways, such as checking the clock on the wall during a session, taking a phone call or text during a session, looking away from the client, or pulling your chair back from the client to create more distance.

Bein (2008) notes that radical acceptance and positive regard not only contribute to client self-acceptance but also provide a container for client risk taking and growth (p. 39). He states, "When clients experience your radical acceptance of them, they become disposed to explore their inner and outer lives with you. They move through this healing space with you secure in the knowledge that you accept them exactly as they are" (p. 31).

APPLICATION EXERCISE 2.2

Positive Regard

A. Overcoming Barriers to Positive Regard and Acceptance

Think about expressing to the client those limitations that may be blocking your sense of liking for the client and those strengths that increase your appreciation for the client. The following steps may assist you in expressing this:

1. Picture the other person in your mind. Begin a dialogue in which you express what it is that is interfering with your sense of positive regard. Now reverse the roles. Become the other person. What does the person say in response? Then what do you say?
2. Complete this process again. This time, express the strengths you see in the other person— what you appreciate about that person. Again, reverse the roles. Become the other person. What does he or she say in response? Then what do you say?

This exercise can be used with any client toward whom you have difficulty experiencing positive regard and acceptance.

(Continued)

B. Expressing Positive Regard and Acceptance

Take a few minutes to think about a person with whom you currently have a relationship and for whom you experience positive regard. What kinds of things do you do to express your feelings of positive regard for this person? Jot them down.

_____

_____

There is no set answer to the preceding exercise because each person has a different style of communicating good feelings for another person. The first step, though, is positive regard—to feel comfortable enough to express warm feelings to someone else. Being free enough to share feelings of regard for another human being spontaneously is a process that can be learned.

Think again for a moment about several of your existing relationships with a few people close to you—perhaps your partner, parent, child, neighbor, or friend. Then respond in writing to the following questions:

1. What is your level of expression of positive regard for these people?
2. How often do you say things like "I like you," "It's nice to be with you," "You're good for me," "I enjoy you," and so forth?
3. What is your feeling when you do express positive regard?
4. What is the effect on the other person?
5. If your expression of such statements is infrequent, what might be holding you back?

Either now or later, seek out someone you like and then try to express these kinds of feelings to that person. Then think again about the previous questions. Share your reactions with your partner. In doing this, you will probably note that warmth and positive regard are expressed both nonverbally and verbally.

CONGRUENCE (GENUINENESS)

Neither empathy nor positive regard can be conveyed in helping relationships unless the helper is seen by the client as genuine. Genuineness is also referred to by Rogers as *congruence,* a condition reflecting honesty, transparency, and openness to the client. Congruence implies that therapists are real in their interactions with clients. As Corey (2013) noted, this means helpers are "without a false front, their inner experience and outer expression of that experience match, and they can openly express feelings, thoughts, reactions, and attitudes that are present in the relationship with the client" (p. 182). Through being congruent, helpers model for clients not only the experience of being real but also the process of claiming one's truths and speaking about them. When this happens, there is usually more vitality and a greater "connection" in the helping relationship. As Jordan (1997) noted, "We all know the deadened, bored, or anxious feelings that occur in interactions in which people cannot risk being in their truth. . . . Inauthenticity takes us out of real mutuality" (p. 350). Take a moment to think about the fact that most clients come into the helping process in a state of incongruence, often either not knowing who they are or not feeling as if they can truly be who they are. In this respect, the congruence of the helper is even more important. It helps clients become more congruent, making it easier for them to own their feelings and express them without excessive fears (Kolden, Klein, Wang, & Austin, 2011).

The beginning helper may find this condition easier to apply in theory than in practice. Questions inevitably arise when congruence is examined. Some examples are the following: What if I really don't like my client? Should I let that be known? Wouldn't it destroy the relationship? Congruence means that the helper is honest but in helpful rather than destructive ways. Expressing your feelings should not take precedence over understanding the client's feelings. The helping relationship does not have all the mutuality present in many other relationships, such as friend to friend, partner to partner, and so forth. Corey (2013) cautioned that congruence does not mean that the helper impulsively shares all thoughts and feelings with clients in a nonselective way. A general guideline is to share your feelings when they are persistent and if they block your acceptance of the client. At times, however, it may be better just to acknowledge these kinds of thoughts and feelings to yourself or to your supervisor. In other words, an important part of congruence means developing a sense of awareness about all that you are and what the impact of this may mean for your clients. For example, Roberto became aware through supervision that the sessions with one particular client, Jessica, seemed to drag on and move more slowly than with his other clients. Roberto was not sure why, but after disclosing this to his supervisor, he realized it was because Jessica talked a lot in the sessions about things that seemed trivial to Roberto compared to what his other clients discussed. Roberto was able to own and be congruent with these feelings with his supervisor, and he noticed these feelings growing less intense as a result. He also found a way to ask Jessica in the following session about her goals for counseling and about her own experience of the sessions so far. Interestingly enough, Jessica disclosed that she wished Roberto could take a more active role in the sessions so they could move along more quickly.

Steps in Congruence: Awareness and Discernment

Because congruence can be a complicated process, consider the following two steps in the development of congruence in the helping relationship. The first step involves self-awareness or acknowledgment. The second step involves discernment or good clinical judgment.

Ask yourself what it means to be genuine. Can you tell when you are being yourself or when you are presenting an image that is different from the way you actually feel? To communicate congruence to the client, you must first learn to get in touch with yourself and your own truth—to become aware of who you are as an individual and what kinds of thoughts and feelings you have. This involves learning to discriminate among your various feelings and allowing them to come into your awareness without denial or distortion. A good question to ask yourself is "What am I experiencing now?" Congruence also involves paying attention to what goes on in your body during a counseling session. Our bodies provide cues to us about what we experience and also what clients experience during sessions. Furthermore, body cues can "leak" out to clients, particularly if we are unaware of them. For example, clients may feel the effects of our prior late night through our lack of energy, sleepiness, and shallow breathing, or they may sense our uptightness through our rushed speech and constricted breath.

Once you develop acknowledgment and awareness of all that you are and what you are experiencing and feeling, a second step in congruence involves discernment or good clinical judgment about expressing your feelings to clients. Sommers-Flanagan and Sommers-Flanagan (2014, p. 140) suggest the following guidelines to develop such discernment:

- Examine your motives: Is your expression solely for the client's benefit?
- Consider if what you want to say or do is really therapeutic: How do you anticipate your client will react?

Once you decide that you are in a situation in which expression would benefit the client—and the client would be helped by such expression—consider the use of both self-disclosure and feedback statements, which we describe in the next section.

SELF-DISCLOSURE Expression of your thoughts, ideas, and feelings follows after your awareness of them. This process might also be called self-expression or self-disclosure. Hill and Knox (2002) defined *self-disclosure* as statements that reveal something about you (p. 255). Self-expression and self-disclosure are important ways of letting the client know that you are a person and not just a role; however, self-disclosure should be used appropriately and not indiscriminately in the counseling sessions. Hepworth and colleagues (2013) cautioned against self-disclosure of hostility in particular. It is important not to interpret self-disclosure to mean that you should talk about yourself; the primary focus of the interview is on the client. However, it is occasionally appropriate and helpful for you to reveal or disclose a particular feeling you may have about the counseling session or about the client. The clue to appropriateness is often determined by the question, "Whose needs am I meeting when I disclose this idea or feeling—the client's or mine?" Clearly, the needs of the former are more appropriate. As Zur et al. (2009) state, "Appropriate, ethical, and clinically driven self-disclosures are intentionally employed with the client's welfare in mind and with a clinical rationale" (p. 24).

Self-disclosure can revolve around several different topics:

- The helper's own issues
- Facts about the helper's role
- The helper's reactions to the client (feedback)
- The helper's reactions to the helping relationship

Usually, disclosure in the latter two areas is more productive. Many times, helpers are tempted to share their problems and concerns when encountering a client with similar problems. In a few instances, this may be done as a reassurance to clients that their concerns are not catastrophic. But in most other instances, a role reversal occurs—the helper is gaining something by this sharing with the client. Some research indicates that the helper who discloses at a moderate level may be perceived by the client more positively than the practitioner who discloses at a high or low level (Edwards & Murdock, 1994). Thus, too much or too little self-disclosure may limit the client's confidence in you as an effective helper. Furthermore, self-disclosure that occurs too frequently may blur the boundaries between helper and client and can be a precursor to problematic multiple or nonprofessional relationships with clients. (We discuss the slippery slope of this situation in Chapter 10.) On the other hand, lack of self-disclosure can turn clients away. Self-disclosure is an important way to build trust with adolescent clients, with clients who have substance abuse issues, and in multicultural counseling situations (Egan, 2014; Sue & Sue, 2013). In other words, the decision about self-disclosure often varies with the *context* of the helping situation, including the setting, the type of client, and the theoretical orientation of the helper (Zur et al., 2009).

APPLICATION EXERCISE 2.3

Dyadic Encounter: Congruence

To assist you in becoming aware of your own thoughts and feelings, select a partner and spend a few minutes with this dyadic encounter experience (Banikiotes, Kubinski, & Pursell, 1981). It is designed to facilitate getting to know yourself and another person on a fairly close level. All you need to do is respond to the open-ended questions as honestly and directly as possible. Both of you should respond to one question at a time. The discussion statements can be completed at whatever level of self-disclosure you wish; there is no forced disclosure!

My name is . . .

The reason I'm here is . . .

One of the most important skills in getting to know another person is listening. To check on your ability to understand what your partner is communicating, the two of you should go through the following steps one at a time.

Decide which one of you is to speak first in this unit. The first speaker is to complete the following item in two or three sentences:

When I think about the future, I see myself . . .

The second speaker repeats in his or her own words what the first speaker has just said. The first speaker must be satisfied that he or she has been heard accurately.

The second speaker then completes the item in two or three sentences. The first speaker paraphrases what the second speaker just said, to the satisfaction of the second speaker.

Share what you may have learned about yourself as a listener with your partner. To check your listening accuracy, the two of you may find yourselves later saying to each other, "Do you mean that . . .?" or "You're saying that . . ." Do not respond to any sentence you do not want to.

When I am new in a group, I . . .

When I am feeling anxious in a new situation, I usually . . .

You're saying that . . . (Listening check)

Right now, I'm feeling . . .

The thing that turns me off the most is . . .

When I am alone, I usually . . .

I feel angry about . . .

Do you mean that . . .? (Listening check)

Checkup

Have a short discussion about this experience so far. Keep eye contact as much as you can, and try to cover the following points:

How well are you listening?

How open and honest have you been?

How eager are you to continue this interchange?

Do you feel that you are getting to know each other?

(Continued)

Then continue with the following:

I love . . .
I feel jealous about . . .
Right now, I'm feeling . . .
I am afraid of . . .
The thing I like best about you is . . .
You are . . .
Right now, I am responding most to . . .

Often, clients may ask questions about the helper: Are you married? Why did you become a counselor? Are you in school? These are common questions clients ask in seeking information about the helper. In this case, it is usually best to give a direct, brief answer and then return the interview focus to the client. However, if this is a common occurrence with a particular client, there are other ways of responding. Continual client questioning of this sort often indicates that the client is anxious and is attempting to get off the "hot seat" by turning the focus onto you. There are better ways to handle this than spending the interview disclosing facts about yourself. Alternative ways of responding include the following:

1. Reflect on the client's feelings of anxiety: "You seem anxious about talking about yourself now."
2. Reflect on the process: "You seem to be asking a lot of questions now."
3. Make a statement about what you see happening: "I think you feel as if you're on the 'hot seat' and that asking me questions is a good way for you to get off it."

SHARING AND FEEDBACK STATEMENTS Some helpers are able to acknowledge their feelings and determine when these can be best expressed in the interview, but they are not sure how to express these kinds of thoughts and feelings to the client. Self-disclosure or expressions of congruence are often characterized by sharing and feedback statements—statements that convey to the client your sense of what is going on and your feelings about it. These kinds of statements are illustrated by the following examples:

"I am glad you shared that with me."

"If that happened to me, I think I'd feel pretty angry."

"I don't feel that we're getting anywhere right now."

Other examples of sharing responses are:

CLIENT: It's hard for me to say so, but I really do get a lot out of these sessions.

HELPER: That makes me feel good to hear you say that. or

HELPER: I'm glad to know you feel that way.

Note that in the helper's sharing statements, the communication is direct; it focuses on the helper's feelings and on the client. It is a better statement than a generalized comment, such as "I hope most clients would feel the same way." A sharing and feedback statement should avoid the trap of counseling lingo or language. To begin a sharing and/ or feedback statement with "I hear you saying . . . ," "It seems that you feel . . . ," or "I feel that you feel . . ." gets wordy, repetitive, and even phony. Say exactly what you mean.

APPLICATION EXERCISE 2.4

Self-Disclosure

Think about yourself in the following instances:

1. You have a client who describes herself as shy and retiring. During the third interview, she says: "I'd like to be like you—you seem so outgoing and comfortable with people. Why don't you just tell me how you got that way?" Do you then consider it appropriate to share some of your experiences with her? Do you think your response to this might vary depending on the client's cultural affiliations? If so, how?

2. You have had one particular client for about seven individual sessions. After the first session, the client has been at least several minutes late for each session and waits until almost the end of the interview to bring up something important to discuss. You feel that he is infringing on your time. This is preventing you from giving your full attention and understanding to the client. You have acknowledged to yourself that this is bothering you. Is it appropriate to go ahead and express this to him? If so, what would you say?

Take a few minutes to think about yourself as the practitioner in these two examples. Now write in the following space what you would do in each example concerning self-disclosure.

There is no right or wrong answer to these two examples; each counseling interaction is somewhat different. Ultimately, you, as the helper, will have to make a decision for yourself in each instance, taking into consideration the client and the context. In the first instance, rather than sharing facts about yourself, there may be more productive ways of helping the client reach her goals. For example, she might be more involved if you suggest role reversal. You become the client; have her be the outgoing and comfortable counselor she sees. In the second instance, the client, by being late, is not fulfilling his share of the responsibility or he is indirectly communicating something about his feelings that needs to be discussed.

APPLICATION EXERCISE 2.5

Expressing Helper Feelings

Sharing and feedback communicate to the client that you have heard or seen something going on and that you have certain thoughts or feelings about it that you want to communicate. Sometimes, you will want to say not only what you feel about a specific instance or experience but also how you feel about the client. This will be more effective if your feelings are expressed as immediate ones—that is, expressed in the present rather than in the past or future. This is the meaning of keeping the process of relationship in the here and now, using what is going on from moment to moment in each session to build the relationship. It is represented by the type of statement that communicates something like the following: "Right now, I'm feeling . . ." or "Right now, we are . . . ."

To experience this here-and-now kind of communication, try to get in touch with yourself this instant. What are you feeling this very moment as you are reading and thinking about this page, this paragraph, this sentence? Write down four or five adjectives that express your present feelings. Tune in to your nonverbal cues too (body position, rate of breathing, tension spots, etc.).

APPLICATION EXERCISE 2.6

Using Sharing Statements

With a partner, engage in some sharing statements that are direct, specific, and immediate. Can you tune in to your feelings as you engage in this kind of communication? What does it do for you, and what effect does it have on the other person? Jot down some of these reactions here. List the sharing statements you have made to your partner.

POSITIVE FEEDBACK STATEMENTS: ENCOURAGEMENT AND STRENGTHS PERSPECTIVE
Positive feedback statements are also related to the quality of congruence. Like self-disclosure, these kinds of statements help clients see their helper as a real human being. Johnson (2014) has pointed out that both self-disclosure and feedback statements can reveal things to clients they do not know about themselves. Like self-disclosure, feedback statements should never be made against the client.

In a review of related research about feedback, Claiborn, Goodyear, and Horner (2002) concluded that positive feedback is more acceptable than negative feedback and that this is especially true early in the helping relationship. Hepworth and colleagues (2013) noted that positive feedback statements can focus on client strengths and effective coping and can empower clients. According to these authors, recordings of sessions between social workers and clients reveal a dearth of responses that underscore client strengths, successes, assets, coping behaviors, and areas of growth.

We spoke of strengths counseling in Chapter 1. Human strengths are important because they protect against illness, both physical and emotional (Vailant, 2000). Also, clients may be more likely to change when helpers focus on strengths rather than deficits (Smith, 2006). This is probably because focusing on strengths builds hope and fosters resilience—in other words, focusing on strengths with clients has "healing effects" (p. 36). One way to focus on client strengths is the intentional use of encouragement—that is, "feedback that emphasizes individuals' efforts or improvement" (p. 41). Positive feedback statements or compliments are key components of the encouragement process with clients (De Jong & Berg, 2013).

Positive feedback statements are useful when you have warm and supportive feelings for clients that are truly genuine. Consider the following examples offered by Hepworth and colleagues (2013, p. 123):

> HELPER TO INDIVIDUAL CLIENT: You have what I consider [an] exceptional ability to "self-observe" your own behavior and to analyze the part you play in relationships. I think this strength will serve you well in solving the problems you have identified.

> HELPER TO CLIENT WHO IS A MEMBER OF A COUNSELING GROUP: I've been touched several times in the group when I've noticed that, despite your grief over the loss of your husband, you've reached out to other members who needed support.

Some guidelines are fundamental to effective feedback processes. Such statements express a feeling of acknowledgment and ownership by the helper, as in "When something happens, I feel . . ." or "When I see you, I think. . . ." Note that these statements use the personal pronoun or "I" messages. They avoid judgment and evaluation. Most of all, they do not accuse or blame, as in the following statement: "You are a real problem to work with because you are always late." In other words, they preserve the dignity and self-respect of the other person involved in the relationship. Furthermore, an effective feedback statement does not contain advice; it is not a "parenting" or scolding statement. It should also concern a behavior or attitude the other person has the capacity to change or modify. For example, it would not be helpful to use the following kind of feedback statement: "I just don't like the way you look. Why don't you do something about your complexion?" Focus your feedback statements on behavior rather than personality traits, and be specific rather than general.

Feedback is usually more effective when it is solicited. Thus, feedback statements that relate to clients' goals or to aspects of the counseling relationship may be better received by clients because of their involvement in this process. In any case, though, you can determine the effects of your feedback by the clients' reactions. If your clients are defensive, give detailed explanations or justifications, or make strong denials, this is a clue that perhaps you have touched on an issue too soon. At this point in the relationship, clients need an indication of your support and acceptance. It is also important to give clients a chance to explore their feelings about and reactions to these feedback statements.

APPLICATION EXERCISE 2.7

Focusing on Strengths: Positive Feedback Statements

A. Characteristics of Feedback

With a partner, try some feedback-type statements similar to the examples described in the preceding section. Be sure your responses include a description of your partner's behavior as well as your reactions to it. For example, you might say something like "I appreciate [your feeling] your taking the time to talk with me [partner's behavior]."

List the feedback statements you make to your partner. What are the effects on you? On the other person? On the relationship?

_____

_____

_____

B. Positive Feedback Statements and Focusing on Strengths

In a small group, construct a positive feedback statement that focuses on a positive ingredient or strength that each member brings to the group. This may refer to a specific behavior you have seen each person demonstrate in the group, or it may refer to something you appreciate about that person. Share your statements verbally in the group. Make sure there is time for the group member to respond to your positive feedback statements.

_____

_____

_____

_____

A CLIMATE OF SAFETY

The conditions of a therapeutic relationship are so important because they are intended to help clients feel safe. When clients feel safe, they feel trusting and free to be open. When clients do not feel safe, they often feel self-protective, guarded, and subdued. It is the helper's responsibility to offer the kind of climate in which clients feel the sense of safety they need in order to ask for and accept help. If a client has come from a particular kind of family or relationship in which there was a lot of stress—such as abuse or incest—then the helper's effort to provide a safe environment will need to be even more intentional and more intensive. Clients—particularly those who have had their trust broken in the past—will often test the helper. They will likely not believe that the therapist's initial efforts to be understanding, sincere, accepting, and warm are really true. They may want to find out if they really mean something—if they really are valued as the helper says they are. This may account for all kinds of client feelings and behaviors that are projected or reflected in or outside a session, including acting out, calling the practitioner on the phone, being late to a session, becoming angry, and so on. It is as if clients long for a warm, caring empathic helper but, due to their history, fear this and, in their fear, they resist, attack, or retreat (Karasu, 1992, p. 21). According to Teyber and McClure (2011), there is nothing that "casual" about these testing behaviors by clients; they are the clients' attempts to assess safety or danger in the helping relationship (p. 327). Establishing a climate of safety means that helpers provide a more effective response to clients than they have received or expect to receive from others; clients feel safer when the helper does not respond in a familiar yet problematic way that they have come to expect (Teyber & McClure, 2011).

A climate of safety is a basic prerequisite to progress in counseling. Efforts to provide a safe, therapeutic environment for clients need to be ongoing and persistent. This is especially true when you are working with clients who do not have privileges and power from the mainstream culture and who have experienced discrimination and oppression.

Summary

Although the helping relationship has some marked differences from other interpersonal relationships, it does serve as a model that the client can use to improve the quality of relationships outside the counseling room. From the view of your clients, the helping relationship is described as a special place outside the usual context of family, friends, and work where they can express themselves freely to a respectful and supportive person (Lilliengren & Werbart, 2005).

Clearly, the helping relationship cannot succeed without the presence of accurate empathy or understanding of the client's world. When you assume that you understand but you do not, you and your client detour from a constructive and helpful course and risk the dangers of false conclusions and failure. In a similar manner, if you do not value your client or if you do not consider the client's problems and concerns to be real, you are denying the most reliable information about your client's perceptions. Lacking this information, you cannot help your client develop in more constructive directions. The degree to which you can be honestly and consistently yourself, know yourself, and share yourself with your client in congruent ways (all of which underlie accurate empathy and positive regard) establishes the ultimate parameters of the helping relationship.

A recent study of clients in counseling described the critical incidents that, from the client's perspective, helped to forge a strong helping relationship (Bedi, Davis, & Williams, 2005). These were described by clients as specific things the helper said or did and included the following:

- Active listening: The counselor remembered what I said.
- Self-disclosure: The counselor recalled an experience similar to my own.
- Encouragement: The counselor focused on what I was doing well.
- Validation of feelings: The counselor understood my fears and my frustration over situations.

Bedi and colleagues (2005) concluded several things about the helping relationship from the client's perspective. First, clients see the strength of the helping relationship as related to things the helper does rather than things the client does. Second, as helpers, we may overlook behaviors and comments that seem simple or benign to us but have tremendous impact on clients for establishing a positive therapeutic relationship.

Although the behaviors presented in this chapter can be learned and incorporated into your style and repertoire, there is a dimension yet to be acknowledged. The integral human element of the helping relationship cannot exist by mechanical manipulation of certain behaviors at given moments. Your relationship with each client contains its own uniqueness and spontaneity that cannot—without the loss of both genuineness and sincerity—be systematically controlled prior to its occurrence. However, your spontaneity will increase rather than decrease once you have become comfortable with a variety of counseling techniques. While you are learning counseling responses, this ease may not be quite as apparent because you will need to overlearn them. However, once the responses suggested in this text have become second nature to you, your spontaneity as a helper will begin to emerge. You will be on your way to becoming the helper you hope to be.

Reflective Questions

1. How do you approach a new relationship? What conditions do you require to be met before you open yourself to a closer relationship?
2. What were the "unwritten rules" in your family and in your culture about interactions with nonfamily members? How might these rules affect the kind of relationship you are able to offer clients?
3. If you were a client, what conditions would you look for in your helper?

4. Under what conditions do you feel safe? Do you feel open and able to disclose? Trusting? Does this vary with persons of different ages, gender, values, and ethnic origins?
5. How have your own childhood experiences influenced your relationships with others as an adult? In exploring this for yourself, can you see potential connections between the childhood experiences of your clients and the way they may relate to you and to others?

MyCounselingLab

For each exercise, log on to MyCounselingLab.

1. Choose the Video Library tab under Video Resources; locate the Process, Skills, and Techniques tab; and select: "Empathy as a Foundation for Engagement." Watch this segment and then comment on how the two practitioners conveyed empathic understanding to this client as her grief unfolds.
2. Click the Process, Skills, and Techniques tab again. Watch "Example of Counselor Self-Disclosure." What did you think about this clinician's use of

self-disclosure in this clip? How was it used? Did it seem to elicit something positive in the session?

3. Click the Process, Skills, and Techniques tab once again. Now watch "Establishing an Egalitarian Relationship." Comment on what you saw the practitioner do to establish a strong helping relationship with the client. Discuss instances in which you were able to identify empathy, positive regard, and congruence on her part. What effects did this seem to have on the client?

Recommended Readings

Bein, A. W. (2008). *The Zen of helping*. Hoboken, NJ: John Wiley & Sons.

Brammer, L. M., & MacDonald, G. (2003). *The helping relationship* (8th ed.). Boston, MA: Allyn & Bacon.

Breggin, P., Breggin, G., & Bemak, F. (Eds.). (2002). *Dimensions of empathic therapy*. New York, NY: Springer.

Chi-Ying Chung, R., & Bemak, F. (2002). The relationship of culture and empathy in cross-cultural counseling. *Journal of Counseling and Development, 80*, 154–159.

Clark, A. J. (2007). *Empathy in counseling and psychotherapy*. New York, NY: Erlbaum.

Cowan, E. W., Presbury, J., & Echterling, L. (2013, February). The paradox of empathy: When empathy hurts. *Counseling Today,* 56–61.

Hepworth, D. H., Rooney, R. H., Rooney, G. D., & Strom-Gottfried, K. (2013). *Direct social work practice* (9th ed.). Belmont, CA: Brooks/Cole, Cengage.

Johnson, D. W. (2014). *Reaching out: Interpersonal effectiveness and self-actualization* (11th ed.). Upper Saddle River, NJ: Pearson Education.

Norcross, J. C. (Ed.). (2011). *Psychotherapy relationships that work: Evidence-based responsiveness* (2nd ed.). New York, NY: Oxford University Press.

Pedersen, P., Crethar, H., & Carlson, J. (2008). *Inclusive cultural empathy*. Washington, DC: American Psychological Association.

Siegel, D. (2010). *The mindful therapist*. New York, NY: Norton.

Zur, O., Williams, M., Lehavot, K., & Knapp, S. (2009). Therapist self-disclosure and transparency in the Internet age. *Professional Psychology, 40,* 22–30.

Communication Patterns in the Helping Process

As the helper-client relationship develops, communication patterns emerge. Issues related to the locus of control and responsibility in the session, choice of topics, timing, and other therapeutic logistics are undefined at the outset of the helping process. In the first few sessions, these issues are resolved—either openly or tacitly—and become apparent through understanding the communication patterns that evolve.

Ivy (2012) defines communication as an ongoing and complex process of sending and receiving both verbal and nonverbal messages for the purposes of sharing meaning (p. 30). She notes that some of us are more effective communicators than others or are more effective in some situations than others, but she stresses that all of us can learn to improve our communication patterns.

There are many ways to think about communication patterns in the helping process. Some patterning takes the form of ritual, whereas other patterning is responsive. That is, some of the behaviors become ritualized as a function of routine; for example, the client always chooses the chair facing the window or the helper always begins by asking, "What is on your mind today?" and so forth. Other patterns are negotiations between the practitioner and client, the intent of which may be to settle matters such as "Are we really going to work today?" or "I want you to take charge because I'm feeling overwhelmed." Frequent topic shifts made by the client in early helping sessions may be an expression of client anxiety and of a need to control something about the process. If the helper is unaware of these shifts in communication and also of the client's underlying affect, progress may be impeded.

Ritualized communication patterns in helping can be useful in some situations because they are predictable and provide security, especially to clients who grow accustomed to them. At other times, however, ritualized patterns of communication can be inhibiting and create blockages instead of growth. Ivy (2012) suggests one way to counteract rigid or stuck communication patterns is to expand your repertoire. As helpers we tend to get fixated in communicating and relating in certain ways, as if we have only one mode of communication and that is "default" (Ivy, 2012, p. 33). The issue with default communication is that we can get stuck in a "relational rut" (Ivy, 2012, p. 33). As she notes, a primary goal of expanding your verbal and nonverbal communication repertoire is to "enlarge your communication 'bag of tools' from which to choose when you confront various communication situations so that you're not locked into some predictable pattern" all the time (p. 33).

As you will see later in this chapter, communication styles and patterns are greatly influenced by cultural variables such as ethnicity, race, gender, disability, sexual orientation, and so on, and particular communication patterns do not always have the same meaning for different clients. It is incumbent upon helpers to adapt communication styles and patterns across diverse groups of clients because one size does *not* fit all.

RITUALIZED PATTERNS OF COMMUNICATION

Ritualized patterns may be either situation-specific or idiosyncratic to the individuals involved. For example, we have already mentioned examples of situation-specific patterning with the client who always chooses a certain chair to sit in. This act of repeated choice may arise out of a very simple condition. It was the chair selected by the client at the initial session, and its continued selection in subsequent sessions offers familiar ground and reflects that the client feels no need to make a different choice. However, if the client arrives for the fifth session and, with no explanation, chooses a different chair, the act of choice may contain unspecified meaning. In other words, through the act of choosing, something is communicated, but what is communicated is unclear until the helper explores this with the client.

Ritualized Helper Patterns

The same situation may apply to the helper. Most experienced helpers develop a style of interaction with their clients. Although their style takes individuals into account, it is nonetheless patterned and, as such, is a kind of trademark of that particular practitioner's work. For example, one clinician may use the first several minutes of the session as relationship time and may communicate this to clients. A different clinician may view the first few minutes as history-taking time. However, should a client arrive in a distraught state, that pattern may be suspended, and therapeutic work may begin immediately.

Ritualized Client Patterns

Clients also become involved in ritualized patterns of communication. Often, these patterns evolve out of assumptions about what the helper wants or expects from the client. For example, a client may assume that the helper expects to hear an account of the week's worries. The fact that this happened in the second session led the client to think such an account is expected, so he or she continues the practice in subsequent sessions. Thus, although the activity may have little to do with the ensuing process, it remains part of the pattern. Often, such patterns are useful to clients because they provide stability and predictability. Occasionally, however, the purpose or intention behind the pattern outlives its usefulness, and the helper needs to challenge the pattern gently.

INTERACTIVE COMMUNICATION PATTERNS
ACROSS DIVERSE CLIENT GROUPS

Interactive communication patterns are influenced by cultural variables such as race, ethnicity, gender, sexual orientation and gender identity, disability, and immigration/refugee status. Most patterning—and certainly the most significant patterning that occurs in helping sessions—is interactive in nature. It has been suggested by Hackney and Cormier (2013) that most clients approach counseling with two conflicting motivations: (1) "I know I need help" and (2) "I wish I weren't here." Given this dual set of motivations, the client may be expected to convey conflicting and even contradictory communications at times. Similarly, helpers must resolve the potential conflict that was mentioned in Chapter 2 regarding unconditional positive regard and congruence, when the helper's feelings about the client may be pulled in two different directions. We mention these conflicting tendencies because they can confuse the communication process. It is essential that the helper remains aware of such conflicts in communication patterns. In addition to these contradictory communications, interactive communication patterns are also influenced by the cultural variables mentioned at the beginning of this paragraph (race, ethnicity, gender, sexual orientation and gender identity, disability, and immigration/refugee status). These cultural variables also affect the quality of the therapeutic relationship.

In the preceding chapter, we discussed how core conditions of empathy, positive regard, and genuineness are necessary for establishing a healing and effective helping relationship with clients. In this chapter, we go beyond that to suggest that helping relationships are strengthened when practitioners can alter their ritualized communication patterns by flexibly offering adaptations to such patterns with clients. This stance has empirical support; the efforts of Norcross (2011) and others have found that adapting or tailoring the helping relationship to specific client characteristics enhances the effectiveness of counseling and psychotherapy (Norcross, 2011). And conversely, less effective helpers "rarely tailor or customize treatment to patient characteristics beyond diagnosis" (Norcross, 2011, p. 427). Such adaptations are particularly potent when it comes to cultural dimensions of client characteristics where flexibility of helper communication patterns is key to effectiveness (Smith, Rodriguez, & Bernal, 2011). In this chapter, we focus on characteristics of clients where communication patterns and styles may be particularly challenging to typical helpers and where adaptation and flexibility are especially important. The dimensions we consider in this chapter include the following:

Race and ethnicity

Gender

Sexual orientation and gender identity

Disability

Immigration and refugee status

Communication and Race and Ethnicity

Sue and Sue (2013) note that different racial and ethnic groups differ in their communication styles. For example, "many cultural minorities tend not to value verbalizations in the same way that Americans do. In traditional Chinese culture, children have been taught not to speak until spoken to. Patterns of communication tend to be vertical, flowing from those of higher prestige and status to those of lower prestige and status. In a therapy situation, many Chinese clients, to show respect for a therapist who is older and wiser and who occupies a position of higher status, may respond with silence. Unfortunately, an unenlightened counselor or therapist may perceive this client as being inarticulate and less intelligent" (Sue & Sue, 2013, p. 187).

Sue and Sue (2008) have provided other examples of different communication patterns, such as the following: "African-American styles of communication are often high-key, animated, heated, interpersonal, and confrontational" and often "African Americans tend to act as *advocates* of a position" (p. 224). In contrast, White, middle-class communication styles are usually characterized more as "being detached and objective, impersonal, and nonchallenging," and Whites often act as a "*spokesperson*" rather than an advocate (Sue & Sue, 2013, p. 224). Unfortunately, a culturally uninformed helper may view varying patterns of client communication in pejorative ways. For example, an Asian client practicing restraint of strong feelings may be viewed by a culturally uninformed practitioner as being "inhibited, lacking in spontaneity, or repressed" (p. 187).

Pedersen and Ivey (1993, p. 14) have identified four possible communication barriers in the cross-cultural helping process: verbal and nonverbal language problems, interference from preconceptions and stereotyping, erroneous evaluation, and stress. For example, clients who are bilingual or trilingual, who do not speak Standard English, or who have a pronounced accent or limited command of Standard English may be misunderstood by helpers. Other language barriers may exist with clients from different geographic locations. For example, a client from Russia may not understand certain English phrases and idioms, or a Jewish client may use Yiddish phrases to describe certain things to the practitioner. Sue and Sue (2013) conclude that the lack of bilingual therapists and the requirement that the culturally different client communicate in English may limit the person's ability to progress in counseling. As you can imagine, from the clients' point of view, having a helper who does not understand the way they talk and express themselves can seriously dampen their desire to return for future sessions.

Generally speaking, clients belonging to different cultural groups are more receptive to communication patterns that are similar to their own and that are respectful of their values. For example, American Indians, Asian Americans, Black Americans, and Hispanic Americans tend to prefer more active and directive forms of helping rather than more passive, nondirective communication (Sue & Sue, 2013, p. 228). A communication mismatch can occur between cross-cultural helping dyads if the helper focuses on more passive-attending skills (such as those described in Chapter 4) and the client prefers a more active communication approach. As Sue and Sue (2013) conclude, "[W]hen the counseling style of the counselor does not match the communication style of his or her culturally diverse clients, many difficulties may arise: premature termination of the session, inability to establish rapport, or cultural oppression of the client" (p. 229). As these authors note, this caveat applies to both White helpers and also counselors of color (Sue & Sue, 2013). Some beginning helpers have difficulty understanding how differences in communication styles in culturally diverse helping dyads may result in these conditions. To that question, Sue and Sue (2008) reply that the helping process represents a "special type of temporary culture" (p. 229). Misunderstandings and breakdowns in the communication process in cross-cultural counseling dyads are more likely to occur if helpers assume that certain rules and patterns of speaking are universal and possess the same meaning.

Implications for Practice

Many helpers develop their communication style from the perspective, standards, and worldview of their own ethnicity and race. As a result, there may be limits on how much practitioners can adapt or change their communication styles to match those of their clients. At the same time, practitioners can stretch, grow, and cultivate nuances and variances within such styles to enhance communication with a wide range of clients. A number of authors have suggested recommendations for practice in effective communication with clients who represent racial and ethnic minorities:

1. Expand your repertoire of helping styles and roles in order to shift your helping style to meet the cultural dimensions of your clients. Recognize that there is not a "one size fits all" approach to communicating with clients in general and with clients of racial and ethnic minorities in particular.

2. Become knowledgeable about how race, culture, and gender affect communication styles.

3. Obtain additional training and education on a variety of theoretical approaches and orientations, particularly those that consider not only individual characteristics but also contextual and systemic factors. Such training helps you to see how systems affect individuals.

4. Think holistically about clients, for example, recognizing that people are not just a product of their thinking or behavior, but are "feeling, thinking, behaving, cultural, spiritual, and political" beings (Sue & Sue, 2013, p. 232).

Communication and Gender

Communication patterns are also influenced by gender. While biological sex is the degree to which a client was born genetically into a male or female body, gender refers to the clients' personal sense of feeling and behaving as a woman or a man. Gender communication is communication both about and between men and women. Ivy (2012, p. 21) states that "communication becomes *gendered* when sex or gender overtly begins to influence your choices—choices of what you say and how you relate to others." Gender roles and schemata cannot help but spill over or infiltrate the helping process, so both ritualized and responsive patterns between same-gender and different-gender helper and client pairs are likely to vary somewhat.

Wood (2013, p. 136) points out that men and women have learned to relate experiences via varying communication styles, which can often result in breakdowns in the communication process. She states:

> Masculine speech tends to follow a linear pattern, in which major points in a story are presented sequentially to get to the climax. Talk tends to be straightforward without a great many details. The rules of feminine speech, however, call for more detailed, less linear storytelling. Whereas a man is likely to provide rather bare information about what happened, a woman is more likely to embed the information within a larger context of the people involved and other things going on. Women include details, not because they are important at the content level of meaning but because they matter at the relationship level of meaning. Recounting details is meant to increase involvement between people . . . Because feminine and masculine rules about details differ, men often find feminine accounts wandering and tedious. . . . (p. 136)

You can probably see how this could play out in a helping session. Male helpers may need to learn patience in listening to female clients' accounts of experiences, while female helpers may need to learn to respect male clients' ways of relating experiences without overtly pushing them to include more detailed information.

A qualitative research study that assessed perceptions of male and female clients by female and male counselors found a great deal of consistency and similarity among the counselors' descriptions of clients of both genders (Vogel, Epting, & Wester, 2003). However, two primary areas of difference emerged. Both female and male counselors tended to view female clients as emotionally vulnerable. At the same time, these counselors viewed the male clients as having difficulties in self-control. What is striking about these differences is that they seem to reflect more traditional gender role notions. As the authors explain, this may be because the clients in this study actually did have different presentations in the session or it may be because there was some unintentional gender bias affecting the counselors' perceptions of the clients (Vogel et al., 2003). In either case, they conclude that practitioners need to "increase the range of affective and behavioral responses that they consider healthy and appropriate for each of the sexes" to promote gender-fair counseling (p. 139).

We think it is important to note that any perpetuation of restrictive gender roles by helpers toward clients is as damaging toward male clients as it is toward female clients. O'Neil (2013) has made a valuable contribution to the helping literature in his cogent article about ways in which mens' psychological issues are related to restrictive gender roles. He has conducted several decades of research to produce evidence-based documentation that "a man's restricted thoughts, feelings, and behaviors about masculine gender roles predict serious psychological and interpersonal problems" (p. 22). He believes that gender-sensitive therapy with men can produce patterns of positive masculinity that can help men and boys "learn alternatives to sexist attitudes and behaviors" and identify "the personal qualities that empower males to improve themselves, their families, and the larger society" (p. 22).

In a comprehensive review of gender issues in the helping process, Enns (2000) observes that "power differentials" are reflected in communication patterns (p. 613). For example, use of language that conveys standards and expectations based on male norms communicates a subtle but biased power differential between the genders. Similarly, heterosexist biases are conveyed when noninclusive language is used to refer to intimate partnerships and parenting. Part of the use of gender-sensitive language means that helpers are sensitive to the ways in which all people—including those who hold unearned privilege—may feel disempowered by patriarchal norms and values. Brown (2010) posits that feminist therapy, an approach as applicable to men as it is to women, is one that has empowerment for clients as "its superordinate goal" (p. 29). She states: "[S]uch empowerment is seen as having the important function of subverting patriarchal influences in the lives and psyches of all of those involved in the therapy process, including the therapist. Because both parties, therapist and client alike, are immersed in patriarchal cultures, the process of uncovering disempowerment and developing strategies toward empowerment is ongoing, with each feminist therapist discovering the deep and subtle ways in which patriarchal assumptions of hierarchy and privilege inform her or his work and the experience of the people who come into the office" (p. 30). In communication with clients, there is a specific focus on helping the client move toward personal power in situations where powerlessness has occurred.

Fixed gender roles not only result in differing communication patterns between women and men but they may also produce gender-role stress and shame-proneness for both, thus affecting communication. As Efthim, Kenny, and Mahalik (2001) assert, helpers need to be attentive to the links among gender, shame, guilt, and externalized communication patterns. They state that "clients who seem rigidly committed to traditional gender role norms may be shame-prone, and so the counselor should exercise care when communication centers around feelings of not 'measuring up' as a woman or man" (p. 79). From their research, these authors also note that "male clients who are stressed about being in contexts in which traditional male dominance is threatened or in which tender emotions are being expressed may rely on externalizing defenses. . . . [That is,] they may speak in the language of threat and counterthreat, particularly regarding the danger of being perceived as 'feminine' or of being seen as failing to prove their masculinity. Female clients, on the other hand, may respond with either overt shame or externalization when coping with stress in domains where male power has a direct impact on them: concerns about body image, feeling vulnerable about victimization, and discomfort with situations calling for assertive behavior" (p. 436).

The overall goal of recognizing gender patterns in communication during helping sessions is to develop awareness of any gender-stereotyped patterns that could potentially harm the client. Pittman (1985) coined the term *gender broker* to describe the function of practitioners in helping clients examine socialization and communication styles, old and new. All the ethical codes of conduct in human services promote the idea of being respectful, informed, and nondiscriminatory in the theory and practice of gender communication.

Implications for Practice

Both women and men are affected by traditional gender-role situations. Hoffman (2001), Bartholomew (2003), Brown (2010), and O'Neil (2013) have offered a number of suggestions for gender-sensitive communication:

1. Support clients' desires to break free from the oppression of traditional gender norms.
2. Communicate empathy for the plight of both genders.
3. Use gender inquiry questions to help understand messages clients have received about gender, such as "Do you remember anything that happened when you were growing up that strengthened your sense of being a girl or boy?" or "What did you learn about how you should be acting as a girl or boy?" and "How do these messages still affect you?"
4. Attend to ways in which other aspects of culture affect gender development in clients' lives. For example, how have dimensions such as religious affiliation, ethnicity, geography, age, and so on, affected the client's sense of being a woman or a man? Have these other dimensions restricted or expanded the client's sense of gender?
5. Be especially attentive to the ways in which powerlessness and helplessness characterize the client's communication and stance in therapy. Be mindful of the ways in which you as the helper may be perpetuating patriarchal assumptions in your communication with clients. We especially like the questions that Brown (2010) recommends for communicating about power with clients, including the following:

"What is the most powerful thing you could do right now?" (p. 35)
"What are the power dynamics in this situation?" (p. 30)

6. Become sensitized and alert to ways in which women and men have been socialized to talk in varying ways and for different purposes. Wood (2013, pp. 134–135) discusses some specific ways in which gendered communication may result in breakdowns and misunderstandings in communication. For example, a female client may talk to obtain a connection and find support from the helper when the male helper responds by giving information or advice. In another example, a male client may feel pushed by a female helper who tries to delve quickly into feelings and vulnerabilities when the male client is quiet or withdrawn. Wood (2013) concludes that respecting gender differences in communication "calls on us to suspend judgment based on our own perspectives and to consider more thoughtfully what others mean in their own terms, not ours" (p. 138).

Communication with Lesbian, Gay, Bisexual, Transgender, and Questioning Clients

In this section, we discuss communication with clients who are identified as lesbian, gay, bisexual, transgender, and questioning (LGBTQ), meaning persons who have an emotional, romantic, sexual, or affectionate attraction to persons of the same sex (lesbian women and gay men); persons who have a sexual attraction to persons of both sexes (bisexuals); persons whose identification with their gender is different from their biological sex (transgender); and persons who are questioning their sexuality. Note that transgender status reflects gender identity and is separate from sexual orientation. In some parts of the world, attitudes toward LGBTQ persons are becoming more accepting; in other areas, attitudes are becoming more punitive and restrictive, and LGBTQ clients still live in a world privileged by heterosexuality. As a result, many LGBTQ individuals face discrimination, prejudice, harassment, and bullying.

Historically, LGBTQ persons were labeled as being sick, disturbed, or pathological, and there have been some attempts in the mental health community to engage in therapeutic practices with LGBTQ clients in which these clients were told they could or should change their sexual orientation with therapeutic practices known as conversion therapy. However, homosexuality was removed from the American Psychiatric Association's list of mental disorders in 1973; in 2009, the American Psychological Association (APA) reviewed the research on sexual orientation and concluded that same-sex attractions and orientation are not pathological conditions and that therapeutic efforts to change clients' sexual orientation are unwarranted and unsubstantiated. APA has also published guidelines for conducting therapy with lesbian, gay, and bisexual clients (American Psychological Association, 2012b).

In spite of these advances, research still suggests that many helpers have prejudicial beliefs that affect the helping relationship with LGBTQ clients and/or engage in biased and inappropriate communication with LGBTQ clients (Shelton & Delgado-Romero, 2011). For example, many helpers still communicate at least implicitly that their clients are heterosexual or suggest that LGBTQ clients are mentally ill or unstable. All helpers should familiarize themselves with competencies for working with LGBTQ clients by consulting a number of resources including the Association of Lesbian, Gay, Bisexual & Transgender Issues in Counseling (ALGBTIC) competencies (Association of Lesbian, Gay, Bisexual & Transgender Issues in Counseling, 2008). Practitioners also should recognize that ethical practice with LGBTQ clients means that helpers are able to label themselves as LGBTQ-friendly or -affirming and are able to avoid communication with LGBTQ clients that fosters oppression and prejudice.

Implications for Practice

A number of suggestions for communication with LGBTQ clients have been offered by Dermer, Smith, and Barto (2010), as well as the national website for the Association of Lesbian, Gay, Bisexual & Transgender Issues in Counseling (2008) and the American Psychological Association (2009). We have summarized these as follows:

1. Develop awareness about how heterosexual privilege (accrued benefits from belonging to a dominant societal group, heterosexual in this instance) can affect both verbal communication and nonverbal aspects of communication with LBGTQ clients. Heterosexual privilege can affect everything from reading material, brochures, intake forms, pictures and calendars on office walls, as well as language.

2. Be sensitive to your language and try to minimize heterosexist bias in your language. This is an important thing to do with *all* clients because the client's sexual orientation may be unknown to you for a period of time. It is always important *never to assume* your client's sexual orientation or gender identity. A big part of using nonheterosexist language also has to do with understanding and using terms that describe this client population accurately. Dermer, Smith, and Barto (2010) have written a very useful article on this topic. As they state, "[A] larger pool of language now exists to describe negative attitudes and actions toward sexual minorities, and it is important for clinicians to understand the various terms and the possible consequences of particular language," especially when it comes to the nuances of terms that describe sexual intolerance. They prefer the terms *homonegativity* and *heterosexism* to *homophobia*. Also, particular clients may have another term to describe themselves, so one way to facilitate effective communication with LGBTQ clients is simply to ask them how they self-identify and prefer to be described or how they describe themselves.

3. The ALGBTIC competencies state that helpers need to be aware that language with these clients is always evolving, varies from person to person, and has been used to oppress LGBTQ clients. They also indicate that certain labels used to describe LGBTQ clients require contextualization to be used appropriately. Be attentive to the language used in your intake forms and your diagnostic questions and history taking. Provide a space for the client to write in gender status in addition to the traditional boxes of male and female, and use terms such as *partnered* and *spouse and relationship dissolution* in addition to the more traditional terms of *married* and *divorced*. Include a question about sexual attraction and orientation.

4. Engage in self-reflection about your own gender identity and sexual orientation, and know how this affects your process and the helping relationship. ALGBTIC standards of competence state that helpers should use self-disclosure about their own affectional status and sexual orientation carefully and only when it is clearly in the best interest of the LGBTQ client to do so. Be aware, however, that an occasional client may ask you if you are straight or not, so be prepared to address their questions about your sexual orientation, your prior experience working with LGBTQ clients, your comfort level discussing LGBTQ issues, and your personal beliefs about LGBTQ issues. It would not be uncommon now, for example, to have a client ask you about your views on gay marriage.

5. Be careful about any communication that suggests negative assumptions concerning pathology or dysfunction in LGBTQ individual clients, couples, and families; at the same time, do recognize and be prepared to communicate about the potential impact of societal stigmatization and poor legal protection for these clients. Realize that a client's LGBTQ identity may or may not be part of their presenting concerns.
6. Recognize the positive impact on communication of becoming an ally for LGBTQ clients. Having a Safe Zone sticker on your office door communicates this information to clients right away. Remember that a Safe Zone sticker lets clients know that you have been through training that means you are supportive toward and sensitive to the needs of LGBTQ persons. Develop your advocacy skills and your comfort level in speaking up and speaking out. Anyone can join ALGBTIC as an ally member.
7. Recognize how ethical practices affect communication with LGBTQ clients. Consult the ALGBTIC competencies, and use other resources as well to be informed and stay abreast of knowledge that affects your work with LGBTQ clients.

Communication with Clients with Disabilities

An increasing number of clients are persons with chronic health issues and conditions that have some disabling effects. Some of these clients have sensory disabilities involving sight or hearing; some have a condition limiting basic physical activities; others have a condition that affects their learning, remembering, or concentration; and still others have a condition that affects their ability to work at a job. While this is not a conclusive list of disabilities, perhaps it does give you a sense of the wide range of clients whom you may see. While some disabilities are more visible than others, the word itself refers to functional limitations a person experiences as a result of an impairment. While some disabilities are the result of progressive, chronic conditions, others are not, and in these instances, the client with a substantial disability may be healthier than the clinician. The area of disabilities has grown in the last several decades by leaps and bounds: Some universities are now offering programs in disability studies.

The potential impact of clients' disabilities on communication styles and patterns may often be either unknown or minimized by helpers. For example, through the American with Disabilities Act, many strides have been made in improving accessibility in buildings, increasing access to education, and opening up employment opportunities for persons with disabilities. However, much less attention has been given in general to communication and interaction with people with disabilities. A helper's sense of discomfort in working with someone with a disability—particularly a client with a visible disability—may consciously or unconsciously result in the helper's communication withdrawal, for fear of saying the wrong things. As a result, the client may feel more invisible or more stigmatized simply by the helper's absence of or limited communication. Issues in communication patterns between helpers and clients with disabilities may include awkward or biased use of language, shorter interactions and prematurely terminated helping sessions, greater interpersonal distance between helper and client during the session, and restricted or stiff oral communication. Helpers also may shut down their communication patterns by not asking questions, by wondering how helpful they should be, or by internal reactions about their own real or potential disability status. For example, as Daughtry, Gibson, and Abels (2009) have observed, many helping professionals have disability-related biases and anxieties that result in considerable interpersonal distance in the interaction. In addition, some clients with disabilities may have conditions such as hearing and visual impairments that require assistive communication devices, and these devices may somewhat alter the communication flow between client and helper. In the following section, we make recommendations for communicating with clients with disabilities.

Implications for Practice

Some of these recommendations come from my own experience, and others are recommended by Daughtry et al. (2009, p. 204), Artman & Daniels (2010), and the American Psychological Association (2012a, 2013).

1. Be aware of and sensitive to language. *Language* has the possibility of healing or hurting.

Use affirmative phrases, such as the "client with a disability" rather than "my disabled client." Avoid using the word *handicapped* to refer to any client! Similarly, a helper can refer to his or her client as a person with a psychiatric disability rather than a crazy person, or a client who uses a wheelchair rather than a client confined to a wheelchair. This is language that considers the person first rather than the disability, avoids sensationalizing the disability, and avoids verbs that suggest images of passivity (Artman & Daniels, 2010). Similarly, it is important to avoid using descriptors that refer to clients with disabilities in ways that evoke pity, such as "afflicted by," "the victim of," "struck by," "crippled with," and so on. As Artman and Daniels (2010, p. 444) point out, these kinds of phrases represent the projections of able-bodied practitioners and are actually expressions of negativity toward clients with disabilities.

2. Use supportive, nonverbal communication. For example, it is appropriate when meeting a client with a disability to offer to shake hands, using either the right or left hand. Also, when working with a client using crutches or using a wheelchair, place yourself at eye level with the person. Do not pat a client in a wheelchair on the head or shoulders. Avoid shouting at a person with a hearing impairment. Look directly at the client and speak clearly, slowly, and expressively, especially if this is a client who is reading lips. Rephrase your communications if necessary but do not keep repeating yourself word for word as this tends to be insulting. If the client is using an electronic communication device, stand in front of the person and refrain from reading over her or his shoulder when engaged in typing. Be mindful of environmental space and potential obstacles and barriers in the office areas. If the client is there with an accompanying individual, be sure to address the client directly rather than the other person.

3. Develop a communication style that is direct and respectful rather than avoidant or condescending. Address clients with disabilities in the same way you would other clients. For example, do not talk with clients with disabilities as though they are childlike or ill. Address clients with disabilities by their first names only if this is a practice you use with all your clients. If some clients have difficulty in speaking or understanding, listen carefully, do not rush the communication in the session, and do not pretend to understand when you do not. Instead, rephrase what you do understand, and give the client time to respond. Avoid finishing or completing sentences for the client. At the same time, if you do not understand a particular client because he or she uses a communication aid or has difficulty with speech, do not automatically assume he or she cannot understand you! If the client with a disability has a communication issue, he or she will probably let you know and indicate a preferred method of communicating. You can facilitate the communication process by *asking the client what she or he needs from you as a communicator and then adapting your communication style accordingly.* Ask rather than assume that a person with a disability automatically needs or requires some sort of assistance from you.

4. Develop cultural competence in working with clients with disabilities and gain as much information as you can, but recognize that reading about disabilities in books and articles is somewhat self-limiting. When possible, seek consultation with mental health professionals who have disabilities such as deafness, visual impairment, and so on (Whyte, Aubrecht, McCullough, Lewis, & Thompson-Ochoa, 2013). Maintain good connections for referral options with other mental health professionals who self-identify as having various disabilities because some clients with disabilities may request or prefer a referral to a helper who is living with a disability. At the same time, remember that you cannot deny services to a client with a disability nor should you separate or give unequal service to clients with disabilities (American Psychological Association, 2013). Remember too that disability status is a relatively porous state; often a person can move in and out of it at any time. Disability activists refer to those who are not physically or mentally impaired as temporarily able-bodied (TAB) to reflect the notion that able-bodiedness is not usually a permanent state of being for any given individual.

Communication with Clients Who Are Immigrants or Refugees

In the national bestseller *Outcasts United,* Warren St. John (2009), a reporter for the *New York Times,* chronicles the transformation that occurs in a small southern town in Georgia after it is designated in the 1990s as a refugee settlement center. Currently, about 40 percent of the town's population is foreign born, and the public high school has students enrolled from over fifty countries in the world. At the same time, the town is also populated with residents who were born in Clarkston and have lived there their entire lives. Some of them have rarely ventured outside its borders. St. John says this about the multilayered situation in Clarkston filled with immigrants and refugees:

> When I think about Clarkston, I sometimes visualize the town as a lifeboat being lowered from a vast, multilevel passenger ship. No one aboard chose this particular vessel. Rather, they were assigned to it—the refugees by resettlement officials they never met, the townspeople by a faraway bureaucratic apparatus that decided, almost haphazardly, to put a sampling of people from all over the world in the modest little boat locals thought they had claimed for themselves. . . . [E]veryone on the boat wanted the same thing: Safety. But to get there, they would first have to figure out how to communicate with each other, how to organize themselves, how to allocate their resources, and which direction they should row. (p. 10)

Migration is a global issue and occurs around the world. In the United States alone, there has been a 44 percent increase in migration since 1990 (Chung, Bemak, Ortiz, & Sandoval-Perez, 2008). Currently, about 1 out of every 10 persons living in the United States comes from a refugee or immigrant background (Chung et al., 2008). Many of these migratory persons have relocated in places like Clarkston, Georgia, communities that are unaccustomed to diversity and with little experience integrating diverse individuals into the local culture. Chung and colleagues (2008) as well as Segal and Mayadas (2005) have contributed to our understanding of the fact that not all migratory clients are the same. There are some distinct differences between immigrants and refugees, although these groups are often lumped together. Immigrants are those who voluntarily migrate; refugees are forced to migrate. As Segal and Mayadas (2005) point out, currently refugees are able to adjust their status to immigrant after a year of residence in the United States, but the "psychosocial profile of a large proportion of the refugee population has little in common with that of most immigrants" (p. 564). Echoing the definition of Chung et al. (2008), Segal and Mayadas (2005) note that most immigrants are *pulled* to the United States or another country by the perceived attractiveness of it; in contrast, refugees are *pushed out* of their country of origin, often due to traumatic and unforeseen events (p. 564). Once resettled or settled here, however, both groups, and also undocumented immigrants, experience issues with discrimination, language barriers, and cultural issues, as well as enormous stressors (Segal & Mayadas, 2005; Birman, Simon, Yi Chan, & Tran, 2014).

In counseling individuals who migrate to the United States, practitioners will most likely encounter various barriers to effective communication. In part, these clients may guard personal information very closely due to fear of exposure, and they may mistrust any person they perceive as being in a position of authority (Segal & Mayadas, 2005, p. 569; Singer & Tummala-Narra, 2013). Sue and Sue (2013) observe that some immigrant clients may view the helper as "an arm of the government" (p. 461).

A significant barrier to communication with immigrants and refugee clients is often a language one because, for many of these individuals, English is not their primary language. As a result, interpreters are often used to facilitate communication in the helping process. The addition of a third person to the typical helping dyad adds a dynamic all its own. The interpreters may have emotional reactions to material or traumas discussed by the client, and the helpers may develop emotional reactions toward the interpreter. Sometimes the clients may develop a stronger attachment base to the interpreter rather than the helper (Sue & Sue, 2013, p. 464).

With refugee clients, it is important to realize the potential impact of their "preimmigration trauma, often life-threatening in nature," which results in greater degrees of stress for this client population than other immigrants (Sue & Sue, 2013, p. 466). Because of prior trauma and resulting shame, refugee clients may even be more reluctant to self-disclose personal information to helpers as well as information about prior traumas. Issues surrounding safety may present in the helping process as paramount.

Implications for Practice

Segal and Mayadas (2005), Chung et al. (2008), and Singer and Tummala-Narra (2013) have offered a number of suggestions for effective communication with immigrant and refugee clients. Communication between Western practitioners and immigrants and refugees can be one of the most challenging because of the potentially substantial gaps of understanding between the practitioner and the client. Communication with immigrants and refugees requires a special skill set that includes knowledge about current local, state, and federal laws and debates regarding immigration (which are constantly shifting), as well as knowledge about the client's country of origin and the immigration process (Sue & Sue, 2013). I have summarized a number of implications for practice with immigrant and refugee clients:

1. Structuring of the initial helping session and of the helping process is important for all clients, of course, but it is especially important in communicating effectively with refugee and immigrant clients. Describe your role very carefully to these clients and emphasize your independence from the government. Provide sufficient and repeated

explanations of what the helping process involves and what your role is, and also inquire about how the clients see their role in the process as well. Be aware that their cultural norms will certainly affect many of these clients' expectations of and receptivity to the helping process (Singer & Tummala-Narra, 2013, p. 293).

2. Pay careful attention to issues of privacy and safety. Make sure that the client feels comfortable in the counseling environment. Sue and Sue (2013) suggest that services to immigrants might fare better if they are offered within the immigration community itself with participation from other immigrant helpers. Explain the concepts of privacy and confidentiality in close detail and make sure that the client really understands and grasps the implications of these concepts for the formation of safety and trust and the disclosure of personal information.

3. Be gentle with clients who may have experienced pre-immigration traumas. Do not push them to reveal their experiences sooner than they feel ready; allow them to determine the pace and timing of disclosure and discussion of such information.

4. Provide full explanations of how the health care system in the United States (or your country) works. Remember that most of these clients will have very little understanding of this process and may seem noncompliant when, in reality, they are just uninformed and confused. One of the most challenging clients I (Sherry) ever worked with was an immigrant professional in the United States on a green card who wanted a consult with a psychiatrist at the local psychiatric hospital. He was incensed that he could not get an immediate appointment. His insistence on being able to obtain an appointment with the doctor as a walk-in made absolutely no sense to me until I inquired about the health care system in his country of origin and discovered that doctors there are available around the clock on a walk-in basis and people rarely schedule appointments in advance.

5. Expect and be prepared to deal with language barriers. Because many of these clients may not speak English as a primary language, expect to use an interpreter or to listen extra carefully to the client's English. In the above example, I (Sherry) did not need an interpreter, but the client had a very strong accent, and I had to be extra-attentive in my listening skills to hear the words accurately. When interpreters are necessary, consider getting training in working with them and also consider providing training for the interpreters because they may be exposed to traumatic material during the process.

6. Make explicit attempts to inquire about both the culture in the client's country of origin as well as the client's immigration experience. Sue and Sue (2013) recommend that helpers obtain a "migration narrative" (p. 468). They state: "This provides an understanding of the individual's social and occupational life prior to leaving his or her country of origin" (p. 468). In addition, inquire about the client's experiences with the transition from the homeland and "any traumas associated with this process" (Sue & Sue, 2013, p. 469). Again, in this process, allow the client to determine the pace because much of this material maybe emotionally challenging.

7. Inquire and communicate about current stressors the client experiences in the United States (or in the country in which you work). Be particularly attentive to asking about issues of language; underemployment or unemployment; differences in values, beliefs, and family structure; lack of resources; and discrimination and prejudice. Demonstrate sensitivity and understanding of how such stressors appear to be affecting your client.

8. Be prepared to extend the usual role that you may provide to clients who are refugees and immigrant clients. These clients may need you to be more directive in your

communication style and also may need direct support and advocacy from you. As Chung et al. (2008) suggest, this may mean "questioning and challenging policies, rules, regulations, and systems that adversely affect the mental health of immigrants when necessary; and, at times, rocking the boat" (p. 314). Chung et al. (2008) suggest that, in particular, it is important with these clients to avoid falling into the trap of the nice counselor syndrome—that is, a helper who is nice and nurturing but fails to "take risks, speak up and speak out, advocating for social justice, fairness, and equality" (pp. 314–315). They state: "It is especially important to demonstrate the courage to challenge unhealthy, unfair, and unjust situations that lead to human rights violations and adversely affect the immigrants' mental health" (p. 315).

9. Be especially alert to clients' communication of instances of injustice, prejudice, and discrimination. Undoubtedly during the course of counseling with refugee and immigrant clients, you will hear about instances of institutional racism and political countertransference (Chung et al., 2008). In addition, be aware of your own potential countertransference. Be honest with yourself and assess your own beliefs about how you feel about immigrants and refugees being in your country. Explore your own beliefs with your instructor or a supervisor so that you do not consciously or unconsciously project negative attitudes onto these clients.

10. Be aware that racial minority immigrant clients are more likely to present psychological symptoms that vary from Westernized notions of health and wellness. For example, some immigrant and refugee clients may experience psychological trauma as physical symptoms, such as stomachaches and headaches. Singer and Tummala-Narra (2013) conclude, "[I]f clinicians are not aware of culturally relevant manifestations of psychological distress, they may misdiagnose the client's distress and/or develop inaccurate formulations and ineffective interventions" (p. 291).

APPLICATION EXERCISE 3.1

Communication Patterns in Helping

A. Race and Ethnicity

In a small group, discuss ways in which communication patterns may vary among clients from differing ethnic groups and of different races. Relate your observations to the helping process. Discuss what your preferred communication style in the helping process seems to be. How might this help or hurt you in working with a client whose ethnic group and race differ from your own?

B. Gender

Observe the way men and women talk, even in ordinary, noncounseling conversations. What similarities and differences do you note? How do you think these similarities and differences affect the helping situation?

C. Sexual Orientation and Gender Identity

What communication experiences have you had with persons who identify as gay, lesbian, bisexual, or questioning? What about with persons who self-identify as transgender? How do your values in this area affect your communication?

(Continued)

D. Clients with Disabilities

Recall your experiences working with clients with disabilities. What do you notice about the communication patterns? If you have not yet had much experience in this area, what do you anticipate as you think about working with clients with disabilities both in terms of your own internal reactions and your oral and nonverbal communications?

E. Immigrant and Refugee Clients

With a partner or in a small group, discuss your experiences in interacting with persons who are refugees or immigrants to the country in which you have citizenship. Explore your beliefs about refugees and immigrants residing in your country. How do you think your beliefs will affect your communication patterns with these clients?

SILENCE

Another kind of pattern that affects helper-client communication is that of silence. For most beginning helpers, silence can be frightening. It seems to bring the total focus of attention on them, revealing their most glaring weaknesses as helpers—at least this is how many helpers describe their experiences with silence. As a result, their tendency is to say something—anything—to prevent silence. Typically, a question is asked. Often, it is a bad question—one that can be answered by a minimal response from the client. The answer to the question is relatively unimportant because the question was not well thought out by the helper. The helper may not even be listening to the answer. Such a state of affairs suggests that it is the helper's responsibility to keep the client talking, that talking is the only evidence that the client is working, and that silence is probably nontherapeutic or a waste of time. None of these assumptions are valid. In fact, a study of the effects of silence during actual counseling interviews found that significantly higher amounts of silence were linked to greater rapport, whereas lower amounts of silence were associated with less rapport (Sharpley, Munro, & Elly, 2005). As Karasu (1992) has noted, the importance of silence is frequently overlooked, as "therapists tend to underestimate the power of listening and overestimate the power of speaking" (pp. 81–82).

Because clients react to silence in this way, you can use silence as a counseling technique and as a way of responding to clients. Silence has another meaning that is important to acknowledge. After a period of hard work in the session or after a moment of significant insight, the client often needs time to absorb the experience—to fit it into his or her existing system. This results in an integration silence—one in which the client is fully experiencing the therapeutic moment. You may not encounter this in your first helping sessions, but you will as you gain experience.

Types of Silence

Silence can be a therapeutic moment as well as a self-conscious moment. But what makes one silence different from another? What are the dimensions of silence in a counseling session? Silence can be broadly categorized as helper-induced or client-induced. Helper-induced silence occurs when the focus of the interview is on the helper. In other words, if the helper—rather than the client—is feeling responsible for the moment and responds with silence, that is a helper-induced silence. Conversely, if the client has been talking, assuming responsibility, and then stops, that is a client-induced silence.

HELPER-INDUCED SILENCE   Helper-induced silence can be examined in two contexts: the helper's intentions and the consequences of the silence. Helper intentions can vary widely and can have a range of effects.

One form of silence occurs unsystematically. It is like being at a loss for words. Its intention is probably to give the helper time to absorb and comprehend all that is going on at the moment. Again, it is not intended by the helper to be a therapeutic moment, although the effect is often therapeutic. Many times, a helper fails to respond to the moment for personal reasons, and the effect is to encourage the client to continue more deeply into the topic or the feeling. When this happens, the helper is more apt to feel lucky rather than competent!

The second form of helper-induced silence is one that the helper has deliberately presented. Maybe the helper has been very active and has decided to reduce that activity, thus transferring more responsibility to the client. Or maybe the helper senses a momentum on the client's part that will lead to insight, commitment, or new relevant issues. In this case, the helper chooses not to respond in order not to interfere with or impede the client's psychological momentum.

CLIENT-INDUCED SILENCE   Client-induced silence also has varied intentions and consequences. As noted with helper-induced silence, client silence is affected by the issue of responsibility and what to do with it. For example, suppose Bettina has developed a life pattern of avoiding some personal issues. When these issues arise, her natural response is to deny or ignore them by deflecting attention from herself. In the counseling setting, she may be aware that these personal issues are the source of her difficulties. Yet her natural reaction continues to be avoidance, deflection, or resistance. In this example, Bettina's silence would reflect an attempt to transfer momentary responsibility to the helper and away from herself. If she is successful, the consequence would be yet another time when important issues are avoided.

Another reason that clients lapse into silence is to try to catch up on the progress of the moment. Counseling sessions sometimes move very quickly, covering a lot of ground and incorporating and relating many issues to one another. There is a need to stop, catch one's breath, and observe the progress or comprehend the implications. This is a very therapeutic type of silence. It allows clients to fit the new growth or insight that has occurred into their existing system. In effect, the client alters the existing system to include what has just been learned. Client-induced silence sometimes results from a client opening some new door to his or her awareness. For example, Robert—who, with his wife Carolyn, had been in counseling for several weeks—lapsed into a silence during a discussion of families of origin (a technique used to identify styles, expectations, and rules of interpersonal living). After a silence of a minute or more, he stated to the therapist and his wife, "I've been living with Carolyn for six years and thinking that I was overcoming the life I had with my parents. Now I can see that I have been more a reflection of my parents' home than I realized. I wonder what I really do believe in and want from my own family I'm creating with Carolyn."

Silence also has different meanings from one culture to another. U.S. Americans experience discomfort with silence and want to avoid it if possible. In contrast, those in Asian cultures usually regard silent pauses as an indicator of respect. Other cultures may equate silence with a need for privacy or a consensual agreement. Patterns of silence may also vary with gender. A woman may wait for a pause in the conversation to make a point; a man may interrupt a conversation to offer a fact. When expressing feelings, a woman may do so with great verbal facility; a man may pause frequently or present his feelings more hesitantly. Silence and pauses can also vary with clients with certain disabilities. For example, with clients using assisted communication devices, rhythms and pauses of communication may change. Or consider the client who is on Social Security disability due to severe and incapacitating depression. With this client, perhaps there are more silent periods during the session than periods of conversation, especially in initial sessions.

How do you know what kind of silence is occurring? The intention of a client-induced silence must always be inferred. By watching the client closely and by being sensitive to the themes, issues, and feelings being expressed, you will be gathering clues to what is happening. Is the client relaxed? Are the client's eyes fixed on something without being focused? This may mean the client is thinking about or pondering something, examining a new idea, or ruminating in his or her mind. Or is the client tense? Does he or she appear nervous, looking from one object to another and avoiding eye contact? If so, this may mean that he or she is avoiding some topic or idea. Again, we remind you to be careful about assigning universal meanings to client pauses and silent periods because these meanings do vary with individuals.

THERAPEUTIC SILENCE   Skilled helpers often use silence as their best technique for specific situations. This does not suggest that they are inactive. There is always nonverbal behavior that adds meaning to the silence, thereby communicating a therapeutic message to the client. The messages that the helper may seek to communicate include: "I want us to move a bit more slowly," "I want you to think more about what you just said," "I don't accept the message you just presented," or "I care very much about you and your feelings in this moment." Silence can also be soothing to clients. Other therapeutic messages can be communicated through silence, but the ones discussed here tend to be the most common.

Pacing the Helping Session

Helping sessions can be compared to a musical score. They have variations in theme, timing, activity, and inactivity. As you acquire self-comfort and skills, you will become aware that different times in an interview have very different qualities. The helper is a conductor of sorts for this therapeutic score. Sometimes the client is hyperactive, babbling, or overreacting, and the desired objective is to slow down the pace of the session. You can always verbally call attention to the client's activity; silence often achieves the same objective. You may not respond with total silence. Occasional verbal responses let the client know that you are still a participant. But you may want to monitor your reactions and not respond to all that stimulates you.

The use of silence to *pace* the session is especially important in initial interviews when the conditions of trust and safety are being built. Especially in these sessions, it is important to let the client determine the pace. As Hutchins and Cole-Vaught (1997) noted, "The helping interview may be one of the few opportunities clients have to express their thoughts and feelings without being rushed or pressed to perform. This luxury of unhurried time allows more complete expression than is typical in most interactions" (p. 104). In using silence to pace a session, it is important to explain the purpose of silence to clients, especially those in beginning sessions, so they are not scared away (Sommers-Flanagan & Sommers-Flanagan, 2014, p. 71).

Silent Focusing

One of the ways in which silence is most useful is to focus attention on the moment. It is like stopping to listen to an echo. Throughout the text, we will be suggesting ways in which you can help clients hear themselves. Silence is the first of these ways. Sometimes, clients make totally irrational statements. By not responding to the statement, you allow the clients' messages to remain present—to continue to be heard even by the clients themselves. Other times, clients may make a statement of such relevance that you want to give them time to absorb the impact of that relevance. This would be the case when a client has just acknowledged a significant insight and needs time to fit this insight into an existing system of meanings.

Responding to Defenses

Occasionally, clients come to the interview filled with emotions that belong to other people or situations, yet they spill them out on you or the helping process. Or you may make a statement to which the client responds defensively. These situations often reflect a lack of client awareness, although they are moments when the potential for awareness is great. The temptation for you may be to give the client insight into the situation. Often, it is more meaningful to allow clients to give themselves that insight. This can be done by using silence as your response.

Silent Caring

Silent caring occurs in those moments when no words are an adequate response to the feelings that are present. It may be a moment of quiet weeping for the client or it may be a moment of heavy melancholy. Whatever the feeling may be, it is one of those moments when experiencing the feeling fully is more important than making it go away. You can communicate your compassion and involvement very clearly with caring silence.

Guidelines for Using Silence

There are specific therapeutic guidelines to follow in using silence effectively with clients. Sommers-Flanagan and Sommers-Flanagan (2014) and Sharpley et al. (2005) have summarized these guidelines as follows:

- When a client pauses after making a statement or after hearing your paraphrase, let a few seconds pass rather than immediately jumping in with further verbal interaction. Given the opportunity, clients can move naturally into very significant material without your guidance or urging. Give them a chance to associate to new material.
- As you are sitting silently and waiting for your client to resume speaking, tell yourself that this is the client's time to express him- or herself, not your time to prove you can be useful. If you assume the role of an "expert" interviewer, you will probably feel greater responsibility (i.e., as if you need to say the right thing or ask the right question).
- Try not to get into a rut regarding your use of silence. When silence comes, sometimes wait for the client to speak next and other times break the silence yourself.
- Avoid using silence if you believe your client is confused, experiencing an acute emotional crisis, or psychotic. Excessive silence—and the anxiety it provokes—tend to exacerbate these conditions. Silence is also not useful in some culturally diverse

helping situations; for example, if a gay client says to a straight helper, "I don't feel safe here at school" and if this report is met with silence, it may make the client feel less safe and more invisible.

- If you feel uncomfortable during silent periods, try to relax. Use your attending skills to look expectantly toward clients. This will help them understand that it is their turn to talk.
- If clients appear uncomfortable with silence, you may give them instructions to free-associate (i.e., tell them, "Just say whatever comes to mind"). Or you may want to use an empathic reflection (say something like "It's hard to decide what to say next").
- Remember that silence is at times the most therapeutic response available.
- Remember to observe your body and face while communicating silence. This is important because there is a big difference between communicating a cold and a warm silence (Sommers-Flanagan & Sommers-Flanagan, 2014, pp. 71–72).
- Give clients the opportunity to stop or terminate the silence that you initiate. This contributes to greater rapport and gives clients the chance to decide when to speak again rather than having this decided for them by you (Sharpley et al., 2005).

APPLICATION EXERCISE 3.2

Being Comfortable with Silence

Some people often have to learn to be silent. Perhaps you find silence to be intense and uncomfortable. If so, this exercise will help you become more comfortable with silence. Team up with two other people. One person will be the talker, one will be the listener, and the third can be the timekeeper. Invite the talker to talk about anything he or she wishes. You will listen and respond. But before you respond, allow a pause to occur. Begin with five-second pauses. Gradually increase the duration of pauses until you are allowing fifteen seconds to pass before responding. The timekeeper should sit in a position from which he or she can signal the number of seconds to you without distracting the talker. After a 10-minute discussion, rotate roles and repeat the exercise until all three of you have had a turn as listener.

As a variation on this exercise, consider your contacts with people you encounter every day. Become conscious of your interaction patterns. Do you interject your reactions as soon as the other person has completed a communication? Do you interrupt the other person, thus preventing the slightest possibility of a silence? During the next few days, monitor your response behavior. When someone speaks to you, pause and think about the message for a few seconds and then give your response. Record any feedback you receive from your friends or acquaintances regarding your communication behavior.

Summary

The practice of helping involves a sense of both personal authenticity and professional skills. Both authenticity and skills are maintained by patterns of behavior that emerge as the helper matures and grows in experience. Similarly, clients evolve patterns of behavior that reflect their personal qualities, their problems, and their culture. We have noted in this chapter how these patterns affect and are affected by the helper's communication patterns and styles.

Helpers must be careful to avoid imposing their communication styles and values on clients and must be sensitive to communication styles from culturally diverse clients because variables such as race, ethnicity, sexual orientation, and gender identity play a large role in communication patterns. Gender expression of language also affects the helping process. Again, it is crucial for helpers to be sensitive to the ways in which gender roles are expressed through language and to be aware of the difficulties that patriarchal gender norms have created for both women and men. As the helper's comfort level with the helping setting improves, these patterns may be examined for their effect on the session. Helpers must also be sensitive to language usage and verbal and nonverbal communication patterns in their interactions with clients with disabilities and also with clients who are immigrants or refugees.

More subtle—and perhaps of greater concern—are the helper communication patterns that become ritualized. Ritualized patterns exist for expediency's sake. They are the behavioral shorthand that allows more efficient functioning. The problem is that efficient functioning may not be effective functioning, particularly in the helping relationship. As we noted at the beginning of this chapter, the helping relationship is more effective when it is adapted or geared toward the contextual and cultural characteristics of clients. This

requires helpers to be therapeutically flexible in their communication styles with diverse clients. As I (Sherry) was writing this chapter, I took a walk on my neighborhood beach. There I encountered a toddler mowing the sand on the beach with a toy lawnmower. I said to his mom: "I guess he is mowing the sand instead of the grass."

"Yup" she said, "that is what happens when you live at the beach."

He was a toddler but he had figured out that something about the situation required a different response than what is usually found or typically expected in a certain context. That is the metaphor for this chapter—while we tend to develop particular or ritualized communication styles with clients, it is in the unique adaptation of such styles that we provide the most effective helping relationship.

Another communication pattern affected by culture, gender, and disability status involves the use of silence. Again, silence can be used therapeutically or accidentally. When accidental, any positive effects may be from luck rather than intention. The intentional use of silence can contribute greatly to the helping relationship and the establishment of rapport between helper and client.

Reflective Questions

1. What types of messages can be communicated with a silence? How many of these messages might occur in a helping session? How can you tell one message from another?

2. What do you think your own tolerance and/or comfort level is with silence? Are you more comfortable with silence that is initiated by you or by the client? What about silences that are terminated by you or by the client?

3. Provide examples that illustrate how the meaning and use of silence may be affected by working with clients with disabilities, those of a different race, and those of a different gender.

4. Discuss some examples in which you have observed communication patterns being influenced by culture, such as race and ethnicity.

5. Describe your reactions to the idea that gender affects communication. What is your comfort level in communicating with clients who share your gender and those who do not? What about with transgendered clients?

6. How do your values affect your communication with clients who self-identify as having a gender identity status or a sexual orientation different than your own?

7. Discuss ways to enhance your communication and interactions with clients with disabilities.

8. Discuss ways to enhance your communication and interactions with clients who are immigrants. Now do the same for clients who are refugees. What differences do you note?

9. How do you think the communication styles and patterns discussed in this chapter relate to you?

10. Discuss the notion that flexibility and adaptability in communication patterns are required for effective helping relationships.

11. Describe ways in which you hold privilege in terms of gender, race, ethnicity, sexual orientation, able-bodiedness, and country of origin. How do you believe these aspects of privilege might affect your communication with clients who vary from you on these dimensions?

MyCounselingLab

For the following exercise, log on to MyCounselingLab and then click the Video Library tab under Video Resources.

1. Click into the Counseling Children and Adolescents collection to locate the "Demonstrating Patience and Silence" clip. After reviewing this clip, consider the following questions:
   a. How comfortable would you be initiating a helping session in the same way that the practitioner did on the clip?
   b. What did you think the function of the silence was that you viewed in this helping interaction?

2. Locate the Ethical, Legal, and Professional collection. Then watch the video "A Cross-Cultural Miscommunication." After reviewing this clip, respond to the following questions:
   a. Did you feel the counselor used an active or passive communication style? What was the effect on the client?
   b. Did you see any evidence of preconceptions or stereotypes displayed in the verbal communication of the counselor? If so, what were they, and how do you think these affected the client?

Recommended Readings

American Psychological Association. (2012). (Division 44 Committee on Lesbian, Gay, and Bisexual Concerns Joint Task Force on Guidelines for Psychotherapy with Lesbian, Gay, and Bisexual clients). Guidelines for psychotherapy with lesbian, gay, and bisexual clients. *American Psychologist, 67,* 10–42.

American Psychological Association. (2013). *Enhancing your interactions with persons with disabilities.* Washington, DC: Author.

Artman, L., & Daniels, J. (2010). Disability and psychotherapy practice: Cultural competence and practical tips. *Professional Psychology, 41,* 442–448. doi: I-1037/a0020864.

Association for Lesbian, Gay, Bisexual and Transgender Issues in Counseling (2008). *Competencies for counseling gay, lesbian, bisexual and transgendered (GLBT) clients.* www.algbtic.org/resources/competencies.html

Bartholomew, C. G. (2003). *Gender-sensitive therapy: Principles and practices.* Prospect Heights, IL: Waveland Press.

Chung, R. C.-Y., Bemak, F., Ortiz, D. P., & Sandoval-Perez, P. A. (2008). Promoting the mental health of immigrants: A multicultural/social justice perspective. *Journal of Counseling and Development, 86,* 310–317.

Daughtry, D., Gibson, J., & Abels, A. (2009). Mentoring students and professionals with disabilities. *Professional Psychology, 40,* 201–205.

Dermer, S. B., Smith, S. D., & Barto, K. K. (2010). Identifying and correctly labeling sexual prejudice, discrimination, and oppression. *Journal of Counseling and Development, 88,* 325–331.

Evans, M. P., Duffey, T., & Englar-Carlson, M. (2013). Introduction to the Special Issue: Men in Counseling. *Journal of Counseling and Development, 91:* 387–389. doi: 10.1002/j.1556-6676.2013.00108.x

Hoffman, R. M. (2001). The measurement of masculinity and femininity: Historical perspective and implications for counseling. *Journal of Counseling and Development, 79,* 472–485.

Nutt, R., & Brooks, G. (2008). Psychology of gender. In S. D. Brown & R. W. Lent (Eds.), *Handbook of counseling psychology* (176–193). Hoboken, NJ: John Wiley & Sons.

Sharpley, C. F., Munro, D. M., & Elly, M. J. (2005). Silence and rapport during initial interviews. *Counseling Psychology Quarterly, 18,* 149–159.

Singer, R. R., & Tummala-Narra, P. (2013). White clinicians' perspectives on working with racial minority immigrant clients. *Professional Psychology, 44,* 290–298.

Sommers-Flanagan, J., & Sommers-Flanagan, R. (2014). *Clinical interviewing* (5th ed.). Hoboken, NJ: John Wiley & Sons.

Sue, D. W., & Sue, D. (2013). *Counseling the culturally diverse* (6th ed.). Hoboken, NJ: John Wiley & Sons.

Vogel, D. L., Epting, F., & Wester, S. R. (2003). Counselors' perceptions of female and male clients. *Journal of Counseling and Development, 81,* 131–140.

Attending Skills

We have identified several conditions that affect the development of the helping relationship in prior chapters. Those conditions—accurate empathy, positive regard, and genuineness or congruence—are called *core conditions* because they are central to the therapeutic process. Also important is the helper's capacity to implement communication patterns in a flexible manner with adaptability to each unique client. In addition, the helper must also bring other skills and knowledge to the therapeutic process. Certainly, the first of these skills is the ability to *attend* actively to the client. This objective is not as simple as it might appear. It involves more than an attentive ear. Have you ever talked to someone who was fiddling with a pencil, staring around the room, or seemed otherwise distracted as he or she listened to you? If you have (and who has not?), recall how this felt. The listener may have heard all that you said, but you probably interpreted his or her behavior as a lack of interest, concentration, or attention. That being the case, you probably found it difficult to continue the conversation. Clients exhibit the same sensitivity to whether the helper is paying attention to what they say. Attending skills are used by the helper to assure, support, and/or reinforce the client. These skills are very important for the client who is feeling vulnerable, uncertain, or insecure. One precondition for the existence of attending behaviors is an awareness of the client's communication. This awareness must then be communicated through your undistracted attentiveness to the client. Attentiveness is one way of saying, "I am following both your message and your metacommunication; I am invested and involved in your story."

Ivey, D'Andrea, and Ivey (2012) summarized decades of research on helper attentiveness in the following two statements:

1. Clients respond better and more positively, verbalize at greater length, and indicate a stronger willingness to return to see helpers who are attentive.
2. Experienced and seasoned helpers typically do better with attending skills, while inexperienced or beginning helpers have room to grow on dimensions of attentiveness.

In the following section, we describe the primary dimensions of helper attentiveness.

COMMUNICATION OF ATTENTIVENESS

Attentiveness is communicated primarily through four dimensions: facial expressions, eye contact, body positions and movement, and verbal responses (Cormier, Nurius, & Osborn, 2013). You may have noted that the first three of these channels are all nonverbal. On the surface, attending to clients appears relatively simple; however, it is easier said than done. Egan (2014) listed a number of obstacles to the attending process:

1. Being judgmental
2. Having biases
3. Pigeonholing clients
4. Attending to facts
5. Sympathizing
6. Interrupting

These are all ways in which we disrupt our attentiveness to and with clients.

Another issue in the communication of attentiveness involves the various meanings that people attach to different gestures or words because such meanings have been learned. Some of the meanings are fairly standardized; others have distinct regional or cultural variances. For example, do you prefer to have people look at you when you talk to them? Most European Americans do, but some American Indians do not, and studies suggest that some inner-city African-American youths do not. It is important to remember that some cultural groups have sanctions on direct visual contact during some types of interpersonal interactions. When you are telling someone what you think, what would be your reaction if that person began to frown? If the frown was not consistent with your feelings, you probably would begin to question the inconsistency between your message and the listener's response. If you feel strongly about a topic and the other person does not seem to care about it, are you likely to continue telling the person about your feelings? No—because most of us want to know that our feelings are heard and understood.

For these and other reasons, your behavior can contribute to your client's feelings of security. The increased sense of security that occurs as clients are talking about themselves can become a self-reinforcing phenomenon. Most of you have probably had the experience of entering a new activity and feeling nervous and unsure of yourselves. But as you stayed with the activity and nothing bad (perhaps even some good things) happened, your self-confidence began to grow. So it is with the helping process. As the client begins to experience your acceptance, your understanding, and your commitment, the feelings of vulnerability, uncertainty, caution, or lack of trust begin to dissipate. In the following sections of the chapter, we describe nonverbal and verbal ways to increase your attentiveness with clients. We also explore the contextual variables surrounding these dimensions because, as we indicated earlier, the meanings of certain gestures or words are learned and vary by region and culture.

Facial Expressions

Knapp, Hall, and Horgan (2014) observe that the face is the primary means by which people communicate information about their emotional states. Facial expressions convey basic emotions such as anger, disgust, fear, sadness, and happiness. Unlike most other aspects of nonverbal attending behavior, facial expressions do not seem to vary much among cultures. These basic emotions seem to be represented by the same facial expressions across cultures, although individual cultural norms may influence how much and how often such emotions are expressed (Mesquita & Frijda, 1992). For example, anger is often conveyed cross-culturally through the eyes and by changes in the area of the mouth and jaw. However, men and women both within and between cultures may express anger in different ways and at different times. For example, some persons may reject the idea of releasing anger because they have learned it is "unchristian" or "unladylike" (Kelley, 1979, p. 24). Your facial expressions communicate messages to the client that are as meaningful as those you receive from the client's facial expressions.

A primary—although often not intentional—way that helpers use their facial expressions is to reinforce client behavior. For example, Almedar, your client, reveals that he was invited to join an honorary society at his school. Because Almedar's prior success at school has been limited, in hearing this, your own face lights up. This in and of itself encourages Almedar to share more of this part of his story with you. Another aspect of facial expressions and attentiveness has to do with *mirroring*. It is important for your facial expressions to reflect those of the client: If the client expresses pleasure, you look happy; if the client conveys sadness, you show concern. The same mirror neurons in the brain that we discussed in Chapter 2 that help to create resonant empathy are also related to the mirroring of facial expressions between helpers and clients.

ANIMATION.   Animation in facial expression gives clients the feeling that you are alert and responding to ongoing communication. An absence of facial expressions (a deadpan look) suggests a lack of interest, awareness, or presence to clients. You can surely remember talking with someone who lacks facial responsiveness and the effect this had on you, and we doubt it was pleasant. The most noticeable expression is the smile. The appropriate use of smiles can have a powerful effect on clients, particularly when used in conjunction with occasional head nods. However, continuous smiling has a negative effect, just as do frequent frowns, which can communicate disapproval. On the other hand, occasional frowns communicate your failure to follow or understand a particular point and are therefore often useful.

Eye Contact

What is the effect of eye contact in the helper-client relationship? Research into interpersonal interaction indicates that eye contact has more than one effect and that these effects do vary across cultures. It may signal a need for affiliation, involvement, or inclusion; it may reflect the quality of an existing relationship; or it may enhance the communication of a complex message. Eye contact can also produce anxiety in the other person. A gaze lasting longer than about 10 seconds can signal aggressiveness rather than acceptance. An averted gaze may hide shame over expressing something seen as culturally taboo.

In some cultures, client eye contact is appropriate when listening. In other cultures, an individual may look away as a sign of respect or may demonstrate more eye contact when talking and less eye contact while listening. Effective eye contact—eye contact that reinforces clients and makes their communication easier—lies somewhere between the fixed gaze and "shifty eyes," or frequent breaks of eye contact. Look at clients when they are talking. Occasionally, permit your eyes to drift to an object away—*but not far away*—from the client. Then return your eyes to the client. Let yourself be natural. At the same time, avoid making stereotypical judgments about the client's eye contact or lack thereof. As Knapp, Hall, and Horgan (2014) comment, the meanings and effects of eye contact vary both within and across cultural groups. For some clients, less eye contact is typical of their culture and should not be construed to mean anything else. In other words, eye contact varies from client to client and within and between cultural groups, and eye contact patterns may involve changes in duration as well as frequency (Knapp, Hall, & Horgan, 2014). Some clients may favor more direct eye contact because their cultural identifications emphasize visual contact during interactions, while other clients identify with cultures that sanction a lot of eye contact during some kinds of interpersonal interactions. Other clients may avoid eye contact because of their clinical disorder. For example, some clients with autism, depression, or social anxiety may not be able to bear the intensity of a gaze between themselves and the helper. Another variable that affects eye contact during the helping process is distance or space between the helper and client. As physical space is increased, eye contact often increases too; as physical space is decreased, eye contact also often decreases. We provide several application exercises for you to work with these nonverbal attending skills.

APPLICATION EXERCISE 4.1

Facial Expressions

A. Facial Attentiveness

With a partner, designate one of you as the speaker and the other as the listener. While the speaker shares one of his or her concerns, the listener's tasks are the following:

1. Do not respond with any facial expression or animation whatsoever while the speaker is talking; maintain complete facial passivity.
2. After two or three minutes, respond with a facial reaction that is opposite to the feelings and concerns being expressed by the speaker. For example, if the speaker is talking seriously, smile and look happy.
3. After another three minutes or so, respond with facial animation and expression that mirror the kind and intensity of feelings being expressed by the speaker.

Discuss the different results produced by these three approaches. Reverse roles and repeat the exercise. What can you conclude about facial attentiveness as a result of this exercise? What have you learned about yourself and your facial gestures? What do you want to change about your facial gestures, and how do you intend to bring about this change? If possible, repeat this activity with a person from a distinctly different culture than your own. Do your conclusions change in any way?

B. Recognizing Facial Cues

Find two people with whom to work. Designate one of you as the speaker for round 1, the second as the listener, and the third as the observer. Roles are rotated for rounds 2 and 3. For each round, the listener feeds each of the four incomplete sentences to the speaker. The speaker repeats the sentence and adds the first completion that comes to his or her mind. The observer watches for changes and cues in the speaker's facial expressions as he or she works with all the incomplete sentences in the round. For this to be most effective, when you are in the role of the speaker, take your time, breathe deeply, and say whatever comes into your mind without thinking about it or censoring it. The observer shares the observations with the speaker after the round is over. When you are in the role of the speaker, only disclose what feels comfortable to you.

1. Anger
    a. When I get angry . . .
    b. I get angry when . . .
    c. I feel disgusted that . . .
    d. One thing that makes me mad is . . .
2. Sadness
    a. When I get sad . . .
    b. I get sad when . . .
    c. I feel "blue" that . . .
    d. One thing that makes me sad is . . .
3. Fear
    a. When I get afraid . . .
    b. I feel afraid that . . .
    c. I get afraid when . . .
    d. One thing that makes me afraid is . . .

APPLICATION EXERCISE 4.2

Eye Contact

Perhaps you can better grasp the effects of eye contact by participating in the following dyadic exercise. With a partner, determine who will be the speaker and who will be the listener. While the speaker speaks, the listener should listen but avoid eye contact with the speaker. Then discuss the following questions: What are the effects on the speaker? How well did the speaker feel that he or she was able to communicate? Try the exercise again, but this time, maintain eye contact with the speaker as described in the previous section. What effect does this have? Reverse roles, and repeat the exercise. Discuss how the effects may vary depending on the gender and culture of the participants.

Body Positions and Use of Space

Body positions serve important functions in a helping session. Body positions and movement are involved in regulating the space or distance between the helper and a client, greeting a client, terminating a session, and taking turns (that is, the exchange of speaker and listener roles within a conversation; Cormier, Nurius, & Osborn, 2013). Body movement and comfort with physical space (closeness or distance) vary among cultures and with gender. Generally, among European Americans, counselors and clients sit face-to-face. Even an intervening object such as a desk is often considered a distraction—a barrier to attentiveness. Ivey, D'Andrea, and Ivey (2012, p. 147) note that, in some Eskimo and Inuit cultural groups, persons sit side by side when discussing a personal issue. European Americans usually prefer several feet of distance between chairs; however, those from contact cultures may be more comfortable with closer distances (Watson, 1970). Many Latino and Latina clients prefer closer distances, as do client and helper dyads of the same race (Knapp et al., 2014). Yet individual differences among clients may be as important in use of space and distance as cultural patterns. For example, the effects of space also vary with a client's expression of feelings. A client who has just expressed a lot of anger often requires more personal space than someone who is feeling sad or experiencing a lot of pain. In short, the concept of space has no universals.

Gender also dictates what is considered appropriate space. Some females may be more comfortable with a closer distance to the helper, especially if the helper is female. However, many female clients may feel intruded upon if a male helper positions himself too close. Clients with a history of severe physical and/or sexual abuse may require greater space, particularly at the beginning stage of the helping process. To be respectful of all clients, it is important to allow *them* to choose the appropriate amount of distance from the helper in the counseling interactions.

One important aspect of body communication involves the amount of tension conveyed by the body. Astute helpers note the degree of tension or relaxation in a client's body. A body that is blocking or holding back a feeling may be tense, with shallow, fast breathing. A relaxed body posture indicates comfort, both with the counseling setting and with the topic being discussed. Selective body tension communicates action. It may reflect a "working" moment for you—involvement with the client, movement toward a goal, or preparation for something new.

Shifts in body position, such as leaning forward or backward, often signify an "important segment of the encounter" (Knapp et al., 2014, p. 139). Body tension that is continuous probably communicates discomfort with the client, the topic, or yourself. To be comfortable with yourself, it is important to begin from a base of relaxation because this is what will be mirrored to the client. Application Exercise 4.3 may help you achieve a desired state of relaxation.

APPLICATION EXERCISE 4.3

Muscle Relaxation

While sitting down, raise your hands and arms three to four inches above the armrests of the chair and then let them drop. Feel the tension flow out of your arms. Repeat this, and try to increase the relaxation. Let your back and buttocks be in contact with as much of the chair as possible. Feel the chair pressing against your body. Tense the muscles in your legs and then release the tension. Feel the surge of warmth in your muscles as your legs relax. Repeat this tensing and releasing of leg muscles several times, each time achieving a little more relaxation. Now take three or four deep breaths slowly. After each breath, slowly release the air from your lungs. Do you feel more relaxed than when you started?

Do this exercise again—this time without any interruptions between different body exercises. This is a good exercise to do just before seeing a client. It is one of the ways by which you can prepare yourself for the session. As you do the exercise more often, you will find it easier and quicker to achieve a surprisingly comfortable state of relaxation.

Visible Behavior

Together, facial expressions, eye contact, and body messages constitute the helper's visible behavior. The impact of visible behavior on communication is considerable, as Application Exercise 4.4 illustrates.

APPLICATION EXERCISE 4.4

The Impact of Visible Behavior

This exercise gives you an opportunity to measure the effect of your facial and body gestures on the person receiving your message. Select as your partner a person you have wanted to involve in a conversation. Sit down facing each other. Both of you close your eyes—and keep them closed throughout the conversation. Talk to each other for about five minutes. Then open your eyes, complete the conversation, and discuss the differences between visual and nonvisual communication. What compensations did you have to make while talking without sight? How successful do you believe you were in your communication attempts? What, in particular, were you missing in terms of visual feedback from your partner?

VERBAL FOLLOWING BEHAVIOR AND SELECTIVE ATTENTION

The things you say will have an immediate impact on your clients. Many studies have shown that the helper's responses can mold and shape the direction of the client's responses. In other words, whatever topic you respond to with a verbal acknowledgment, the client will probably continue to talk about it. Topics that you do not respond to often get cut off or interrupted. This process is called *selective attention*. Egan (2014) has aptly noted that if helpers think everything that their clients say is key, then nothing is key. One of the implications of this is that, as helpers, we are constantly sorting out all the various messages and story lines we get from clients. What is important? What is more relevant? Less relevant? Are there patterns of messages or story lines we do not want to respond to with attentiveness, such as with the client who is always talking about how everyone else is the problem?

Ivey, Gluckstern Packard, and Ivey (2006) have suggested that what the helper chooses to focus on says more about the helper than the client. These authors also stated that it is important to notice what topics the helper selectively attends to so the clients are not inadvertently or unconsciously steered away from topics they need to discuss just because they are uncomfortable for the helper. If you become aware of this happening, it is useful to consult your supervisor (see also Chapter 10).

Several points should be considered in terms of your verbal impact. Fit your comments or questions into the context of the topic at hand. Do not interrupt clients or quickly change topics. Stay with the topics that clients introduce, and help them develop and pursue them. This implies more than a technique; it is a highly conscious awareness of what is going on between you and your client. It is called *verbal following*, and it is an important way to show your attentiveness to clients. Egan (2014) proposed some useful questions that may help you listen and attend to clients, especially with the skill of verbal following:

- What are the main ideas reflected by the client's message?
- What are the most important experiences described in the client's messages?
- What themes are apparent in the client's messages?

- What is the client's worldview?
- What is most important to the client?
- What does the client need you to understand?

Of course, the helper does not distract clients by asking these questions directly. Rather, these questions are part of the helper's process in listening and attending to clients, and they reflect the helper's interest in the client's world. Try your skills in verbal following in Application Exercise 4.5.

APPLICATION EXERCISE 4.5

Verbal Following

A. Role Play of Verbal Following

In the roles of helper and client, choose a partner and sit in pairs. Concentrate on using the verbal-following behaviors discussed in this chapter. In your responses, react only to what the client has just said; do not add a new idea. Let your thinking be as close as possible to that of the client.

Prevent your facial gestures, body gestures, and verbal responses from distracting the client. After five minutes, stop the exercise and then discuss the following with your client: What was your client most aware of in your behavior? How well did your client think you understood his or her communication? What, if any, of your behavior got in your client's way? Now reverse roles, and repeat the exercise. What effect did your own gender and culture have on this activity? What about the client's gender and culture?

B. Verbal Following and Shifts in Focus

Shown here are some client statements followed by helper responses. Describe each helper response: Do you feel that it is a response to the client's statement? If not, describe the nature of the inappropriate response, such as shift of topic, focus on others, or focus on past.

CLIENT A: I think I just have to go away for a while. The pressure is really building up.
HELPER: What would Bob say to that?

The helper did/did not (circle one) respond to the client's statement. If the helper did not respond to the client's statement, the nature of the inappropriate response was _____.

CLIENT B: She doesn't really care anymore, and I've got to learn to accept that.
HELPER: You are fairly sure that she doesn't care.

The helper did/did not (circle one) respond to the client's statement. If the helper did not respond to the client's statement, the nature of the inappropriate response was _____.

CLIENT C: Grades are the biggest problem I have in school. I can't get poor grades and bring shame to my family.
HELPER: What did you do last year?

The helper did/did not (circle one) respond to the client's statement. If the helper did not respond to the client's statement, the nature of the inappropriate response was _____.

CLIENT D: The job I have isn't fun, but I'm afraid that if I quit, I might not get another job.
HELPER: Jobs are really getting hard to find.

The helper did/did not (circle one) respond to the client's statement. If the helper did not respond to the client's statement, the nature of the inappropriate response was _____.

Feedback: Part B

These exchanges illustrate some of the common pitfalls that await the helper. In the exchange with client A, the response was probably inappropriate. The helper seems to have jumped topics by bringing up Bob. In addition, the helper ignored the client's reference to the pressure and its effect on him. The response given to client B could be quite appropriate, although it is not the only possible appropriate response. The helper is responding directly to what the client said. The inappropriateness of the response to client C is more obvious. The helper really did not respond to any of the key ideas in the client's statement. Instead, for some reason, the helper decided to collect information about the client. The helper also ignored the social and cultural implications of the client's situation. Finally, the response to client D is also inappropriate. The client is talking about feelings ("isn't fun," "afraid"). The helper's response has nothing to do with the client. Instead, the helper shifted the focus to a social commentary on the current economic scene.

COGNITIVE AND AFFECTIVE MESSAGES AND DIFFERENTIATION

Because your responses to client messages greatly influence the nature of topic development, you will be faced with the decision of which kind of content to respond to and thus emphasize. Very often, the client's particular response contains both a cognitive message and an affect message. Cognitive messages usually deal with facts and information as well as people, places, and things, whereas affect messages primarily reflect feelings and emotions. Typically, in early interviews, the affect message is disguised. The disguises may be thin but nonetheless necessary to the clients. It is their way of protecting themselves until they can determine the kinds of things to which you are willing to listen. Once you are able to hear the affect message (and this comes with practice), you will have to make some decisions. It is important that you respond to that portion of the client's communication that you think is most significantly related to the client's concerns.

The process of choosing whether to focus on client cognitive and affective topics is called *differentiation*. Whether you choose to respond to the cognitive portion or the affect portion depends largely on what is happening in the interaction at that moment and on what the client needs. In other words, choosing to respond to the cognitive content serves one objective, whereas choosing to respond to the affect content serves another objective. This process of differentiation not only involves the client's comfort level but also the helper's comfort level (or lack thereof). Some helpers are too uncomfortable with feelings or emotions to focus on affect even when the client is leading them in that direction, while others seem to focus always and exclusively on affect and feelings while ignoring important and relevant insight and cognitive understanding. It is helpful during work with your supervisor or faculty advisor to determine if your own tendency is to respond more naturally to either cognitive or affective content. Whatever your natural inclination, you can work to broaden your range of responses, thus enhancing the potential of the helping process.

Some theoretical approaches to counseling (e.g., person-centered, existential, gestalt) favor an emphasis on affect, whereas others (e.g., rational-emotive, cognitive-behavioral, reality therapy) suggest that the primary emphasis should be on the cognitive process. Of course, many variables influence this sort of emphasis. In working with one client who intellectualizes frequently, the helper may focus primarily on affect in an effort to get the client to recognize and accept his or her feelings. However, the same helper—with another client who intellectualizes—may choose to emphasize cognitive elements if the counseling time is too limited for the client to feel comfortable with emotions. There are certainly times when emphasis on the affective takes precedence over the cognitive, and vice versa. Generally, though, during the interview process, it is important to respond to *both* affective and cognitive topics because, for all clients, feelings sometimes govern thoughts, and thoughts and their consequences sometimes govern or influence feelings. The important point is not which comes first but which type of intervention is likely to be the most effective for each client.

EFFECTS OF RESPONDING TO COGNITIVE CONTENT

Responding to cognitive content can be an anxiety-reduction tool for clients easily threatened by feelings. Thus, rapport with clients is sometimes established more quickly by discovering how they think before wondering how they feel. It is also important to realize that behavior incorporates both feelings and thoughts. To solve problems and make decisions effectively, clients have to be able to think as well as feel. Responding to cognitive content assists clients in developing and expressing those thought processes involved in problem solving and decision making.

Although exploration of feelings is useful to most clients, it is often not sufficient for goal achievement. Once the helping goals have been established, action plans must be developed to produce goal attainment. Responding to cognitive content goes one step further than responding to affect in that it focuses directly on behavior change. On the other hand, responding primarily to cognitive content presents the following limitations:

1. It may reinforce the intellectualization process; that is, it may encourage the client to continue to abstract and deny feelings that are actually influencing his or her behavior.
2. It may not provide the opportunity that the client needs to share and express feelings in a nonjudgmental setting. The helping relationship may be the only one in which a client can feel that his or her emotions (and consequently the self) will not be misunderstood.
3. It may continue to repeat a pattern similar to the rules in the client's family of origin in which talking about feelings is not allowed, encouraged, or explored.

Again, it must be stressed that the initial strategy in the differentiation process is an exploratory one. All clients respond differently to your emphasis on feelings or on cognitive content. In the next section, we discuss attentiveness to client affective messages and possible helping responses to them in the differentiation and selective responding process. You can work on responding to cognitive messages in Application Exercise 4.6.

APPLICATION EXERCISE 4.6

Identifying and Responding to Cognitive Content

For additional practice in identifying cognitive content—thoughts or ideas pertaining to problems, situations, people, or things—carefully read the following client statements. Then identify and list the different cognitive topics within each client response.

1. "I'm thinking about either going to graduate school or getting a job—whichever would be the better experience is what I'll do."

   _____

   _____

   _____

2. "When I was growing up, I never thought about being a CEO of an organization. I always thought I'd just be a stay-at-home mom. And people can say what they want to about it, but for me, this job is a very good fit, and I don't think my kids suffer just because I'm busy with work."

   _____

   _____

   _____

Feedback

The answers to the preceding exercises are as follows:

1. **a.** I'm thinking about going to graduate school.
   b. I'm also thinking about getting a job.
   c. I'll do whatever provides the best experience.

2. **a.** When I was growing up, I didn't think about becoming an organizational CEO.
   b. I always thought I'd be a stay-at-home mom.
   c. People can say what they want to about it.
   d. For me, this job is a good fit.
   e. I don't think my kids suffer just because I'm busy at work.

TYPES OF AFFECTIVE MESSAGES

Although there are many different kinds of feelings, most distinct, universal feelings that are identified by words fit into one of four categories: joy, anger, fear, or sadness. Many lists of affect words are now available, both in published books and also online. We have a sample list of affect words available in Table 5.1 in Chapter 5, which you can peruse now if you wish.

Positive Affect—Joy

Feelings of joy reflect positive or good feelings about oneself and others and indicate positive feelings about interpersonal relationships. Many of them can be identified by certain affect words such as _happy, content, peaceful, grateful, pleased, satisfied,_ and so on.

Certain nonverbal cues often occur simultaneously with affect word cues. The most obvious of these cues are facial ones. The corners of the mouth may turn up to produce the hint of a smile. The eyes may widen slightly. Facial wrinkles disappear. Often, there is an absence of body tension. The communicator may move his or her arms and hands in an open-palm gesture of acceptance. When the client is describing feelings about an object or event, there may be increased animation of the face and hands.

You might be wondering why we include positive affect, asking yourself, "Don't people who come to see helpers do so because of emotions such as anger, depression, anxiety, and so on?" Yes, that is partly the case. It is also true that intense positive affect can be as difficult as or even more difficult for some clients to own and tolerate than negative or disruptive feelings. Positive affect can make some clients feel "embarrassed, self-conscious, out of control, and vulnerable" (Fosha, 2000, p. 70). And it is all too easy in the helping process to bypass any positive feelings in the course of the counseling sessions to focus solely on negative or problematic feelings (p. 257). Positive affect is important because clients can feel pride and joy in acknowledging and focusing on their ability to deal with and experience frightening or painful emotions. As Fosha has observed, "Joy, pride, self-confidence, and a new appreciation of one's abilities are some of the affective experiences that follow after the unbearable feelings become bearable" or, stated another way, "Joy can be the other side of fully faced and overcome fear" (p. 165).

Anger

Anger represents an obstruction to be relieved or removed in some way. Different kinds of stimuli often elicit anger, such as frustration, threat, and fear. Conditions such as competition, jealousy, and thwarted aspirations can become threats that elicit angry responses. Anger often represents negative feelings about oneself and/or others. Many times, fear is concealed by an outburst of anger. In such cases, the anger becomes a defensive reaction because the person does not feel safe enough to express fear. Anger is also a cover-up for hurt. Beneath strong aggressive outbursts are often deep feelings of vulnerability and pain. And anger can sometimes be hidden underneath smiles or verbal denials that anything could be wrong, such as an "I'm doing fine, thank you!"

Remember that anger covers a broad group of feelings and can be expressed in many ways. With the expression of anger, the body position may become rigid and tense or it may be characterized by gross changes in body position or movement. Sometimes, anger toward another person or the self may be expressed by hitting, which consists of fault-finding or petty remarks directed at the object of the anger. For example, one partner in couples counseling may express this sort of anger by continual verbal attacks on the other person or by incessant remarks of dissatisfaction with the partner. Hitting can also be expressed through nonverbal cues, such as finger drumming or foot tapping.

Certain vocal qualities can be associated with anger. Many times, the voice becomes much louder as the person becomes more rigid in what he or she is saying; if the anger is very intense, the person may even shout. In some instances of intense anger, the feeling may be accompanied by tears. Many times, the expression of anger causes vocal pitch to become higher. With some people, however, the vocal pitch is actually lowered, becoming more controlled and measured. This often means that the person experiencing the anger is attempting to maintain a level of control over his or her feelings.

Fear

Fear represents a person's reaction to some kind of danger to be avoided. Often, this reaction is a withdrawal from a painful or stressful situation, from oneself, or from other people and relationships. As such, the person experiencing the emotions of fear may also be isolated and sad or depressed. Fear can also be described as a negative set of feelings about something or someone that results in a need to protect oneself.

Several facial cues are associated with fear. The mouth may hang wide open as in shock; the eyes may also dilate. Fear may cause a furrow to appear between the eyebrows. Fear of the helper or of the topic at hand may be reflected by the client's avoidance of direct eye contact; remember, however, that the meaning and use of eye contact vary among cultures.

Body positions and movements are also associated with the expression of fear. At first, the person experiencing fear may appear to be still in body position or may draw back. After this initial period, however, body movements usually become greater as anxiety increases, resulting in jerky and trembling motions. Although parts of the body may shake, the hands are often tightly clasped, as if giving protection. Tension may also be indicated through actions such as leg swinging, foot tapping, finger tapping, or playing with a ring or another piece of jewelry.

Voice qualities are also indicators of the level of anxiety the client is experiencing. As the level of anxiety increases, the breathing rate becomes faster and breathing becomes shallower. As anxiety and tension increase, the number of speech disturbances increases. This yields a greater number of cues, such as errors, repetitions, and omissions of parts of words or sentences. The rate of speech also increases as anxiety mounts.

Sadness

Some of the more common conditions expressed by clients are feelings of sadness, loneliness, or depression. These emotions may be a response to a variety of client conditions, including unsatisfying interpersonal relationships, environmental conditions such as disempowerment and oppression, physiological imbalances, or even poor nutrition. Sometimes, sadness can be a response to the helper's compassion or empathy. Having the helper's care and understanding can make the client more aware of not having it or not having had it in other life situations or with other persons (Fosha, 2000, p. 227).

Vocal cues can also provide clues about this emotional state. The intonation of a depressed person is also a departure from the normal intonation. The voice quality may become more subdued, with less inflection, so the voice takes on more of a monotonic quality.

It is important to recognize that sadness has different meanings among cultures. In fact, in some societies, depression is not even recognized as an illness or a sign of something being wrong but rather an indication of spiritual insight (Castillo, 1997). O'Neill (1993) found that among American Indians living on reservations, sadness had positive connotations because "it signified maturity and recognition of the tremendous loss they experienced through domination by Anglo American society" (O'Neill, as cited in Castillo, 1997, p. 208). Grief is also a phenomenon that is embedded in sociocultural contexts. For example, in Greece, a widow grieves for five years after her partner's death (Kramer, 1993). While sadness in Western society is often characterized by a cognitive feature such as self-talk, in many non-Western societies, it is represented more by somatic symptoms (Castillo, 1997). Application Exercise 4.7 has several components to help you identify nonverbal and verbal affect messages and cues.

APPLICATION EXERCISE 4.7

Identifying Affect Cues

To give you practice in identifying nonverbal and verbal affect cues, complete the following exercises.

A. Identifying Nonverbal Affect Cues

Select a partner. One of you will be the speaker; the other will be the respondent. The speaker should select a feeling from the following list. (Note how any cultural affiliations affect this process.)

- Contentment or happiness
- Puzzlement or confusion
- Anger
- Discouragement
- Disgust
- Worry or anxiety
- Embarrassment and self-consciousness
- Excited or thrilled

Do not tell the respondent which feeling you have selected. Portray the feeling through nonverbal expressions only. The respondent must accurately identify the behaviors you use to communicate the feeling and should infer the feeling you are portraying. After he or she has done so, choose another and then repeat the process. When you have portrayed each feeling, reverse roles and then repeat the exercise.

An alternative way to do this application exercise is in two small groups or teams. Each team picks one emotion to act out, and the other team has to guess what it is just from the nonverbal affect cues. If the other team guesses correctly, they get one point. If they do not, the first team can continue to try to act it out or they can pick another emotion to act out. As soon as the second team guesses the emotion accurately, it is their turn, and they can pick an emotion to act out. If it is identified accurately by the other team, that team then gets one point. Continue until both teams have acted out all the different emotions on the list. Afterward, you can process this activity with the following sorts of questions:

1. Which feelings were easiest to act out? Easiest to identify?
2. Which feelings were hardest to act out? Hardest to identify?
3. What have you taken away from this activity about nonverbal affect cues?

B. Linking Body Cues and Emotions

Many emotions are expressed graphically by descriptions about the body. Smith (1985) has provided an excellent list of some of these. We have adapted his exercise, which is to enact each of them with your own body and note the feelings and body sensations that accompany each enactment.

- He holds his head high.
- She has a tight jaw.
- He turns away.
- She has shifty eyes.
- He sticks his chest out.
- Her shoulders are stooped.
- He stoops low.
- She sits tall and straight. (pp. 60–61)

C. Identifying Verbal Affect Cues

The speaker should select a feeling from the following list:

- Surprise
- Elation or thrill

- Anxiety or tension
- Sadness or depression
- Seriousness or intensity
- Irritation or anger

Do not inform the respondent which feeling you have selected. Verbally express the feeling in one or two sentences. Be certain to include the affect word itself. The respondent should accurately identify the feeling in two ways:

1. Restate the feeling by using the same affect word as the speaker.
2. Restate the feeling by using a different affect word but one that reflects the same feeling.

Here is an example:

SPEAKER: I feel good about being here.
RESPONDENT: You feel good?
    or
RESPONDENT: You're glad to be here.

Choose another feeling and then complete the same process. When you have expressed each feeling, reverse roles and then repeat the exercise.

D. Identifying Affective Components

Read the following client statements taken from actual interview typescripts. Identify the affective component(s) in each statement by writing first-person sentences and by underlining the affect word of each client's communication. Here is an example:

> CLIENT: I'm not the type that would like to do research or, uh, things that don't have any contact directly with people. I like to be with people, you know—I feel at home and secure with people.

In this statement, the affect word *like* is identified, and the following affective components are identified by written sentences in the first person:

1. I enjoy being with people.
2. People help me feel secure.

If there is more than one affective component within a given client communication, place an asterisk (*) next to the one that you feel has the greatest bearing on the client's concern. In the preceding example, asterisk either 1 or 2 depending on which has the greater bearing in your opinion.

Client Statements

1. "Well, uh, I'm happy just being with people and having them know me."
2. "And, and, uh, you know, they always say that, you know, some people don't like to be called by a number; well, I don't either."
3. "In speech, I'm, uh, well, in speech, I'm not doing good because I'm afraid to talk in front of a bunch of people."
4. "I can't afford to lose my place on the honor roll and bring shame to my family."

Feedback: Part D

CLIENT 1: I'm *happy* being with people who know me.
CLIENT 2: I *don't like* being called by a number.
CLIENT 3: (1) I'm not *doing good* in speech and (2)* I'm *afraid* to talk in front of people.
CLIENT 4: My family and I would be *shamed* if I lose my place on the honor roll.

EFFECTS OF RESPONDING TO AFFECTIVE MESSAGES

The importance of responding to client feelings as an anxiety-reduction tool has already been mentioned. Generally speaking, responding to affect diminishes the intensity of feelings. For example, responding to (accepting) strong feelings of anger expressed by the client reduces the intensity of the feelings and assists the client in gaining control of them so the client is not overwhelmed by feelings. The expression of feelings may be an important goal for some clients. Some people have had so few opportunities to express their feelings openly that to find an acceptant listener provides highly beneficial relief.

Responding to affect with acceptance and understanding can also assist clients in incorporating personal feelings and perceptions into their self-image. In other words, the helper's acceptance of feelings that have been previously denied and labeled as "bad" by the clients suggests that they may have mislabeled these feelings and thus themselves. In this way, helpers model affective competence for clients. They help clients learn how to manage their feelings instead of denying them or shutting down and not functioning.

Responding to affect is often the best way to communicate your warmth and involvement with clients. That is, responding to client feelings establishes a high level of trust between you and your clients. It is precisely this kind of trust that enables clients to own their feelings, behaviors, and commitment to behavior change. Fosha (2000) described this process in a very clear way:

> Why is it more effective to say something to somebody than merely to think it and feel it, even if the other does little more than listen? Why should it make such an enormous difference to communicate something to another person? In expression—and reception by the other—the full cycle of processing core affect is complete. . . . The difference between aloneness and the sense of being integrated in the mainstream of mutuality—community—is created by the act of affective communication with one other person, who is open and interested. (p. 28)

Although responding to affect early in the helping process can be the best strategy for reducing client anxiety, with some clients, your response to their affect message may only induce greater anxiety. With this kind of client, you have to modify the strategy and respond to cognitive topics in order to find out how the client thinks and what kind of ideas he or she has. Helpers who always emphasize feelings to the exclusion of cognitive content impose certain limitations on the helping process. Some of the limitations of responding only to feelings include the following:

1. Responding only to feelings is unrealistic and therefore reduces the client's ability to generalize aspects of the helping relationship to other relationships. For most clients, it is highly unlikely that any of their friends or family take only their feelings into account.

2. Responding only to feelings fosters an internal focus to the exclusion of the world around the client. Clients may become so preoccupied with themselves that the level of their other relationships deteriorates even more. Also, responding to an internal focus reflects a European-American worldview that will not be compatible with the worldview of some clients from other cultural groups.

3. Responding to affect induces catharsis—the ventilation of pent-up feelings and concerns. For some clients, this may be all that is necessary. For other clients, this is not a sufficient goal. With catharsis, there is a greater possibility of reinforcing "victim mythology"; that is, the helper's responses to feelings may only generate more client negative self-referent statements.

In this chapter, we discussed verbal following and selective attention, in which the helper makes discriminations or differentiations—sometimes subtle ones—that affect the outcome of a session. Choosing to respond to the cognitive dimension of a client's problems leads the session in one direction. Choosing instead to respond to the affective dimension leads in a quite different direction. The cultural and contextual affiliations of both helper and client help to shape this process.

ATTENDING TO CONTEXT

Egan (2014) observed that clients are more than the sum of their verbal and nonverbal messages. In its deepest sense, attentiveness means listening to the ways in which clients are influenced by the contexts in which they live, move, and have their being. Egan added that key elements of this context become part of the client's story, whether they are mentioned directly or not. Many of the elements of context were discussed in Chapter 1. They have to do with things such as the client's religion or faith heritage, race, ethnicity, gender, sexual orientation, social and economic class, occupation, geography, age, and so on. These elements of context often form a central part of the client's identity, and not to attend to them is to render the client invisible. For example, for some clients, being Jewish may be a core aspect of their identity and being in the world, whereas for others, the core aspect may be race, sexual orientation, money, social class, or health status. Listening for context not only involves attending to and acknowledging these elements of context surrounding clients but it also involves attending to and clarifying the meaning that clients give to these contextual elements. The next section, Case Example: Listening for Context, illustrates this process.

Case Example: Listening for Context

Sondra is a lesbian who came out many years ago—so many years ago that, at this point in time, being a lesbian was an important but not the only important part of her identity. Sondra stated in your counseling session that she sometimes felt annoyed because people were always responding to her sexual orientation as a rather singular factor; that is what they paid attention to. Sondra believed there were many other interesting aspects to her life and her identity, and she felt annoyed when other people were not interested in learning more about these. On the other hand, your client Angela was upset when you did not mention in the session the fact that she was African American. She felt you overlooked something that was critical to how she saw herself and that you were not attentive to this important part of her identity. She wondered aloud how well the two of you would be able to work together in counseling because you had "missed" communicating your awareness and attentiveness about this important part of her narrative, her story.

APPLICATION EXERCISE 4.8

Helper Attentiveness and Culture

Now that you are aware of behavioral descriptions of inappropriate social behaviors and attending behaviors in the counseling setting, can you deduce some appropriate behaviors? Be specific about nonverbal components (face, eyes, tone of voice, rate of speech, etc.), body language components (head, arms, body position, etc.), and verbal components (choice of words, types of responses, etc.). List them on a sheet of paper.

For the second part of this activity, go back over the list you just created. Consider instances in which your list of helper attentiveness behaviors may not be culturally appropriate for some clients. Think about examples, and discuss them with a partner or in a small group.

Summary

One of the major goals in counseling is to listen attentively and to communicate this attentiveness through the use of eye contact, intermittent head nods, a variety of facial expressions, relaxed posture, modulated voice, and verbal responses that follow the client's topics. As we have seen in this chapter, many of these components of attentiveness vary depending on the gender and culture of both helper and client.

Because helpers cannot attend to everything, attentiveness is selective, and in counseling sessions, helpers make moment-by-moment decisions about what is most important. In this chapter, we discussed the role of selective attention in identifying and responding to cognitive and affective client messages and the varying potential effects of responding to these kinds of messages.

In addition to listening to verbal and nonverbal messages, helpers also need to pay attention to the context surrounding client stories and lives. Like cognitive and affective messages, contextual messages may be explicit or implicit. It is the helper's attentiveness that assists clients in identifying and developing the important contextual themes of their stories and lives. Ivey, Gluckstern Packard, and Ivey (2006) concluded, "The acts of attending and listening are very powerful. Through your careful listening, the client will come to find new perspectives and ways of being in the world." (p. 14). In the following chapter, we discuss some verbal helping skills that practitioners use to listen accurately and sensitively to clients.

Reflective Questions

1. Recall an incident in which you were sharing a significant moment with another person and that person displayed some distracting behavior. What was the effect of that person's behavior on you? What did you decide was the reason for that person's behavior?

2. What do you notice about nonverbal behavior among persons from varying cultures?

3. What effect does your own culture have on the way you seem to attend and respond to clients?

4. When a client's message contains both cognitive and affective components, what conditions might lead you to respond to the affective element? How might this be influenced by the client's culture?

5. If you were a client, would you prefer a helper whose natural inclinations were toward feelings or toward rational thinking? What would be the advantages for you if you had the helper you preferred? What would be the disadvantages for you with such a helper?

6. Clients are often less aware of their feelings than of their thoughts. How might you assist clients to become more aware of their feelings by the way you choose to respond?

MyCounselingLab

Click on MyCounselingLab and locate the Video Library under the Video Resources tab in the left-hand navigation bar.

1. Click the Process, Skills, and Techniques collection. Watch the following two selections: "Encouraging Clients to Listen to Their Center" and "Examples of Active Listening in Session." Review these two clips and then answer these questions:
   a. In the first clip, the client talked a great deal in the session. How did the practitioner use attending skills to listen to her?
   b. In the second clip, what nonverbal and verbal attending skills did the practitioner use, and what effects did these seem to have on this particular client?
   c. In these two clips, the helper and client differed on several cultural dimensions, including race, gender, and age. Did you think the helper's attending skills were affected by these differences? If so, how?

Recommended Readings

Cormier, S., Nurius, P. S., & Osborn, C. J. (2013). *Interviewing strategies for helpers* (7th ed.). Belmont, CA: Brooks/Cole, Cengage.

Egan, G. (2014). *The skilled helper* (10th ed.). Belmont, CA: Brooks/Cole, Cengage.

Ivey, A., Gluckstern Packard, N., & Ivey, M. B. (2006). *Basic attending skills* (4th ed.). North Amherst, MA: Microtraining Associates.

Knapp, M. L., Hall, J., & Horgan, T. G. (2014). *Nonverbal communication in human interaction*, (8th ed.). Boston, MA: Wadsworth, Cengage Learning.

Listening Skills

Perhaps there is no more powerful medicine in the world than the gift of having someone really listen to you. Mark Nepo writes in *Seven Thousand Ways to Listen* that "listening is an animating process by which we feel and understand the moment we are in: repeatedly connecting the inner world with the world around us, letting one inform the other" (Nepo, 2012, p. xiii). Nepo points out all the different languages that have a word for listening: *hylsnan*, in Old English, meaning "to pay attention, to wait for a sound or signal"; *ascoltare* in Italian, *kiku* in Japanese, *lytte* in Norwegian, *escuchar* in Spanish, *dinlemek* in Turkish, and so it goes. Each word sounds very different, and yet each word represents the same process. Nepo says that one thing that all these various words have in common is that they describe a process that pulls us out of human isolation in order to experience our connection with one another. Nepo (2012, p. 49) asks:

- *Have you encountered a great listener in your life?*
- *What can you add to your own practice of listening from their great example?*

Nichols (2009) describes listening as a lost art, saying that culturally we've gained access to so much information but have lost the capacity to focus our attention on other persons and what they are communicating to us. He says "to listen is to pay attention, take an interest, care about, take to heart, validate, acknowledge, and be moved . . . appreciate" (p. 14). He describes two primary purposes of listening: taking in information about someone and also bearing witness to another person's experience. Both of these two purposes are very important reasons to engage in effective listening in the helping process.

Reading this, perhaps you are thinking: "Listening? Really? How hard can that be?" Listening is often one of the toughest challenges for beginning helpers possibly because of an almost inherent tendency to want to jump into the conversation with clients and fix them. It is actually far easier to move into action with clients than to stay present and listen. Ivey, Gluckstern Packard, and Ivey (2006, p. 4) suggest that the helping process can be summarized in the following maxim: *"Listen, listen, listen, and then listen some more before taking action."* Following this maxim requires a great deal of patience that often has to be cultivated and practiced sufficiently before helpers feel comfortable to listen, listen, listen, and then listen . . . some more!

In this chapter, we write about listening to clients. Specifically, this chapter is about helping you develop a repertoire of verbal responses that communicate to clients that you are listening to them and hearing their messages, both verbal and nonverbal. These responses include the following: the paraphrase, the reflection of feelings, the summarization of content, and the summarization of feelings. In Chapter 6, we discuss the role of problem solving in the helping process and present the verbal action skills of questions, reflection of meaning, and challenging responses. Together these two chapters, along with the prior chapter on attending skills, constitute a wide range of basic helping skills. This set of helping skills has been garnering empirical support for their use in working with clients since the mid-1970s when several key textbooks describing these skills first appeared on the market, including *Counseling Strategies and Objectives* (Hackney & Cormier, 1973), *The Skilled Helper* (Egan, 1975), *Basic Attending Skills* (Ivey, 1971), and *Basic Influencing Skills* (Ivey, 1971). Since that time, many texts describing these skills in one way or another have appeared on the market. Essentially these skills represent the notion that beginning helpers can acquire a basic set of skills to use in helping interviews, much like a golfer has a set of golf clubs, taking out one club to use in one situation and yet another golf club to use in another situation. The attending skills we discussed in Chapter 4 are usually learned first. The listening skills we describe in this chapter are learned next. The action skills we describe in Chapter 6 are usually emphasized in the later stages of training.

PARAPHRASE: LISTENING FOR CONTENT

We begin with the paraphrase response because it is usually the easiest of the listening responses for beginning helpers to learn. Paraphrasing is the rephrasing of all or a selected portion of the client's previous communication, and it neither adds to nor detracts from the basic communication. It confirms for the client that the helper has heard the communication in a nonjudgmental way. Operationally, the paraphrase may be defined as a simple, compound, complex, or fragmentary sentence that mirrors the client's previous communication by *using your own words.* Paraphrasing is sometimes referred to as a reflection of content because this response usually picks up on the cognitive part of the client's message, whereas the reflection of feelings response picks up on the affective part of the message. The paraphrase can be used effectively as long as it is interspersed with other types of helper responses. Otherwise, it can produce a parrotlike effect that has an adverse effect on clients. When using a paraphrase response, it is helpful to use the most important words and ideas expressed in the client's message. When you do this, your response lets clients know you have heard their message accurately and that you are able to respond to it in a way that does not simply copy or mimic their expression. The following examples of paraphrases will help you understand this particular response:

CLIENT: I'm hoping to get a good job this summer.

HELPER: You're counting on getting the job you need this summer. (paraphrase)

CLIENT: It doesn't look like we'll get a vacation this summer.

HELPER: It looks like a vacation is not going to happen for you this summer. (paraphrase)

CLIENT: I like people, but I sure get tired of them.

HELPER: After a while, being around people can be fatiguing for you. (paraphrase)

Using paraphrases to listen effectively to clients has several purposes:

- Communicating your understanding of the client's situation.
- Encouraging client elaboration of the previous client message.
- Helping the client to focus.

The client will usually let you know when a paraphrase is accurate by a confirming or affirming response to you, such as "that's it" or "yes, you're right." On the other hand, if your paraphrase is not on target, it usually gives the client an opportunity to clarify the meaning of the message.

Here are the steps you can use to formulate the paraphrase response:

1. Attend carefully to the client's message. If you are listening closely, you will be able to recall the client's verbal and nonverbal communications so that you can rephrase them for the client. If you are not paying attention or you are distracted, however, you may have difficulty in formulating an accurate paraphrase (or other listening responses too!) because you simply can't remember what the client said. This is a prime example of where listening involves more than just accurate verbal responses to clients; it also involves presence on your part.

2. Listen for the content part of the message in particular and note what idea, fact, person, object, or situation the client discusses through the message.

3. Translate the key part of the content message by using your own words to rephrase it for the client. You may wish to begin your paraphrase with the client's name or with what is called a sentence stem such as "It sounds like . . .," "It appears as though . . .," "and You're saying that . . .," and so on.

4. Note carefully the client's response to your paraphrase. Does the client confirm your message or not? The client's response gives you feedback about the accuracy of your paraphrase.

Try some paraphrases of your own in Application Exercise 5.1.

APPLICATION EXERCISE 5.1

Paraphrasing: Listening for Content

Practice the steps we noted in this chapter to formulate a couple of sample paraphrase responses for each of the four client messages. Feedback follows.

1. CLIENT: This has been a really rough year for me.
   YOU: _____

2. CLIENT: Probably the worst class I have is literature.
   YOU: _____

3. CLIENT: I never thought I would enjoy living alone, but now that I have been doing it for a while, I'm used to it and I prefer keeping my own company.

You: _____

4. CLIENT: I thought getting an abortion might be a moral issue for me, but honestly I just didn't see any other option.

You: _____

Feedback

With client 1, did your paraphrase sound something like one of the following?

It seems like this year has been especially tough for you. Is that true?

Apparently this year in particular has been really challenging for you in several ways.

With client 2, did your paraphrase sound something like one of the following?

It sounds like your literature class has been a difficult experience for you.

It seems like your literature class has been something you have disliked.

What about client 3?

It seems like you like living alone much more than you anticipated you would.

Now that you have gotten accustomed to living by yourself, you find you actually enjoy the experience of it.

And with client 4?

It sounds like you thought having an abortion might be more of a moral struggle for you than it turned out to be.

It sounds like this situation turned out to be less complicated for you than you anticipated, especially since you felt it was your only choice.

REFLECTION OF FEELINGS: LISTENING FOR AFFECT

As we already indicated in this chapter, the paraphrase response is used primarily to attend to the content portion of a client's message. In contrast, the reflection of feelings response is used to attend to the affective portion or the emotional tone of the client's communication. A reflection of feelings is similar to a paraphrase, but it has an added emotional component that is missing in the paraphrase. To help you see the differences in these two listening skills, consider the contrast in the following example:

CLIENT:	This sure has been a crappy week. Nothing went right at the job, and my wife and I argued all the time.
HELPER PARAPHASE:	It sounds like this has been such a tough week for you in a lot of respects.
HELPER REFLECTION:	Wow. I imagine you must be feeling disappointed in the way your week has turned out, with nothing going right for you.

Reflection of feelings accomplishes precisely what its name indicates: a mirroring of the feeling or emotion present in the client's message. This response helps clients to own and express feelings. The value in reflection of feelings is helping clients to recognize their feelings and to accept those feelings rather than fear them. Initially, clients may defend against feelings because they seem dangerous. People who feel sad may do everything in their power to avoid feeling sad or blue. Ultimately, the client needs to learn to trust his or her feelings; it is the experiencing and expressing the sadness rather than the blocking or numbing out of it that is healing (Brammer, Abrego, & Shostrom, 1993). The reflection of feelings response also helps clients name and validate their emotions within a safe context. This response also helps clients feel understood, especially at an important emotional level.

The reflection of feelings response is the primary listening skill used to convey basic empathy to clients. Many clients come to us with unmet emotional needs or with histories in which their feelings have been negated or judged. As a result, clients lose trust in the validity of their own experiences and feelings. This may be even more apparent in working with clients from marginalized groups with histories of cultural oppressions as well. When helpers convey such understanding to clients through effective and accurate reflection and validation, clients "feel that they have been seen and are no longer invisible or alone, different or defective, dismissed or unimportant, and so forth. At that moment, the client begins to perceive the therapist as someone who is different from many others in her life, and possibly as someone who can help" (Teyber & McClure, 2011, p. 72).

The reflection of feelings response can occur at different levels. At the most obvious level, the helper may reflect only the surface feeling of the client. At a deeper level, the helper may reflect an implied feeling with greater intensity than that originally expressed by the client. The more obvious level occurs when the helper reflects an affect message that is overtly present in the client's message by using a different affect word but one that captures the same feeling and intensity expressed by the client, as in the following example:

CLIENT: I feel really mad that you interrupted me.

HELPER: You're very angry about being interrupted.

The second kind of reflection occurs at a deeper level. This one mirrors an affect message that is only covertly expressed or implied in the client's message. For example, consider the implied affect message in "I think we have a really neat relationship." The feeling inherent in the words refers to a positive affect message of *like, enjoys, pleased,* and so forth. Thus, a reflection that picks up on the implied feeling in this communication might be among the following:

- "Our relationship is important to you."
- "Some good things are in it for you."
- "You're pleased with the relationship."

This reflection that occurs at a deeper level not only mirrors the covert feeling but also must at least match the intensity of the client's feeling and perhaps even reflect greater intensity of feeling. The most effective reflection is one that emphasizes what the client anticipates—in other words, one that acknowledges the implied admission of the client's message. Consider this sort of reflection in the following example. Note that the helper reflects back the covertly implied feeling with a greater intensity of affect and acknowledges the implied admission—that is, what the client would like to do or feel, as shown here:

CLIENT: I feel like I have to be so responsible all the time.

HELPER: Sometimes, you'd feel relieved just to forget all that responsibility—to say, "To hell with it"—and really let go.

There are several steps in formulating effective reflection of feelings responses. First, listen carefully for any overt or obvious feeling or affect words in the client's message. Table 5.1 lists a variety of commonly used words to describe feelings at three levels of intensity: mild, moderate, and intense. We suggest you familiarize yourself with these and other affect words to add to your own affect vocabulary. This activity will help you expand the choices you have when trying to reflect myriad client feelings and emotions.

TABLE 5.1 Sample List of Affect Words

Feeling	Mild	Moderate	Intense
Joy	good	wonderful	tremendous
	glad	happy	overjoyed
	happy	joyful	jubilant
	satisfied	pleased	excited
	contented	optimistic	delighted
Anger	displeased	irate	infuriated
	bothered	mad	enraged
	ticked off	indignant	fuming
	slighted	insulted	offended
	dislike	disgusted	hate
	annoyed	frustrated	furious
Fear	concerned	alarmed	agitated
	apprehensive	anxious	overwhelmed
	tense	frightened	terrified
	uneasy	threatened	panicked
	wary	suspicious	petrified
	mistrustful	foreboding	dread
Sadness	uninterested	bored	dispirited
	down	unhappy	depressed
	sad	pessimistic	crushed
	low	discouraged	hopeless
	unhappy	sorrowful	heartsick
	isolated	lonely	abandoned

Second, listen as well for any hidden or less obvious ways the client has described feelings or emotions in her or his communication. Sometimes the affect message is disguised by clients and is conveyed implicitly rather than explicitly. This is often the case when clients are less aware of their feelings, are unable to name feelings, or are unsure about revealing feelings directly to the helper.

Third, give your full and undivided attention to *how* the client is communicating in addition to *what* the client is saying. Recall from Chapter 4 that affect messages are often conveyed by nonverbal means, so listening for nonverbal cues from the client's eye contact, body position, vocal tone, gestures, and facial expressions is crucial to the formulation of an effective reflection of feelings response.

Fourth, after you have identified the feelings from carefully attending to the explicit and implicit verbal messages and the client's nonverbal cues, reflect the predominant feelings you have picked up using different affect words than any used by the client, but use words that reflect the same emotional tone at the same intensity. For example, suppose a client says to you, "I'm so pissed off at her," while another client says, "I got kind of bothered by her." Both clients are speaking of affect that has to do with anger but at much different levels of intensity. The first client is clearly expressing a deeper level of an angry feeling than the second, and it would be inaccurate for the helper to reflect a low-intensity affect word back to the first client or a strong-intensity word back to the second client. Can you imagine the mismatch if a helper said to the first client: "Yeah you do seem a little bit annoyed with her," or if the helper said to the second client, "Boy, you seem really, really mad at her." After you choose a different but appropriate affect word, add it to a sentence stem, such as "You're feeling _____."

Fifth, add to your response the context of the feelings or the situation in which these feelings occur. This can usually be detected from the content portion of the client's message. Essentially, this addition takes the form of a brief paraphrase. For example, suppose the client says, "I feel so frustrated. Nothing I have done this week has worked out. I feel like everything I have done has just turned out the wrong way!" In this message, the affect is frustration, and the context or content is having her experiences not work out to her expectations or satisfaction. A sample reflection of feelings response to this client would be, "You're feeling upset (affect) since nothing you have accomplished this week has worked out the way you had hoped for (content)."

Finally, assess the client's response to your reflection. If you are accurate, the client will confirm your message by saying something like: "Yes, that's exactly what's going on" or "Yup, I am feeling like that!" If you have missed the mark, usually the client will let you know by indicating something like: "Well, it's not quite like that. It's more like this. . . ." and then you can attempt an additional reflection.

To reassure you, even very experienced helpers don't always hit the mark with responses that are entirely accurate. It is not as important that you have perfect responses every time you respond to a client, but it is essential for you to try your best to understand where the client is coming from. If your intentions are good, even if you misunderstand the client's communication, most clients are very forgiving because they can sense that you are working on their behalf! If a client lets you know that you are a bit off the mark with your response, you can say something like this: "I sure want to be able to understand this. Could you clarify for me what you are experiencing in this situation so I can be sure to get it this time?"

Some clients may deny their feelings if you have introduced attention to the affect message prematurely. As Ivey, Ivey, and Zalaquett (2014) note, "[C]lients are not always ready to address or share with you the way they feel. . . . Remember that not all clients will appreciate or welcome your commenting on their feelings. . . . Less verbal clients may find reflections puzzling at times . . . and with some cultural groups, reflection of feelings may be inappropriate and represent cultural insensitivity." They conclude that, although "noting feelings in the session is essential, acting on your observations may not always be in the best interests of the client. Timing is particularly important with this skill" (p. 175).

The reflection of feelings response is a very important tool in the repertoire of the helper, but it can be a challenging skill to learn and apply. Young (2013) notes some of the more common issues that helpers face in learning to reflect feelings, including waiting too long into the session before responding to the client's feelings (usually because of the helper's own discomfort), stating the reflection as a question rather than as a statement, and adding or tacking a question to the end of the reflection and essentially giving the client two responses rather than one to respond to. Try some reflection of feelings responses in Application Exercise 5.2.

APPLICATION EXERCISE 5.2

Reflecting Feelings: Listening for Affect

This exercise gives you some opportunities to develop reflection of feelings responses for selected client messages. Feedback follows.

CLIENT 1:   I knew he was sick, but I didn't know that he could be terminally ill. I guess I am just in shock from learning this.

YOU: _____

CLIENT 2:   I have just been feeling really incompetent right now. This job is so new to me and I keep feeling like I'm making lots of mistakes.

YOU: _____

CLIENT 3:   I wasn't sure if this would be a good move for me or not. But now that I've been here for several years, I'm on top of the world. Things couldn't be better, really!

YOU: _____

CLIENT 4:   This constant snow and ice has really gotten to me. I have been cooped up and unable to get to the gym and I'm totally out of my routines too.

YOU: _____

Feedback

For client 1, does your reflection go something like this: "It sounds like you're feeling alarmed from learning about the severity of his illness which came as such a surprise to you"?

What about client 2? Our sample reflection goes like this: "It sounds like you're feeling somewhat ineffective with the way you're performing at your new job."

For client 3, here is a sample reflection: "Wonderful. How exciting that you made a move, felt unsure about how it would turn out, but now find yourself living a dream."

For client 4, here is a reflection example: "It seems like this weather pattern has really done a number on your routines and you're feeling frustrated with being so confined to your house right now."

SUMMARIZATION: LISTENING FOR MULTIPLE ELEMENTS OF CONTENT AND AFFECT

The summarization helping skill is just what it seems—it represents a way for helpers to summarize or tie together various elements of the client's communications, both verbal and nonverbal. We can define a summarization response as a statement that condenses client verbal and nonverbal messages by combining two or more paraphrases and/or reflections. The summarization can be a skill that is used to respond to immediate client messages as well as to a number of messages that occur within an individual session or even over a period of time encompassing a few sessions. As such, it is probably one of the more challenging basic helping skills to acquire because it involves "deeper concentration over time" to a number of client messages (Ivey et al., 2006, p. 93).

Summarization is useful in helping interviews in many ways. First, it forms a more cohesive picture of various components of the client's messages and communications, helping both client and helper make sense of the meaning of the communication. Related to this, the summarization is a good tool to help identify a theme or pattern that may not become apparent until after a few messages or even after a few sessions.

Another purpose of a summarization response is that it can bring focus to a client who rambles. Summarization is also an effective way to regulate the pace of an individual session. If the helper feels the session may be moving too quickly, the use of this response provides emotional space in the session for both client and helper to catch up on the quick progression of communication. Summarization is also a great way to review progress and is a common skill used in terminating an individual session or even terminating with a client (client being an individual, group, couple, or family). We depict some examples of this in Chapter 7.

Young (2013) says that a summarization "helps the client make some sense of the tangle of thoughts and feelings," thus serving a "reflecting purpose, letting the client hear his or her viewpoint in a more organized way. The summary ties some of the major issues that have emerged into a compact version of the story" (p. 151). Ivey et al. (2006) point out that "clients who come to you are often confused. They may have so many things going on in their lives that they don't know which way to turn. They may experience mixed emotions. Important facts regarding decisions may be overlooked" (p. 93). Like Young, Ivey and colleagues see summarization as an important skill for helping clients track and organize their thoughts and feelings.

We find that it is easier to beginning helpers to learn this skill if we separate it initially into summarization of content and summarization of feelings. As such, this is the way we present it in the next two sections of the chapter. This is a good way to practice this skill initially, but in reality, the effective summarization ties together *both* content and feelings of multiple client messages.

Summarization of Content Response

A *summarization of content* is a rephrasing of at least two or more different content or cognitive messages expressed by the client. As Ivey et al. (2006) note, the summarization of content is very similar to the paraphrase except in the dimension of time. Whereas the paraphrase is a response "to the client's last few sentences or a short paragraph," the summarization of content puts together a "number of paragraphs, an entire session, or perhaps even issues expressed over a series of several interviews" (p. 95). Consider the following examples of the summarization of content response:

CLIENT: I've been pretty tired for the last few months. I just don't seem to have my usual energy. I am sleeping okay, but by early afternoon, I just run out of steam. Maybe it's because so much has happened around me lately—my partner just lost his job and my dog died about a year ago.

HELPER: (Summarization of content with at least two paraphrases) Wow—it seems like a lot of pretty significant things has been happening in your life and you have noticed these affecting your energy level.

CLIENT: (Early in the session) I don't think I have a big problem with pot. I mean, I do smoke it every day, but it doesn't seem to interfere with anything I need to do. Well, sometimes I guess I do feel a little concerned because I like the feeling I get from it [pot], so I don't want to give it up.

CLIENT: (At the end of the session) Well, maybe I am more dependent on pot than I should be. I do like to get high every day. I like the feeling I get from smoking pot. And it helps me not wig out about things that stress me out or piss me off.

HELPER: (Summarization of content with at least two paraphrases) You have said a couple of things during this session about your smoking pot—sometimes you wonder if you're too dependent on it. Other times you think maybe you could give it up easily if you wanted to.

In the next section of the chapter, we will explore how summarization can be used to respond to affective messages as well as in the summarization of feelings response. Before that, try your hand at summarization of content responses in Application Exercise 5.3.

APPLICATION EXERCISE 5.3

Summarization of Content

For the following three client–helper interactions, please observe these directions:

1. Attend carefully to the client messages.
2. Identify in writing the cognitive or content portions of the client communication.
3. Formulate a summarization of content message.

Feedback follows.

CLIENT 1:   I find it easier to relate to my stepson than my own son. I think it's because we're not biologically related, if you know what I mean. There just seems to be so much less conflict between us.

Cognitive Messages:

_____

_____

(Continued)

Summarization of Content:

_____

_____

_____

CLIENT 2:   My partner confronted me about my drinking and got me to agree to come in here to see you, but I really don't want to be here. I don't think how much I drink is anyone else's business but my own.

Cognitive Messages:

_____

_____

Summarization of Content:

_____

_____

_____

CLIENT 3:   (Early in the session) I think this woman is my soul mate. We have been together now for about five years and we share the same goals and values.

CLIENT 3:   (At the end of the session) Lately though, she and I have been having lots of conflict. She wants to move to an urban area and I have a great job here and don't think I should have to give it up

Cognitive Messages:

_____

_____

Summarization of Content:

_____

_____

_____

Feedback

Client 1

Cognitive Messages: (1) It is easier to relate to my stepson than my own son. (2) I think it is because we are not biologically related. (3) There is less conflict between me and my stepson than between me and my biological son.

For client 1, does your summarization of content look like this: "You've noticed quite a difference in the way you, as a parent and adult, relate to your son and your stepson, and you've realized it actually seems easier to get along with your stepson than your biological son"?

Client 2

Cognitive Messages: (1) My partner confronted me about my drinking. (2) I came to see you at my partner's request. (3) My drinking is really just my business, not yours.

Check out your summarization of content for client 2. Here is our sample: "You're really here only because your partner prodded you to come here, and that is because he thinks you have a drinking problem, but you don't agree."

Client 3

Cognitive Messages: Early in the session: (1) This woman is my soul mate. (2) We've been together about five years. (3) We share the same goals and values.

At the end of the session: (1) Lately she and I have been having conflicts. (2) She wants to move to an urban area. (3) I have a great job here.

For client 3, did your summarization of content pick up the client messages at both the beginning and at the end of the session, as in the following example: "You know early in the session you were describing your partner as your soul mate and how you two were on the same page, but as you have continued to talk about this relationship during our session, you have also mentioned some growing areas of conflict between the two of you"?

Summarization of Feelings Response

Summarization of feelings is very similar to reflection of feelings in that it is a response that discriminates between different affective components of the client's communication and communicates understanding of the client's feelings by the helper. The basic difference in the two responses is one of number, or quantity. The reflection of feelings responds to only one portion of the client's communication, whereas the summarization of feelings is an integration of several affective components of the client's communication. Thus, summarization of feelings is really an extension of reflection of feelings. In this response, the helper is attending to a broader class of client responses and must have the skill to bring together seemingly diverse elements into a meaningful gestalt (Ivey et al., 2012). Like the reflection of feelings, summarization of feelings involves reflecting the feelings of the client in your own words. Again, this encompasses not just one feeling but a bringing together of several feelings into a significant pattern.

Although clients sometimes present one predominant feeling, there are other instances in which clients have several feelings going on at the same time. Teyber and McClure (2011) noted that two common affective constructions with mixed components include anger-sadness-shame and sadness-anger-guilt. In the first sequence, the primary feeling is often anger, but it is usually a response to hurt or sadness. Often, experiencing the anger and sadness provokes shame. In the second sequence, the predominant feeling is sadness, but it is often connected to anger that has been denied because the expression of it produces guilt. These affective sequences are typically acquired in childhood and are a result of both family of origin rules and culture. Teyber and McClure (2011) suggest that when clients are not progressing, one reason may be "that therapists have only responded to the clients' single presenting affect . . . rather than the constellation or sequence of feelings (the "firing order") that clients often present (p. 204). They state: "Therapists help clients change by responding to the entire sequence of feelings in their affective constellation, rather than just responding to the first or initial feeling in the sequence—the client's primary presenting affect" (p. 205).

The summarization of feelings response can identify the various affective states the client describes or experiences. Consider the following examples and note how the helper does not just respond to the initial or primary presenting feeling in the client's communication but rather the sequence of various feelings.

CLIENT: I'm so pissed off at my mother and my wife. They're always on my back, telling me what to do, where to go, how to think—planning my

> whole life for me. It's been this way for years. I wish I could do something different, but I just feel hopeless about it. I wish for once I could be a man and stand up to them, but I just keep giving in and giving in.

HELPER: You seem to be feeling several things in this situation: First, you're obviously angry about their behavior. Also, you feel sad and perhaps ashamed about your powerlessness to effect any change—is that accurate?

CLIENT: I'm really feeling down about my job. It's so hard to find the energy to keep going in day after day. I don't really mind the work, but over the years, the people there have been so nasty that I don't want to be around them. I know if I weren't the nice person that I am I would probably really tell them a thing or two.

HELPER: You're feeling discouraged about your job. It also sounds like you're feeling pretty angry and fed up with your coworkers, but because of your own niceness, you feel a little guilty or reluctant to express your irritation with them.

As we can see in these examples, the summarization of feelings response is often used instead of reflection of feelings when a client's communication contains many different affective elements rather than just one or two. Like the summarization of content and paraphrase, the summarization of feelings response "covers a longer time period" than the reflection of feelings response (Ivey et al., 2006, p. 95). Application Exercise 5.4 gives you an opportunity to develop some summarization of feelings responses.

APPLICATION EXERCISE 5.4

Summarization of Feelings

For the following helper–client interactions, please observe the following directions:

1. Read each interaction carefully.
2. For each client statement, identify—by writing sentences—the various affective components of the communication.
3. For each client statement, write a summarization of feelings for each client statement.

Feedback follows.

CLIENT 1: Uh, I'm unsure why I'm having such a hard time letting my family and friends know I'm gay. I mean, I watch TV now, and I see a whole sort of cultural revolution going on there. But when it comes to me, I feel very hesitant. After all, I'm a jock. Who wants a gay in their locker room?

Affective Components: _____

Summarization of Feelings: _____

_____

CLIENT 2: My daddy won't want to meet you because you're black and I'm half black. And he treats my mom and me like dirt. And he thinks only white people deserve to be treated well. I just wish I had a dad who was good to me and my mom. I miss that.

Affective Components: _____

Summarization of Feelings: _____

_____

CLIENT 3:   (In session one) I've been single now for a really long time. And after a couple of failed marriages, I don't think I'm marriage material. I think I'm really destined to live alone. I get lonely but I don't feel confident about being in a relationship again.

CLIENT 3:   (In session five) Well, I've been talking to my women friends about this relationship issue. Some of them have started to date again. I don't know though about this whole online thing. I haven't dated for years. It's a whole different world out there. It feels sort of scary. But maybe I don't want to be the only one in our group of friends who doesn't date. Maybe I do want to construct a profile and see who's out there for me. I guess I feel more optimistic that someone could come along and we could match.

Affective Components:

_____

Summarization of Feelings: _____

_____

Feedback

Client 1

Affective Components: (1) I'm unsure why I'm having a hard time letting my family and friends know I'm gay. (2) I feel hesitant.

Summarization of Feelings: "You're really feeling uncertain and puzzled about why it's so hard to come out to your family and friends and yet, at the same time, you recognize you do feel like holding back on this."

Client 2

Affective Components: (1) My daddy treats me and my mom like dirt. (2) I miss having a dad who is good to me and my mom.

Summarization of Feelings: "It sounds like it's so hard to be treated this way by your daddy, without respect, and you sure long for a daddy who would treat you and your mom well."

Client 3

Session One, Affective Components: (1) I feel lonely but don't feel confident about being in a relationship again.

Session Two, Affective Components: (1) Dating again feels sort of scary. (2) I don't want to be the only one in my group of women friends who doesn't date. (3) I guess I feel more optimistic I could find a match.

Summarization of Feelings for Both Sessions: You seem to recognize your various feelings about this dating issue. You feel lonely and at times you feel unsure about whether you want to be in another relationship. It feels a little daunting. At the same time, you want to fit in and feel a sense of belongingness with your group of women friends and feel more hopeful about finding someone to date.

In using both the reflection of feelings and the summarization of feelings responses, be careful to heed our earlier caution about the potential effectiveness of these two responses depending on the race, gender, and ethnicity of clients, particularly in initial sessions. Ivey et al. (2006) note that, "in cross-cultural counseling situations, trust needs to be built before you can expect in-depth discussion of emotions" (p. 76).

Combining the Two Summarization Responses to Multiple Client Messages

Although we have separated the summarization of content and summarization of feelings responses in this chapter for learning purposes, once you acquire these responses, it's time to think about putting the two together. They are often combined in actual helping interviews with clients so you can integrate both feelings and content with clients. Here are some examples of putting the summarization of content and feelings responses together that reflect both cognitive and affective components of multiple elements of client messages:

CLIENT: (Serena, a young girl who has been having some issues with another girlfriend, sniffling and shedding tears while she talks) Amanda can just be so mean to me. Like she's nice at school to me, and I seem like her best friend there, but when we get to Miss Mary's house for after school, she gets mean. She ignores me and just plays with Marina instead. If I try to play with them, she and Marina go off somewhere else and leave me behind, all alone.

HELPER: **(Summarization of content *and* feelings)** Serena, I can see how upset you're feeling about Amanda's behavior with you, acting one way with you at school and then turning her back on you at Miss Mary's, leaving you to play by yourself.

Can you identify the summarization of content and of feelings in this example? The content has to do with her friend Amanda's changing behaviors in the school and after-school settings, while the feeling involves Serena's distress over this situation.

CLIENT: (Maria, a mother of a twenty-something daughter, shaking her head, speaking slowly) You know, this week, I decided there's a reason your twenty-something daughter shouldn't be living at home with you. I mean the last few years things have been fine. But ever since she broke up with her steady boyfriend a few months ago, I have felt worried sick about her. She goes out at night and on weekends and I don't know where she is or who she is with or what she is getting into now. I wish there was a way she could actually move out so I wouldn't have to worry as much as I do.

HELPER: **(Summarization of content *and* feelings)** Maria, I can tell that this evolving situation with your daughter is very worrisome to you, especially in the last few months, because she has changed her routines and you find yourself clueless concerning her whereabouts.

This example summarization combines the situation of the daughter's change in routine, the content part of the message, with Maria's feelings of worrying, the affective part of the message.

Here are the steps involved in putting together an effective summarization response that focuses on both content and affect messages: First, listen carefully, not just to the prior message of the client but also to the series of messages from the client, both verbal and nonverbal. This is often the most challenging part of learning to summarize because it means you have to concentrate on a number of different messages from a client over a period of time. This requires focus and attention. If you are truly attending to the client, you will notice that you can remember many things about the client and their communication. Attentiveness enhances memory and recall. Second, identify all of the cognitive and affective elements of these messages in a way that distills the primary issue or theme and also the primary affective tone of the verbal and nonverbal messages. Look for repetition in words and feelings and nonverbal messages because these are often significant clues to major cognitive and affective themes. Third, from this distillation process, think of a paraphrase that essentially reflects the content theme, and think of a reflection of feelings that reflects the major affect theme. Fourth, put these two together in the form of a summary statement, and you will have a summarization of content and feelings response.

Two caveats must be noted here. Occasionally, a lengthy client message or even series of messages may appear to contain almost exclusively cognitive content. In these instances, the affective messages are implicit and inferred. Or maybe the opposite is true: A long message or series of messages may describe multiple feelings with the situation or cognitive component being inferred or implicit. Second, because you are often summarizing some implicit messages, it is useful to follow up your summarization response with a query that checks out the accuracy of what you've heard. So you may summarize and then say something to the client like, "Have I heard you accurately?" or "Does this sum up what you've been telling me?" Application Exercise 5.5 gives you an opportunity to develop summarization responses that respond to both content and affect messages in the same response.

APPLICATION EXERCISE 5.5

Summarization of Content *and* Feeling

For each of the following client messages, identify the explicit and implicit cognitive and affective themes, and formulate and write a summarization of content and feeling response. Feedback follows.

CLIENT 1: (Session one) I have mixed feelings about this man I'm seeing now. I like being with him. I'm clearly attracted to him. He is a super nice man, and he seems to really get me. But I feel reluctant to commit to him on a long-term basis because he really doesn't take care of himself in any substantial way and he has already developed several kinds of chronic illnesses.

CLIENT 1: (Session two) I haven't really addressed this with him directly. I mean we've had conversations, I've sent him e-mails about exercise and nutrition and things. But I haven't just out right told him that I don't think I see a long-term future with him given his current health habits.

CLIENT 1: (Session three) We've been dating about a year now. I don't know what to do. At my age meeting single men is pretty tough. I enjoy his companionship. And for the present time, it is fine. Do you think I need to address my hesitations and concerns

(Continued)

more directly with him? I think he would like to get much more serious as he keeps hinting around about living together, traveling together, maybe even getting married someday.

Your summarization of content and feeling response:

_____

_____

CLIENT 2: (Session one) It's been a pretty interesting experience living next door to my new neighbors in the last year. They moved in during the fall, really late fall and I didn't see much of them until the spring. I did notice when they looked at the house they brought about 50 folks over with them. No, I'm not kidding, 50 people! Can you imagine?

CLIENT 2: (Session two) Things changed when warm weather arrived though. They have a huge back yard and I mean huge. Every couple weeks they have a big outside get-together. This is a young couple, no kids, in their twenties. We all live in a quiet neighborhood, and the rest of us are middle-age or older, with responsibilities.

CLIENT 2: (Session three) The cars of people at their house take up the entire street on our block, both sides. I don't really understand why they didn't buy a house with a lot of parking space in a driveway for their events. Sometimes I've gotten blocked in by someone at their party.

CLIENT 2: (Session four) They're actually nice kids. Good kids. They both have good jobs. But they do seem clueless about the noise and the parking and sometimes when I've had a few people over, there are no spots on the street for my guests to park.

Your summarization of content and feeling response:

_____

_____

CLIENT 3: (Session one) We've been married a long time now, but it's a second marriage for both of us. Sometimes James does drive me really crazy though. I'm not sure in retrospect what drew me to him, or why I ended up remarrying him in particular.

CLIENT 3: (Session two) James is very quiet and keeps to himself. He spends a lot of time up in his study working out math problems, which is what he used to do before he retired. He was a math professor. But we just don't ever really talk to each other. We do things together, go to movies and plays, but I don't feel that much of an emotional connection between us.

Your summarization of content and feeling response:

_____

_____

Feedback

Client 1, Sample Summarization: "You've been talking about your relationship with this man for the last several sessions and how you feel pulled in different directions, enjoying the time you spend with him but feeling uncertain about committing to him given his health habits."

Client 2, Sample Summarization: "In the last couple sessions you've mentioned an ongoing situation with your new neighbors, commenting on how nice they are and at the same time, I surmise, feeling sort of irritated about the changes their events have created for you in your quiet and peaceful neighborhood."

Client 3, Sample Summarization: "It seems like you're becoming more aware of the distance between you and James, who spends a lot of time alone, and you're left feeling isolated and lonely, wondering how much the two of you really have in common."

PUTTING IT ALL TOGETHER: USING LISTENING SKILLS IN A HELPING INTERVIEW

Although in most helping interviews, listening skills are usually combined with the action skills we discuss in the next chapter, it is possible to conduct an interview using only the basic attending and listening skills. At this point, because we have introduced each of the skills separately to help you learn them with ease, your task is to combine them in a way that helps you use them together during a helping session.

Young (2013) suggests that, even though clients tell their story in a certain way and at a certain time, there is a cycle of listening that occurs in a repetitive way throughout a helping interview. He describes this listening cycle as "a way of conceptualizing a normal or average helping session during which you use the most common building blocks. The listening cycle is repeated with each major topic the client presents" (p. 152). Generally this cycle reflects the order of the skills as we have presented them in Chapter 4 and in this chapter. That is, helpers begin with verbal following and nonverbal attending skills (eye contact, body position, and vocal qualities and cues) and then respond to client messages with paraphrases or reflections of content, followed by reflection of feelings and finally with summarization.

The reason for this cycle is twofold. First, use of verbal and nonverbal attending skills helps to promote an atmosphere of safety in the session so that the client feels more comfortable in self-disclosing. Second, clients usually feel safer disclosing content than they do disclosing affect, so paraphrases that focus on cognitive or content messages are typically used prior to reflection of feelings, which focus on affective messages. Summarization is used later after a number of different client messages are expressed. Application Exercise 5.6 provides you with an opportunity to combine the listening skills you read about in this chapter in a role-play interview.

APPLICATION EXERCISE 5.6

Practice in Action: Listening Skills

Complete the following exercise with two other people:

1. One of you—designated as the speaker—should share a personal concern with the respondent.
2. The respondent's task is to listen to the client messages, both verbal and nonverbal, and respond by using only the listening skills covered in this chapter: paraphrase, reflection of feelings, and summarization. Remember that you might use the cycle of listening that Young (2013) describes to help you combine these skills.
3. The observer will use the observer rating chart in Figure 5.1 to keep track of the number and kinds of responses used by the listener. This feedback should then be given to the listener.
4. After interacting for approximately 10 minutes, reverse the roles.

	Helper Paraphrase	Helper Reflection	Helper Summarization
1.			
2.			
3.			
4.			
5.			
6.			
7.			
8.			
9.			
10.			

FIGURE 5.1 Observer Rating Chart

OBSTACLES TO LISTENING

Egan (2014) discusses what he refers to as the "shadow" side of listening, that is, traps that helpers can fall into when listening to clients that reflect various kinds of distortions. Among these obstacles are the following:

- *Filtered listening:* The more filters we have when we listen, the stronger our biases. And as Egan (2014, p. 101) points out, "[T]he stronger the cultural filters, the greater the likelihood of bias." To avoid the trap of filtered listening, we have to listen for our own prejudices and make sure they don't get projected onto clients.

- *Evaluative listening:* This trap represents the tendency to be judgmental when we listen, to label what we hear clients say as good, bad, indifferent. The well-known poet Jelaluddin Rumi says, "Out beyond the idea of wrong doing and right doing there is a field . . . . I'll meet you there." In evaluative listening, it's all too easy to not meet in the field and to label the client communications as wrong or right. While Egan (2014) aptly suggests that it's unlikely helpers will never judge clients, setting aside judgment during the listening process is important so clients know that helpers are on their side.

Sometimes helpers fall into these traps because they equate listening with an open mind "as being the same as approving what the client is saying" (Egan, 2014, p. 103). To us, listening with an open mind is like listening from your heart. You are neither approving nor disapproving of what you are hearing; rather, you are simply trying to understand and respond in an open-hearted way that helps clients feel safe with you.

Summary

In this chapter, we built on the helping skills, introduced in the prior chapter, of attending behaviors by expanding our focus to include helping responses that communicate listening and understanding to clients. We discussed the importance of listening to clients and described ways in which listening can help clients heal. We introduced you to several listening skills to use with clients, including the paraphrase, which reflects content or the cognitive parts of client messages; the reflection of feelings response, which reflects the affective or emotional parts of the client messages; and the summarization of content and feelings response, which responds to both content and affective client messages over a period of time. We also discussed ways in which some forms of listening, such as filtered listening and evaluative listening, can impede the therapeutic work with clients. Finally, we stressed the role of listening before problem solving and taking action with clients.

We present several action-based helping skills in the following chapter and want to stress that listening is the best foundation of all.

> While there is much to do we are not here to do.
>   Under the want to problem-solve is the need to being-solve.
>   Often, with full being the problem goes away.
>
> (Nepo, 2012, p. 53)

Reflective Questions

1. Can you think of instances when it might be easier for you to listen to some clients than others? What about instances where you might be challenged to listen? What do these situations have in common? How can you learn from them to improve your listening skills with clients?

2. What does it mean to you to listen with the facts versus to listen with the feelings?

3. How do you think you listen to verbal and nonverbal messages that are unspoken?

4. Can you think of an instance or two where you engaged in filtered listening? In evaluative listening? What were the effects?

5. Describe times when someone else listened to you with filters and evaluation. How did you feel and how did you react when this happened?

6. This question comes from Mark Nepo's wonderful book *Seven Thousand Ways to Listen* (Nepo, 2012, p. 80). Trace your history and development as a listener. Describe several key experiences that have shaped your journey.

7. This question comes from Nichols's illuminating book on *The Lost Art of Listening* (Nichols, 2009, p. 108). Identify any defensive parts of you (hurt, anger, fear) that have interfered with your ability to listen effectively to others. Where did these defensive parts come from? How might you work with them so they don't keep showing up either in your significant relationships or with clients?

MyCounselingLab

For each exercise, log on to MyCounselingLab.

1. Log onto My Counseling Lab and click on the Video Library under Video Resources. Open the Theories of Counseling collection and watch the video "Attending, Joining, and Active Listening." Comment on the helper's attentiveness to the client's nonverbal behavior in this clip. What did you notice about this and what were the effects? Also explore the helper's attentiveness to cultural dimensions of the client's behavior. What did you note about the helper's use of reflection of feelings with this client?

2. Under the Family Therapy collection, look at the clip "Facilitating Understanding-Part 1." Discuss how the practitioner gets both partners to listen to each other using listening responses.

3. Also in the Family Therapy collection, watch the clip "Continuing to Clarify Specific Issues." Note all of the ways in which this counselor listened in this video. Can you identify the times in which the therapist paraphrased content and also reflected feelings? Did you see any use of summarization?

Recommended Readings

Cormier, S., Nurius, P. S., & Osborn, C. J. (2013). *Interviewing and change strategies for helpers* (7th ed.). Belmont, CA: Brooks/Cole, Cengage.

Egan, G. (2014). *The skilled helper* (10th ed.). Belmont, CA: Brooks/Cole, Cengage.

Ivey, A. E., Gluckstern Packard, N., & Ivey, M. B. (2006). *Basic attending skills* (4th ed.). Hanover, MA: Microtraining Associates.

Nepo, M. (2012). *Seven thousand ways to listen.* New York, NY: Free Press.

Nichols, M. (2009). *The lost art of listening* (2nd ed.). New York, NY: Guilford.

Teyber, E., & McClure, F. (2011). *Interpersonal process in therapy* (6th ed.). Belmont, CA: Brooks/Cole, Cengage.

Young, M.E. (2013). *Learning the art of helping* (5th ed.). Upper Saddle River, NJ: Pearson.

Action Skills

In Chapter 5, we discussed the use of listening skills to facilitate your helping interviews with clients. We emphasized how attentive listening can promote healing for clients. At the same time, there are certainly instances when helpers establish rapport with clients and lay a foundation of listening in the session and then, as sessions ensue, help clients move toward change. This is accomplished in helping interviews with the use of action skills. Ivey, Gluckstern, and Ivey (1997) explain the use of action skills this way:

> Just having our life stories heard by another person is a powerful and empowering experience. With some clients listening to the story line empathically and warmly is enough. Others, however, need new stories, fresh ways to think about themselves, and more effective methods to act to change their lives. (p. 4)

Ivey, Gluckstern, and Ivey (1997) and Ivey, Ivey, and Zalaquett (2014) identify action skills as influencing responses and, as Egan (2014) notes, "[A]ll attempts to help others involve, to one degree or another, influencing them" (p. 135). Egan states:

> Helpers influence their clients. The trick is to influence them to do such things as discussing difficult problems; developing new life-enhancing perspectives on themselves, others, and the world; working on the right issues; exploring possibilities for a better future; choosing and committing themselves to problem-managing goals; exploring ways of achieving these goals; and engaging in the kind of effective and efficient action needed to accomplish all of this—to influence them, certainly, but without robbing them of their freedom. (pp. 135–136)

A major decision that helpers face in using action skills involves the timing or the point in the interview or series of interviews that such skills are used. If action skills are used too early or too often with clients, these gentle nudges may backfire, causing clients to become reactive, resistant, or even drop out of counseling prematurely. In using action skills effectively, think of the image of a tightrope walker. The helper is like a person walking on the tightrope, balancing the use of listening empathically to build the relationship and foster rapport, while at the same time moving into action to help the client make progress and get unstuck. If the helper stays on the listening side of the tightrope too long, the helping sessions can get bogged down and the client can repeat the same story and feel discouraged about lack of progress. On the other hand, if the helper moves to the other side of the tightrope too quickly and starts nudging the client too soon, this may be off-putting to clients who then lose their own sense of balance and feel threatened by too much change coming too soon.

In this chapter, we describe a variety of action skills that helpers can use to help nudge clients into making effective choices so they do not remain stuck in old stories, feelings, or beliefs that are disempowering. The action skills that we discuss in this chapter include questions, reflection of meaning, and challenging responses.

QUESTIONS

Some models of helping skills consider questions to be a listening response (Ivey, Gluckstern Packard, & Ivey, 2006; Ivey et al., 2014). In Ivey's model, questions are described as an invitational response. This description of questions is echoed by Young (2013). In our model of helping skills, however, we classify questions as an action or influencing skill (Cormier, Nurius, & Osborn, 2013). We greatly respect our colleagues who classify questions as a listening response, and we agree that open questions in particular can have an invitational quality about them. In our clinical experience, however, we have found that questions—even seemingly innocuous ones—are often perceived by clients as intrusive. This is especially true if questions are introduced too early in the helping process or used too frequently by practitioners. Intrusiveness of questions may be even greater with clients from non-Western cultures and also with mandated clients and adolescent clients.

When a client is asked a question, there is an implicit expectation for the client to respond or to answer in some fashion that is not apparent with listening responses we described in the previous chapter. Some clients may even feel burdened or pressured by this expectation for response. Other clients are simply put off by questions because they are not ready to share private or personal information with helpers, again another expectation delivered by the question response. Cormier, Nurius, and Osborn (2013) observe that "questions have the potential for establishing desirable or undesirable patterns of interpersonal exchange, depending on the skill of the therapist. Beginning interviewers are prone to err by assuming that a helping interview is a series of questions and answers or by asking the wrong kind of question at a particular time. These practices are likely to make the client feel interrogated rather than understood . . ." (pp. 151–152).

Questions are usually categorized as *open-ended* or *closed* or *focused* questions. The primary difference between an open-ended question and a closed question is that an open-ended question encourages client elaboration, while a closed question can be answered with a single word response such as yes or no or even "I don't know." Open-ended questions begin with words such as *what, when, how, who,* and *where,* while closed questions typically start with *is, are, can,* or *do.* Consider the following examples of open-ended and closed questions that a helper used with a client who described an issue with being betrayed by a close mentor and friend.

Open-Ended Questions

Helper: Who do you feel has betrayed you?

How were you betrayed?

What happened with that person?

When did this betrayal occur?

Closed Questions

Helper: Is this betrayal something you're still concerned about a lot of the time?

Do you think the betrayal was intentional or not?

Are you consumed with thinking about it on a daily basis?

Can you find a way to stop focusing on it?

Generally, we recommend the use of open-ended questions in helping interviews; as you will see, however, there are certain situations in which closed questions can be helpful. As Ivey and colleagues (2006) note, questions are an important way "to help an interview move along. They open new areas for discussion, they assist in pinpointing issues, and they can be used to facilitate [client] self-exploration" (p. 37). Whether you choose to use an open-ended or closed question really depends on the purpose of your question and the timing of it in the interview. As Ivey and his colleagues suggest, "the art of questioning lies in knowing which questions to ask when" (2014, p. 117).

Open-ended questions serve several purposes, and they can be used in many situations with clients. Such questions are useful to begin a session. For example, a helper may say to a client, "Where would you like to begin today?," "How are you doing today?," or "What has happened since we saw each other last week?" Open-ended questions can also encourage client elaboration and elicit additional client information. Closed questions are used more sparingly but yet can be appropriate when the helper needs a specific piece of information. Closed questions can be especially useful during problem identification sessions, such as those we describe in Chapter 8. Hepworth and colleagues (2013, p. 143) suggest that closed questions can also be helpful "if the client is unresponsive and withholds information or has limited conceptual and mental abilities." Young (2013) compares open-ended and closed questions to types of questions on an exam. He likens open-ended questions to essay exams that show you a deeper level of understanding, and closed questions to multiple-choice exams that check your knowledge of specific facts (p. 94).

The use of questions comes with several pitfalls, in addition to the possibility of overuse that we mentioned at the beginning of this section. These pitfalls include *leading* questions, *stacking* questions, and *accusatory* questions. As Young (2013) suggests, leading questions have "an embedded message" and "are usually grouped together as a subtle argument or a secret way of giving the client advice" (p. 93). These questions are leading because "they are really disguised attempts to push through the client's acceptance of the helper's agenda" (Young, 2013, p. 93). Consider this example dialogue, which includes leading questions:

CLIENT: Now that I'm in grad school, I just don't think I have time to work. So I will probably quit my job. Of course, that gives me time to study more, but I wouldn't have any money other than my student loan. I probably couldn't keep seeing you or doing other things that cost money.

HELPER: Do you think quitting your job is the best or only solution to your study issues?

CLIENT: Well so far, it seems to be.

HELPER: Don't you think you might be better off dropping a class so you can still keep your job and find more time for studying?

CLIENT: Well, maybe.

In this example, can you see how the counselor's own agenda was reflected in the two leading questions (also closed questions) to help shape the client's behavior? Most parents have usually had plenty of experience with leading questions with their children ("Don't you think it's time to go to bed now?") and will tell you after a while that such questions are eventually likely to produce resistance to change!

Another pitfall of using questions is the possibility of what I refer to as stacking questions. Stacking questions simply means asking multiple (two or more) questions at once, before giving clients time to respond. Stacking questions can be confusing to clients and is especially problematic with clients who may need more time to process information or to formulate responses. Consider the following dialogue that contains examples of stacked questions:

CLIENT: We just decided to separate. We found that we had drifted apart. My wife actually had moved away for a short period of time to take a new job and I discovered that I was happier living alone than living with her. I think she felt the same way. So we separated. We are friends now but that's it. It's just better this way.

HELPER: Okay, so when did this happen? Did it just happen or has it been a while ago? What is the separation doing for you? What is better about it?

As you can see from this example, in the helper's quest and urgency to obtain information, a series of questions are almost fired at the client, leaving the client little if any time or space to respond. And the client is likely to feel confused. What does the client respond to?

The third pitfall of questions has to do with accusatory questions. In our description above of open-ended questions, you may have noticed that we did not include the word *why* as a potential way to begin an open question. This was intentional because often the word *why* puts clients on the spot, and the use of *why* questions is considered accusatory. *Why* questions place a special burden on clients because they ask clients to provide reasons or to explain motives. There is an implicit accusation inherent in *why* questions, and they are likely to make clients feel defensive, uncomfortable, or even shamed. If clients really knew the reasons and motives for their behavior, they would probably not be seeking help from you because they would have it all figured out already! Yet as Young (2013) observes, it can seem enticing to helpers to ask *why* questions because this form of inquiry seems "psychological and appears to be getting at the root of a problem" (p. 92). Exploring reasons, rationales, and motives is important in the helping process, but there are more effective ways to do so than asking *why* questions. In the following section, you will see how you can use a reflection of meaning response to explore reasons and motives without having to rely on *why* questions. Also you can often obtain the same information you are seeking by using a *what* question instead.

To formulate questions effectively, consider the following two steps. First, determine your purpose for the question. What is your intention? What do you hope the question will accomplish? The answer will help you decide if you use an open-ended or a closed (focused) question at a particular point in time. Second, given the purpose of your question, what wording will you use to begin your question most effectively? Remember to begin your open-ended questions with words such as *how, what, when, where,* and *who,* but avoid starting your open-ended question with *why.* In contrast, start your closed or focused question with a word such as *is, can, do,* or *are.* Application Exercise 6.1 gives you an opportunity to practice both open-ended and closed questions.

APPLICATION EXERCISE 6.1

Questions

For each of the four client responses, develop a sample open-ended and closed question. Check your questions with those provided in the feedback section.

1. Client: I don't need pity, but I am down on my luck right now. I just lost my job; I don't have a place to stay no more. I've been living out of my car, but it's kind of on its last leg too. I'm not sure where I'll go after my car goes too.

Helper open-ended question: _____

Helper closed question: _____

2. Client: A man's gotta do what a man's gotta do. She asked for it. She was bugging me all night long. Nagging. Yelling at her was the only way I could get her to stop it. She has to learn to shut up sometimes. I have so much I can handle and her stuff just puts me over the edge.

Helper open-ended question: _____

Helper closed question: _____

3. Client: I've met this new woman and I really like her. But I think she is very interested in me sexually and I don't know how to tell her about my ED [erectile dysfunction]. I never used to have this problem, but after the prostate cancer and radiation, unfortunately that has been a big side effect. I'm afraid it will be a real turnoff for her.

Helper open-ended question: _____

Helper closed question: _____

4. Client: I'm feeling so stressed out at work. Every time I turn around there's another deadline. I work all the time, but I'm always behind. There is so much pressure. I think I'll be lucky to get even a short vacation this year.

Helper open-ended question: _____

Helper closed question: _____

Feedback

Here are some sample questions. See how yours match up. Also consider sharing yours with a peer, a colleague, or your instructor.

(*Continued*)

Client 1

Open-ended questions: "What do you think is your next best step in this situation?," "What other resources have you located that might be helpful?," "Who do you know that could be helpful without pitying you?"

Closed questions: "Have you contacted the local homeless shelter yet?," "Are you actively looking for work?," "Can you identify any other options available to you other than living in your car?"

Client 2

Open-ended questions: "What feelings does her stuff trigger in you?," "How else have you tried to manage your anger and her talking?," "What happens after you yell at her?"

Closed questions: "Do you feel bad after you yell at her, or not?," "Have you tried handling this situation in any other way besides yelling at her?," "Are you frustrated with her or with yourself?"

Client 3

Open-ended questions: "How have you thought about approaching this situation with her?," "What do you feel most concerned about in letting her know of this?," "When do you think might be the right time and place to have this discussion with her?"

Closed questions: "Are you more concerned about just having to tell her this or is it more about her reaction to it?," "Have you thought about the different ways she might respond to this and how you'll handle it then?," "Do you have a plan in mind for sharing this with her?"

Client 4

Open-ended questions: "What kinds of stressors in particular are you experiencing at work that are especially challenging?," "How does the stress show up for you?," "When do you usually experience the most stress?"

Closed questions: "Are there any things in particular you've tried or used to reduce the stress?," "Can you tell me exactly what happens to you when you get this stressed out?," "Have you found any effective ways to cope with the stress and pressure?"

REFLECTION OF MEANING RESPONSE

The reflection of meaning response is an advanced reflection compared to the reflection of feelings response, which is a basic reflection. In fact, sometimes reflection of meaning has been referred to as advanced or additive empathy, while reflection of feelings is called basic empathy (Egan, 2014). This differentiation reflects the idea that the reflection of meaning response is a skill designed to help clients uncover deeper messages embedded in client communication. Young (2013) says that "if a helper wants to really understand a client, he or she must be willing to go beyond facts and feelings and uncover the deeper meaning that the client assigns to life events" (p. 139). The reflection of meaning response is a skill designed to do just that, to convey your understanding and empathy about the meanings of the client's messages. According to Carl Rogers, the founder of an approach known as client- or person-centered therapy, empathy involves sensing meanings of which the client is hardly aware (Rogers, 1951). In analyses of sessions that Rogers conducted with multiple clients, most of Rogers's responses to clients were actually reflections of meaning rather than reflections of feelings.

Young (2013) states that "human beings are meaning makers by nature" (p. 138). Ivey, Ivey, and Zalaquett (2014) note that "meanings are organizing constructs" (p. 288). Indeed, reflection of meaning highlights the fact that what happens in a situation is usually not as important to understand as how the client perceives or interprets the situation. This view of client communication is consistent with another approach to helping called constructivism, which emphasizes the client's "unique, subjective perspective or self-constructed narrative" as contrasted with an objective or consensual reality (Prochaska & Norcross, 2014, p. 406). Another way to think about this is that knowledge about a situation cannot be constructed independently of the knower (Prochaska & Norcross, 2014). Further, constructed reality reflects one's culture, perceptions, and language (Prochaska & Norcross, 2014, p. 406). The well-known couples therapist and researcher John Gottman and his colleagues explain how conflict can occur in any particular dyadic exchange by a constructivist perspective. They note that, given a common situation, each person in the dyad has one's own subjective reality about the situation (Gottman, Gottman, & DeClaire, 2007). This explains, for example, why two partners might have a disagreement about the same situation. One person in the dyad constructs his or her subjective reality of the situation, and the other person constructs an entirely different subjective reality of the very same situation, thus leading to conflict. (No doubt all of us have experienced this in one dyadic exchange or another!)

The reflection of meaning response is an extension of the reflection of content or paraphrase, which helps us to understand the situation or context, and the reflection of feelings response, which helps us to understand the client's feelings about the situation. In the reflection of meaning response, we strive to understand the meanings and perspective the client has about the situation. Young (2013) notes that "if we know the meaning of the story, we will have learned why the client is troubled by it" (p. 140). This skill helps answer the question "Why are we talking about this topic?" (Young, 2013, p. 140). When helpers simply stay at the level of reflecting content and feelings and don't go deeper, therapy usually comes to a standstill. Young (2013) alludes to this, stating that this can be a particularly thorny issue for beginning helpers. He observes that "beginning helpers are often confused when the client's story seems to have run its course . . . This is because the helper has not gone deeper into the meaning of the story" (p. 142).

Young (2013, p. 142) provides another way to think about depth in a helping session by examining whether your responses are lateral or horizontal ones, which keep things at the same level of depth, or whether they are vertical, which go much deeper. For me, this brings up the image of the difference between a swimmer swimming on the surface of a pool versus a diver jumping off a board and plunging into the deep end of the pool. Every client story and situation has varying levels or layers. Reflecting meaning shifts the discussion to a deeper level. Imagine peeling an onion. The first layer to come off might be like paraphrasing or reflecting content, while the second layer is like reflecting feelings. The third layer is like reflecting meaning. What can make this skill so challenging to learn and use, however, is that clients often don't talk like divers diving into a pool. They talk like swimmers swimming on the surface of the pool. Clients typically are most likely to share content before sharing feelings, and they are even more reluctant to share meaning because, as the depth increases, so does the perceived threat. Clients feel as if content is the safest kind of information to share. They are not likely to dive deeper until they know and trust the helper and feel safe in the relationship and the helping process. Generally speaking, clients often don't share meaning, even though it might be very important to their issue. Sometimes they might be unaware of the potential meaning of the situation as well. With less verbal clients, or with clients who are less psychologically minded, more concrete, or more reluctant, exploring meaning may be even more challenging.

The reflection of meaning response is defined as a statement that reflects implicit significance and perspectives below the surface of the client's overt communications. It is designed to help make the implicit client message explicit and to elicit a fuller expression of what the client is implying instead of saying directly or overtly (Egan, 2014). Consider the following example of this skill; notice the contrast between paraphrase, or the reflection of content, and reflection of feelings, and finally reflection of meaning.

> CLIENT: I just don't really know how she could have died. She was so young, and she was always the picture of health. She was the last person I would have ever thought would have developed end stage colon cancer. It completely boggles my mind. I just keep asking myself over and over one question: Why did this happen? What did she do to deserve it? What did I do to deserve it?

> HELPER 1: (Paraphrase of situation or content) Sounds like you are still questioning why she got ill and had to die so prematurely.

> HELPER 2: (Reflection of feelings) Seems like you're really feeling confused and puzzled about this, maybe even feeling in shock about the suddenness of it, even the improbability of it.

> HELPER 3: (Reflection of meaning) It seems like the facts in this situation just don't add up for you. You find yourself wondering how an awful thing like this could have happened to a good person like her—and even you.

Can you see in this example how each response moves vertically instead of horizontally? How, like the diver jumping into the pool, response 3 is at a deeper level than response 2, and at an even deeper level than response 1?

Reflection of meaning can be a challenging skill to implement. This is true for several reasons. As we mentioned above, clients often don't share meanings of events, and when they do, these are often shared covertly. You have to listen very carefully and read between the lines to discover the meanings.

Using the reflection of meaning skill in a session or a series of sessions has several purposes. We have already mentioned one. This is a skill that helps clients explore issues and situations at a deeper level, which in turn contributes to client self-exploration and awareness, precursors to client change. In addition, this response "allows the client to recognize that the story [he or she is] telling is not necessarily the facts but is, instead, a perspective. The helper holds up a mirror to the client, 'reflecting' rather than agreeing with what the client says" (Young 2013, p. 141). This has the potential to help the client develop alternative views, perspectives, and meanings about the situation that might prove helpful. Ivey and colleagues (2014) suggest that the art of supplying clients with different perspectives and ideas helps them to find new ways of thinking, feeling, and behaving (p. 268). This skill also helps clients understand and reflect on any core assumptions, values, and beliefs that are affecting the issue. It is also useful for helping clients identify themes in their story, identify missing connections or pieces in the story, "own" their story, and see things in the story they have been overlooking or missing (Egan, 2014, p. 181). Reflection of meaning also helps clients to develop insight and to identify causal relationships and patterns (Hepworth & colleagues, 2013).

We've identified reflection of meaning as a skill that is more challenging to acquire and use than other skills that we have discussed. What are the guidelines and steps involved in reflecting meaning? First, to use this response effectively, it is important to know the client and to have developed a safe space in which you and the client can work together. For this reason, reflection of meaning is not usually used in initial sessions but rather later in the helping process. It is also a response that is used when clients appear to be ready to engage in self-exploration. Also, because this response can be potentially powerful, it is important to use these responses more sparingly and not overwhelm the client all at once (Hepworth & colleagues, 2013, p. 537). Finally, when reflecting meaning, it is essential to make sure that your response is consistent with cultural meanings for the client and doesn't just reflect your own cultural biases. In a similar vein, because this response involves mirroring for the client but also involves your own intuition and hunches, it is helpful to be aware of your own blind spots so you are really mirroring the *client's* meaning and not your own projections (Cormier, Nurius, & Osborn, 2013).

Several steps are involved in formulating an accurate reflection of meaning response:

1. Listen carefully to identify implicit meanings of client communication. Listen for what the client conveys subtly and indirectly. Listen for behaviors, patterns, feelings, implied goals, actions, wishes, core beliefs and assumptions, and even unused resources and opportunities, strengths, and potentialities (Cormier et al., 2013; Egan, 2014; Hepworth et al., 2013). There are several ways to accomplish this task. First, ask yourself questions about what you are hearing below the surface of the client's messages. We recommend the following questions suggested by Egan (2014, p. 197):

   What is the client only half saying?
   What is the client hinting at?
   What is the client saying in a confused way?
   What is the covert message behind the explicit message?

   Another way you can listen for meaning is to ask an open-ended question that invites the client to focus on the perceived significance and meaning of the situation (Ivey et al., 2014; Young, 2013). For instance, you might say something to the client like the following:

   When you find yourself thinking about this situation, what about it is most salient to you?
   What about this situation is most meaningful and relevant to you?
   How would you describe your perception and interpretation of this situation?
   What exactly does this situation represent for you?

   A third way you can listen for meaning is to listen for key words and phrases, especially those that may be expressed over time in a repetitive fashion (Ivey et al., 2014). And finally, you can identify implicit meanings by using your own personal intuition or hunches as well as your knowledge of the client. Perhaps you can see in our discussion of this response how important your attending and listening skills will prove to be in being able to develop effective reflection of meaning responses!

2. Formulate what you want to say in your head; that is, think before you leap! You can use a sentence stem if that is helpful to you in formulating a reflection of meaning

response. A simple sentence stem recommended by Ivey and colleagues (2014, p. 277) changes the "you feel" in a reflection of feelings to a "you mean" for a reflection of meaning: "You mean _____." Make sure that, when you formulate your reflection of meaning, it is culturally accurate. Cultural meanings vary among different cultural dimensions of clients. To formulate this response effectively, it is important to have some understanding of the client's cultural context. Ivey and colleagues note that, in Western cultures, it is more often than not the individual that determines the meaning. In many non-Western cultures, however, meaning is given "in accord with the extended family, the neighborhood, and religion. If individual meaning is not in accord with cultural beliefs, making that meaning work in daily life will present major challenges to the client" (2014, p. 278).

3. Determine the degree of depth in your reflection of meaning response carefully. According to Cormier, Nurius, and Osborn (2013, p. 171), depth refers to "the degree of discrepancy between the viewpoint expressed by the helper and the client's beliefs." Hepworth et al. (2013, p. 541) recommend pitching this response just "to the edge of the client's self-awareness." These authors suggest avoiding a response that is too deep or too distant from the client's current level of awareness because this is likely to engender client defensiveness and/or resistance.

4. Check out the accuracy of your response directly with the client. Be attentive to both verbal and nonverbal reactions. Egan (2014) observes that, in using reflection of meaning, clients might not immediately recognize themselves in your response; thus, they might "experience a bit of disequilibrium" (p. 177). If the client confirms the accuracy of your response, the discussion will move ahead progressively to a deeper level more quickly. On the other hand, if the client rejects your response or reacts adversely to it, acknowledge your misunderstanding and move back to responses that work with content and feelings, such as paraphrasing and reflecting feelings.

Ivey and colleagues (2014, p. 277) note that the skill of reflecting meaning becomes more challenging when the meanings and values expressed by the client are conflicted. For example, some clients may feel caught in an acculturation conflict, divided between values and meanings of their original cultural group and those of the new cultural referent group. Another client may feel divided or confused about whether to pursue an occupation of his or her choice or whether to pursue an occupation recommended by his or her parents. In these instances of conflicted meanings and values, an action skill that usually works better than a reflection of meaning is the challenging response. We discuss this response in the next section, after you have completed Application Exercise 6.2.

APPLICATION EXERCISE 6.2

Reflection of Meaning

For each of the following four client messages, develop a reflection of meaning response. Then check your responses with the feedback section at the end of this application exercise. You may also wish to compare notes with a peer and your instructor.

Client 1: Well, I guess I feel guilty because, even though I really miss my brother, and I hate that he died so young, I am still going on with my life. I'm able to go to college and work toward a career for myself, and even find myself partying these days and having some fun.

Question: What is the client hinting at? What is the client expressing covertly? _____

_____

Your reflection of meaning: _____

_____

Client 2: I've been injecting crystal meth on and off now for a couple of years. And when I can't afford it, I just resort to using weed and booze. My family disowned me, so I live on the streets or sometimes in shelters, but that is hard 'cause of the drug use. A couple of times I've had sex with other men to get money for drugs but it's been with good men so I suppose all in all, I'm okay given everything that has happened.

Question: What is the client hinting at? What is the client expressing covertly? _____

_____

Your reflection of meaning: _____

_____

Client 3: Since I returned from active duty, I've had some trouble adjusting to life back here. I've noticed it's been hard to sleep. I haven't been able to find a good job. Sometimes I get real mad at my girlfriend for no obvious reason I guess. I just moved here a couple months ago. And I feel real good about the move, even though I did it alone and left my girlfriend behind. It's just easier to live alone right now.

Question: What is the client hinting at? What is the client expressing covertly? _____

_____

Your reflection of meaning: _____

_____

Client 4: Being a gay Asian American man can be tough. But I am in a good, committed relationship with another man I really care about. Still, I've been feeling pretty anxious and even panicky. I just wake up with a panic attack or, out of the blue, I'll feel panicky at work or at a party or something. I haven't told anyone about feeling this way, not even my partner. And I've also hid the fact I'm gay from people I work with and even my family. Do you think I'm okay?

Question: What is the client hinting at? What is the client expressing covertly? _____

_____

Your reflection of meaning: _____

_____

Feedback

Client 1

Question: The client seems to be hinting at survivor's guilt.

A sample reflection of meaning: "You feel guilty because you're alive and he's not."

Client 2

Question: The client is hinting that things aren't as okay as the client is suggesting they are.

A sample reflection of meaning: "You're feeling concerned because while things are okay now, you're uneasy about how your current lifestyle might affect you in the long run."

(Continued)

Client 3

Question: The client is hinting that it must be safer if he is alone.

A sample reflection of meaning: "You mean that being overwhelmed means that you have to go it alone, as if somehow it's safer being cut off from others."

Client 4:

Question: The client is hinting that he may feel stigmatized.

A sample reflection of meaning: "You mean that perhaps your feelings of panic have something to do with having to hide your true self from people who are important to you."

CHALLENGING RESPONSES

Challenging responses are sometimes also referred to as confrontation responses. Because the word *confrontation* has a negative connotation, however, the helping literature has moved more toward the use of the term *challenging responses* instead. In reality, neither term aptly describes the purpose of this response with clients. This is a not a response used to test, dare, dispute, oppose, provoke, or argue with a client. Instead, the purpose of challenging clients is to promote an environment in which clients learn to challenge themselves, especially their self-defeating thoughts and behaviors as well as self-limiting possibilities. Egan (2014) states that "all effective helping is some kind of mixture of support. . . . Finding the right mixture is essential because challenge without support is harsh and unjustified; support without challenge can end up being empty and counterproductive" (p. 160).

Like the other action skills of questions and reflection of meaning, the challenge response is also used to enhance client self-awareness and to promote effective client change. The major use of the challenging response is to confront "discrepancies, inconsistencies, and dysfunctional behaviors (overt and covert)" that contribute to client issues and block forward movement (Hepworth et al., 2013, p. 549). Ivey and colleagues (1997, p. 48) define the challenge/confrontation response as "gently and respectfully aiding clients to look at themselves and the discrepancies and incongruities in their lives." In a later work, Ivey and colleagues (2014) describe the challenging response as an action skill "that invites clients to examine their stories for discrepancies between verbal and nonverbal communication, between expressed attitudes and behaviors, or conflict with others (p. 236). As these authors point out, this action response is not going against the client, it is going with the client, and it is based on attending and listening to clients in an intentional and careful way (p. 236).

Challenging responses are not typically used early in the helping process; rather, they are used later, when trust has been firmly established in the therapeutic dyad. The exception to this general guideline would be in instances where there is imminent danger to the client or someone else, or when there has been a legal violation (Hepworth et al., 2013). In initial stages of helping, practitioners are providing high levels of support. As helping ensues, however, what emerges will include distortions, inconsistencies, and blind spots in the client's communications. As Young (2013, p. 167) suggests, the essential aim of this action skill is to "help clients operate with unclouded information about themselves." In essence, this action skill represents "an educational process that brings information to the client's attention that has been previously unknown, disregarded or repressed" (Young, 2013, p. 171).

While this is not a skill that is used frequently with clients, it is a tool that has significant effects. Consider the fact that almost all client stories present some form of conflict in which a discrepancy is embedded, at least covertly if not overtly. Such discrepancies create tension and anxiety, which the client is motivated to reduce, or incongruence, which the client is motivated to resolve. This is because according to cognitive dissonance theory (Festinger, 1957), people are motivated to keep experiences and beliefs consistent in order to avoid the anxiety and tension people feel from inconsistencies. When helpers challenge clients, these inconsistent attitudes and beliefs come to light. That's when clients experience arousal or anxiety about the inconsistency and usually work hard to reduce the tension by making experiences congruent.

Consider the following examples of the challenging/confrontation response:

CLIENT: (Said with tears in her eyes, and a low, soft voice) I will go live with my mother and that will be okay.

HELPER: I notice you are saying it will be okay for you to live with your mom, and at the same time, though, I see the tears in your eyes and I hear some sadness in your voice.

CLIENT: (Session one) I could retire, I am sure old enough, really past the retirement age. But I don't think it's a good idea. You know what happens to people after they quit work? They usually drop dead.

CLIENT: (Session three) I have some big decisions to make. I am going to be retiring soon and I have to figure out if I will stay around here or try to move to a less expensive state.

HELPER: I noticed you've told me two different things about retiring. In the first session you mentioned that you didn't think retiring was a good idea for you, and now you're indicating you plan to retire and figure out where to move. How do you put these two things together?

Cormier, Nurius, and Osborn (2013) assert that the challenging response should be used in a way that helps clients explore their behavior rather than making them defensive about it. They state that this response "must be used carefully in order not to increase the very behavior or pattern that the helper feels may need to be diminished or modified." (p. 175). We summarize a number of guidelines about how to use the challenging response most effectively with clients.

First, be clear about why you are challenging a particular client at a particular time. Make sure that the challenge is for the benefit of the client and not just the result of your frustration with the person. This is actually a potential ethical issue because misuse of confrontation violates the stance of the ethical codes of helping, which indicate that the helper's first priority is to protect the welfare of the client. As Young (2013, p. 183) asserts, the challenging response should not be delivered in any way that potentially shames the client by communicating that the helper has caught the client in a trap.

Second, when you deliver the challenging response, make sure you deliver it with a hefty dose of emotional support. Support can be conveyed through your nonverbal behaviors as well as through your tone of voice and specific words you choose to deliver the message.

Third, remember that the timing of this particular response is very critical. Generally it is saved for later sessions and is not used until trust and rapport between the helper and client are firmly established. Also, it is a response that is used sparingly and in small doses.

Johnson (2014) says that, because of the potential potency of this response, it is probably not something that should be used unless the helper is willing and able to maintain and increase one's involvement and commitment to the helping relationship. For example, if you're a graduate student and you're in a semester-long field experience, using a challenging response at the end of the semester, right before you're terminating your clients, is not a great idea because you don't have enough time to follow up on the effects. Similarly, you would not want to confront at the end of any session because you wouldn't have enough time to process the client's reactions before the session is over. Johnson (2014) describes this as a potential "hit and run" confrontation and should be avoided except when the client introduces material near the end concerning danger to self or others. Cormier, Nurius, and Osborn (2013) recommend that the perceived ability of the client to act on the confrontation is a major criterion for deciding on when to use this skill (p. 176).

A final guideline about effective challenges has to do with potential client reactions to the use of this skill. For example, client reactions to being challenged can vary greatly among cultural groups. Some traditional Asian and American Indian clients might experience the challenging response as disrespectful and insensitive (Sue & Sue, 2013). On the other hand, as Ivey and colleagues (2014) point out, clients from some European American and African American cultures may respond well to appropriate confrontations and challenges. The kind of clinical disorder may also affect the client's response. A "narcissistic and self-centered" client may resist being challenged, while manipulative or acting-out clients may need a challenge that is more firm (Ivey et al., 2014, p. 237). Hepworth et al. (2013) caution against challenging clients who are under "extreme emotional strain" because this response does mobilize client anxiety and could make the client's anxiety worse (p. 548). Ultimately what matters about the client reaction to the challenge response is how the client works with it. General reactions from clients to challenges can range from denial and confusion to false or partial acceptance, to full acceptance. And once a challenge response has been delivered, it is important to go back to basic listening skills and reestablish the relationship base with empathy and understanding.

You can follow several steps to develop a useful challenge response with clients. Keep in mind, of course, the guidelines that we just discussed. First, this skill requires concentrated observation and listening on your part for a period of time with the client so that you can identify verbal, nonverbal, and behavioral inconsistencies. This is what makes the skill difficult for beginning helpers. It's almost like you have to train your eyes and ears to listen and look for discrepancies, conflicts, and states of incongruence before you can even formulate the challenging response. Here is a list of the major types of discrepancies you will find in helping sessions with clients.

Verbal and Nonverbal:

The client says one thing, yet the nonverbal behavior doesn't support the words.

Example: "I'm really happy we are moving in together" while the client frowns and looks down at the floor with a glum facial expression.

Verbal and Behavior:

The client says one thing, yet the client's behavior represents another thing.

Example: The client commits verbally to doing homework outside the session but comes in the next week and says that she forgot to do it.

Verbal and Verbal (Two Stated Inconsistencies):

The client's words and verbal messages convey two different or mixed messages.

Example: "I'm definitely not a racist; I just don't want those people moving into my neighborhood."

Nonverbal and Nonverbal (Two Nonverbal Inconsistencies):

Example: The client is laughing and crying at the same time in the session.

As you accumulate experiences with clients, you will begin to note even additional kinds of discrepancies, but the list above includes the major ones to pay attention to as you start working with the challenging response.

Second, once you've identified a type of discrepancy, evaluate the purpose and timing of your challenging response. Is there a sufficient relationship base for you to implement it? Is it workable based on the client's gender, age, ethnicity, and race? Is it based on some purpose related to progress for the client and not on an artifact of your own frustration with the client?

Third, formulate in your mind a challenging response that *summarizes* rather than disputes the essential elements of the discrepancies. We recommend using a sentence stem such as "On the one hand this, *and* on the other hand, this." Note the use of the word *and* rather than *but*. Beginning helpers often make this simple but important mistake in formulating an effective challenging response.

Fourth, deliver your challenging response using supportive nonverbal behaviors and assess the client's reaction to it, which may not always be immediate. Follow your challenging response with basic empathy and listening responses, such as paraphrasing and reflecting feelings. You can develop some challenging responses of your own in Application Exercise 6.3.

Now that you've learned about and had some practice in these three action skills of questions, reflection of meaning, and challenging responses, it's time to put your skills together in a more comprehensive fashion. Application Exercise 6.4 gives you an opportunity to do just that.

APPLICATION EXERCISE 6.3

Challenging Responses

This application exercise presents a twofold task. For each of the four examples, first identify the type of discrepancy you note in the example; second, formulate and write an example of a challenging response that summarizes the discrepancy using the "on the one hand _____ and on the other hand _____" sentence stem. Feedback follows the exercise. You may also wish to check your responses with a peer or your instructor as well.

> Client 1: The client is looking at the floor with downcast eyes and speaking in a soft, low vocal tone while also smiling brightly when discussing the situation about her low grades with you.
>
> Identify the discrepancy: _____
>
> _____
>
> Your challenging response: _____
>
> _____

(Continued)

Client 2: I'm not really mad at him. He's just a big jerk.

Identify the discrepancy: _____

_____

Your challenging response: _____

_____

Client 3: (While smiling and talking in an animated fashion) I'm so unhappy with my parents. They practically have disowned me since I told them I'm gay."

Identify the discrepancy: _____

_____

Your challenging response: _____

_____

Client 4: I joined the gym because I really want to work out. I just haven't made it there since I joined up a month ago.

Identify the discrepancy: _____

_____

Your challenging response: _____

_____

Feedback

Client 1

Discrepancy: The discrepancy is between the client's two different nonverbal behaviors.

Sample challenge response: "On the one hand, you are smiling about the situation, and on the other hand, when you talk about it, you are looking down at the floor and also speaking in a very low voice."

Client 2

Discrepancy: The discrepancy is between the client's two different verbal messages.

Sample challenge response: "You say, on the one hand, that you're not mad at him, and on the other hand, you also say he's a big jerk. How do you put these two things together?"

Client 3

Discrepancy: The discrepancy is between the client's verbal message and her nonverbal message, which does not support her words.

Sample challenge response: "You're telling me, on the one hand, that you're very unhappy with your parents, and at the same time, you're smiling and talking animatedly about this situation."

Client 4

Discrepancy: The discrepancy is between the client's verbal message and the client's behavior.

Sample challenge response: "Juan, I hear you saying, on the one hand, that working out is really valuable for you, and at the same time, you are telling me you've been a gym member for a month and haven't gone to work out yet. How do you put this together?"

APPLICATION EXERCISE 6.4

Helping Skills Integration

Complete the following exercise with two other people.

1. One of you—designated as the role-play client—should share a personal concern with the helper.
2. The helper's task is first to listen to and observe the client and her or his messages and communication, and then respond with the listening skills learned in Chapter 5 and the action skills learned in this chapter. These six skills include paraphrase of content, reflection of feelings, summarization, questions, reflection of meaning, and challenging responses.
3. The observer can use the observer rating chart in Figure 6.1 to keep track of the number and kinds of responses used by the listener. After completing about a 15- to 20-minute role play, the observer can provide feedback to the helper not only about the quantity of responses but also about the quality of responses. What does the feedback tell you about your own helping style? Were you more comfortable with listening skills or action skills, or were you balanced between the two?
4. After the initial role play and discussion of feedback, switch roles two more times so that each person has an opportunity to be a client, a helper, and an observer.

Helper	Type of Helper Response					
	Paraphrase	Reflection of Feelings	Summarization	Question	Reflection of Meaning	Challenging
1.						
2.						
3.						
4.						
5.						
6.						
7.						
8.						
9.						
10.						
11.						
12.						
13.						
14.						
15.						
16.						
17.						
18.						
19.						
20.						

FIGURE 6.1 Observer Rating Chart

Summary

This chapter described the purpose of action skills with clients and discussed three important actions skills to use: questions, reflection of meaning, and challenging responses. We noted the differences and potential uses of both open-ended and closed questions. Open-ended questions are designed to obtain much more expanded information from clients; closed questions can be used sparingly to obtain a specific piece of information or fact. We cautioned against excessive use of questions, which could turn the helping interview into more of an interrogation session. We defined the reflection of meaning as an advanced empathic tool that reflects the meaning that a situation or issue has for a client. We noted some of the difficulties in learning to use this response effectively because clients often don't dive deep enough to discuss issues of meaning. We discussed the effective and ineffective use of challenging responses with clients. We described various types of discrepancies or inconsistencies that clients present, and we noted how the challenging response can identify and summarize these inconsistencies in a supportive rather than a punitive manner. We also observed how action skills may be more or less effective depending on the cultural affiliation(s) of the client.

Reflective Questions

1. Now that you have read both chapters on listening and action skills, where do you see yourself on this continuum of listening and action? Do you naturally gravitate toward listening skills with clients and people, or do you think you are more inclined to gravitate toward action skills? How might your natural inclinations work for you and against you in helping sessions with clients?

2. We discussed the idea that questions can be considered intrusive by some clients. Have you been in situations where you experienced someone's questions directed toward you as intrusive? Not intrusive? What were the differences between the situations for yourself?

3. What do you think about the constructivist notions that are present in the reflection of meaning responses? How does the idea that people have their own subjective reality about any given situation correspond or not to your worldview?

4. What kinds of discrepancies do you notice about yourself? About close friends and family members? How do you like to be challenged by others? What is your typical response to being challenged?

5. Can you contrast the listening skills and the action skills in terms of their potential use with diverse kinds of clients? Consider factors such as the client's presenting issue and the client's age, gender, race, ethnicity, and so on.

MyCounselingLab

For each exercise, log on to MyCounselingLab.

1. Click on Video Library under the Video Resources tab, select Family Therapy. Find and watch the clip "Clarifying Specific Issues." In this clip, what kind of questions did the helper use? Did they seem useful or not?

2. Also in the Family Therapy collection, watch the clip "Facilitating Understanding-Part 2." Did this helper seem to take more of a listening role or more of an action role with the clients? How did this seem to play out with this couple? Assess this helper's use of questions in this clip.

3. Also in Family Therapy, watch the video "Facilitating Open Emotional Expression." What did you think about this helper's use of open-ended questions in this clip? Did you see instances in this clip where the helper reflected meaning? If so, where?

4. In the Process, Skills, and Techniques collection, look at the video "Examples of Active Listening." Were you aware of the helper's use of reflection of meaning to reflect what was under the surface of this client's communication? What seemed to be the impact of this response with the client?

5. Also in Process, Skills, and Techniques, look at the video "Confrontation: Dayle." Identify this client's inconsistent messages. How did this helper challenge the client and what was the effect with this client?

Recommended Readings

Cormier, S., Nurius, P., & Osborn, C. (2013). *Interviewing and change strategies for helpers* (7th ed.). Belmont, CA: Brooks/Cole, Cengage Learning.

Egan, G. (2014). *The skilled helper* (10th ed.). Belmont, CA: Brooks/Cole, Cengage Learning.

Hepworth, D. H., Rooney, R. H., Dewberry-Rooney, G., & Strom-Gottfried, K. (2013). *Direct social work practice: Theory and Skills* (9th ed.). Belmont, CA: Brooks/Cole, Cengage Learning.

Ivey, A. E., Ivey M. B., & Zalaquett, C. R. (2014). *Intentional interviewing and counseling* (8th ed.). Belmont, CA: Brooks/Cole, Cengage Learning.

Johnson, D. W. (2014). *Reaching out: Interpersonal effectiveness and self-actualization* (11th ed.). Upper Saddle River, NJ: Pearson.

Sommers-Flanagan, J., & Sommers-Flanagan, R. (2014). *Clinical interviewing* (5th ed.). Hoboken, NJ: Wiley.

Strong, T., & Zeman, D. (2010). Dialogic considerations of confrontation as a counseling activity: An examination of Allen Ivey's use of confronting as a microskill. *Journal of Counseling and Development, 88,* 332–339.

Young, M. E. (2013). *Learning the art of helping* (5th ed.). Upper Saddle River, NJ: Pearson.

Managing the Helping Session

We have discussed the qualities of a therapeutic relationship and how effective helpers attend to and understand the client, but we have not yet discussed the structure within which all this occurs. Experienced helpers enter each session with a sense of who they are, what they wish to do and to be in the session, and how they will represent themselves to the client. This is true in the first session as well as in the twelfth. As we mentioned in the previous chapter, experienced helpers develop a personal style that they carry into the relationship. That style provides the structure for how to begin the process, how to develop it, and how to end it.

In this chapter, we will consider some awkward and sensitive times in the helping relationship that require structure. Many helpers and clients have difficulty with beginnings and endings, whether the beginning or ending of a helping interview or the beginning or ending of a helping relationship. As you read this chapter, you will find suggestions and thoughts that may help you make smoother transitions into and out of these moments. There are two types of beginnings that will be examined: beginning the first interview you have with a client and beginning subsequent interviews. Similarly, we examine the two types of termination: termination of a session and termination of the helping relationship. In addition, we explore the ethical issues surrounding these two key transitional times in helping sessions and also some ideas for managing between helping sessions.

THE FIRST INTERVIEW

Your first interview with a client will have a special set of dynamics. It is the beginning of a potentially significant relationship. As such, there are hopes and expectations, fears and reservations, acute awareness of some conditions, and an amazing lack of awareness of other conditions—all of which have a bearing on the session. With so many emotional issues operating, you might be wondering how you can possibly have a successful first interview. Helpers deal with this issue in one of two ways. Some practitioners choose to work with the relationship dynamics that are operating. Others choose to make the first session an *intake interview* and collect needed information about the client. Whichever choice you make, you must still attend to the opposite choice later. If you focus on interpersonal dynamics in the first session, in the second or third interview, you will want to collect information. If you use the first session as an intake session, you will soon afterward need to acknowledge relationship dynamics. If you wish to focus on relationship dynamics, then the content of Chapter 2 is particularly relevant. Specifically, you will want to achieve an accurate sense of the client's world and communicate that understanding back to your client. Learning to understand means putting aside your own agenda long enough to allow the client's world to enter your awareness. It means not worrying about yourself (Am I doing the right thing? Am I looking nervous?) and trying to avoid "analysis paralysis" (C. Helbok, personal communication, Nov. 20, 2002). Until you have had the experience of several beginning sessions, this will be a difficult task. Of course, you will have an underlying set of objectives in the beginning session:

- To reduce your client's initial anxieties to a level that permits him or her to begin talking
- To refrain from excessive talking because that takes time away from your client
- To listen carefully to what your client is saying and attempt to reconstruct in your mind the world that he or she is describing
- To be aware that your client's choice of topics gives insight into his or her priorities for the moment

CULTURAL VARIABLES AND THE FIRST INTERVIEW

Whether you choose to focus primarily on establishing a relationship or on gathering information in an initial counseling session often depends somewhat on your setting as well as the client's cultural affiliation. Some settings specify that the initial session be an intake interview; this initial history-gathering session may even be conducted by an intake worker rather than the counselor assigned to work with the client. The client's culture also influences your focus in an initial interview. Sue and Sue (2013) observed that some culturally diverse clients may approach the helper initially with caution, not feeling safe to self-disclose until and unless the helper self-discloses first. This trepidation may be reinforced with White counselors whose sole focus in the initial session is individualistic rather than contextual—that is, viewing the client's problems as residing within the individual rather than society or the context and environment in which the client resides. Some research reported by Sue and Sue (2013) has found that many Asian-American and African-American clients prefer a more structured and logical approach (e.g., an intake information session) to an affective and reflective one. In any initial session, regardless of approach, helpers need to exert caution and move slowly. Asking very personal questions in an initial session may be perceived as lacking respect (Sue & Sue, 2013). It is important to be flexible enough in your helping style to adapt your style in an initial session to meet the cultural diversity of your clients.

STRUCTURING OF INITIAL MOMENTS

In opening an interview, some logistics require your attention. An initial guideline is to be on time. This communicates respect. The beginning point can be as simple as a smile and greeting from you, along with a simple introduction and a motion to show the client where to sit. For example:

> "Hello. I'm Bill Janutolo. Please have a seat here or in that chair if you wish. I realize this is our first meeting together, and I'm interested in getting to know you and something about what brings you here today."

In initial moments with clients, the helper sets the tone. Initially, you want to welcome the client and begin the interview in a warm and friendly fashion. Then proceed to give the first interview some structure. Questions must be resolved. How long will the interview be? (Often, the length of the interview depends on the age of the client, with shorter interviews for children and elderly clients.) How do you want your client to address you? What should your client expect the sessions to be like? What are your client's rights? What will be your role? Answers to these and other questions provide the structure for the relationship.

Structuring has been defined as the way the clinician defines the nature, limits, roles, and goals within the helping relationship (Brammer, Abrego, & Shostrom, 1993). It includes comments about time limits, number of sessions, confidentiality, possibilities and expectations as well as supervision, observation, and/or other procedures. Describing the helping process and providing structure reduces the unknowns and thus reduces clients' anxiety. It also permits clients the opportunity to check out their expectations. Structuring conveys to clients the message that they are not going through the counseling process alone (D. Fosha, personal communication, Jan. 13, 2006). Kottler (1991) summarized the ingredients of effective structuring in initial sessions as follows:

- Providing a general overview and preview of the helping process
- Assessing the client's expectations and promoting positive ones
- Describing the helper's expectations
- Orienting the client to a new language and new behaviors
- Helping the client to increase tolerance for frustration and discomfort
- Obtaining client commitment (pp. 141–144)

Not only does structuring provide a sense of safety for clients, but it also fulfills the helper's ethical obligation to inform clients about the nature of the helping process at the outset (American Counseling Association, 2014b; National Association of Social Workers, 2008). There are also aspects of structuring to consider in working with diverse clients. For example, with children, structuring is more limited, and much of it occurs with the adult who is giving consent for the minor to be seen by a helper. With culturally diverse clients, structuring needs to occur in a way that generates "a mutually satisfying set of procedures that honor the cultures inherent to the therapy, the therapist, and the client"

(Helms & Cook, 1999, p. 169). One of the most important aspects of providing structure to clients has to do with giving information about the helping process—known as informed consent—and clarifying concerns about confidentiality.

Informed Consent

Simply put, informed consent has to do with providing information to clients about the potential helping process, the benefits and risks of being a client, and securing the client's agreement about the process. While writing this section, I (Sherry) and a friend recently attended training in an energy healing modality. Well into the training, we learned that there was a special diet we should have followed several days prior to the training as well as during the training, including no chocolate. While we were told of this information, Sherry was melting her daily piece of antioxidant dark chocolate in her mouth! We were also notified near the end of the training that we might experience some unusual sensations for a few weeks after the training. Needless to say, had we been informed about this kind of information prior to the training, we may have made different decisions. Because the trainer did not provide informed consent either before or at the very beginning of the training day, we did not have the option of deciding to forego the training. (*Note:* This training was for personal development only and was not a continuing education–approved event).

In the helping professions, we are required by our ethical codes to disclose to clients some information about the benefits, risks, and alternatives to treatment procedures. As Corey, Corey, Corey, and Callanan (2015) observe, "professionals have a responsibility to their clients to make reasonable disclosure of all significant facts, the nature of the procedure, and some of the more possible consequences and difficulties" (p. 155). Informed consent is also a legal issue. It is not just a matter of providing information to clients about the helping process (also called *notice*) but also of negotiating an agreement with the client based on such information and facts. Clients must have the capacity to make an informed decision, the comprehension to understand the information supporting their decision, and the competence to make an informed consent decision without being pressured or coerced.

Corey et al. (2015) list some of the primary issues that helpers need to address to assist in obtaining consent with clients at the beginning of a helping relationship. As we will see later in this chapter, these issues affect the beginning of the helping process, and they potentially structure and give notice about the termination of the helping process. The particular issues recommend by Corey et al. (2015, p. 156) include the following:

- What are the goals of the therapeutic endeavor?
- What services will the helper provide, and what are the qualifications of the helper to provide these services?
- What is expected of the client, and what is the client's role in the process?
- What are the benefits and risks of engaging in counseling for the client?
- What are the financial arrangements?
- What might the approximate duration or length of the helping sessions be?
- What are the limitations of confidentiality, and in what situations does the helping professional have mandatory reporting requirements?

We discuss this last question in the following section.

Confidentiality

According to Welfel (2013), "confidentiality refers to an ethical duty to keep client identity and disclosures secret" (p. 118). You will want to emphasize the issue of confidentiality to new clients. Does it mean you will talk to no one? What are the implications if you are observed by a supervisor or if you are recording the session? Will you keep a written record? If so, what are the client's guarantees that the record will be kept confidential? What about e-mail communication? Or faxes?

According to ethical guidelines for helping professions, the helper is generally obligated to treat the client's communication in a confidential manner; that is, the helper agrees not to share information given by the client with other persons. There are some exceptions to this general policy, however, such as when the client requests release of information, when a court orders the release of information, when the client is involved in litigation, and when the client's condition indicates harm to self or others. The current ethical codes of most helping professional organizations are written so that mental health professionals can disclose confidential information (with certain restrictions) when they believe the client is of immediate danger to others, based on some kind of a risk assessment procedure that assesses the client's capacity for and history of violent behavior. This exception to confidentiality stems from a court case in 1974, which has evolved over the years so that in some (but not all) states, the helper has a *duty to warn* and/or a *duty to protect* the one in danger or at risk from the client's threatened actions. These actions often include notifying or warning the intended victim and protecting the victim by securing protection from loved ones or police, by increasing the frequency of the sessions with the client, or by hospitalizing the client. In the case of self-danger (when the client is at immediate risk of suicide), the "legal and ethical responsibility to protect the client from harm is unequivocal" (Welfel, 2013, p. 134). All 50 states in the United States also have legal statutes that require helpers to report instances of both child and elder abuse. All 10 provinces and three territories in Canada have mandatory reporting for child abuse, while some have mandatory reporting for elder abuse. Because these statutes vary from state to state and from province to province, it is important to know the guidelines for your particular state or province, to consult with supervisors and colleagues about clients at risk, and to document in writing all actions and decisions.

With respect to clients and initial interviews, the important point is to discuss with clients both the protection and the limits of confidentiality as part of the structuring process. Here is how one helper begins a session with structuring:

> Juanita, we have about an hour together. I'm not sure what brings you here, but I'm ready to answer any questions you have and also to listen to whatever you tell me. You can talk about whatever you wish—this is your time. And whatever you do talk about is kept between you and me. We call this confidentiality. It means that I keep what you say to myself. This is very important to me and to you. However, I do need to let you know there are some exceptions to this that I need to share with you up front so that you're aware of what they are. If you tell me about abusing a child or an elderly person, I'm mandated to report this, as these are both against the law in this state. And the other exceptions would be if I was ordered by a court of law to provide information or if you were involved in litigation, and also if you requested that I share information. Finally, if you gave me information that led me to conclude there was serious risk of harm to yourself or someone else, there would also be some limits to the complete confidentiality of this material. I want to be sure that you understand what

this may mean before we get started here today, so let's take some time to talk about this because your safety and privacy are important to me as well as to you. Do you have any questions about what this might mean before we get started?

If you are working under supervision, also add that you will be consulting with your supervisor, who is also obligated to honor the confidentiality of the client's communication except in the instances you just noted to the client. Sample informed consent documents for adults, children, and mandated clients are available through the website at the Center for Ethical Practice at the University of Virginia (centerforethicalpractice.org/ethical-legal-resources/practice-resources/sample-handouts/).

TIMING OF CONFIDENTIALITY   Most ethical codes for helping professions require that confidentiality and its limitations be discussed as early as possible—usually at the beginning of the helping process during the initial interview. This early timing is important for several reasons. First, it is intended to give clients enough information to help them become informed about and consent to the conditions under which counseling occurs. Many clients are unaware that confidentiality is not always absolute. Second, should a disclosure by the counselor become necessary during the course of subsequent sessions, lack of information about it is not only unethical but also contributes to a client's sense of betrayal.

PRIVACY REQUIREMENTS   A federal government rule called the Health Insurance Portability and Accountability Act (HIPAA) also affects helpers and confidentiality in the United States. While technically HIPAA applies strictly to health care providers and electronic communication, it is also applicable to any provider (called a "covered entity") who employs an e-mail, fax, or sends a text to even one client. Part of the HIPAA law is designed to protect client privacy by delineating the steps that providers have to take to secure client information. Under HIPAA, all health care (including mental health) professionals are required to provide clients with a notice of privacy practices (NPP) that tells clients what information can be released under HIPAA without explicit consent and what clients can do if they believe their personal health information was disclosed in unauthorized ways. (This notice does not substitute for an informed consent discussion, which we described earlier). This notice of privacy practice must be posted publically in the office setting, with a copy given and explained to each individual client. Each client signs an acknowledgment of receipt and understanding of the notice. HIPAA applies not only to direct health care providers but also now extends to business associates, such as billing services and document storage companies, that an agency or practice may employ.

In addition to the privacy rule of HIPAA, the security rule requires the health care provider to implement a number of safeguards to ensure the confidentiality and availability of electronic records. The law that covers the security safeguard for electronic client records is known as the Health Information Technology for Economic and Clinical Health Act (HITECH). For example, clients may now ask for copies of their electronic records in electronic form. If a security breach is detected, the health care provider must perform a risk assessment and try to mitigate the breach, and also report the breach to the client. (A breach means the improper acquisition, access, use, or disclosure of protected health information.) For additional information on HIPAA, we recommend the website for the U.S. Department of Health and Human Services at hhs.gov/ocr/privacy/hipaa/understanding/. On this website you will find a link for covered entities and business associates, as well as a link for consumers. In the United States, be aware that many states also have established laws regarding client privacy. If the law in your state differs from the federal law, the more stringent law takes precedence. Because issues around confidentiality and privacy are complex, it is wise to consult with your supervisor, a colleague, or a trusted attorney when questions about these issues arise. We also discuss some of the ethical challenges around these issues in Chapter 10. Application Exercise 7.1 gives you an opportunity to role-play aspects of informed consent.

APPLICATION EXERCISE 7.1

Working with Informed Consent and Notice

Because informed consent is such a critical and integral part of the helping process, this activity gives you an opportunity to develop and refine your skills in providing informed consent. Recall that the activity of providing *notice* gives clients information about the helping process at the outset, while *informed consent* involves obtaining the client's agreement about the information you have provided.

In this activity, we suggest you divide into triads, with one person assuming the role of helper, one person assuming the role of a new inexperienced client, and the third person assuming the role of observer and feedback provider. As the helper, your task is to conduct a 15- to 20-minute beginning helping interview in which you provide information to the client about the helping process. Make sure that you cover thoroughly issues of privacy, confidentiality, and limits to confidentiality, as well as issues that may affect termination, such as insurance reimbursement limits, financial responsibilities, expectations of clients, and so on. Following the practice interview, the observer should provide feedback about the thoroughness of your informed consent process. Each of you can trade roles so that you are in each of the three roles at least once. We suggest you attempt to discuss the following issues in these practice sessions:

- The goals of helping
- The kinds of services you provide to clients
- Your qualifications
- What you expect from the client
- The potential benefits and risks of helping
- The financial arrangements and responsibilities
- Privacy, confidentiality, and the limits of confidentiality

Encouraging the Client to Talk

After providing this initial structure, you and your client are ready to begin work. The obvious beginning is to get your client to talk, to indicate his or her reason for entering counseling, and perhaps to indicate in some form what he or she hopes to achieve as a result of counseling (the client's first statement of goals). Your beginning will be an invitation to the client to talk. The nature of this invitation is important. A good invitation is one that encourages but does not specify what the client should talk about. This is called an unstructured invitation or an open-ended lead.

UNSTRUCTURED INVITATIONS The unstructured invitation has two purposes: It gives the client an opportunity to talk, and it prevents the helper from identifying the topic the client should discuss. An unstructured invitation is a statement in which the helper encourages clients to begin talking about whatever is of concern to them, such as:

- "Please feel free to go ahead and begin."
- "Where would you like to begin today?"
- "You can talk about whatever you'd like."
- "Perhaps there's something particular you want to discuss."
- "What brings you to counseling?"
- "What brings you to see me now?"

By contrast, a structured invitation—one that specifies a topic—gives clients little room to reflect on the motives, goals, or needs that brought them to counseling. An example of a less desirable structured invitation to talk might be "Tell me about what careers you're considering." The client is obviously tied down to a discussion of careers by this invitation, thus delaying or even negating a more relevant issue. (*Note:* If careers are what the client wants to discuss, an unstructured invitation allows this topic to emerge the same as a structured invitation would.) Other responses that solicit information include open-ended, closed, and clarifying questions.

OPEN-ENDED AND CLOSED QUESTIONS   As you learned in the previous chapter, open-ended questions require more than a minimal or one-word response by the client. This type of question is introduced with either *what, where, when,* or *how.* You will find that it is very difficult to ask questions that clearly place the focus on your client. Helpers fairly often ask questions that allow the client to respond with either a yes or a no. The result is that the client assumes no responsibility for the content of the interview. The purpose of the open-ended question is to prevent this from happening. However, when you want the client to give a specific piece of information, a closed question can be the best approach.

Application Exercise 7.2 will help you develop the skills involved in initiating a helping interview.

APPLICATION EXERCISE 7.2

Initiating a Helping Interview

This class exercise requires a video-recording system. Have class members select partners. Each pair is to decide who is to be the helper and who is to be the client. The exercise is to last for 5 minutes. The helper is to work toward achieving the following goals:

- Set the client at ease (body relaxed, voice without tension).
- Help the client to start talking about anything (use unstructured invitation).
- Get the client to identify a current concern (acknowledge that the client came to counseling for a reason; ask about the reason).

When each pair is finished, reverse roles and repeat the procedure. Then, when all pairs have had the opportunity to do the exercise, replay the recordings and discuss the encounters by using the following format:

- Ask the helper for his or her reaction to the recording.
- Describe those behaviors that were helpful in the exercise.

CLIENT REACTIONS TO INITIAL INTERVIEWS

Client reactions to initial interviews often depend on whether they have had any prior experience with counseling and, if so, whether that experience was positive or negative. Clients who have had positive experiences with the helping process are not as likely to have the same fears and reservations as clients who have had negative or mixed experiences, or who have never seen a helper before. Most clients approach initial helping sessions with some mixture of both dread and hope (D. Fosha, personal communication, Jan. 13, 2006). All clients need to feel a sense of safety or they are unlikely to return for more sessions. It is the helper's task to provide safety and security and to recognize and address any client fears and reservations. From the start, helpers want to create a new kind of environment for clients. A general principle to remember in initial sessions is that the safer a client feels, the wider the range of self-exploration that ensues (D. Fosha, personal communication, Jan. 13, 2006). Sommers-Flanagan and Sommers-Flanagan (2014) noted that common client fears at the beginning of the helping process include concerns about whether the practitioner is competent, helpful, understanding, and trustworthy, as well as anxieties about being pressured or judged (p. 177).

Sue and Sue (2013) add that, for some culturally diverse clients, their fears and trepidation are initially centered on concerns such as self-disclosure, racism, and cultural understanding on the part of the helper. These kinds of client concerns are likely to appear in initial interviews, regardless of whether you approach the initial interview as a time to establish the relationship or as a time to gather pertinent information, as in an intake interview. We describe the intake interview in the following section.

INTAKE INTERVIEW CONTENT

We have described the intake as an information-gathering interview, but we have not indicated what that information should be. This section presents a suggested outline of topics to cover and the rationale for their importance. Morrison (2014) has written a helpful guide for the first interview.

An assumption behind the intake interview is that the client is coming to counseling for more than one interview and intends to address problems or concerns that involve other people, other settings, and the future as well as the present. Most helpers try to limit intake interviews to an hour or perhaps 90 minutes, or probably no more than 45 minutes for younger clients. To do this, you must assume responsibility and control over the interview. The following is a suggested outline. Variations in this outline will occur depending on the setting and on certain client variables, such as age, gender, race, class, ethnicity, sexual orientation, and health and ability/disability status.

    I. Identifying Data

        A. Client's name, address, and telephone number at which client can be reached. This information is important if the helper needs to contact the client between sessions. The client's address also gives some hint about the conditions under which the client lives (large apartment complex, student dormitory, private home, etc.).

        B. Age, gender, gender identity, ethnic origin, race, partnered status, occupational status, and educational status as well as languages, citizenship, and immigration/refugee status. This is information that can be important. It lets you know if the client is still legally a minor, and it provides a basis for understanding information that will come out in later sessions.

II. Presenting Issues—Both Primary and Secondary

It is best when primary and secondary presenting issues are described in exactly the way the client reported them. If the issue(s) has behavioral components, these should also be recorded. The following questions can help reveal this type of information:

A. How much does the concern interfere with the client's everyday functioning?

B. How does the concern manifest itself? What are the thoughts, feelings, and so on, that are associated with it? What observable behavior is associated with it?

C. How often does the concern arise? How long has the concern existed?

D. Can the client identify a pattern of events surrounding the concern? When does it occur? With whom? What happens before and after its occurrence?

E. What caused the client to decide to enter counseling at this time?

III. Client's Current Life Setting

How does the client spend a typical day or week? What social, spiritual, and religious activities, recreational activities, and so on, are present? What is the nature of the client's vocational and/or educational situation? What is the client's living environment like? What are the client's most important current relationships? What sorts of financial stressors is the client experiencing?

IV. Family History

A. Recognize the plurality in contemporary practice of the definition of families. Be careful not to assume that the client's family is like your own. For example, leave room for the possibility that the client may have a family of choice to describe rather than a biological family. Once the client has identified something about his or her family, you can assess for family history by using the following as examples.

B. Names, ages, and order of brothers and sisters, and relationship between the client and siblings if siblings, either biological or adopted, are present.

C. Is there any history of emotional disturbance and/or substance abuse in the family?

D. Description of family stability, such as number of family moves, significant losses, and so on. This information provides insights in later sessions when issues related to client stability and/or relationships emerge.

E. If the client is a minor and the biological or legal custodial parents are divorced, obtain a notarized copy of the custody agreement because this will have an impact on informed consent for counseling. (You cannot counsel a minor of divorced parents unless all custodial parents give consent.)

V. Personal History

A. Medical history: Has the client had any unusual or relevant illness or injury from the prenatal period to the present, including hospitalizations, surgeries, or substance use? Does the client have any disabilities?

B. Educational history: What is the client's academic progress through grade school, high school, and post–high school? This includes extracurricular interests and relationships with peers.

    C. Military service record: Has the client served on active duty? Has the client or members of the client's family been deployed? Has the client experienced war, terrorism, or natural disaster service of any kind? Note setting and duration.

    D. Vocational history: Where has the client worked, at what types of jobs, for what duration, and what were the relationships with fellow workers? Has the client suffered any employment termination or job losses?

    E. Spiritual and religious history: What is the client's prior and current faith heritage, religious values and beliefs, and spiritual practices?

    F. Legal history: Has the client had any run-ins with the law, such as speeding tickets, accidents, time in prison, bankruptcy, divorce and custody issues, fights, weapons, or violence?

    G. Substance use history: What is the client's past and current use of substances? Note the client's drug(s) of choice, including prescription medicines, frequency of use, the amount of substance use daily and weekly, and any particular consequences of substance use the client has experienced.

    H. Sexual relationship history: Be careful not to assume the client's sexual orientation in exploring sexual history. Use with discretion questions such as the following: Where did the client receive sexual information? What was the client's dating history? Any engagements, marriages, and/or partnerships, legal or nonlegal? Other serious emotional involvements prior to the present? Reasons that previous relationships terminated? How and in what way, and with what effects? Are there any children?

    I. Counseling experience: What experience has the client had with counseling, and what were the client's reactions? Who referred the client?

    J. Traumatic experiences: Has the client encountered neglect or physical, emotional, or sexual abuse? Medical traumas or accidents? Natural disasters? Oppression? Discrimination? Immigration? Wars or war-related trauma, dislocations from country of origin?

VI. Description of the Client during the Interview

In this section, you can overview some of your primary observations and impressions about the client. Be very careful, however, not to impose your own cultural biases, norms, and value judgments. Examples of observations and impressions that could be included here are the client's physical appearance, including height and weight, dress, posture, gestures, facial expressions, voice quality, and tensions; how the client seemed to relate to you in the session; the client's readiness of response, motivation, warmth, and distance; and so on. Do there appear to be any perceptual or sensory functions that intrude on the interaction? (Document with your observations.) What are the stream of thought and rate of talking? Are the client's remarks logical? Connected to one another? What is the client's first language? Second language? What information have you gathered about the client's race, ethnicity, and general cultural affiliations? How might this information affect your impressions and observations?

VII. Summary and Recommendations

Acknowledge any connections that appear to exist between the client's statement of a problem and other information collected in this session. What is your understanding of the problem? What are the anticipated outcomes of counseling for this person? What type of counseling do you think would best fit this client? If you are to be this client's clinician, which of your characteristics might be particularly helpful? Which might be particularly unhelpful? How realistic are the client's goals for counseling? How long do you think counseling might continue? Is there anything in the client's history that seems like a red flag to you?

In writing the intake interview, the following cautions should be noted. First, avoid psychological jargon. It is not as understandable as you might think. Second, be as concise as possible and avoid elaborate inferences. Remember, an inference is a guess—sometimes an educated guess. An inference can also be wrong. Try to prevent your own biases from entering the report. Only include information that is directly relevant to the client and the counseling services to be offered. Remember that it is your responsibility to take steps to safeguard client privacy and confidentiality of communication. Make sure that the word *confidential* is stamped on the report itself—on each page if it is more than one page in length. Do not leave drafts of the reports around on your desk or in your mailbox or open on your computer screen.

Using Intake Interview Information

Following the intake interview but before the second session, review the write-up of the intake interview. Helpers develop different approaches to using this information. Some practitioners look primarily for patterns of behavior. For example, one helper noted that her client had a pattern of incompletion in life: He received a general discharge from the army prior to completing his enlistment, dropped out of college twice, and had a long history of broken relationships. This observation provided food for thought. What happens to this person as he becomes involved in a commitment? What has he come to think about himself as a result of this history? How does he anticipate future commitments? Another practitioner uses the intake information to look for signals that suggest how this client might enter the helping relationship. Is there anything to indicate how the client might relate to females? Is there something in his life at present that common sense would suggest is a potential area for counseling attention? For example, is the client in the midst of a divorce? Is the client at a critical developmental stage? The main caution is to avoid reading too much into the intake information. It is far too early for you to begin making interpretations about your client.

Many practitioners supplement the intake interview information with some additional sort of structured assessment that may include diagnostic questions about the client's presenting concern, such as depression, anxiety, or substance abuse. It may also include the use of formalized, written questionnaires and instruments, such as inventories that measure depression or anxiety and that yield yet additional information about potential diagnoses and client concerns and strengths. Such instruments can often be administered at the end of the intake interview or near the beginning of the follow-up interview. These can be introduced to the client simply by indicating that you would like the client to complete a form or two to assist you in determining more about the client's presenting concerns and in formulating a plan for treatment. Once such forms are used, it is important to score them promptly, use the information they provide efficiently, and provide feedback to the client about what the instrument yielded.

HANDLING SUBSEQUENT INTERVIEWS

Handling subsequent interviews involves several dimensions and tasks, including reestablishing rapport, eliciting essential information, and focusing in depth (Hepworth et al., 2013). Once you have established a relationship or rapport with your client, subsequent interviews require that you reinstate the relationship that has developed. Reinstating the relationship usually amounts to acknowledging the client's absence since the last interview. This includes being sensitive to how your client's world may have changed since your last contact and your reactions in seeing the client again. This can be done with a few short statements, such as "Hello, Marvel. It's nice to see you again." This might be followed by some observation about the client's appearance: "You look a little hassled today" or "You're looking more energetic today." Or you might begin by asking, "How are you feeling today?" These types of questions focus on the client's current or immediate condition and reduce the likelihood that the client will spend the major part of the session recounting how the week has gone. If your client needs a bit of small talk to get started, it probably means that he or she needs time to make the transition into the role of help seeker or client. The important point is that you probably do not need to go to the same lengths in establishing rapport as was necessary when counseling was first initiated. However, keep in mind that some degree of relationship building occurs in each and every session.

In addition to rapport building, subsequent interviews are also characterized by information gathering and focusing in depth. The question becomes "What does the helper do with information that's gathered during the helping interviews?" Basically, the helper uses such information to make clinical judgments and inferences; such judgments and inferences are the basis for the clinician's assessment of the client's personal style and level of functioning, determinations about who is the actual client and how much therapy may be needed, decisions about the client's diagnosis—including diagnostic formulations and areas of strengths, and ideas about the most appropriate or efficacious approach to take with a particular client.

Another way in which helpers make use of clinical information is to help clients focus in depth in subsequent interviews. For example, some clients—out of fear or lack of trust—may withhold important parts of their story in initial interviews and may not reveal issues that bear significant weight until they feel very safe with the helper. Sometimes, clients presenting issues will shift significantly in subsequent situations, often due to internal processing, to external situations, or both. For example, Eduardo was working with Sammy, who was exploring issues related to his partner when Sammy's mother passed away suddenly and unexpectedly. At this point, the focus of the sessions shifted somewhat away from the initial concern to the more immediate situation at hand and to Sammy's resulting grief and sadness. At a later point, additional sessions shifted back to Sammy's ongoing concerns with his partner.

Practitioners can help clients focus in depth in several ways, as suggested by Hepworth et al. (2013). One way is for the helper to explore and assess the cognitions of the clients because thought patterns, beliefs, and attitudes are also "powerful determinants of behavior" (Hepworth et al., 2013, p. 53). For example, focusing in depth on cognitive patterns may reveal dogmatic or rigid thinking, misinterpretations, and nonproductive beliefs. Hepworth et al. (2013, p. 53) recommend the following kinds of questions to focus in depth on cognitions:

- How did you come to that conclusion?
- What meaning do you make of that?

- How do you explain what happened?
- What are your views (or beliefs) about that?

We suggest additional strategies to focus in depth on cognitive processes in Chapter 9.

Another way is for the helper to assess and tune into the client's affective or emotional functioning because these patterns can affect the client's behavior in many contexts and can also provide clues about the client's interpersonal functioning. For example, the helper may use questions to focus in depth on affective functioning, such as the following questions recommended by Brooks-Harris (2008, p. 199):

- What feelings related to this concern have you been experiencing?
- Do you ever feel sad, afraid, angry, or ashamed in this situation?
- Do these feelings help you resolve things or do they make things worse?
- Are there other emotions you might be feeling at a deeper level?
- Are there feelings you express in order to get a reaction from someone?
- Which emotions are you likely to express, and which do you tend to hide?
- Are there times when your feelings seem too intense for the current situation?
- Do you ever feel like your emotions are restricted or muffled or you can't express what you're really feeling?

We suggest additional strategies to focus on affective dimensions in Chapter 9.

TERMINATING THE INTERVIEW

The beginning practitioner is often unsure about when to terminate the interview and may feel ready to conclude either before or after the client is ready. A general guideline is to limit the interview to a certain amount of time, such as 45 or 50 minutes. Rarely does the helping interview need to exceed an hour in length because both client and helper have a saturation point. With children, sessions may only be 20 to 40 minutes in duration, and some part of this time may be spent in play therapy.

There is also a minimal amount of time required for counseling to take place. Interviews that continue for no more than 10 or 15 minutes make it very difficult for the helper to know enough about the client's concern to react appropriately. Indeed, helpers sometimes require 5 to 10 minutes just to reorient themselves and to change their frame of reference from their preceding attention-involving activity to the present activity of counseling.

Acceptance of time limits is especially important when the client has a series of interviews. Research has shown that clients, like everyone else, tend to postpone talking about their concerns as long as possible. Without time limits, the presumed one-hour interview may extend well beyond an hour as a result of this postponing tendency. It is the one instance in which the client can easily manipulate the helper. If the client introduces a new topic near the end of a session, the practitioner can suggest discussing it at the outset of the next session. The rare exception to this would be when the client presents a truly urgent and immediate concern.

Other Termination Strategies

Often, a brief and to-the-point statement by the helper is sufficient for closing the interview:

- "It looks as if our time is up for today."
- "Well, I think it's time to stop for today."

This type of statement may be preceded by a pause or by a concluding kind of remark made by the client. Another effective way is to use *summarization*. Summarization provides continuity to the interview, is an active kind of helper response, and often helps the client to hear what he or she has been saying. As you learned from Chapter 5, this response is essentially a series of statements in which the helper ties together the main points of the interview. It should be brief, to the point, and without interpretation. An example of a helper's use of summarization at the end of an interview is the following:

> Essentially, you've indicated that your main concern is with your family—and we've discussed how you might handle your strivings for independence without their interpreting this as rejection.

Another possible termination strategy is to ask the client to summarize or to state how he or she understood what has been going on in the interview, as in the following example:

> As we're ending the session today, I'm wondering what you're taking with you; if you could summarize this, I think it would be helpful to both of us.

Mutual feedback involving both the client and the helper is another possible tool for termination of an interview. If plans and decisions have been made, it is often useful for both individuals to clarify and verify the progress of the interview, as in the following example:

> I guess that's it for today; I'll also be thinking about the decision you're facing. What things do you want to do before our next session?

Mutual exploration involves the client and helper assessing the experience of the helping session or sessions together. Whether the process has gone well or poorly, mutual exploration provides an opportunity to process what the experience has been like, as in the following example:

> Now that we're about out of time for today, can you share with me what it's been like for you?

Boundary Issues in Terminating an Interview

It is up to the helper to set boundaries for terminating a session; however, some clients challenge these limits for various reasons, such as anxiety, dependence, or reactivity. For example, a client may abruptly end a session and say, "That's it for me today," before the allotted time has occurred. Other clients may wait until you initiate termination and then say something provocative, such as "Well, actually the real reason I came today is because I had to file for bankruptcy yesterday" or "I have something urgent I must tell you before I leave today."

In both of these situations, it is the helper's responsibility to maintain time boundaries established at the beginning of the session—which, as we mentioned earlier, will vary with the age of the client and the setting in which you work. The rare exceptions to this would be with a client who is desperately anxious to leave early and with a client who brings up a recent traumatic event or a serious threat against oneself or someone else, such as "Last night, I got in the car with a loaded gun and drove over to the house of the man who is having an affair with my wife."

As Sommers-Flanagan and Sommers-Flanagan (2014) have noted, beginning interviewers often feel guilty about maintaining time boundaries. But according to the authors, disregarding these boundaries usually does not serve clients well in the long run (p. 204). Application Exercise 7.3 gives you an opportunity to practice the skills associated with opening and terminating a helping session.

APPLICATION EXERCISE 7.3

Opening and Terminating the Interview

Use the following triadic exercise to review styles of opening and terminating an interview. With one class member as the speaker, another as the listener, and a third as the observer, complete the following tasks by using the observer rating charts in Figures 7.1 and 7.2.

Counselor Response	Order
Unstructured invitation	
Open-ended questions	
Closed questions	

FIGURE 7.1   Observer Rating Chart: Opening the Interview

Counselor Response	Order
Time limits	
Summarization	
Mutual feedback	
Structuring next session (time, date, etc.)	

FIGURE 7.2   Observer Rating Chart: Terminating the Interview

Opening the Interview

- For the speaker role: Talk about yourself; share a concern with the listener.
- For the listener role: Respond to the speaker as if you were opening an interview. Try out the responses mentioned in the chapter: unstructured invitation and open-ended and closed questions.
- For the observer role: Observe the kinds of responses made by the listener. Keep a frequency count of the types of responses made. Share your report with the listener.

Rotate the roles and then follow the same process so that everyone plays the part of the speaker, the listener, and the observer.

Record the order and frequency of responses used. If the counselor's first response was unstructured invitation, place a 1 in the space provided in the observer rating chart in Figure 7.1. If the second counselor response was an open question, place a 2 in the appropriate space, and so forth.

(Continued)

Terminating the Interview

- For the speaker role: Continue to explore the same topic you introduced in the preceding interaction.
- For the listener role: Respond to the speaker as if you were terminating an interview. Try at least one of the procedures mentioned in the section as approaches for termination of the interview (acknowledgment of time limits, summarization, or mutual feedback). If you, as the listener, did not use any of the termination procedures or if termination did not occur with your speaker for some reason, complete the interaction again.
- For the observer role: Observe the procedure for termination used by the listener. Share your report with the listener.

Rotate the roles and then follow the same process so that everyone plays the part of the speaker, the listener, and the observer.

Record the order and frequency of responses used in Figure 7.2.

TERMINATING THE HELPING RELATIONSHIP

The process of terminating a helping relationship can evoke various and even conflicting reactions for the helper. Some may think of it as a loss experience or certainly as a "letting go" if the relationship has been highly meaningful (Murdin, 2000). Others may consider termination to be an index of the helper's success or failure. From the client's point of view, termination may be a symbol of success or it may be a reenactment of many former goodbyes in life. Whatever the interpretation, it is apparent that termination possesses an emotional dimension that can be intense. Often, it evokes an awareness of what the client means to us, and vice versa. Through the process of termination, both helper and client are usually changed (Murdin, 2000, p. 211).

Perhaps the most useful way to conceptualize termination is to think of it as a transition rather than an event (Hackney & Cormier, 2013). As the helping relationship develops and as the client is able to address and resolve the issues that necessitated counseling, the prospect of termination becomes a therapeutic stage in the process. More often than not, the helper becomes aware of the approaching termination first. Concerns related to the timing of termination, the preparation for termination, and the anticipation of therapeutic problems related to termination become dominant in the helper's mind.

When Should Termination Occur?

Some counseling theories provide guidelines for the timing of termination, including possibilities such as letting the client determine the timing or having the clinician establish the date of termination at the outset of the helping process (Hackney & Cormier, 2013). Such issues depend on your own theoretical orientation. However, there are some pragmatic factors that contribute to the question of timing. For example, the client may be under a managed health care plan that dictates a certain number of sessions per year, such as 20. At the end of the specified number of sessions, several scenarios could occur. The helper may be able to negotiate with the client's plan for a few more sessions if the goals have not been reached. Alternatively, the helper and client may reach some kind of private payment agreement if termination does not seem clinically indicated. If the client is unable to pay and the insurance company does not authorize additional sessions, however, helping professionals "still have a fiduciary obligation to assist, stabilize, and/or refer" those clients who continue to need care (Younggren & Gottlieb, 2008, p. 501).

Hackney and Cormier (2013) have summarized some of these pragmatic considerations in termination as follows:

- When counseling has been predicated on a behavioral or another form of contract, progress toward the goals or conditions of the contract presents a clear picture of when counseling should end.
- When clients feel that their goals have been accomplished, they may initiate termination.
- When the relationship appears not to be helpful termination is appropriate.
- When contextual conditions change—for example, the client or helper moves to a new location—termination must occur.

Preparing Clients for Termination

Clients should be made aware throughout the helping process that there will come a time when counseling is no longer appropriate. This does not mean that they will have worked out all their issues nor will it mean that they have acquired all the tools and awareness necessary for a satisfying life. It does mean that they have grown to the point at which they have more to gain from being independent of the helping relationship than they would gain from continuing the relationship. Murdin (2000) observes that an important indicator of client readiness for termination is the client's ability and willingness to discuss reasons for wanting to terminate (p. 41). We believe that human beings are happier and more self-fulfilled when they are able to trust their own resources. Of course, healthy people rely on others, but they do so out of self-perceived choice rather than self-perceived necessity.

Occasionally, you will know in the first session with your client that the relationship will last a certain length of time. For example, if your client is seeking premarital counseling and the wedding is to take place in two months, the time constraints are apparent. People going to university counseling centers may know that vacations dictate the amount of time allowed for counseling. In such cases, it is appropriate to acknowledge throughout the relationship that these time constraints exist.

When the relationship is more open-ended and determined by the client's progress, the termination stage begins well before the final session. The client's presenting concerns, goals for counseling, and progress in counseling should be reviewed from time to time (Vasquez, 2005). Hackney and Cormier (2013) refer to this as termination by degree (p. 34). We believe that for any relationship that has existed more than three months, the topic should be raised at least three to four weeks prior to termination. This allows the client time to think about and discuss the ramifications of ending counseling with the helper. In addition, termination should also take into account both the nature of the client's issues and the nature of the helper's theoretical or treatment approach (Younggren & Gottlieb, 2008, p. 503). Clients with more severe issues usually require a longer termination period that provides more follow-up care than those with less severe issues. Also, terminating with a client after a long-term psychodynamic relationship is somewhat different than terminating with a client who was seen briefly with a cognitive-behavioral approach.

Cultural Variables and Termination

It is important to recognize that not all cultural groups share the same values and beliefs about the dimension of time, and this can also affect the termination process. For example, European Americans generally have a highly structured and future-oriented view of time, but some clients from other cultural groups have a much more casual view of time (Ivey, D'Andrea, & Ivey, 2012). In cross-cultural helping situations, the time element of termination also needs to be discussed, negotiated, and understood from the client's perspective.

Also, many clients of color terminate the helping process at a much earlier time than other clients. Often, these clients are the decision makers about when to stop counseling, presumably because it is not relevant enough to them and their experiences, particularly their culturally linked experiences (Sue & Sue, 2013). Therefore, it is presumptuous to assume that in all situations, control of the termination process is in the helper's hands.

Introducing Termination

Introducing termination can be done by saying something similar to this:

> We've been dealing with a lot of issues, and I believe you've made a lot of progress. One of our goals all along has been to reach the point where counseling is no longer needed. I think we're reaching that point, and probably in about three or four weeks, we'll be stopping.

You can try to anticipate some of your client's reactions to this. They may feel good about their progress, nervous about the prospect of being on their own, or sad to see a significant relationship ending—to name but a few reactions. It is also important for the client to summarize both what has been achieved and what remains undone (Murdin, 2000, p. 150).

Occasionally, it is appropriate to terminate gradually. This can be done by spacing the time between interviews. If you have been seeing your client weekly, change the appointments to every other week or once a month. Or you may schedule a six-month check-in that gives your client the sense of an ongoing relationship—one that leaves the door open—should that be necessary. Even with these gradual transitions, you still have as a major concern the transition of a significant relationship.

In all cases, it is important to emphasize the client's continued growth once counseling has ended. This includes summations of what the client has learned, discussions of other resources and support systems the client can make use of in her or his life, and the invitation for follow-up sessions as necessary. Kottler (1991) observed that "some people believe that therapy never ceases, that clients continue their dialogues with us (as they do with deceased parents) for the rest of their lives" (p. 173).

Occasionally the ending of a helping relationship has a character of finality. Perhaps you or your client is moving. Or you may be referring your client to another helping provider. In such instances, there may be a grieving process connected with termination. It is appropriate to view this grieving process as necessary and therapeutic in its own right. It is as important for the helper as for the client. A client may occasionally terminate simply by canceling the next appointment and there is no formal termination that occurs, yet the helper may still feel some grief. It is a symbolic or ceremonial conclusion—an acknowledgment that the relationship had importance and that reality dictates that it ends. In such cases, it is better not to hang on to it because that would only make the transition more difficult. If you are making a referral to another practitioner, you must give up your role as helper for both ethical and practical reasons.

Challenges to Termination

Murdin (2000) summarized a number of possible different challenges to the termination of counseling and psychotherapy. For example, she noted that clients sometimes leave suddenly and/or prematurely for fear of losing their own power. She observed that "the whole ending process involves questions about who has the power and whether or not it can be given up or shared" (p. 38). Studies have revealed that one-third of all clients do not return to counseling after only one or two sessions (Vasquez, 2005). These are likely to be clients who did not find counseling to be very useful for them. In other instances, clients just stop coming to see you because they feel ready to leave but are afraid to raise the issue of termination or do not see a way to exit. Other clients may terminate the helping process prematurely because they have difficulty in regulating affective reactions, are emotionally unstable, and may be upset or irritated with the helper and yet avoid communication about their feelings. In these situations, a note or phone call may be useful to collaborate with clients about various options: Do they want their file terminated? Do they want to come in for a review session? Do they want to return to counseling—either with you or with someone different (Vasquez, 2005, p. 21)? A review of over 35 years of scientific literature on premature termination resulted in a number of other recommendations for preventing counseling dropout, including preparation, time-limited counseling, negotiation, case management, motivational interviewing and enhancement, strengthening the therapeutic relationship, and facilitating a safer environment for the expression of client feelings (Ogrodniczuk, Joyce, & Piper, 2005).

At the other end of the continuum are clients who fight the termination process and have trouble saying goodbye for fear of losing the helper and his or her compassion (Murdin, 2000, p. 37). Even in instances where the termination point has been decided at the outset of the helping process—such as in time-limited counseling—challenges to the termination process can and do still occur. For instance, it is not uncommon for clients to have a crisis as the end of the contract approaches. Often, these clients may try to persuade the helper to work beyond the agreed-upon ending time. Murdin (2000) recommends that, in most cases, the helper should keep faith in the client and abide by the agreed-upon ending date (p. 151). She states that "in time-limited work, the therapist must be prepared to work for an ending right from the beginning and must not waver from the view that an ending is desirable" (p. 155). Murdin recommends that, before agreeing to any changes in the termination date, helpers should search themselves and their own motivations for extending the time (p. 153). For any exception that may be made to the original contract, she also believes it is better to initiate a new contract than to extend the existing one (p. 153). Challenges to termination often occur because the attachment produces a fear of loss. The greatest difficulty in termination of counseling lies in "hidden anxieties" about this loss (p. 37). The fear of loss can result in emotions such as anger and jealousy (in addition to the sadness we mentioned earlier). Occasionally, clients' fear of loss may be so great that they even pursue helpers by stalking them. Obviously, there is a great deal that helpers can do to promote a healthy attachment with clients and to avoid an unhealthy attachment, such as extreme dependence or adoration (Murdin, 2000).

Ethical Issues in Termination

In the United States, Canada, and the United Kingdom, numerous ethical complaints made by clients have to do with termination issues that clients felt were handled improperly (Murdin, 2000). Terminating the helping relationship does pose potential ethical and legal issues for helpers if not managed appropriately. Generally, it is important for helpers to avoid sudden endings. If a situation—such as a helper's severe illness—requires a sudden termination, the helper still has continued responsibilities for the welfare of the client. "When incapacity or absence suddenly strike, psychotherapists must make sure that those being treated have access to emergency resources, and if the psychotherapist is unable to return to practice within a reasonable time, appropriate referrals must be arranged" (Younggren & Gottlieb, 2008, p. 502). And the helper has certain ethical responsibilities in the referral process, including protecting the client's privacy and confidentiality unless there is a written client release on file, providing the client with choices of several other professional helpers, ensuring that these other helpers are regarded as competent and ethical professionals, and facilitating a smooth transition (Welfel, 2013). When a helper is incapacitated in a sudden and severe manner, other qualified helping professionals will need to fulfill these responsibilities.

Helpers cannot terminate services with a client "just because"—just because they feel like it, don't like working with the client, don't agree with the client's values and/or worldview. This constitutes abandonment and has legal as well as ethical implications. The one exception allowed by most of the helping professions' codes of ethics is in the rare case when a client or someone connected to the client poses a risk of harm to the helper.

It is also important to remember that clients who have not received any structuring about the termination process at the outset of the helping process may be more likely to feel abandoned and angry when the practitioner suggests termination is appropriate or when the practitioner becomes ill or moves away. Therefore, an important ethical issue in terminating the helping process effectively involves discussion of this issue as part of the informed consent process that we described earlier in this chapter. As Younggren and Gottlieb (2008) note, in reality, "effective termination begins during the initial psychotherapy session or another early session in which matters of informed consent are discussed. . . . Through this mechanism, practitioners explain the details of the treatment relationship and make contracts with patients regarding what the psychotherapist will and will not do. This is also the time for the practitioner to explain what he or she expects of the patient. It is through this clarification of the professional–patient relationship that much of the difficulty associated with the closure of psychotherapy can be avoided" (p. 502).

Part of this discussion about termination should very clearly include client financial obligations and insurance limitations. If a client is using health insurance and has a very restricted plan, it is important to explain this before counseling ensues to ensure that client expectations are reasonable and realistic and that the client still retains the potential choice to consent or not consent to treatment under these conditions.

Another potential ethical issue in termination involves continuity of care. Perhaps the client decides to terminate and return to see you at a later point. Or perhaps the client takes a break and later returns to your setting and sees another practitioner. In either case, a written summary of your progress with the client provides the basis for you or someone else to begin sessions with the client at a later date without having to start all over again. The structure of *discharge summaries* or *termination reports* varies among settings. Generally speaking, however, most termination reports consist of the following kinds of information:

- Identifying information about the client (name, age, gender)
- Duration of counseling; dates and number of sessions with the client
- Summary of client's presenting issues and possible diagnostic codes for problems
- Type and method of counseling (treatment and intervention strategies)
- Summary of counseling and therapeutic progress
- Recommendations for future treatment (including referrals)

The need for a more detailed summary is evident when the termination occurs prematurely and/or when the client objects to it. In these cases, "the record should include documentation that allows the reader to understand the rationale for ending therapy as well as the ethically appropriate and clinically indicated steps the practitioner took to do so in a reasonable manner" (Younggren & Gottlieb, 2008, p. 503).

Summary

Beginning interviews, subsequent interviews, and ending interviews all present different challenges for both helpers and clients. At the outset of the helping process, both helpers and clients might experience some anxiety and uncertainty. It is important for practitioners to establish safety and trust from the beginning of the process because many clients have both fears and reservations about the helping process. This is especially true for many culturally diverse clients and for clients who have had either no prior experience or negative experience with counseling. Structuring and disclosure can ease client fears and insecurities about the process. Both rapport and information gathering are important tasks in the initial stage of the helping process. One of the most important topics to address at the beginning of the helping process is confidentiality and its limits. Through the process of providing notice and informed consent, the helper provides information to the client about the helping process and secures client agreement based on such information and facts. This sort of process not only facilitates the beginning of counseling but also affects subsequent helping sessions and even potential termination issues.

Termination—both of helping sessions and of the helping process—evokes its own set of challenges and emotions. It is important for helpers to terminate an interview as well as the helping process in a way that empowers clients. Clients who feel disempowered, such as some culturally diverse clients, might choose to terminate early or suddenly, often because counseling does not feel relevant to them, the helper does not understand their worldviews, or aspects of oppression and discrimination are re-created for them in the helping process.

Both the termination of interviews and the termination of the helping process require the helper to manage a transition effectively. This transition becomes more difficult if either the helper or the client has any hidden anxieties about separation and/or loss. It is important for helpers to address feelings of loss, to prepare clients for termination over a period of time, and to help clients find ways to support their growth after counseling has ended.

Reflective Questions

1. Discuss what it might be like to be a client seeking help for the first time from an unknown practitioner. Now discuss this as it applies to a cross-cultural dyad.
2. Discuss the positive and negative perceptions that a client might have after going through an intake interview.
3. Discuss the transition that the helper needs to make from a beginning interview or two to a subsequent session. What changes for the helper? For the client?
4. From a helper's perspective, what do you think are the most important elements in terminating a significant relationship? What are the most important elements from the client's perspective?
5. Describe what you see as potential ethical issues in the termination of a helper–client relationship.

MyCounselingLab

For each exercise, log on to MyCounselingLab.

1. Go to the Ethical, Legal, and Professional Issues collection in the Video Library under the Video Resources tab. Watch the "Misinformed Consent" clip. Discuss what mistakes this beginning helper made in the notice and informed consent process with this client.

2. In the Assessment and Diagnosis collection, locate the clip "Diagnostic Assessment: Reviewing Intake Information with Clients." After watching this clip, describe how this therapist encouraged his client to talk during this initial session.

3. Click on the Theories of Counseling collection and watch the video clip entitled "Closing an Initial Interview." In this clip, two different practitioners end a session with a client. Contrast the two different endings you see in this clip. What did you like and dislike about each of the two session terminations?

Recommended Readings

Hackney, H., & Cormier, L. S. (2013). *The professional counselor* (7th ed.). Upper Saddle River, NJ: Pearson.

Morrison, J. (2014). *The first interview* (4th ed.). New York, NY: Guilford Press.

Murdin, L. (2000). *How much is enough: Endings in psychotherapy and counseling*. London: Routledge.

Ogrodniczuk, J. S., Joyce, A. S., & Piper, W. E. (2005). Strategies for reducing patient-initiated premature termination of psychotherapy. *Harvard Review of Psychiatry, 13*, 57–70.

Sommers-Flanagan, J., & Sommers-Flanagan, R. (2014). *Clinical interviewing* (5th ed.). Hoboken, NJ: John Wiley & Sons.

Sue, D. W., & Sue, D. (2013). *Counseling the culturally diverse* (6th ed.). Hoboken, NJ: John Wiley & Sons.

Welfel, E. (2013). *Ethics in counseling and psychotherapy* (5th ed.). Belmont, CA: Brooks/Cole, Cengage.

Younggren, J. N., & Gottlieb, M. C. (2008). Termination and abandonment: History, risk, and risk management. *Professional Psychology, 39*, 498–504.

Conceptualizing Client Issues and Setting Change Goals

It is appropriate now to consider some of the larger issues of counseling—namely, the nature of client concerns and the establishment of goals that are realistic antecedents to the solution of those concerns. Philosophical questions underlie these issues because there is no one way of conceptualizing human problems, and we will not be able to resolve the philosophical problems for you. In fact, it may require the greater part of your career to do that. But we will present a viewpoint that represents our stand at this time. We find it useful because it focuses not only on our clients but also on the world that they return to after each helping session—a world in which their problems are real.

THE CLIENT'S WORLD AND UNMET NEEDS

What brings clients to counseling? The answer to this—more than any other question—will reveal your role as helper. It is a disarmingly simple question but not one to be taken lightly. We begin with this response: Clients enter counseling when they experience issues and needs that they are unable, on their own, to understand or when their particular coping strategies to meet needs or resolve issues no longer work.

All human beings share certain basic needs. These include the need for security, nourishment, survival, affiliation, love, and self-esteem. In a classic article, Jourard (1963, pp. 33–38) has conceptualized these needs in a way that is useful for counseling. They include the following:

1. *Survival needs:* All people are concerned with self-preservation and safety. This includes psychological safety as well as physical safety. Although people may not always recognize threats to their psychological safety, they do recognize their responses to those threats—namely, increased anxiety, inaccurate or restricted perceptions of the world, and increasingly inappropriate behavior.

2. *Physical needs:* These include the needs for nourishment, shelter, income, freedom from pain, rest, and replenishment of energy. When these needs go unmet or become distorted (e.g., via overeating or migraine headaches), people's responses may inhibit the satisfaction of still other needs (e.g., the migraine sufferer finds it difficult to achieve love and sex needs). As another example, clients whose physical needs are eliminated as a result of a natural or human-made disaster are necessarily so focused on survival and basic physical needs that higher level needs—such as attachment, ambition, mental health, freedom, and so on—are overtaken by this basic, almost instinctual preoccupation with safety and survival.

3. *Love and sex needs:* These are the needs to become involved in a close personal way with another human being. People grow in their development of these needs and often recognize their intensity only when they have suddenly experienced the loss of a close personal relationship. When these needs are unmet, people question their potential to love and to be loved, to be in an extended relationship, or to be able to give to or take from another person. When such loss occurs, it is not hard to understand why grief theorists discuss loss as rejection.

4. *Status, success, and self-esteem needs:* These needs motivate people to achieve in the eyes of their peers and to gain respect, confidence, and/or admiration. When these needs are unmet, people lack self-respect and self-confidence or overreact with excessive and manufactured self-respect and self-confidence.

5. *Mental health needs:* When these needs are met, people feel like functional human beings. When they are unmet, people are incongruent, disillusioned, disoriented, and vulnerable to despair.

6. *Freedom needs:* These are the needs to feel autonomous, free to make personal choices, or free not to choose. When these needs go unmet, people feel restricted, undervalued, or unappreciated.

7. *Challenge needs:* These are the needs for activity, future orientation, and opportunity. When they are missing, people are vulnerable to boredom, meaninglessness, or emptiness.

8. *Cognitive-clarity needs:* These needs reflect the drive to resolve the conflicts in values, ideas, and commitments that exist in people's lives and the need to live one's life with honor and integrity.

Perhaps you would add to or take away from this list, according to your view of human experience. However, the point is that all human beings experience needs as part of living. To experience a need does not set a person apart as unusual, inadequate, or in some other way lacking. On the other hand, human beings are not always adept at recognizing (comprehending) experienced needs nor do they necessarily possess the skills required to meet needs once the needs are recognized. To recognize and meet one's needs is not necessarily a natural part of the process of living; it must be learned.

The place where people learn or do not learn what their needs are and how to get them met is in their family of origin. This is where needs are either affirmed and met or shamed and rejected. Teyber and McClure (2011) suggest that when childhood needs are consistently ignored or shamed, persistent psychological problems may result. As an example, once a child's need is blocked by a caregiver, the child often grows up and blocks the same need as an adult. Or the child may grow up and try to deny having the need, or attempt to satisfy the need through a particular way of coping.

For example, an adult client whose early needs for affection were shamed may block current needs for affection and claim, "I don't need anybody's love. I can make it on my own." Yet at some level, the unmet need for affection will still try to seek expression, and when it does, the client will try to cope with it in a particular way but usually in an unsatisfying or troublesome way.

In addition to this intrapsychic view of needs, we also need to recognize the role of external stressors and environmental events in creating needs. For example, clients also experience needs in terms of current life events and may enter therapy when various life stressors or developmental issues become too hard to handle. For example, consider an adult woman who is coping well with her partnered relationship and her job. But as her aging father unexpectedly develops Alzheimer's disease, her world starts to fall apart; she experiences needs now that were either not there or not apparent to her before this event.

Current life events and environmental stressors are particularly important in shaping needs of clients who feel marginalized because of race, gender, sexual orientation, religion, health and/or disability status, ethnicity, or socioeconomic status and who experience the effects of stereotyping, discrimination, and oppression on a frequent and repetitive basis. In these situations, emotional distress resulting from current needs is often more the result of a lack of both real and perceived power in a client's daily, current life rather than unmet developmental childhood needs (Brown, 2010). For example, consider the situation of a financially challenged Latina woman who is raising her three children single-handedly. She has no living parents to help her in child rearing, and her two brothers were shot and killed in an urban gang fight. She has a part-time job and is in danger of losing it because she has needed to take days off to care for her sick children. Furthermore, in riding the subway to her place of work, she is met with racial taunts. Clearly, the context of her current world is a major factor in her presenting needs.

Thus far, we have drawn a picture of the client as a person who is (1) continually experiencing issues and needs, (2) not always understanding or even recognizing some of those issues and needs, and (3) seeking your assistance when unrecognized and/or unmet issues and needs become the bigger issue of living. Although this may be an adequate description of the person entering counseling, it fails to embrace the total situation of the client. Any description of clients must also include the world in which they live, including significant others, employment or the setting in which they spend the major portion of the day, expectations for self and others, habits and routines, dreams and fantasies of the future, attitudes toward the past, values and the meanings of life, and methods developed for survival (survival of responsibilities, tensions, disappointments, expectations of others, dashed hopes, etc.). You might wish to refer to our discussion of the initial interview in Chapter 7 for a review of all these components, where the helper and the client worked on conceptualizing client issues to begin the initial session.

Sometimes, clarity about the client's real issues does not come quickly or easily. For example, a young man comes to the helper, and at the end of the session, it is still unclear what led him to seek the services of a helper, although he is speaking generally about his family stress. In fact, not until the third session does the client allude to his sexual orientation. Finally, by session five, he discloses that he is bisexual and has been thrown out of his house by his parents, who have told him that they never want to see him again. He now has to support himself financially but is not yet prepared to do so. As a result, he has been living for the last six weeks in his car, unaware of any community resources that may be available to him. In addition, he is starting to feel tremendous guilt about his bisexuality because of his parental reaction and his religious upbringing. In this case, it has taken about six weeks for the client to feel safe enough with the helper to get to the heart of what is really troubling him.

THE ROLE OF THE HELPER IN ASSESSING CLIENT CONCERNS

Based on what we have said about the client who is entering counseling, it follows that you would have some fairly clear responsibilities. These responsibilities are above and beyond creating a favorable climate for counseling—even beyond being a good and caring listener. It is your role to hear the issues as clients describe their concerns and also to help them hear those needs and issues, recognizing from our earlier example about the young man that such clarity may be ambiguous at first. Next, it is your role to help clients formulate goals that will help them meet the needs or resolve the issues. From these goals, plans of action may be constructed, implemented, and evaluated. Finally, you must help clients recognize that they are making progress. When clients have lived with problems too long or the problems seem too overwhelming to clients, it is difficult for them to trust any progress.

The helping process may often be viewed as an unfolding process in which the outer, more obvious issues precede the more subtle, less obvious concerns. As an example, consider an Asian-American man who comes to counseling with an obvious dilemma: He cannot fall asleep at night. He has a physical need to sleep. After the insomnia problem has been addressed, and the goals and strategies have been formulated to help with this need, focus is then directed toward those pressures that led to the insomnia in the first place. The man's insomnia could be the result of old wounds or unmet needs that have become reactivated recently, as well as cultural and environmental factors that are overlaid on top of these old wounds or unmet needs. For example, this client reports that he recently lost his job as a result of layoffs; he now feels lacking in self-respect and self-confidence, and may have esteem needs, wanting to be respected, valued, and appreciated by himself and by others. He does not want to lose face among his family members and the members of his cultural group. These may be carryover needs from family and culture that are now being felt again because of a major loss. He also faces survival needs related to loss of income in his current life.

As you attempt to conceptualize or understand client issues, it is important that you keep in mind that client issues and needs are complex and multidimensional, consisting of multiple elements. In other words, it is the exception rather than the rule for a client to come in and say, "I'm just having one problem with my best friend. That's it." And even in the case of children, an issue with a best friend usually has many more layers than what appears at first. The child may be angry with the friend or may feel betrayed by the friend. The child may have concluded that he or she is unlikable. The child may be putting up barriers between him- or herself and the friend. The child may have a learning disability that contributes to misperceptions about or miscommunications with the friend or to troubles in the classroom. Or the child may be reacting to a breach in the friendship as a result of something that happened at home, at school, or in the larger community or cultural network. In assessing client concerns, it is helpful to see a broader picture rather than a narrower frame. Both Cook (2012) and Shallcross (2013b) describe ways in which helpers assess client problems through broad lenses. This broad lens, known as a meta-theoretical ecological approach, raises a number of questions about client issues that addresses questions such as *what, who, where, when,* and *how much.* An ecological assessment of client issues encompasses not only dimensions about the individual client but also about the client's environment and the interaction between the two.

ASSESSING KEY COMPONENTS OF CLIENT ISSUES

Using a broad lens framework, we describe six dimensions of client issues, which we illustrate below with sample assessment questions:

1. ***Narratives:*** The narratives and stories that the client constructs about self, others, and the world as well as the literal and evaluative use of language.
   Sample questions
   Tell me your story—what brings you here?
   If this issue was a story, what would the title be? And what character and role do you play in this story?
   What is the story you keep telling yourself about this problem?
   What do you need to re-vision your story? And when that need is met, how will you feel?

2. ***Feelings:*** The emotional responses to the problem that often exaggerate the problem, impede the comprehension of the problem, or become the problem.
   Sample Questions
   What feelings are predominant in this story?
   What feelings help keep this story going?
   What feelings make the story better? What makes it worse?

3. ***Behavior:*** The habits and routines that are inappropriate responses and perhaps contributors to the problem.
   Sample Questions
   What are some specific things that you do or don't do that contribute to the story about this issue?
   How do these things make the issue better? How do they make them worse?
   Are you aware of some things that you do that are helpful? Some that are not helpful?

4. ***Beliefs:*** The client may already have beliefs that contribute to the problem, impede the solution, or become the problem.
   Sample Questions
   What patterns of thinking or self-talk are you aware of that are involved in your story?
   How do these beliefs or thinking patterns make the problem better? How do they make the problem worse?
   How do these beliefs or thinking patterns contribute to this story?

5. ***Interactional and relational patterns:*** The client's established ways of reacting to familiar others, including the miscommunication channels, expectations, self-fulfilling prophesies, coping styles, and so on.

Sample Questions

Who else is involved in this story? For example, if you are the primary character, who are the secondary characters?

Do these persons play a positive or a negative role in this story?

How does your way of relating to these other persons affect the story?

6. ***Contextual factors:*** Time, place, concurrent events, and cultural and sociopolitical issues.

Sample Questions

What is the context surrounding your story?

Can you tell me something about the *where* and the *when* of this story?

What are the cultural factors involved in your story?

These six dimensions of client issues derive from orientations to counseling that we call theoretical approaches or counseling theories. (We summarize the major theoretical approaches in Chapter 9.) Some of these approaches emphasize the role of feelings or beliefs and cognitions in the development and maintenance of client issues, whereas others emphasize the role of behaviors, language, systems, and cultural factors. We take an integrative position that emphasizes the importance of all six dimensions in assessing client issues.

Assessing Key Components of Client Issues: The Case of Manace

In this section, we provide some sample questions to illustrate how a practitioner might use particular questions to assess these six components of client issues and concerns. These sorts of questions help guide the problem-solving sessions and also help the practitioner develop a case conceptualization of the client's presenting issues. We typically recommend beginning with the narrative component as a natural place to start talking with the client about the issue, as in the following case example.

CASE EXAMPLE: MANACE Manace is a tenth-grader at the school in which you are employed as a counselor. He came to the United States during the summer months and this is his first year at your school. You met his mother at the parent–teacher night, and she expressed concern about her son because he seemed to be having nightmares during the night. She said that he wakes up screaming and then has a lot of trouble going back to sleep. Several of his former teachers had reported that he falls asleep frequently during classes. His mother explained to you that they came to the United States following the terrorization of the local village in which they lived. Her husband and his father as well as another sibling had died in the attack on their village. She and Manace came here on the sponsorship of a local church (they had converted to Christianity some years ago). She said that the teachers thought it would be helpful if Manace came to talk with you.

When Manace initially comes to meet with you, he is soft spoken and does not look directly at you, staring instead at the floor. You can sense that he is unsure about why he is there and what to say. You explain to him who you are and what your role is at the school, and you also provide information to him about confidentiality and privacy. You assess his use and understanding of English and note that, even though it is not his primary language, he speaks English fairly fluently and seems to understand what you are saying. You begin the session by asking him about his adjustment to a different country with new customs, language, and so on, and inquire about how he likes the school situation. Gradually he begins talking with you and tells you that he misses his homeland very much and also his father and brother, who perished. He says, "I feel so alone here, and I feel like I need to take care of my mother and be strong for her. That is what my father would wish for me."

You begin your assessment and conceptualization by asking him questions about the *narrative:* "Manace can you tell me the story of what happened to you in your village, what your life was like there? And now, what it is like here?" As the conversation ensues, you follow up with additional narrative questions such as the following: Can you give this story a title? And what role do you play or have in this story? You find that it takes several sessions for Manace to feel comfortable enough with you to share what has happened to him and his mother. Little by little, he adds details and discloses more information.

Gradually you ask him about the feelings, behaviors, and beliefs that are also connected to the narrative. You ask questions like the following:

When you think about what has happened to you and your mom, how do you feel?

Have you noticed anything that you do that makes it better for you to deal with this? What about anything you do that makes this worse for you?

What do you think about this story of your life so far? What conclusions have you drawn from what has happened?

As Manace is able to share his feelings, behaviors, and thoughts related to the situation, you gradually also explore the interactional and relational patterns and cultural and contextual factors surrounding the story. You ask him, for instance, about the most significant people involved in the story. He discusses his mother and also his deceased father and brother. You note that most of his focus is on his family, and while this is culturally relevant given his history, you also want to explore his relationships in his new community. You ask about people he is involved with at school. He mentions that he has very few friends here and feels somewhat "picked on" by a certain group of students. You explore how these students adversely affect his life at school and also explore his ties to the local church that brought them to the community. You ask him to put the story in a contextual place by describing his village both before and after the attack. He notes what a small, peaceful, prosperous place it had been before the attack and how no one had any resources or access to much food after the attack. You also explore contextual factors by asking him to talk about how life in the community here is different and how it fits or does not fit with his worldview. Manace indicates that his country of origin is very family-oriented, whereas the kids here seem to want to do things apart from their families and parents.

As noted earlier, conceptualization of client issues does not come quickly. It comes progressively. You can see from the case example that Manace and the school counselor spent a number of sessions exploring Manace's situation. After your first session with clients, you will begin to have some hunches about them, their world (and how they view it), and their concerns (and how they view them). In subsequent sessions, these initial hunches will be modified as you understand your clients better and as your clients understand and report their world to you. There will be mistaken hunches along the way, and they are to be accepted as part of the process too. Acknowledge and discard them. The remainder of this chapter is an extension of the conceptualizing process—that is, conceptualizing the client's goals. First, you have an opportunity to work with key components of an issue in Application Exercise 8.1.

APPLICATION EXERCISE 8.1

Assessing Key Components of Issues

Select an issue in your life right now that you find troublesome. Make sure that it is an issue that you feel comfortable disclosing to others. This may be a small issue such as finding more time to study for graduate school, or it may be a larger issue such as resolving a long-standing conflict with a significant person. With a partner or in a small group, identify and describe the issue. With the help of your partner or the members of the group, assess the six key components of this issue using the graph below.

Narratives	Feelings	Behaviors	Beliefs	Interactional Patterns	Contextual Factors

PROCESS AND OUTCOME GOALS

The helping process involves two types of goals: process goals and outcome goals. *Process goals* are related to the establishment of therapeutic conditions necessary for client change. These are general goals, such as establishing rapport, providing a nonthreatening setting, and possessing and communicating accurate empathy and unconditional regard. They can be generalized to all client relationships and can be considered universal goals. Process goals are your primary responsibility; you cannot expect your clients to help you establish and communicate something like unconditional regard.

Unlike process goals, outcome goals will be different for each client. *Outcome goals* are the goals directly related to your clients' changes—to be made as a result of the helping process. As you are able to help your clients understand their concerns, you will want to help them understand how counseling can be used to respond to these concerns. The two of you will begin to formulate tentative outcome goals together. As counseling continues, the original goals may be modified through better understanding of the issues and through the development of new attitudes and behaviors that will resolve them. Goal setting should be viewed as a flexible process, always subject to modification and refinement. Most important, outcome goals are shared goals that both you and your clients agree to work toward achieving.

Outcome goals that are visible or observable are more useful because they allow you to know when they have been achieved. However, not all outcome goals are stated as visible goals. For example, consider these two outcome goals:

1. To help your client develop more fully his or her self-actualizing potential.
2. To increase the frequency of positive self-statements at home and at work by 50 percent over the next six weeks.

Both of these could be considered outcome goals. They might even be so closely related as to be the same in terms of outcomes. Your clients may be much more attracted to goals such as developing their self-actualizing potential. You may want to view the development of self-actualizing potential as a composite of many smaller and more specific goals. To state it a little differently, self-actualizing is a hypothetical state that cannot be observed. It can only be inferred through certain visible and audible behaviors. Using this goal, you have no way of knowing the types of activity that your clients will enter into while proceeding toward the goals. As a result, you and your clients will know very little about what they could be doing in the relationship, and you will have no way of assessing progress toward the desired results. Consequently, the first goal listed is not as satisfactory as the second because it does not provide you or your clients with specific guidelines for change.

When outcome goals are stated precisely, both you and your clients have a better understanding of what is to be accomplished. This better understanding permits you to work more directly with your clients' problems or concerns and reduces tangential efforts. Equally important are the benefits you are able to realize in working with specific behavioral goals. You are able to enlist the cooperation of your clients more directly because they are more likely to understand what is to be done. In addition, you are in a better position to select viable techniques and strategies when your clients have specific objectives. Finally, both you and your clients are in a better position to recognize progress—a rewarding experience in its own right.

It is also important to realize that specific observable statements of outcome are now required as part of treatment planning by almost all counseling agencies that receive both state and federal funding because they are clues to client progress and effectiveness of the helper's strategies and interventions. Outcome goals form the basis of *treatment plans* in counseling. A treatment plan describes the client's presenting issues, outcome goals and ways to measure such goals, and intervention strategies. It also includes a projected time line of treatment and is required by most health care insurance companies for third-party reimbursement.

CULTURALLY APPROPRIATE HELPING GOALS

Clients who feel marginalized from the mainstream culture may find mental health services based on long-range goals irrelevant. Clients faced with financial challenges, discrimination, and disempowerment may be far more concerned with survival and physical needs and with short-term goals that are oriented toward resolution of current life issues.

Sue and Sue (2013) noted that culturally diverse clients do not always share many of the values evident in both the goals and the processes of the helping relationship. It is important for helpers to identify their own cultural biases and values and to ensure that they do not steer clients in a direction that disavows the beliefs and values of the client's culture. To do so is to enact a form of racism, sexism, ageism, and so on, because it suggests the helper is in a superior position, while the client is in an inferior position (Sue & Sue, 2013).

The duration of helping goals also plays a role in culturally sensitive goal formation. Many clients from culturally diverse backgrounds do not return to counseling or end the helping process early because they feel the helper is committed only to the pursuit of long-term counseling goals. Long-term goals are often less suitable for some diverse clients, such as those from lower socioeconomic levels or those who want short-term, concrete, direct action results (Sue & Lam, 2002; Sue & Sue, 2013). Application Exercise 8.2 gives you an opportunity to work with culturally relevant outcome goals for a specific client case.

APPLICATION EXERCISE 8.2

Goal Setting and Culture

Aaliyah, a young Muslim woman, is a college junior in the United States who requests a female counselor. In the first few helping sessions, she expresses great reluctance to seek help because her Muslim parents—who still live in Turkey—do not approve of seeking help outside their extended family for problems, believing instead that they are "tests from Allah." She is hesitant to describe her pressing concerns; however, over time, she does reveal that she has a non-Muslim live-in boyfriend. Her parents are coming to the United States to visit her, and she is very afraid of having them find out about this relationship. She is fraught with anxiety about their upcoming visit and is experiencing ambivalence about disclosing or concealing the relationship from them. She is experiencing some sleeplessness and some general "aches and pains" that are new for her.

Identify a few goals that you think might be appropriate in working with Aaliyah, given what you know about her and her cultural affiliation so far.

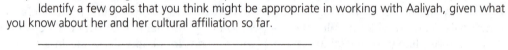

Are your goals specific or vague? How would you and she know when you had achieved these goals? Are your goals process or outcome goals? If they are outcome goals, how would achieving them affect Aaliyah? Are your goals consistent with Aaliyah's cultural affiliation? How do you know? Discuss your goals with your instructor or supervisor.

ELEMENTS OF EFFECTIVE OUTCOME GOALS: SMART GOALS

Effective outcome goals have certain elements in common. These include the following: *i*ntention, *s*pecificity, *me*asurability, *a*ttainability, *r*elevance, and *t*ime-bound. The latter five we just mentioned comprise an acronym known as SMART goals (Doran, 1981). This acronym will help you remember how effective outcome goals are stated. SMART goals make goal statements clear and easy to understand for clients, and they are also useful for documentation in treatment plans and progress notes.

Outcome goals begin with a statement of *intention*—that is, a recognition of what the client hopes to accomplish through counseling. Intentions are often elicited by what is known as the "magic wand question," which helpers pose to clients, as in the following example:

CLIENT: The truth is that I feel like I have sort of messed up my life. I wish I could have a do-over.

HELPER: If I could wave a magic wand, what exactly would you want to happen or what would you want to achieve as a result of this do-over?

CLIENT: Well, I got involved with some people who I guess were a bad influence on me. I got hooked on some drugs and although I am clean now, I wasted a lot of years. My wife divorced me, and I don't have any contact with my two kids right now. I just wish I could start over. I know I can't start over with my ex but I sure would like to be able to start over with my kids.

Once the client is able to identify his or her intention, then the practitioner can help the client refine the outcome goal intention by going through the five elements of SMART goals. Basically this process occurs as follows:

Specific The helper asks the client *what specifically* the client would like to be able to do, and *where* and *when* the client would like to be able to do this. The elements included in this specificity of an effective outcome goal are the behavior to be changed and the conditions in which this change will occur.

Note these elements in the following example:

HELPER: Mario, how do you see yourself starting over with your kids? What exactly would you like to do? And where and when would this occur?

CLIENT: Well, I would like to reestablish some kind of contact with them. I guess initially this would just maybe be a letter or an e-mail to them. I'd like to do this right away.

In the above example, the client's behavior is to write a letter or an e-mail; the conditions in which this will occur are right away and with his kids.

The specificity part of an outcome goal is really important in the helping process because it translates vague intention statements into concrete statements of action.

Measureable The second part of the SMART goal is to help the client define the goal in *measureable* terms. In other words, how will both you and the client know when the goal has been achieved? This happens only when you can establish benchmarks of progress or goal attainment. The measureable part of the SMART goal determines how much or how often the goal will be performed. Consider the following example:

HELPER: Okay, Mario, do you see this as something you do as a one-shot thing, like one letter or e-mail, or do you think several or multiple letters or e-mails are necessary? I guess what I'm asking is how much initial contact do you want to have?

CLIENT: Well, ultimately I would like to be in regular contact with them. But initially, because it's been several years since I have had any contact with either of them, I would probably think in terms of sending an initial letter or e-mail and then following that up with another one.

HELPER: Okay, so it seems like initially you are saying you would have two points of contact via letter or e-mail.

CLIENT: Yup.

Attainability The third part of establishing a SMART outcome goal has to do with *attainability*. Another way to think about attainability is feasibility. The practitioner helps the client determine how feasible the goal is. Is the goal something under the client's control or not? The goal should not be out of the client's reach so the client does not get discouraged about lack of change, but the goal should also set the bar high enough for meaningful change. Consider the following example:

HELPER: Mario, I think you just hit on something we need to talk about. That is how attainable you think this change is. It is one thing to send a couple of letters or e-mails from you to your kids. This seems like something under your control that you can do. It is another thing to reestablish contact with your kids in that you have no control over how and whether they respond; at least, I assume you don't, is that accurate?

CLIENT: Basically. I mean I am legally entitled to have contact with them but since I was the one who stopped responding to their contact, I assume they may be pissed off at me. So you're right, I don't know what to expect after sending a letter. It is possible they might trash it. I guess that's why I thought I might have to send a couple of them so they know I'm sincere now.

HELPER: Okay, so just so we're clear, you can determine what you can do in this situation to change it, but you really can't determine their response.

CLIENT: Correct, I do understand this. But I'm willing to try to do something different on my part.

HELPER: And that is an important thing to grasp and, Mario, I think you do! It seems to me like you want to take responsibility in this situation to try to rectify something in the situation that will help *you* feel better about yourself, but recognizing that you cannot make them respond to you.

CLIENT: Exactly.

Relevance The fourth part of the SMART goal is helping the client ensure that the goal is *relevant*. In other words, is what the client wants to do worthwhile? Is it meaningful? Has the client chosen a goal that really matters? Clients are more likely to work toward goals that are relevant and meaningful to them. Helpers need to make sure that the SMART goal is related to what the client wants ultimately to achieve; in other words, the goal should be connected at a deeper level to the client's overall magic wand intentions, as in the following example:

HELPER: So Mario, I think you also just said something I want to pursue. And that is how relevant is this to you? I mean, let's look at this initial goal of you sending a letter or e-mail or two. I want to make sure you feel this is relevant to your overall intention about wanting to have a do-over in your life that you discussed at the beginning of our session today.

CLIENT: Right. Well you know sending the letter is the initial step. Ultimately I want to have face-to-face contact with my kids, but I know that is not realistic right away given my past behavior.

HELPER: Makes sense to me. I guess I am also asking this: Assuming that your kids wouldn't respond to your letters, at least not initially, does pursuing this still matter to you?

CLIENT: Well sure, it does. Because I have to start somewhere, somehow.

Time-bound The last part of the SMART goal is helping clients identify the time-bound nature of the goal. In other words, the helper assists the client set a time frame for goal achievement. This can overlap with the specificity goal, but sometimes you and the client also want to set a target date for when the client will have completed the SMART goal, as in the following example:

HELPER: Okay, Mario, so let's talk about a time line. When do you plan to have your initial letter of contact sent out?

CLIENT: Really, I'd like to go home today and take care of this.

HELPER: That's super. So you plan to send a letter today. And then how long do you want to wait before sending a follow-up?

CLIENT: I think I would like to give them a couple of weeks to think about it. So if I have not heard anything back from them in three weeks, I would plan to send a follow-up.

HELPER: Sounds like you have really thought through your time frame. And I like your idea of giving them some time but not too much time before you send another follow-up, which I think confirms interest and intentionality on your part.

Try your hand at developing SMART goals in Application Exercise 8.3.

APPLICATION EXERCISE 8.3

Outcome Goals: SMART Goals

Part One

In the following exercise, examples of client outcome goals are presented. Determine which of the five elements of a SMART outcome goal may be missing. After each example, list the missing parts by using S for specificity, M for measurability, A for attainability, R for relevance, and T for time-bound. Feedback is provided at the end of the exercise.

Identify the missing parts of a SMART goal in the following three outcome goals:

1. To decrease temper tantrums.
2. To increase exercise.
3. To decrease the number of arguments at home with my (the client's) partner in order to improve long-range marital satisfaction.

Feedback

1. This goal states the behavior to be changed but needs to include the conditions under which the change will occur to meet the specificity criterion. It also needs to include how much or how often the tantrums will decrease to meet the measurability criterion. The measurability criterion needs to be manageable enough to make the goal attainable. A statement of purpose would ensure the goal's relevance. How would reducing temper tantrums help the client in the client's family and school settings? Finally, the goal needs to include a time frame to meet the time-bound criterion.
2. This goal again states the behavior to be changed but needs to include the conditions under which this change will occur to meet the specificity criterion. It also needs to include how much the client will exercise to meet the measurability criterion. This level of change should be enough to be meaningful but not so drastic that it is not attainable. We assume, but it should be stated explicitly, how increasing exercise will improve the client's physical and emotional well-being, thus ensuring relevance of the goal to the client. Finally, the goal needs to have a time line to meet the time-bound criterion.
3. This goal statement is specific: It states what the client wants to do and with whom and where. But it lacks a statement of measurability: reduction of arguments by how much? And it also lacks a related attainability criterion: Is this feasible? It does include a statement of relevance: helping the long-term growth of marital satisfaction for this couple. But it lacks a time frame.

(Continued)

Part Two

In this part of the application exercise, your task is to develop a SMART goal for yourself! We suggest doing this activity with a partner who can help talk you through the exercise. Start by identifying an *intention* you wish to make in your own life. Address the following question: What do I want to achieve? Next, translate this intention into a SMART goal using the following SMART Goal Worksheet.

SMART Goal Worksheet	
Goal Characteristics	**Your SMART Goal**
Specific: Identify what, where, when, and by and with whom.	
Measureable: Identify how much or how often.	
Attainable: Identify if your goal is realistic given time and available resources.	
Relevant: Identify the importance of your goal to your long-term intentions.	
Time-bound: Identify the time frame and target date for goal completion.	

TRANSLATING VAGUE CONCERNS INTO SPECIFIC GOALS: SUBGOALS

Rarely does a client begin by requesting assistance in achieving specific behavior changes. Instead of saying, "I want to be able to talk to people without getting nervous," the client is likely to say, "I'm shy." In other words, a personal characteristic has been described rather than the ways in which the characteristic is experienced. It then becomes the helper's job to help the client describe the ways in which the characteristic could be changed.

Taking nonspecific concerns and translating them into specific goal statements is no easy task for the helper. You must understand the nature of the client's concern and the conditions under which it occurs before the translation can begin.

What can you expect of yourself and your clients in terms of setting specific goals? First, the goals that are set can never be more specific than your understanding and the client's understanding of the problem. This means that, at the outset of counseling, goals are likely to be nonspecific and nonbehavioral. But nonspecific goals are better than no goals at all. As you and your client explore the nature of a particular concern, the type of goal(s) appropriate to the problem should become increasingly clear. This clarification permits both of you to move in the direction of identifying specific behaviors that—if changed—would alter the problem in a positive way. These specific behaviors can then be formulated into goal statements; as you discuss the client's problems in more detail, you can gradually add the circumstances in which to perform the behaviors and how much or how often the target behaviors can be altered.

After you and your client have established the desired outcome goal together, you can identify some action steps that might help the client achieve the overall goal or target. These action steps can be thought of as subgoals. Subgoals consist of a series of smaller or intermediate steps or tasks that help the client perform the desired behaviors gradually. When several subgoals are identified, they are usually arranged in a sequence or hierarchy. The client completes one subgoal successfully before moving on to another one. By gradually completing the activities represented by subgoals in a successful manner, the client's motivation and energy to change may be reinforced and maintained. Successfully completing subgoals may also reduce potential failure experiences by giving the client a greater sense of control and empowerment and by helping the client achieve the overall desired change in a more gradual manner. Application Exercise 8.4 gives you a chance to work with subgoals.

APPLICATION EXERCISE 8.4

Outlining SMART Goals: Subgoals

Assume that Brent has come to you for counseling and is complaining of insomnia. As you and Brent probe the facets of his concerns, you can consider the specific changes Brent would like to make. Gradually, these changes can be developed into an outline of desired goals. We refer to this as an outline because the major headings (I and II) represent the two overall or primary outcome goals for Brent; the subheadings reflect the subgoals or activities that Brent can perform to achieve the overall goal gradually. Remember that goal setting is a flexible process and that the goals listed in this outline might change as counseling with Brent progresses.

Outcome Goal I To be able to go to sleep within an hour of going to bed at least four nights of the week at home, starting next week, in order to improve alertness for Brent on the job.

A. To identify in writing all his prior solutions for trying to go to sleep (counting sheep, daydreaming, eating a snack, etc.).

B. To substitute these prior activities with trying-to-stay-awake activities.

C. _____

  _____

D. _____

  _____

Outcome Goal II To acquire another job at a higher salary range within the next year in order to improve standard of living and job satisfaction.

List below the type of subgoals that would be likely to help Brent achieve this second outcome goal:

A. _____

  _____

B. _____

  _____

C. _____

  _____

D. _____

  _____

(Continued)

Notice the process by which outcome goals are established:

1. They begin as overall goals that are directly related to the client's specific or general concerns or descriptions of a set of problems; they are consistent with the client's culture.
2. Specific and observable subgoals are established that—if achieved—permit the realization of the overall goals.

Thus, goal setting moves from general to specific goals; the specific goals are directly related to the general goal, and the general goal is a reflection of the client's problems and needs presented to the helper.

CLIENT RESISTANCE TO GOAL SETTING AND THE STAGES OF CHANGE MODEL

Occasionally, a client may be hesitant about setting goals or reluctant to work toward change. For instance, after completing a helping session with her client, a helper said, "This was the fifth interview, and I still can't get him to talk about goals." When this happens, the helper must deal with the question "What's the client resisting?"

In working with clients who are resistant to goals, it is helpful to realize that such behavior is purposeful. That is, what the client does or avoids doing achieves some desirable result for the client. Consequently, you may find that the client who resists setting goals may be protecting the behavior that is in need of modification because that behavior is doing something desirable. An example is the chronic smoker. Although an individual may recognize the negative consequences of smoking, he or she also clings to the habit, believing that it is a helpful way to deal with a tense situation, that it is relaxing, that it increases enjoyment of a good meal, and so forth. Almost all addictions to substances are examples of this. Another example of this is avoidance. Although some clients may wish to change something, their avoidance of the very thing they want to change can feel so protective that the negative consequences engendered by the avoidance outweigh the potential positive consequences of change.

It becomes your task to get clients to identify what they gain from their current behavioral and interpersonal patterns. In so doing, you may determine whether that gain or outcome can be achieved in more desirable ways. For example, a young student may throw paper airplanes out the school window in order to receive attention from peers. Gaining attention may be a desirable outcome. It is the method that is the problem. Therefore, you and your client may consider more appropriate means for gaining increased attention other than throwing paper airplanes out the school window! In a more complicated scenario, consider the student or worker who engages in procrastination, missing critical deadlines, resulting in poorer grades or negative job evaluations. For some clients, such real or imagined negative feedback may motivate them to meet deadlines, but for others, the gain of putting off the task once again may actually mask the potential pain of a lower grade or lower evaluation. Some clients may present with interpersonal patterns that may seem problematic, such as nagging their friends or partner, yet the control they seek from such behavior stops them from thinking seriously about changing the pattern.

A useful way to think about client resistance to goal setting is to reflect on how resistant most people are to change itself. Outcome goals request clients to change. Prochaska, DiClemente, and Norcross (1992) developed a well-tested model of change called the *stages of change model* that helps to explain client resistance to change. Essentially, the stages of change model represents "specific constellations of attitudes, intentions, and behaviors related to an individual's readiness in the cycle of change" (Prochaska & Norcross, 2014, p. 459). Their model has six stages of change that a client progresses through:*

1. *Precontemplation:* The client is either not aware of a need to change or does not want to change; he or she often views the problem as belonging to someone else. When clients at this stage of change show up for counseling, it is often at the request of someone else. Clients at the precontemplation stage are not aware of their problems and also unaware of any risks of their behaviors. A large number of persons who engage in risky or unhealthy behaviors fall into this category. Clients at this stage of change need to acknowledge there is an issue and increase their awareness of the negative aspects of the issue in order to move ahead to the next stage of change (Prochaska & Norcross, 2014).

2. *Contemplation:* The client becomes aware of a need to change and thinks about it but has not decided to do anything about it. Some people can stay "stuck" in contemplation for years, often because, in weighing the pros and cons of change, they feel ambivalent about change itself, and such ambivalence keeps them stuck. To move ahead to the next stage, clients in contemplation "must avoid the trap of obsessive rumination for years—what we call chronic contemplation—and make a firm decision to begin to take action" (Prochaska & Norcross, 2014, p. 460). One of the ways that practitioners can help clients do so is through the use of baby steps. Sometimes, a life crisis such as a poor health diagnosis or the death of a loved one can also spark a move out of chronic contemplation.

3. *Preparation:* The client has decided to take some action in the near future, perhaps as soon as the next month or two. Also in this stage, the client has perhaps tried some action in the past but was unsuccessful. Helpers can detect clients who are in this stage because they report some small behavioral changes that they have already made and because they have started to move out of ambivalence about change as they recognize that the advantages of change outweigh the risks of not changing. As Prochaska and Norcross (2014, p. 461) observe, "Like anyone on the verge of momentous actions, individuals in the preparation stage need to set goals and priorities. In addition, they need to dedicate themselves to an action plan they choose." As you can see, clients at the preparation stage are more likely to be able to set outcome goals, while those clients still stuck in precontemplation and contemplation tend to benefit more from process goals.

4. *Action:* The client is ready to change and has usually begun to take some action toward the desired outcome, although the issue has not yet been successfully resolved. However, clients in this stage are highly motivated to do the work and make the commitment necessary to change the problem. The stages of change model assumes that clients are in the action stage if they have successfully altered a problem behavior for a period of 1 day to 6 months (Prochaska & Norcross, 2014). Clients in the action stage often terminate the helping process quickly but appropriately because they implement action effectively. Clients at this stage tend to "recognize the pitfalls that might undermine continued action, whether these are cognitive, behavioral, emotional, and/or environmental" (Prochaska & Norcross, 2014, p. 461).

---

*From Prochaska and Norcross. *Systems of psychotherapy: A transtheoretical analysis,* 8th ed. © 2014 Cengage Learning. Reproduced by permission. www.cengage.com/permissions

5. *Maintenance:* The client reaches his or her goals through various action plans, and the client maintains the change for a period of at least 6 months. Now the focus is on consolidating the gains that have been made and on preventing relapses. However, maintenance is not a "static stage" but rather "a continuation, not an absence, of change" (Prochaska & Norcross, 2014, p. 461). For some individuals, especially those with chronic issues, maintenance becomes a lifelong stage—or at least needs to become a lifelong stage lest these persons fall into relapse mode. "Stabilizing behavior change and avoiding relapse are the hallmarks of maintenance," according to Prochaska and Norcross (2014, p. 461).

6. *Relapse and Recycling:* As Prochaska and Norcross (2014) indicate, many persons taking action do not maintain the change after the first or even second attempt. Often, clients maintain a gain for a short time, but the gains do not endure for the 6-month period required by the maintenance phase we discussed earlier. This is especially evident in the treatment of serious clinical disorders and addiction issues. When relapse occurs, many of these clients return to helpers for recycling—also referred to by some as booster sessions. For example, in the couples counseling I do, it is not uncommon for couples to come back for refresher sessions when they are starting to lose ground on changes they have made in prior sessions.

It is important to note that the stages of change model is not presumed to be a linear model in which people move through one stage to the next in a progressive fashion; it is instead a cyclical model in which clients spiral through change. For example, when clients relapse, they may recycle back to a much earlier stage of change, such as precontemplation—or, more likely, contemplation or preparation. Prochaska and Norcross note that "[t]he spiral pattern suggests that most relapsers do not revolve endlessly in circles and that they do not regress all the way back to where they began. Instead, each time relapsers recycle through the stages, they potentially learn from their mistakes and can try something different the next time around" (2014, p. 463). As you can imagine from this spiral pattern, when clients do relapse and regress to an earlier stage, the goals of helping will usually shift back with them. For example, this process may mean that the helper has to become more attentive once again to process goals in order to help the client recover from the distress of falling back. It may also mean that the client and helper revisit the outcome goals and devise altered or entirely new ones.

As an example of this model, consider a person who has felt consistently anxious for the last few years. This anxiety is chronically debilitating in that it prevents her from doing certain things that she finds particularly anxiety-arousing. She comes to a mental health practitioner and reveals that she has been feeling this way for several years. During this time, she has sought out a lot of information online and from books about anxiety. But it has taken her two years to decide to seek the help of a helper and to inquire about the use of medication. When this client was in precontemplation, she was not aware of having an issue with anxiety nor was she aware of its consequences for her. When she did become aware of this but did not yet do anything about it, she moved into the contemplation stage. As she sought information from books and online and as she thought about what the information meant to her, she moved into the preparation stage. When she visited the practitioner and sought help and wondered about using medication, she had moved into the action stage. When—through the assistance of the helper—she engages in behaviors to resolve the anxiety, she will move into the maintenance stage, at which point her task will be to continue her action plans to reduce the anxiety.

Research on the stages of change model has the following implications with respect to client resistance to change (Prochaska & Norcross, 2014):

1. The stages of change model can predict client dropout from counseling across a variety of client issues. Most of the clients who drop out early are in the precontemplation stage.

2. The amount of progress clients make during counseling depends on the particular stage of change they are in at the beginning of the helping process. Clients in precontemplation and contemplation have not yet made a commitment to change. Clients in the preparation stage have made a tentative commitment to change but are only ready for small steps toward the desired goal. As Prochaska and Norcross observe, "the further along clients are in the stages of change at the beginning of therapy, the more quickly they can be predicted to progress" (p. 463).

Although people in the action stage are ready to work quickly toward an outcome goal, they represent a minority of clients actually seeking help. As a result, to work effectively with clients in the precontemplation, contemplation, and preparation stages, helpers must be more proactive in the change intervention strategies they use, and they also need to match their change strategies to each client's stage of change (see also Chapter 9). It is also useful to help clients set goals that are both realistic and feasible so they may be more able to move from one stage of change to the next (Prochaska & Norcross, 2014).

A recent self-help book that I recommend for my own clients, *Changeology*, has been written by John Norcross (2012). It summarizes the 30 years of scientific research on the stages of change model and helps clients define and work toward their goals in very concrete ways. A unique feature of this book is the description of pragmatic change strategies that clients can actually use to make progress toward their goals and prevent relapse. The print edition of the book is also supplemented by online support and resources.

Sometimes, clients resist attempts to establish goals because they feel that the helper (either overtly or subtly) is pushing them in a certain direction. As we mentioned earlier, this may be a particular issue with clients who feel marginalized. Unless clients can determine some personal goals of counseling, the probability of any change is minimal. You can avoid creating client resistance to goals by encouraging active client participation in the goal-setting process. We recommend working with the stages of change model by completing Application Exercise 8.5.

APPLICATION EXERCISE 8.5

Stages of Change

Review the stages of change model presented in this chapter. Select two or three current issues in your own life. Apply the stages of change model to each of these issues. What do you notice about the stages of change with respect to these two or three issues? What conclusions can you draw from this activity? You may want to complete this activity by yourself, with a partner, or in a small discussion group in your class.

CLIENT PARTICIPATION IN GOAL SETTING

Often, goal setting is construed to mean that you listen to the client, make a mental assessment of the problem, and prescribe a solution or goal. In fact, such a procedure is doomed to failure. The nature of the helping process is such that the client needs to be involved in the establishment of goals. Otherwise, the client's participation is directionless and renders the client a nonparticipant. As difficult as change is for human beings, it is compounded when clients are left out of the change process! An example will illustrate this idea. A beginning helper was seeing a client who was overweight, self-conscious about her appearance, reluctant to enter into social relationships with others because of this self-consciousness, and very lonely. The helper informed the client that one goal would be for her (the client) to lose one to three pounds per week under a doctor's supervision. With this, the client became highly defensive and rejected the helper's goal, saying, "You sound just like my mother."

Goal setting is highly personal. It requires a great deal of effort and commitment on the client's part. Therefore, the client must select goals that are important to the client. In the preceding example, the client's resistance could have been prevented if the helper had moved more slowly, permitting the client to identify for herself the significance of her weight and the importance of potential weight loss for herself. The helper also needs to remain open to the possibility that there are other outcomes desired by this client. The helper presumed that the goal or desired change involved weight loss. In this particular situation, after several sessions, the client disclosed that she was being sexually molested by her father and still living at home. Then she identified resolution of this situation and related trauma as her desired goal for counseling.

Sperry, Carlson, and Kjos (2003) suggested some useful questions to elicit client participation in the goal-setting process:

- How have you tried to make things better—and with what results?
- How do you think the issue is best handled? What do you see as your part in this change process? What do you see as my part in this process?
- When will things begin to change and get better for you?
- What will your life look like when things get resolved for you—and how will this feel? (p. 68)

Finally, we stress again the importance of the client's cultural beliefs and values in deciding what goals to pursue for counseling. In the preceding example, consider the fact that most European-American girls and women in the United States are preoccupied with weight and body image in a way that many men and girls and women of color are not. It is up to the client, not the helper in the mainstream culture, to decide what goals are relevant and appropriate.

Summary

In this chapter, we entered into the therapeutically active portion of the helping process. In addition to the interactive process that takes place between helper and client, the helper begins to establish an internal conceptualization process in which the client's world is studied. That study is both within the client's context and in the larger context of the family, the culture, and the society in which the client lives.

Clients become involved in this study—often quite naturally—as they unfold their experiences, feelings, and thoughts about themselves, others, and their current world. Interwoven in this process is an emerging awareness of a different or perhaps better set of conditions, which become translated into goals. Some of these goals are related to the helping relationship. Others are more related to the client's world. Through the recognition and establishment of these goals, the helper begins to understand the direction counseling will take and can begin to help the client reach that same awareness. Helpers assist clients in translating issues and vague intentions into outcome goals that are SMART, that is, specific, measureable, attainable, relevant, and time-bound. In conceptualizing client issues and goals, it is useful to remember the stages of change model (Prochaska, DiClemente, & Norcross, 1992). Not all clients are ready for change or for change in big ways. We continue this exploration of the process of change in the following chapter, where our focus turns to the use of helping intervention strategies.

Reflective Questions

1. Both the client and the helper bring their worlds into the helping session. We indicated that goal setting evolves out of an understanding of the client's world. How might the helper's world affect that process of goal setting? Should the helper be concerned about this issue? Explain your answer.

2. In the beginning of this chapter, we discussed how unmet childhood needs can be reactivated in adult life. As an exercise—first for yourself and then with a client—consider completing the following question posed by Steinem (1992): "Write down on [a piece of paper] . . . the things you wish you had received in your childhood and did not" (pp. 104–105). When you have completed this exercise, you have discovered your own needs now.

3. How might the needs of a financially challenged low-income client differ from the needs of a client with a high-paying and secure job? What about the needs of a company manager who was recently laid off due to downsizing? How would these needs affect the outcome goals?

4. Discuss the stages of change model with respect to several different client issues. For example, consider this model with a child who is afraid to come to school, an adolescent who became pregnant after a night of intoxication and does not know what to do, an adult who is addicted to painkillers after suffering a severe back injury at work, and an elderly person who is starting to suffer from dementia and does not want to move out of her home.

MyCounselingLab

For each exercise, log on to MyCounselingLab.

1. Go to the Theories of Counseling collection and choose "Assessments as Basis for Interventions." After watching this video clip, respond in your class or with a partner to the following questions:
   a. Given these video clips, what can you say about this client's world?
   b. Can you identify specific needs of this client? Can you also identify various dimensions of the client's presenting problems?

2. Stay with the Theories of Counseling collection and watch the following two selections:
   a. "Assessing the Stage." How does Dr. Norcross assess which stage of change the client presents within his cocaine addiction?
   b. "Client Responsibility." How does Dr. Norcross enhance the client's motivation to change with respect to his alcohol use? Can you determine from this clip an outcome goal that the client commits to pursue?

3. Locate the Addictions/Substance Abuse collection. Select the video clip "Arriving at Goals through Commitment." After watching this clip, respond to the following questions:
   a. Which of the five stages of change does the client appear to be in at this time? Explain your answer.
   b. How would you describe the client's intention statement?
   c. Which of the five elements of SMART goals did you see displayed in this scenario?
   d. What kinds of process goals between Dr. Norcross and the client were evident to you? What kinds of specific actions did you see Dr. Norcross do to establish these process goals with this client?

Recommended Readings

Cook, E. (2012). *Understanding people in context: The ecological perspective in counseling.* Washington DC: American Counseling Association.

DiClemente, C. C., Doyle, S. R., & Donovan, D. (2009). Predicting treatment seekers' readiness to change their drinking behavior in the COMBINE study. *Alcoholism Clinical and Experimental Research, 33,* 879–892.

DiClemente, C. C., Schumann, K., Greene, P. & Earley, M. (2011). A transtheoretical model perspective on change: Process focused interventions for mental health and substance abuse. In D. Cooper (Ed.), *Principles of intervention in mental health— substance use.* London: Radcliff.

Egan, G. (2014). *The skilled helper* (10th ed.). Belmont, CA: Brooks/Cole, Cengage.

Norcross, J. C. (2012). *Changeology: 5 steps to realizing your goals and resolutions.* New York, NY: Simon & Schuster.

Prochaska, J., & Norcross, J. C. (2014). *Systems of psychotherapy: A transtheoretical analysis,* (10th ed.). Belmont, CA: Brooks/Cole, Cengage.

Shallcross, L. (2013b, April). Building a more complete client picture. *Counseling Today,* 31–39.

Sue, D. W., & Sue, D. (2013). *Counseling the culturally diverse.* Hoboken, NJ: John Wiley & Sons.

Using Integrative Helping Strategies and Interventions

In the previous chapter, we mentioned a variety of factors that contribute to client issues, including feelings, behaviors, beliefs, language, interactional patterns, and cultural factors. To deal effectively with such complex issues, helpers need to equip themselves with a variety of strategies and interventions designed to work with all the various ways in which concerns are manifested. We believe that helpers who have a variety of tools to use with clients are in a better position to address client issues than those who are limited in their knowledge and experience to a single approach.

In this chapter, we examine a number of helping strategies or interventions. Those presented here have been selected because they are used by helpers of varying theoretical orientations and because—when used in conjunction with each other—they treat the whole person. The strategies we describe are used to help clients work with (1) feelings, (2) behaviors, (3) beliefs and attitudes, (4) language and narratives, (5) interactional patterns and relationships, and (6) cultural and social systems. Table 9.1 illustrates a variety of counseling strategies that are based on different theoretical orientations to helping. This table also shows manifestations, or markers, of six dimensions of client issues. The theoretical orientations, highlighted in bold at the top of Table 9.1, constitute the major approaches to counseling practices and interventions. Although these theoretical orientations approach the helping process, the helping relationship, and specific helping interventions in different ways, each theoretical orientation has "useful dimensions" (Corey, 2013, p. 5).

Sharf (2012) has concluded that practitioners today use different parts of various theories in actual practice and have become much more integrative in their work. Efforts to integrate theoretical approaches stem primarily from the increased awareness that each

TABLE 9.1 Treatment Strategies and Corresponding Manifestations of Client Problems

Affective	Behavioral	Cognitive	Language	Systemic	Cultural
Person-centered therapy, gestalt therapy, body awareness therapies, psychodynamic therapies, experiential therapies, emotion-focused therapies.	*Operant conditioning, counter-conditioning, social learning, multimodal therapy.*	*Rational-emotive therapy, cognitive therapy, transactional analysis, reality therapy.*	*Acceptance and commitment therapy, social constructivism, narrative therapy, solution-focused brief therapy.*	*Structural therapy, strategic family therapy, intergenerational systems.*	*Multicultural counseling; cross-cultural counseling: gender-sensitive therapy.*
Active listening, empathy, positive regard, genuineness, awareness techniques, empty chair, fantasy, dream work, bioenergetics, biofeedback, free association, transference analysis, dream analysis, focusing techniques, emotional awareness and regulation techniques.	Guided imagery, role-playing, self-monitoring, physiological recording, behavioral contracting, assertiveness training, social skills training, systematic desensitization, contingency contracting, action planning, counterconditioning, relaxation and stress management, exposure therapies.	A-B-C-D-E analysis; reframing; automatic thinking and cognitive distortions; cognitive restructuring; ego grams; script analysis; choice theory and personal responsibility; wants, direction, evaluation, and planning (WDEP) system.	Cognitive defusion, metaphors, mindfulness, behavioral tasks, commitment to valued actions, identification of self-narratives, re-storying and restructuring of symbolic meaning of narratives and resulting conclusions.	Instructing about subsystems; enmeshment and differentiation; addressing triangulation, alliances, and coalitions; role restructuring; clarifying interactional systems; reframing; prescribing the problem (paradox); altering interactional sequences; genogram analysis; coaching; defining boundaries; shifting triangulation patterns.	Meta-theoretical, multimodal, culturally based interventions; focus on worldviews, cultural orientation, cultural identity; liberation and empowerment perspectives; culturally sensitive language, metaphors, rituals, practices, and resources; collaboration; networking; consciousness raising; advocacy.

Manifestations:
Emotional expressiveness and impulsivity, instability of emotions, use of emotions in problem solving and decision making, emotional constriction and/or lack of emotional regulation.

Manifestations:
Involvement in activities; strong goal orientation; need to be constantly doing something; receptive to activity, action, getting something done, perhaps at expense of others.

Manifestations:
Intellectualizing; logical, rational, systematic behavior; reasoned; computer-like approach to problem solving and decision making; receptive to logic, ideas, theories, concepts, analysis, and synthesis.

Manifestations:
Cognitive fusion, evaluative and comparative language, experiential avoidance, overreliance on reasoning, overidentification with one's story or narrative to construct a particular sense of self or a single "truth."

Manifestations:
Enmeshed or disengaged relationships, rigid relationship boundaries and rules, dysfunctional interpersonal patterns.

Manifestations:
Level of acculturation; type or worldview; level of cultural identity; bi- or trilingual; presenting problems are, to some degree, culturally based.

Source: Adapted From Harold Hackney, Sherry Cormier, *The Professional Helper: A Process Guide to Helping* (7th ed.). Table 7.1, p. 120, 2013. Reproduced by permission of Pearson Education, Inc.

singular approach may be inadequate in and of itself and the recognition that each approach offers something of potential value to clients. A recent poll of psychotherapy experts who were impaneled to forecast trends in psychotherapy found that cognitive-behavioral, multicultural, and integrative theories were likely to increase the most in popularity and use (Norcross, Pfund, & Prochaska, 2013). We touch briefly on various theoretical approaches in this chapter because they are linked intrinsically to different helping strategies and interventions, but for thorough explorations of the major theoretical approaches to helping, we urge you to consult a number of useful texts that focus specifically on theories of counseling and therapy (see Corey, 2013; Prochaska & Norcross, 2014; Sharf, 2012; Sommers-Flanagan & Sommers-Flanagan, 2012; Wedding & Corsini, 2014).

WORKING WITH CLIENT FEELINGS

Why do people have feelings, and how do they relate to well-being? In discussing this topic, Greenberg (2012) offers the following perspective: Feelings and emotions (also referred to as affect) are important to our well-being. Rather than being an inconvenience, feelings are signals that give us clues about our relationships and communication with others. In his address following receipt of the Psychology Award for Distinguished Professional Contributions to Applied Research, Greenberg further notes that emotions can be both our greatest friends and also our greatest enemies! He concludes that emotions are an adaptive component of human functioning and not "simply secondary to cognition" (p. 698). He states, "To access their adaptive benefits, emotions need to be processed rather than avoided or controlled" (Greenberg, 2012, p. 698).

An important part of working with client feelings involves the recent concept of *emotional intelligence (EQ)*—that is, the art of learning when and how to express a feeling and when expression of a feeling will not help. EQ can be contrasted with IQ, the standard measure of intellectual intelligence. Someone could have a high IQ, for example, but a low EQ. Emotional intelligence is rooted in the brain, particularly the prefrontal cortex, a sizable part of the brain located just behind the forehead (G. Miller, 2006). Emotional intelligence forms the basis of the interventions we suggest here for working with client feelings. These interventions support clients' work with their feelings in three ways that specifically promote EQ:

1. To identify and assess feelings through *awareness interventions*
2. To elicit and express feelings through *expression interventions*
3. To understand and regulate feelings through *reflection and regulation interventions* (Greenberg, 2011)

The strategies we present are derived primarily from experiential theoretical approaches to helping, such as gestalt therapy, and from psychodynamic and interpersonal therapies.

Identifying and Assessing Feelings: Awareness of Feelings Interventions

Helping clients become aware of their feelings enables them to identify what they are feeling deep down in their core and helps them in problem solving. Awareness of feelings is fundamental to all affective interventions with clients (Greenberg, 2011).

We describe two strategies to help clients identify and assess their feelings: verbal leads and emotion logs.

VERBAL LEADS One strategy to encourage clients to identify feelings is often simply accomplished by using *verbal leads* or open-ended questions that focus on client feelings and that help clients elicit different facets of their emotions. Some examples of verbal leads to identify feelings are

> Where do you experience that feeling in your body?
>
> If your feeling were a book or a movie, what would the title be?
>
> Does this feeling seem new or old? If old, how long have you experienced these feelings?

EMOTION LOGS You can also use a daily *emotion log* to help clients identify feelings. You can easily construct an emotion log for a client. List the days of the week across the top of the page, in the horizontal direction. In the vertical direction on the left side of the page, from top to bottom, list a number of different affect words. You can obtain these affect words directly from our affect word lists in Chapter 5. When the clients have identified and tracked their feelings on this log, they can bring the completed log to the next session. Together, the helper and client can explore the following questions to assess the feelings recorded on the log, as recommended by Greenberg (2002, pp. 128–129):

1. What is your name for the emotion?
2. Was it a more sudden onset emotion or a more enduring mood?
3. Did you have body sensations with your emotion?
4. Did thoughts come into your mind?
5. Did you act or feel like doing something or expressing something?
6. What brought on the emotion or mood?
7. What information is your emotion giving you?

As Greenberg (2002) points out, changing one's emotion requires experiencing it: "To change in therapy, clients cannot just talk intellectually about themselves and their feelings, they need to viscerally experience what they talk about . . . as total suppression of emotion is unhealthy" (pp. 8, 10). In the next section, we describe three interventions to help clients elicit and express their emotional experience: increasing body awareness of feelings, breathing, and incomplete sentences.

Eliciting and Expressing Feelings: Expression of Feelings Interventions

It's important to realize that expression of feelings is not synonymous with venting or catharsis. Rather, as Greenberg (2011) suggests, these interventions help clients overcome prior avoidance to experiencing feelings and also express primary emotions that were previously constricted (p. 75). However, there is no universal rule about the therapeutic usefulness of always having clients express feelings in therapy. In life, containing feelings is often more useful interpersonally than expressing them (Greenberg, 2011, p. 75). Generally speaking, these interventions in therapy are designed to help clients approach emotion and also learn to tolerate uncomfortable emotions. They are offered to help clients be in "live contact" with their feelings during a helping session (Greenberg, 2011, p. 75).

INCREASING BODY AWARENESS OF FEELINGS Clients can learn to get in touch with their feelings through the use of strategies that encourage greater awareness of what is occurring within one's body. When a person feels tense, it is usually seen or experienced in the contraction of a muscle or group of muscles. Continued tension results in pain, such as a headache or numbness, which occurs from nerve pressure accumulated from the tension. Smith (1985) has recommended the following intervention to help clients acquire body awareness:

> Helper: Close your eyes and just relax for a few moments. Breathe comfortably. (Pause.) (Repeat the directions to relax and the pauses until the client seems to be involved in the exercise.) Check out your body to see what you find. Note anything in your body which calls attention to itself. Just monitor your body, inch by inch, from the tips of your toes to the top of your head and down to the tips of your fingers. In particular, note any hot spots, cold spots, tight or tense muscles, pains, tingling, or anything happening in your body. Don't try to edit or change anything; just be aware and note what is happening. (Pause for a minute or two.) Take your time. When you are finished, open your eyes. (Wait until client opens her or his eyes.) (p. 107)

Following this, the helper asks the client to describe whatever he or she noticed.

Perls (1973), a gestalt therapist, suggested that clients can also identify and express feelings by being asked to exaggerate a particular body action. This strategy is useful because people often make bodily movements that suggest an action that reflects a current and present emotion; it is considered a "slip of the body," much in the way a person says something unintended yet meaningful, as in a verbal "slip of the tongue." As Smith (1985) noted, by inviting the client to repeat the action in an exaggerated form, the meaning of the body action usually becomes apparent. Smith (1985) gave the following illustration:

> An example of this is the patient who, while talking about her ex-lover, begins slightly swinging her leg which is crossed over the other leg, knee on knee. The therapist asks her to be aware of her leg and she says, "Oh, I'm just nervous today." So the therapist asks her to exaggerate the movement. She swings her leg in a larger arc, with more force, and declares, "I must want to kick him. But I didn't know I was angry today. Oh, I just remembered what he said last week. I am mad at him!" (p. 110)

By asking the client to exaggerate the body movement, the helper encourages the client to see that she has both repressed and inhibited a feeling of anger. When a client's movement is directed toward oneself—for example, if she has been chewing her cheek—the exaggeration of this would also illustrate how she had taken the feeling of anger toward the ex-lover and directed it toward herself. Additional strategies to promote body awareness in clients can be found in a primer on gestalt counseling and therapy by Joyce and Sills (2010).

BREATHING Another way to help clients get in touch with and express feelings is through work on *breathing*. According to Lowen (1965), a bioenergetics therapist, every emotional problem is manifested in some sort of disturbance in breathing. Perls (1969), the founder of gestalt therapy, connected shallow breathing and sighing with depression, yawning with boredom, and restricted breath with anxiety. Smith (1985) observed that effective breathing is necessary for vitality; that insufficient breathing leaves the person in a state like "a fire with an inadequate draft" (p. 119). Healthy breathing involves the entire body (p. 120).

There are numerous ways to work with breathing. The first is to point out to the client the occasions on which he or she holds a breath or breathes in a shallow or constricted manner. For some clients, it may be useful to teach them the art of deep breathing, in which the breath is started (inhaled) in the abdomen, moves up through the chest, and is released thoroughly in the exhalation, often with the aid of a vocal sound. When clients can breathe deeply and do not hold back or interrupt the breathing cycle, they are more likely to experience what they feel. Another way to increase breathing awareness is to instruct the client to count the "in" breath and the "out" breath (Gilligan, 1997). For example, you might say, "As the breath comes in through the nostrils, filling up the lower diaphragm, say silently, 'Breathing in, one.' As the breath goes out, say silently, 'Breathing out, one'" (p. 76). The next breath is counted as two, then three, and so on. Other clients may use word mantras with their breath, such as *let in* on the "in" breath and *go out* on the "out" breath.

Gilligan (1997) noted that the restriction of breathing is often such a chronic activity that it becomes unconscious, or without awareness. He has suggested asking clients to recall an "antagonistic image, thought, or a feeling" and whether they sense it "inside" or "outside" their breath (p. 76). He observed that usually "difficult processes are experienced outside the breath" (p. 76). When the difficult experience is brought inside the breath, an important shift in relationship to the troubling experience usually occurs.

One of the advantages of breathing interventions is that breathing is a universal phenomenon. All people—regardless of differences in race, gender, age, class, religion, sexual orientation, and so on—breathe. Many have learned, over time, to shut down their breathing, resulting in a variety of somatic and emotional symptoms. At the same time, certain medical conditions, such as low blood pressure, insulin-dependent diabetes, recent surgery, or pain, may make breathing interventions contraindicated without the expressed approval of the client's health care provider (Cormier, Nurius, & Osborn, 2013).

INCOMPLETE SENTENCES   Another possible intervention to help clients elicit and express feelings is with the use of *incomplete sentences*. Usually, after some work has been done on breathing, the helper "feeds" the client with an incomplete sentence stem and then the client finishes the sentence with the first thing that comes to mind, continuing to say the same root of that sentence with different completions until there is a point at which the client seems finished. Then, another sentence stem is "fed" by the helper. Examples of incomplete sentences developed by Branden (1971) to elicit feelings include

- Something I'm feeling is . . .
- When I look at you, I feel . . .
- As you look at me, I feel . . .
- If I felt mad (or scared or shy or happy, etc.) . . .
- One of the things that I do when I feel mad is . . .
- One of the things that might make me feel mad is . . .
- One of the ways that feeling mad helps me is . . .
- A good thing about feeling mad is . . .
- A bad thing about feeling mad is . . .
- The rule we had in my family about feeling mad was . . .

Understanding and Regulating Feelings: Reflection and Regulation Interventions

The expression of feelings is useful, but such expression needs to be accompanied by making sense of these feelings and learning how to integrate them effectively into daily life and relationships with self and others. Emotional arousal or expression of emotions alone is insufficient for good therapeutic outcomes; expression needs the added component of reflection about the feelings (Greenberg, 2011). Reflection or making meaning of emotional experience helps clients to understand their feelings and to regulate them. Regulation of emotions is especially important when clients experience despair, hopelessness, shame, aggression, and severe anxiety and panic. Emotion diaries are a way for clients to write a narrative about their emotional experiences. Emotion logs, which we described earlier, are a visual tool that clients can use to help them recognize and record selected aspects of their emotional experiences.

EMOTION DIARIES *Emotion diaries* help clients understand feelings by writing a narrative account or story about one's emotional experience of a traumatic event. Pennebaker (1990) found that writing about the feelings associated with an upsetting event for 20 minutes at a time—with at least four different entries in the diary—had a significant effect on improving health and immune system functioning as well as a reduction in the disturbing memories of the event. The positive effects of emotion diaries include not only writing about current incidents as a client experiences them but also about events that occurred at an earlier time that still elicit painful feelings for the client. Emotion diaries are a good way to help clients cope with and understand the sad and tragic events of everyday life, including but not limited to terrorism and disasters (Greenberg, 2011; Halpern & Tramontin, 2007).

AFFECT REGULATION: DEALING WITH DIFFICULT EMOTIONS In addition to understanding feelings, regulating affect is a way for clients to contain feelings so they are not overwhelmed by them. *Affect regulation* has an increasingly important role in the modern world, which is filled with both natural and human-made disasters. Disturbing emotions, such as sadness, shame, fear, anger, and powerlessness, can overwhelm a client. Many clients believe the only way they can regulate these overwhelming feelings is to shut them down, but as Greenberg (2012) and others have found, this strategy is not useful in the long run. Other clients try to avert experiencing these feelings by self-medicating through the abuse of substances or by self-harming, such as cutting themselves. These clients in particular can benefit by learning to regulate undesirable emotions with more self-soothing feelings. The following strategy described by Greenberg is useful for helping clients learn affect regulation skills:

1. Imagine a situation or personal interaction that produces this difficult emotion. This might be a conversation with a parent or partner that leaves you feeling difficult emotions of rage, worthlessness, or undesirability.
2. As the emotion emerges, shift your attention to the process of sensing. Describe the sensations. Describe their quality, intensity, and location and any changes in these. Breathe.
3. Pay attention to accompanying thoughts. Describe the mental process in which you are engaging, whether it be thinking, remembering, or criticizing. Breathe.

4. Focus on another softer, good feeling, such as love, joy, or compassion. Imagine a situation or personal interaction in which you feel this. Feel it now. Allow the feeling to fill you.

5. Talk to the old, difficult feeling from your space in your new, healthier feeling. What can you say to the bad feeling that will help transform it to a better feeling? Say this (Greenberg, 2002, p. 214)

In using interventions to work with client feelings, it is important to be aware of cautions regarding culture. Some clients from some cultural groups may feel uncomfortable with these kinds of strategies because their cultural group does not focus on feelings or on revealing feelings to a nonfamily member. Other clients may be much more concerned with survival, class, and social issues, so focusing on affect seems irrelevant to them.

Greenberg (2012) suggests two issues in working with client emotions that helpers need to consider carefully. The first is whether it is useful to help a particular client to feel feelings or instead to help the client to distract him- or herself from or regulate the feelings. He cites this principle to help practitioners figure this out. "Clients need to be guided to accept and feel their feelings when they are not too overwhelming but to distinguish when the intensity of their emotions is so high that they become dysfunctional, and then learn to regulate them by soothing or distracting" (p. 702).

The second issue has to do with whether to focus primarily on affective content or cognitive content with a particular client. Greenberg recommends focusing on cognition when the client's problems are based on faulty thinking or skill deficits. When reason cannot penetrate thinking, however, accessing emotion is then the key in the helping process. In some instances, emotions are controlled primarily by a part of the brain known as the primitive brain or the amygdala, which does not respond very well to reasoning and direct problem solving.

WORKING WITH CLIENT BEHAVIORS

A variety of strategies are designed to help clients modify their behaviors. Behavioral interventions are based on the assumption that behavior is learned; therefore, inappropriate or maladaptive behavior can be unlearned, while more adaptive behavior can be acquired (Antony & Roemer, 2011). Behavioral approaches also rely heavily on a scientific method. This means that the therapeutic interventions and their outcomes are tested in some empirical way to establish the efficacy of the strategy or strategies being used. In this section, we describe three strategies designed to work with client behaviors: behavioral skills training, self-management, and exposure therapies.

Behavioral Skills Training

Behavioral skills training is used to help clients acquire skills to perform particular tasks in particular situations. For example, a client comes to see you because she falls silent in many interpersonal situations. She reports having difficulty expressing her opinions in group settings and with her husband. She would like your help in increasing her frequency and range of assertiveness skills. Another client comes in and reports that he has yet to ask someone out on a date, spends most of his time alone, and is feeling very lonely because he does not know how to use the interpersonal skills necessary for the development of relationships. He would like your help in acquiring some effective social skills. A child's parents come in to see you and report that they feel like failures because they cannot find effective ways to parent their child, who is acting out at home and in school. They need your help in developing useful parenting skills and strategies. On another day, you see a couple who is in frequent conflict. They tell you that they spend much of their precious time together arguing, even though they cannot recall the next day what the content of the argument was about. They know how to argue very well. They both grew up in families where arguing was a common occurrence. Yet they do not know how to be friends with each other, and sadly, they suggest that they simply do not know much about listening and communicating with one another. Expressing positive feelings to the other person is just about unheard of for this couple. They want your assistance in developing effective communication skills to enhance their relationship. In all these situations, and more, helpers can use behavioral skills training to help clients develop skills that are not yet in their repertoire or, at the least, may be known to the client but not used in necessary contexts and situations. Skills training promotes freedom for clients by providing them with an increased range of responses and with alternative ways of responding and behaving across a variety of contexts (Spiegler & Guevremont, 2010).

SOCIAL MODELING An important part of behavioral skills training is social modeling. *Social modeling* is based on observational learning and imitation (Bandura, 1969). From early childhood, children learn to watch and imitate—a fact that parents who speak too freely in front of their small child know all too well. In modeling, the helper demonstrates a skill or a set of skills to the client, who observes what the helper does. Sometimes, symbolic models—such as stories, DVDs, and movies—are also used with clients as very cost-effective methods. In addition, helpers can encourage clients to find natural models or people in the client's everyday environment who exhibit behaviors and skills the client needs to learn and practice (Spiegler & Guevremont, 2010). Modeling can promote significant change in and of itself in a very brief time—often in one or two counseling sessions. Most often, it is combined with other modalities, such as behavior rehearsal, in a skills training package.

BEHAVIOR REHEARSAL *Behavior rehearsal* literally means what it says. It involves having the client practice performing or demonstrating newly learned or newly expressed skills. In practical terms, behavior rehearsal consists of a series of graduated practice attempts in which the client rehearses the desired behaviors, starting with a situation that is manageable and not likely to backfire. Often, the practice attempts are arranged in a hierarchy according to level of difficulty. For example, the client described previously whose concern was social skills deficits in dating situations may practice social skills with persons he does not care about before he practices with persons whose opinion matters to him. Adequate practice of one situation is important before moving on to rehearse a more difficult or complex skill or situation.

FEEDBACK An important part of behavior rehearsal and behavioral skills training is *feedback*. Feedback is a way for the client to recognize both the problems and successes encountered in the rehearsal and practice attempts as well as a way of observing and evaluating one's performance and of initiating corrective action. However, feedback used indiscriminately in skills training may be ineffective. Feedback is most helpful when the client is willing to change, when the type and amount of feedback given is adequate but not overwhelming, and when the feedback helps the client discriminate between effective and ineffective skills and performance of such skills. Feedback can be supplied by the helper, by persons in the client's environment, by the client, and by video- and digitized recordings.

Because much of skills training is based on *shaping*—or the idea that skills are learned when successive approximations of the desired behavioral responses are reinforced—feedback that focuses on gradual improvement and stresses client strengths is most effective. A final aspect of behavioral skills training involves promoting transfer and generalization of the newly learned skills to settings in which the effective use of the skills is important. This is often accomplished with homework assignments or in vivo tasks in which the client practices the skills in situations in the natural environment. One important overall caveat in behavioral skills training is to make sure both the skills selected and the training itself are culturally relevant to the client. There may be situations in which clients from some cultural groups would not feel safe being assertive. Sue and Sue (2013) point out, for example, that clients from traditional Hispanic and Asian cultures—depending on their level of acculturation—often value restraint in expressiveness of strong feelings and opinions.

Self-Management

Many people are legitimately concerned about the long-term effects of helping. In an effort to promote enduring client changes, helpers have become more concerned with client self-directed change. This interest has led many counseling researchers and practitioners to explore the usefulness of a variety of helping strategies called *self-control* or *self-management* (Wilson, 2010). The primary characteristic of a self-management strategy is that the client administers the strategy and directs the change efforts with minimal assistance from the helper. Like modeling, self-management strategies are cost-effective. One of the most commonly used self-management strategies is self-monitoring.

SELF-MONITORING   *Self-monitoring* involves having clients count and/or regulate given habits, thoughts, or feelings. Self-monitoring seems to interfere with the learned habit by breaking the stimulus-response association and by encouraging performance of the desired response, which is then often reinforced by the individual's sense of progress following its accomplishment. In implementing the procedure, you need to consider what, how, and when to self-monitor.

   • *What to Monitor:* An initial step involves selecting the behavior to monitor. Usually, individuals achieve better results with self-monitoring if they start by counting only one behavior—at least initially. For example, clients may count positive feelings about themselves, or thoughts of competency, or—as we saw earlier in this chapter—feelings and emotions. The counting encourages greater frequency of these kinds of thoughts and feelings. Clients may count the number of times they tell themselves to do well on a task, or they may count the number of behaviors related to goal achievement (e.g., the number of times they tell their partner "I love you," the number of times they initiate conversations or participate in class discussions). Clients also can monitor both process and outcome behaviors. For example, a client could monitor the outcomes of a study program, such as grades on tests, reports, and papers. Equally if not more important is the act of self-recording the processes involved in studying, such as going to the library, finding a quiet study place, preparing for a test, researching a report, and so on. As Watson and Tharp (2014) stated, "You may want to keep track of your progress toward some goal, but the important thing to pay attention to *via* recording is the *process* you are going through. . . . Pay attention to the *process* so you can improve the process, and the goal will happen" (p. 98). In other words, noting the processes involved in changing the behavior is as useful as noting the behavioral outcome itself. For example, consider the client we described who failed to express important opinions and was engaging in self-monitoring. In addition to monitoring the *outcome* of self-expression, monitoring the *processes* involved in assertive self-expression (such as finding contexts or situations for self-expression, practicing phrases of self-expression, watching other people engage successfully in self-expression, and any other behaviors that lead to assertive self-expression) would be just as helpful. Clients also need to select behaviors to monitor that they care about and that are consistent with their values and their cultural affiliations and identities.

• ***How to Monitor:*** The particular method the client uses to count the target response depends on the nature of the selected response. Generally, clients count either the frequency or duration of a response. For example, if they are interested in knowing how often the response occurs, they can use a frequency count to note the numbers of times they smoke, talk on the telephone, initiate social conversations, or think about themselves positively. Sometimes, it is more useful to know the amount of time the behavior occurs. A person can count the duration or length of a behavior in these cases. For example, clients might count how long they studied, how long they talked on the telephone, or the length of depressed periods of thought. Often, it makes sense to use frequency counts if it is easy to count the number of separate times the behavior is performed and to use duration counts if separate occasions are not easy to count or if the target behavior continues for several minutes at a time. Obviously, a client may sometimes monitor both frequency and duration—for example, the number of cigarettes smoked in a day as well as the amount of time spent smoking cigarettes in a day. Sometimes, it is also important to know something about the *intensity* of a target response. In these instances, clients can also monitor the intensity or severity of a response on a rating scale, such as a 1 to 10 or a 0 to 100 rating scale. For example, with a client who reports a lot of daily stress, this client could rate his or her stress level at several points (at least four) during each day on a 1- to 10-point scale, with a 1 representing no stress and a 10 representing severe, incapacitating stress.

In addition, it is important to balance the self-monitoring with attention to *both* positive and negative behaviors. Having a depressed or anxious client self-monitor only depressed or anxious thoughts or feelings can lead the client to feel worse and more discouraged. And for clients who are having panic attacks or ideas of self-harm or suicide, self-monitoring may be contraindicated (Watson & Tharp, 2014, p. 115–117). Similarly, clients who record only the number of times they binge-eat or drink or smoke cigarettes may decide—after noticing all these negative behaviors—that change is too difficult after all. An antidote is to have clients also self-monitor positive behaviors—for example, times when they feel happy or calm rather than depressed or anxious. With clients who overeat or smoke, they can record the times they had the urge to eat or smoke but resisted the urge. Even small and infrequent successes need to be recorded in order to have this type of balance in an effective self-monitoring plan.

Clients will need to record with the assistance of some recording device. These can range from simple devices—such as note cards, logs, and diaries for written recordings—to more mechanical devices—such as a wrist counter, a kitchen timer, a wristwatch, a recorder, or a handheld computer. The device should be simple to use, convenient, portable, and economical.

• ***When to Monitor:*** It is important to self-record the target as soon as it occurs for several different reasons, as summarized by Watson and Tharp (2014). First, immediate recording is more accurate. When we wait until a later time to record a response, our delayed recall is usually not as accurate. Second, immediate recording is more complete. In waiting to record a response, we often omit important information. Finally, if a client waits until the end of the day to engage in self-recording, his or her emotional state may be different at this time, and his or her recordings may be positive or negative. Also, it is the actual act of recording itself—not just thinking about recording—that seems to produce change—through a process called *reactivity*. Reactivity simply means that behavior is reactive or responsive to the process of self- or other observation; for example, when we are told we are going to be observed—either by someone else or by ourselves—our behavior usually shifts. And if the behavior is something we really value, the shift is usually in the positive direction.

A critical issue in the effective use of any self-management strategy has to do with encouraging the client to use the strategy consistently and regularly. Clients may be more likely to do so when they can see the advantages of self-management and when the helper maintains some contact with the client during the self-management process.

Exposure Strategies

Many clients who benefit most from behavioral strategies present to helpers with problems of anxiety and trauma. For example, a female college student was raped while walking from the parking lot to her dorm and now she does not want to walk to the parking lot again. A person in the military involved in a war or natural disaster zone witnesses the death of a comrade and does not want to go back into the war or disaster zone. Another client develops a fear of flying and avoids airplanes even when required by work to travel quickly. One of the most common ingredients of anxiety- and trauma-related concerns involves *avoidance,* or the act and process of staying away from a feared object, person, or situation. Unfortunately, the act of avoidance greatly strengthens and reinforces the client's anxiety. You are probably familiar with the old saying "get back in the trenches." This saying underscores the idea of *exposure therapies.* While exposure therapies are varied in type and duration, the common underlying process is that they all work to get the client "back in the trenches" by helping the client engage in the behaviors and situations that have been avoided, "under carefully controlled and safe conditions" (Spiegler & Guevremont, 2010, p. 206).

IMAGINAL AND IN VIVO EXPOSURE   Exposure strategies can be imaginal or in vivo and brief or prolonged. In *imaginal exposure,* a client imagines encountering the avoided, feared, or traumatic situation(s) with the helper's guidance. Clients are asked to imagine the events on a repeated basis in some kind of a consecutive or chronological narrative. Often, virtual exposure sessions are available for the client to listen to at a later time. With *in vivo exposure,* clients reduce learned fear and avoidant responses by confronting the feared, avoided, or traumatic situations and objects in the actual environment (hence, the phrase "in vivo"). Sometimes, the helper (or preferably, for safety reasons, two or more helpers) accompanies the client in the in vivo situations. The goal of in vivo exposure strategies is for clients to become so accustomed to the feared objects or situations (referred to as "habituated," defined as a 50 percent reduction in anxiety to the feared object or situation) that they no longer need to avoid the situation or object. In vivo exposure is frequently used in treating phobias and panic.

BRIEF EXPOSURE   In *brief exposure,* clients are exposed to the threatening event(s) both (1) for a short period of time—usually ranging from a few seconds to a few minutes—and (2) incrementally—beginning with the aspects of the situation producing the least anxiety or threat proceeding to the aspects producing the greatest amounts of anxiety or threat (Spiegler & Guevremont, 2010, p. 206). To accomplish this, the helper and client usually first generate an anxiety hierarchy—that is, a list of the feared events and/or objects graded by either amount of emotional distress, time, or some other variant related to the event. For example, a client who presents with a fear of driving would generate an anxiety hierarchy based around distance and setting, starting with the idea of driving a short distance—perhaps only out of one's driveway. At the top of the hierarchy, the client would be driving a long distance, perhaps on an unfamiliar highway. This type of exposure was developed in the 1950s by Wolpe (1958) in a procedure referred to as *systematic desensitization.*

PROLONGED EXPOSURE   More recent developments in exposure are credited to Foa (see Foa, Keane, & Friedman, 2009). In *prolonged exposure,* the client is exposed to the threatening object or situation (1) for a more lengthy period, ranging from 10 minutes to one hour and (2) directly and immediately rather than gradually (Spiegler & Guevremont, 2010, p. 207). Prolonged exposure—also referred to as *flooding*—maximizes the client's anxiety with large rather than small doses of the feared object or situation at the outset. The core condition of prolonged exposure is that the client is exposed to a highly aversive situation long enough for the client's discomfort to peak and then decline (Spiegler & Guevremont, 2010). In prolonged and intensive exposure, the helper is always present during all exposure assignments, either imaginal or in vivo. Prolonged exposure is considered one of the evidence-based interventions for a clinical disorder common in war veterans known as post-traumatic stress disorder (PTSD; Makinson & Young, 2012).

All forms of exposure are accompanied by a strong rationale with informed consent and lots of homework practice. As McNeil, Kyle, and Nurius (2013) observe, while informed consent is necessary in any form of helping, it is especially important in exposure therapies because clients can have concerns about this process, worrying that it may progress too quickly or that it may make them feel worse (p. 481). Exposure may also be used in conjunction with breath work, cognitive coping, and muscle relaxation. Brief and graduated exposure has some advantages over prolonged and intense exposure. Because clients typically experience less distress with brief and graduated approaches, they are more likely to consent to this strategy and are more likely to stay the course and not drop out of counseling. Smyth (1999), who has generated an exposure-based cognitive-behavioral therapy (CBT) treatment for post-traumatic stress, recommends the following guidelines for helpers who use exposure-based strategies:

1. Start with brief and graduated exposure before using any prolonged and intensive exposure.
2. Avoid using prolonged and intensive exposure until brief and graduated exposure has yielded strong cognitive coping effects and moderate anxiety reduction effects.

3. Use imaginal exposure before using in vivo exposure, with either brief or prolonged exposure strategies.
4. If using prolonged and intensive exposure seems to overwhelm the client emotionally, return to brief and graduated exposure strategies. (pp. 77–78)

The essence of exposure-based strategies is to help clients approach rather than avoid a feared object or situation in the absence of any real threat and to reduce the client's emotional distress through repeated practice, passage of time, and cognitive coping (Smyth, 1999, p. 65).

Many behavioral strategies have been used quite effectively with diverse groups of clients, perhaps because these strategies focus on action and change rather than insight and exploration (Hays & Iwamasa, 2006). Still, it is important to remember that some of the notions underlying behavioral interventions are decidedly Eurocentric in that they focus on an internal locus of control and responsibility.

WORKING WITH CLIENT BELIEFS AND THOUGHTS

Beliefs and thoughts represent attitudes and assumptions a client has about a situation—often referred to as *cognitions*. Beliefs are potent because they affect clients' perceptions about themselves, others, and their lives. Clients encounter all sorts of difficulty based on their beliefs and thoughts because they may be habitual and automatic and/or distorted and based on incomplete information. For example, clients who are depressed or highly anxious tend to view themselves, others, and the world in a negative way (A. T. Beck, 2005; A. T. Beck & Alford, 2009; Clark & A. T. Beck, 2010; J. Beck, 2011).

A major focus of these interventions is on changing the way the client thinks. *Cognitive therapists* believe that by changing the way a client thinks, his or her emotional distress and problematic behavior can also be changed (Dobson, 2012). There is now a substantial body of research that shows the effectiveness of cognitive therapy in reducing both symptoms and relapse rates—with or without medication—in a number of different kinds of mental health disorders (J. Beck, 2011). There is also recent research supporting the notion that cognitive therapy does help some clients regain emotional control (Siegle, Carter, & Thase, 2006). In this section of the chapter, we describe two related but somewhat different ways of working with client beliefs and thoughts: A-B-C-D-E analysis and cognitive restructuring.

A-B-C-D-E Analysis

A-B-C-D-E analysis is an intervention strategy based on a cognitive counseling approach known as *rational-emotive therapy* (RET), developed by a psychotherapist named Albert Ellis. (Ellis has relabeled RET as REBT, for rational-emotive behavior therapy.) According to Ellis, emotional distress is created by faulty, illogical, or irrational thoughts. In other words, if someone feels emotionally upset, it is not a person or a situation that creates the emotional upset but rather the individual's beliefs or thoughts about the situation. Reduction in emotional distress is brought about when the individual's irrational thinking is changed to rational thinking through interventions such as A-B-C-D-E analysis.

In the first part of this strategy, the client learns to recognize the activating event (A), usually a situation or person that the client finds upsetting. The activating event is often what prompts the client to seek counseling ("My relationship is on the rocks," "I lost my job," "My partner is a jerk," "I don't have any friends," "Why don't boys like me?" "I got passed over for the team," etc.). The most important aspect of this part of the strategy is to refocus clients from attributing their distress to this activating event to their thoughts about it. For example, the helper might respond with "I realize it's upsetting to you not to make the team; however, it's not this situation in and of itself that's making you feel so bad but rather your thinking about this situation." In the next part of the strategy, the client's specific thoughts or beliefs (B) about the activating event are explored and identified. The client may have both rational and irrational thoughts, but it is the irrational thoughts that contribute to the emotional distress and that need to be targeted for change. Rational thoughts are consistent with reality, are supported by data, and result in moderate levels of emotional upset (e.g., "I didn't play as well as other people in the tryouts, and they got picked and I didn't"). Irrational thoughts are not based on facts or evidence and lead to high levels of emotional distress (e.g., "Because I didn't make the team, I am a jerk"). Irrational beliefs often take the form of either catastrophization ("It will be awful when . . .") or "musturbation" ("I must . . . ;" "I should . . . ;" "I have to . . .").

The helper then links the irrational beliefs with the resulting emotional and behavioral consequences (C)—that is, what clients feel and how they act as a result (e.g., "I feel so bad. I just can't seem to snap out of it. I didn't want to go back to school because I'm so ashamed of not making the team."). The helper shows the client how his or her specific irrational beliefs led to these consequences. For example, the therapist might respond with: "You're feeling awful and staying away from school because you now view yourself as a nobody—it's not that you got passed up that is making you feel and act this way; it's the way you're now thinking about yourself."

The real work of the strategy comes next in the disputation (D) phase. Disputation involves disputing or challenging the client's irrational beliefs with the intent of eliminating them and helping the client acquire more rational thinking. The helper uses questions to dispute the client's irrational beliefs. Some examples of questions suggested for cognitive disputation by Walen, DiGiuseppe, and Wessler (1992) include

- Is that true? Why not?
- Can you prove it?
- How do you know?
- Why is that an overgeneralization?
- What would happen if . . . ?
- If that's true, what's the worst that can happen?
- How would that be so terrible?
- Where's the evidence?
- Can you be happy even if you don't get what you want?
- What is the probability of a bad consequence?
- How will your world be destroyed if X happens?
- As long as you believe that, how will you feel? (pp. 97–99)

Dryden (2009) notes that the disputation process (which she refers to as the examination process) can occur through a variety of methods and helper styles, including not only the Socratic-like questions listed above but also with didactic, declarative psychoeducation, humor, and metaphors or stories.

When the disputation process has been effective, it will be apparent in new effects (E), such as lessened emotional distress and changes in behavior (e.g., "I still don't like the fact I didn't make the team, but I know I'm not a jerk just because of that"). It is important for the helper to help clients recognize when and if these emotional and behavioral shifts in effects occur. Some recent research has suggested that, for individuals who ruminate (the maladaptive tendency to focus repetitively on the causes and consequences of negative moods), the acts of identifying and disputing negative cognition may actually increase rather than decrease rumination (Joorman & Gottlib, 2008). This effect was found to be particularly evident with college students who ruminated and felt stressed and received the A-B-C-D-E model via a self-help workbook. The author of this study concluded that "self-taught cognitive skills such as identifying and disputing negative cognitions may render cognitive interventions ineffective (or potentially harmful) for college students, particularly those who ruminate" (Haeffel, 2010).

Cognitive Restructuring

Cognitive restructuring is based in theory from the work of Aaron T. Beck, a cognitive therapist, and on the practice of Donald Meichenbaum, a cognitive-behavioral therapist. *Cognitive restructuring* is based on the notion that clients generate emotional distress due to the dysfunctional ways they interpret the events of their lives (A. T. Beck, 1976; J. Beck, 2011). The procedure helps clients to recognize and alter or to loosen and change troublesome thoughts, beliefs, and *schemas*—schemas are core or basic beliefs that clients regard as "truths," but in this instance, the schemas are dysfunctional. Cognitive restructuring involves not only helping clients learn to recognize and stop self-defeating thoughts and beliefs but also to substitute positive, self-enhancing, or coping thoughts and beliefs. A. T. Beck (1976) and J. Beck (2011) suggested three approaches to restructuring self-defeating thoughts, beliefs, and schemas:

1. "What is the evidence?" These are known as the **evidence** questions.
   What is the evidence that supports this idea and what's the evidence against this idea? (J. Beck, 2011, p. 172)
2. "What is another way of looking at it?" This is known as the **alternative explanation** question.
   Could there be another explanation or way of viewing this? (J. Beck, 2011, p. 172).
3. "So what if it happens?" This is known as the **decatastrophizing** question (J. Beck, 2011, p. 172).
   What is the worst result if it did happen, and how would you cope with this? What is the best possible result? What is likely to happen?

In the first part of cognitive restructuring, clients learn to stop obsessive, illogical, or negative thoughts as they occur. This involves discrimination training in which they are made aware of what "they tell themselves" before, during, and after problem situations. Clients might be instructed to note and record their negative thoughts and beliefs before, during, and after stressful or depressing situations for one or two weeks. As Newman (2003) noted, "[S]pecifically, clients are asked to notice their episodes of excessive anger, despair, fear, and the like, and to choose not to accept them at face value. Rather, clients are instructed to ask themselves, What could be going through my mind right now that could be triggering or worsening how I'm feeling right now?" (p. 92). This sort of discrimination process yields themes and patterns that provide clues about the cognitive schemas or core "truths" the client believes, such as failure or rejection or abandonment.

After clients are aware of the nature and types of their self-defeating thoughts and belief systems, the helper helps them work toward identifying more positive or coping thoughts and beliefs that can replace the negative ones. These coping thoughts and beliefs are considered to be incompatible with the self-defeating thoughts and beliefs.

Coping thoughts are designed to help clients picture dealing with problem situations effectively, although not perfectly. In this way, they are considered better than mastery thoughts, which focus on perfection, because they expose the clients to possible mistakes and prepare them to recover from errors they may make in life (McMullin, 2000). It is best to personalize these coping thoughts for each client. Clients also need to learn coping thoughts to use before, during, and after problem situations. For example, a client who fails tests due to anxiety might concentrate on thoughts such as "I will be calm" or "Keep your mind on your studies" before an exam. During an exam, clients learn to concentrate on the exam and to stay calm instead of worrying about flunking or thinking about their nervousness. After using some coping thoughts, clients can be taught to reward or congratulate themselves for coping instead of punishing themselves for worrying.

When clients have identified some possible alternative coping thoughts to use, they can practice applying these thoughts through overt (role-play) and covert (imaginary) rehearsal. The rehearsal may take the form of a dialogue or a script and may be read aloud by the client or put on index cards or digitized. McMullin (2000) observed that, for most clients, a period of at least six weeks is necessary for the practice of coping thoughts.

A sample cognitive restructuring dialogue used for rehearsal by a high school client who feared competitive situations is provided by Cormier, Nurius, and Osborn (2013):

> Okay. I'm sitting here waiting for my turn to try out for cheerleader. Ooh, I can feel myself getting very nervous. (*anxious feeling*) Now, wait, what am I so nervous about? I'm afraid I'm going to make a fool of myself. (*self-defeating thought*) Hey, that doesn't help. (*cue to cope*) It will take only a few minutes, and it will be over before I know it. Besides only the faculty sponsors are watching. It's not like the whole school is here. (*coping thoughts*) Well, the person before me is just about finished. Oh, they're calling my name. Boy, do I feel tense. (*anxious feelings*) What if I don't execute my jumps? (*self-defeating thought*) Okay, don't think about what I'm not going to do. Okay, start out, it's my turn. Just think about my routine—the way I want it to go. (*coping thoughts*) (p. 380).

Identifying and internalizing coping thoughts and beliefs seem to be crucial in order for clients to benefit from cognitive restructuring. Gradually, clients should be able to apply their newly found coping skills to the in vivo situations as these occur. If cognitive restructuring is successful, clients can detect an increased use of coping thoughts and a decreased level of stress in their actual environment. In vivo practice seems crucial for the efficacy of this strategy in order to promote the clients' confidence in their newly learned beliefs (Meichenbaum, 2007).

Schulte (2013, p. 53) has provided an effective summary of the six steps involved in teaching cognitive restructuring to clients:

- Recognize cognitive distortions.
- Slow down thinking.
- Take note of negative internal monologues.
- Identify and pay attention to any triggers.
- Practice a nonjudgmental stance.
- Use effective counterstatements.

The use of cognitive strategies with diverse groups of clients has received increased attention in the last few years. As Hays and Iwamasa (2006) point out, however, the values inherent in cognitive interventions reflect those of the mainstream culture. Also, as Brown (1994) asserts, for some clients, the supposedly irrational beliefs may sometimes be reasonable or even lifesaving, given the individual's life and environmental context (p. 61). However, the process of challenging or disputing these beliefs may not fit with some clients from particular cultural groups. Therefore, a useful caveat is to cultivate awareness in using cognitive strategies. Be flexible in the way you implement these strategies, and be sensitive to the client's reaction. J. Beck (as cited in Kaplan, 2011) suggests that cognitive therapy is effective with clients from various cultures, but she also states that it is important in working with culturally diverse clients "to find out whether maladaptive ideas are idiosyncratic to the individual or whether they actually represent a belief of the culture." (p. 37). She gives the example of an American practitioner working with a Chinese client and encountering the client's belief that it is very important to show respect to one's elders and parents and not to do anything that would make the elders unhappy or disgraced. She states, "[A] counselor who is unfamiliar working with the Asian culture might not recognize that at first and be surprised to find the belief pretty intractable. Understanding that it's also a cultural belief is helpful" (p. 38). In situations of cultural diversity, she recommends that practitioners help clients look for evidence that a feared outcome is likely to happen and, if it does, how the client is likely to cope. She also suggests talking with the client about how some other persons in the client's cultural reference group might have a "more moderate idea" (p. 38).

WORKING WITH CLIENT LANGUAGE, SYMBOLIC MEANING, AND STORIES

In the preceding two sections of the chapter, we discussed intervention strategies that focus on client behaviors and cognitions. These types of strategies have been referred to as the first wave and second wave of behavior therapy—the *first wave* being interventions that focus primarily on reducing maladaptive behaviors and on establishing more effective behavioral responses, with the *second wave* including interventions that focus primarily on reducing maladaptive cognitions and on establishing more effective ways of thinking. Currently, there is a *third wave* of behavior therapy that includes a variety of approaches, such as *dialectical behavior therapy (DBT;* Linehan, 1993; Koerner, 2012), which is used to treat a disorder called borderline personality disorder; *mindfulness-based cognitive therapy (MBCT;* Segal, Williams, & Teasdale, 2013), which is used to treat depression; and an approach we will focus on in this chapter called *acceptance and commitment therapy (ACT;* pronounced as one word rather than as separate letters), which was developed by Hayes and colleagues (Hayes, 2004; Hayes, Strosahl, & Wilson, 2012).

Acceptance and Commitment Therapy Strategies

To some degree, ACT interventions share some commonalities with behavioral and cognitive approaches. For example, ACT also focuses on the use of science or research to collect data about positive and negative therapy outcomes and has a well-supported empirical basis for its model (Hayes, Luoma, Bond, Masuda, & Lillis, 2006). Also, like traditional cognitive-behavioral approaches, ACT focuses on the function of both behaviors and private events, such as thoughts, feelings, and body sensations. ACT interventions are based on an approach to human language in which literalization, evaluation, and comparison are viewed as contributors to psychopathology. For ACT therapists, clients become fused or overidentified with beliefs and schemas that are created and maintained by language. For example, a client with an eating disorder becomes fused with the role of being bulimic or anorexic.

DEFUSION   What do ACT helpers do in these situations? First, they employ a series of processes designed to tackle the fusion to literal language, called *defusion techniques* (*defusion* being a technique they invented). One of the major ways they do this is through the use of language metaphors. Defusion aims to help clients look *at* their thoughts rather than *from* their thoughts (Hayes & Smith, 2005; Ciarrochi & Bailey, 2008). Stated another way, defusion techniques are "methods for learning how to get present in the here and now in a broader and more flexible way, with the point being to break through the illusion of language" in order to notice the process of thinking (p. 21). In the example of the client with bulimia, the client would be encouraged to defuse by stating, "I'm having the thought that I'm bulimic" instead of "I'm bulimic." Hayes and Smith (2005, p. 21) explain it this way: "When you think a thought, it structures your world. When you see a thought you can still see how it structures your world, but you also see that you are doing the structuring. . . . It would be as if you always wore yellow sunglasses and forgot you were wearing them. Defusion is like taking off your glasses and holding them out, several inches away from your face; then you can see how they make the world appear to be yellow, instead of seeing only the yellow world" (notice the metaphor in this description). Defusion methods are used in ACT to deal with problems linked to language but not with situations such as abuse that require action and are based on client values.

EXPERIENTIAL AVOIDANCE   ACT helpers also note and focus on *experiential avoidance*—that is, the private events or experiences that clients try to avoid, such as the sadness and despair a client may feel as a result of her eating disorder. Unlike the cognitive therapist who uses disputation processes to challenge faulty beliefs and negative emotions, ACT endeavors to help clients develop acceptance of these private or internal experiences. If the client says, "I'm a terrible person," the ACT helper may respond by saying, "Notice the thought you're having. Thank it. Don't give your life over to it if it plays a negative role in your life." ACT has found that, by trying to eliminate a particular thought or belief, it actually takes greater hold and becomes more central. In ACT, acceptance helps clients move out of the narrowing process that comes as a result of experiential avoidance and aversive control with the goal of increasing psychological flexibility. ACT methods focus on changing the *function* or *context* of the thought rather than the specific form of the thought or even the frequency of thoughts and beliefs.

VALUES AND COMMITMENT   Another somewhat unique aspect of ACT is the emphasis it places on values and commitment. ACT practitioners help clients get in touch with what they deeply want in their lives. Unlike a goal—which is something you can obtain and has a beginning and an end—a value is more of an ongoing process. A value is what and who you want to be in your life. A typical ACT homework assignment might be to have the client develop narratives about what she or he wants to be in specific life domains, such as intimate relationships, family, social networks, employment and work, education and training, spirituality, and citizenship and community. After exploring this question, ACT practitioners help clients enact actions to support these values and anticipate barriers that may impede the actions. A particular area of focus in counseling would be when clients indicate that something is important to them and yet they have limited success in that domain. For example, a client may want to be in a loving relationship but is living alone. When clients discover what they deeply value, they may experience strong emotions and also a renewed sense of vitality.

MINDFULNESS ACT also promotes awareness of the present moment through *mindfulness*. Based on the work of Kabat-Zinn (2012), mindfulness simply means having the client get in touch with experiences as they occur moment to moment (note from Chapter 1 that mindfulness is also useful for helpers because we need to model this for our clients). Sometimes, it is referred to as simply being in the moment. In ACT, the purpose of mindfulness is to help clients separate or defuse from literal, evaluative language and thoughts. Mindfulness is also an important component of DBT and MBCT, which we mentioned earlier in this section. Brown, Marquis, and Guiffrida (2013) suggest that mindfulness meditation perhaps is used most effectively when combined with other counseling approaches.

Mindfulness mediation has a host of positive effects on the body, ranging from increased immune function to decreased hypertension. In the past few years, research on mindfulness has exploded, and currently there is a strong empirical base on the usefulness of this approach for a variety of psychological conditions such as anxiety, depression, borderline personality disorder, eating disorders, and drug addiction (Brown, Marquis, & Guiffrida, 2013). A recent study found that high school students who practiced mindfulness in a school setting were less depressed and less stressed than students in the control group (Kuyken, Weare, Ukoumunne, Motton, Burnett, Cullen, Hennelly, & Huppert, 2013). In this study, the students who practiced mindfulness also had higher well-being scores and less depression and less stress over a longer period of time.

One of the most promising aspects of mindfulness is the impact this intervention has on the brain. Known as brain plasticity, which simply means the brain's capacity for change, regular practice of mindfulness can change both the structure and functioning of the human brain (Davidson, 2012). Simply speaking, regular practice of mindfulness meditation has the capacity to help brains work better by decreasing negative pathways and increasing positive pathways in one's brain. You may recall from Chapter 1 that we mentioned mindfulness as one of the characteristics of being an effective helper. Helpers who practice mindfulness seem to stay centered and are less reactive to difficult clients than those who don't. Entire books have now been written on mindfulness, and a recent poll of experts in psychotherapy predicted that the use of mindfulness strategies is expected to increase dramatically in the future (Norcross, Pfund, & Prochaska, 2013). Mindfulness appears to be useful for a variety of diverse clients, although research with diverse clients is more limited (Brown, Marquis, & Guiffrida, 2013). Contraindications for mindfulness include clients with extreme cognitive impairments, profound developmental disabilities, psychoses, and severe depression (Brown, Marquis, & Guiffrida, 2013).

Mindfulness seems to have two primary components: noticing and observing one's experience and accepting one's experience in a nonjudgmental stance. Brown, Marquis, and Guiffrida (2013) suggest that helpers use mindfulness meditation with clients by first providing them with psychoeducation about the approach, followed by instruction in mindfulness techniques, and finally with homework assignments for regular practice.

Psychoeducation In the first part of this intervention, helpers introduce clients to the practice of mindfulness meditation by describing the elements of it. They also educate clients about the benefits of mindfulness and summarize the existing research literature about its outcomes. We recommend you consult a workbook on mindfulness skills authored by Burdick (2013) to see some excellent examples of psychoeducation in mindfulness with clients. The helper often recommends a workbook such as the one mentioned above by Burdick (2013) or a primer in mindfulness with an instructional CD, such as *Mindfulness for Beginners* by Jon Kabat-Zinn (2012). I also like to use a book and CD called *Yoga Nidra: A Meditative Practice for Deep Relaxation and Healing* by psychologist and yoga master Richard Miller (R. Miller, 2010).

Instruction in Techniques While there are many ways to be mindful, a basic one is simply to sit quietly for an extended period of time and follow your breath—notice it coming into the body and notice it going out of the body. Burdick (2013, p. 60) suggests an acronym, SOLAR, to help clients learn this sitting technique:

Stopping

Observing

Letting it go

And

Returning

Burdick (2013) and Cormier, Nurius, and Osborn (2013) suggest a number of breathing techniques to complement this sitting practice, such as belly breathing and counting breath, where the client simply breathes from the belly and inhales and exhales, each one on a count of 4.

Another commonly used mindfulness technique is known as the *body scan*. During an extended period, usually about 45 minutes, clients go through a series of attention to physical sensations in a sequential and nonjudgmental manner. For a detailed description of the body scan technique, consult Burdick (2013, p. 128) or Cormier, Nurius, and Osborn (2013, p. 454).

Homework and Practice We know from research that a great deal of the value of mindfulness meditation comes from its ability to change the brain in useful and positive ways. This occurs only through regular, systematic practice of mindfulness meditation rather than a haphazard use of this technique. The third part of using this intervention with clients involves assigning homework that encourages and enables clients to devote a small amount of time on a daily basis to incorporating mindfulness meditation into their routines. There are several ways this can be accomplished. Some persons recommend the use of a bell on one's computer. Every time the bell rings, it cues the client to practice mindfulness (stop, observe, breathe, and repeat). Other clients can schedule the practice of mindfulness into their day with the use of a daily self-recording log sheet, such as the kind we described earlier in the chapter in self-monitoring. The practice of mindfulness meditation can also be incorporated into daily activities such as eating, driving, answering the telephone, and walking. The overall therapeutic goal of mindfulness is to help clients develop an attitude of equanimity that transfers from the mindfulness practices into the client's everyday life.

Narrative Therapy Interventions

Interventions based on social constructivism are called *narrative therapy (NT)*. Like ACT, NT has also been referred to as a third wave in psychotherapy. Both ACT and NT stress the symbolic meaning resulting from clients' literal language processes and the narratives or stories they have developed about themselves and their lives. For example, a client who is afraid to leave the house has usually constructed a narrative or story that is titled "I'm an agoraphobic." This story gets told, retold, and repeated so many times that the client identifies with it and believes it represents a single "truth" about him- or herself. In NT, a "story" is something that has a recognizable structure (a beginning, middle, and end) and also a plot. The story contains events that occur in sequence in time, and the plot accounts for this sequence. Stories may be past, present, or projected into the future. They may be held by clients in secret or repeatedly shared to others. The aim of constructivist and narrative therapy interventions is to help clients engage in restorying so alternative stories are available in addition to the one they brought to the helper's door. White and Epston (1990), who are associated with the development of narrative therapy, believe that clients' identities become fused with their initial story.

EXTERNALIZING QUESTIONS   In a collaborative way, the narrative therapist uses a series of questions to help clients deconstruct this narrative. These kinds of questions include *externalizing questions* to help the client separate from the problem. For example, with the client who self-identifies as agoraphobic, examples of externalizing questions used in NT would be:

> What does your anxiety require of you, and how do you adjust to meet these requirements?

> or

> What's the mission of your anxiety in your life? How do you participate in this mission?

In this example, these externalizing questions make the anxiety or the agoraphobia an occurrence rather than the way the client self-defines.

QUESTIONS OF UNIQUE OUTCOMES   These externalizing questions are followed by questions exploring *unique outcomes;* it is in the account of unique events or memories of "forgotten exceptions" that alternative stories and narratives are developed. In the previous example about agoraphobia, a question of unique outcomes would be:

> Were there ever times in your life when you resisted, not allowing the anxiety to take over? How? What was your experience then?

These questions of unique outcomes in narrative therapy are very similar to the kinds of questions used in solution-focused therapy to introduce possibilities and to help clients generate alternative reality-based solutions (Cormier, Nurius, & Osborn, 2013).

Basically, NT assumes that the client's presenting and primary story can be called a first draft, and the task of the narrative strategy is to help the client create additional drafts that are more accurate, accepting, and inclusive. This is accomplished through a series of questions, such as those noted previously, over a period of time. These questions often require repetition, patience, and time to allow a newer version of the old story to emerge. NT also requires careful listening by the helper. For additional information about this approach, consult the NT website (narrativeapproaches.com) and also see White (2011).

One of the characteristics that ACT and NT have in common is their emphasis on the client's fusion to literal language. Like ACT, NT also uses a lot of metaphors to introduce new language to clients. And also like ACT, NT questions clients' definitions of themselves as "abnormal" and promotes self-acceptance. Another characteristic ACT and NT share is their emphasis on client knowing. ACT helpers encourage clients to trust themselves and their experiences. Narrative therapists emphasize to clients that they—not others—are the authors of their stories and they have the power to revise them because they hold the "privileged position" as the story's author and creator (White, 2007).

Currently, narrative approaches are valuable for clients with trauma issues. Clients are encouraged—with the support of the helper—to construct a conscious narrative of their traumatic experience so their story of it is complete, without gaps, from beginning to end. The purpose of the narrative in trauma therapy is to help clients gain access to memory stored in the nonverbal mind, to organize traumatic memory fragments into a coherent nonverbal narrative, and to bring closure to the experience by translating the nonverbal narrative into a conscious historical memory.

Narrative therapy has also been used extensively in working with older adults and with clients recovering from loss. B. Miller (2011) describes the use of narrative gerontology as a means to help older adults review life history and focus on strengths and successes. Neimeyer (2012) discusses the use of narrative therapy as a means of promoting adaptation to loss within the context of grief counseling and therapy. As part of his narrative strategies for working with loss recovery, he uses journaling as one method to foster meaning from the narrative of loss, suggesting that clients write stories about the loss for at least 15 minutes per day for four days in a row or more.

A great deal of the current work in narrative therapy has been produced by the Foley Center for the Study of Lives at Northwestern University in Chicago. In a series of interdisciplinary research projects, the Foley Center uses the Life Story Interview, which emphasizes the narratives of adult lives. The interview structure is basically a story of the person's life and includes the past as the person remembers it and the future as the person imagines it. The person is asked to describe major life chapters, key scenes in one's life story, challenges, future chapters, personal meaning, and life theme (see sesp.northwestern.edu/foley).

NARRATIVE STRATEGIES TO PROMOTE GAINS IN WELL-BEING In a series of studies of narrative therapy and psychotherapy, Adler and his colleagues have found some fascinating results. As Adler (2012) indicates, "stories are the currency of psychotherapy. . . . [Clients arrive at the initial session] "with a collection of past chapters that explain to the therapist how they came to be in need of help" (p. 595). As Adler (2012) points out, therapists also construct stories about their clients' therapy, but it is the clients' stories that are "most strongly associated with clinical improvement" (p. 602). Adler and his colleagues found that shifts in client narratives precede shifts and sudden gains in clinical symptoms (Adler, Harmeling, & Walder-Biesanz, 2013). Adler (2012, p. 602) recommends several ways that helpers can use a narrative approach to facilitate client improvement in well-being:

- Pay attention to the client narratives in your formulation of the client's case.
- Cultivate a practice of asking clients about their therapy stories as part of your clinical assessment and progress tracking.
- Listen for "agentic" language, that is client language that speaks of autonomy, achievement, and mastery.
- Help clients reframe thoughts when "agentic" language is missing.
- Use the termination process to help clients make sense of what they have accomplished in therapy.

NARRATIVE STRATEGIES TO PROMOTE CULTURAL AND RACIAL DIALOGUES Although many clients arrive in counseling with individual stories, many others have stories connected to families and cultures. NT is a predominant approach in family therapy as well as in individual counseling (Bitter, 2014). One of the things that NT can do is help enlarge the space of the dominant story to allow room for marginalized perspectives and narratives that get squeezed out by the dominant story. NT has been referred to as an approach of social justice.

Sue (2013) has written extensively about cultural dialogues and narratives in which the cultural narrative of the dominant group is likened to storytelling where historical and cultural themes based on the dominant group narrative are predominant. He describes two different cultural narratives, "the dominant group master narrative, and the less powerful, socially devalued group counternarrative (that of persons of color)" (p. 665). Sue and his colleagues have conducted a series of studies to see what factors facilitate "race talk," or effective dialogues between persons of majority and minority races. The factors that they have found helpful in fostering cross-cultural narratives of race talk include understanding of ourselves as a racial cultural being, acknowledging our cultural biases, increasing our comfort level with discussing race issues and the accompanying emotions, and understanding differences in communication styles used in cross cultural narratives (p. 670).

In some ways, the ACT and NT approaches have much in common with effective multicultural counseling. Both approaches employ an accepting rather than an evaluative position. ACT has generated several studies of its efficacy with diverse kinds of clients (Hayes et al., 2006). NT is essentially a pluralistic approach that values diverse and multiple realities and underscores the importance of inclusion for marginalized perspectives. A potential limitation of these approaches identified by Corey (2013) is that the "not knowing" stance of the helper and the "client-as-expert" stance of the client may engender a potential lack of confidence in the helper's ability to be helpful with clients from some cultural and ethnic groups.

WORKING WITH CLIENT INTERACTIONAL PATTERNS AND RELATIONSHIPS

With any individual client who seeks counseling, the client is part of a larger interpersonal network, sometimes referred to as an *interpersonal system*. In any interpersonal system, such as a marriage, family, work department, or peer group, all segments of the system are interrelated, and change in one part affects the entire system. In those interpersonal systems to which the client belongs, the client typically interacts in predictable patterns. These patterns can be seen within the context of the helping system as well as within the various systems to which the client belongs. In other words, the helper can see the client's typical interpersonal pattern not only in the kinds of interactions the client reports with other persons but also in the way this interpersonal pattern is reenacted within the helping relationship. Thus, in working with interactional patterns of the client, the helper can intervene at two different levels: use of interventions that deal directly with the helper–client system and use of interventions that have an impact on the client's interactional style with other persons.

Reenactment of Interactional Patterns in the Helping Process

Clients begin to develop predictable interactional patterns in their family of origin. *Interactional patterns* are affected by many factors, including family construction and birth order (Adler, 1958), family rules and communication patterns (Watzlawick, Beavin, & Jackson, 1967), and general level of health or dysfunction of the family system (Haley, 1997; A. Miller, 1981). For many people who become clients, their family of origin experience was problematic in three major ways:

1. There was a lack of a strong bond between the parents—sometimes referred to as a lack of a "primary parental coalition" (Minuchin, 1974).
2. There were disruptions or interruptions in the ways parents met children's developmental needs for nurturance, structure, separateness, and attachment.
3. There were child-rearing practices that were either too authoritarian or too permissive in nature.

To cope with this, children—as they grow older—develop a characteristic way of interacting with others. People who use an Adlerian counseling model refer to this as a lifestyle (Adler, 1958); those who use a transactional analysis model refer to this as a script (Woolams & Brown, 1979).

We will talk about three characteristic interpersonal patterns from a developmental/dynamic model (see also Horney, 1970). Clients generally cope in interpersonal systems by (1) moving toward people, (2) moving away or withdrawing from people, or (3) moving against or resisting other people.

MOVING TOWARD OTHERS People who move toward others are likely to be perceived by others as understanding and accommodating. These sorts of people are usually helpful and cooperative but have trouble being appropriately assertive; direct; and, above all, angry. This sort of lifestyle or interpersonal pattern is designed to elicit from others the support and nurturing that was missed as a child. With a client who behaves like this toward the helper, the helper must be careful not just to provide acceptance but also to focus on the general interpersonal style of the client—what the client has missed from his or her family and is trying to elicit from the helper as well as—no doubt—from numerous other people. Clients who move toward others are likely to have issues with being overly compliant and not assertive enough about one's feelings, rights, and opinions. Teyber and McClure (2011) note that a great many helpers themselves fit into this interpersonal pattern!

MOVING AWAY FROM OTHERS Clients who characteristically move away or withdraw from people demonstrate the same behavior in the counseling relationship. They may seek help, but they attempt to maintain as much emotional distance as possible and to remain emotionally unconnected from the counseling per se. These clients have learned to be very independent and are reluctant to ask for help from others, perhaps because of a "heightened sensitivity to rejection and shame" (Teyber & McClure, 2011, p. 288). Although at one level these clients are trying to push the helper away, at another level, they want desperately for the helper to stay connected to them. These clients pose quite a challenge for helpers. To respond reflexively and give up on the client is nontherapeutic. At the same time, if the helper attempts to become too emotionally connected, these clients will feel alarmed and anxious because this is so unfamiliar. The helper needs to stay present and engaged at a pace that follows the client's lead, but above all, the helper must not give up on these individuals.

MOVING AGAINST OTHERS Clients who move against people are on the opposite end of the spectrum from those clients who move toward people. Clients who move against people are assertive to the point of being aggressive in interpersonal relationships. These clients try to maintain control in interpersonal relationships by being dominant and, in plain language, bossy. As clients, they are likely to try to intimidate the helper directly or to resist the helper's efforts passively. They may behave in ways either to take control of the session or to "push the helper's buttons" and make the helper feel inadequate. These kinds of clients may be especially difficult for beginning helpers who may respond counter-therapeutically with fear, competition, or hostility (Teyber & McClure, 2011). Again, as in other instances, it is important for the helper not to respond reflexively and give these clients what they are trying to elicit. The practice of daily mindfulness helps practitioners respond to such clients with equanimity. With these individuals, the helper must avoid getting involved in a battle or power struggle and focus instead on what the clients may be trying to get and/or avoid with their interpersonal styles and the likely impact on their lives.

These three interpersonal coping styles create challenges because they are used in all types of situations, including life choices such as careers and partners, in a rigid or inflexible way (Teyber & McClure, 2011). Lack of psychological flexibility is a major reason why clients come to see helpers.

INTERPERSONAL TESTS OF HELPERS Why do clients act out their typical interactional patterns with helpers? Quite simply, it is a form of a test. They feel that the helper will respond in the same old way as most everyone else, but they hope against hope that the helper will provide a different and more helpful response. When the helper does, they will not have to keep reenacting their same old pattern and can move beyond the point at which they become stuck—not only with the helper but also with other people. Teyber and McClure (2011) conclude, "The therapist can fail the client's test by responding in a way that unwittingly repeats the hurtful relational patterns and confirms pathogenic beliefs—setting the client back. Alternatively, the therapist can pass the test and provide a corrective emotional experience by behaviorally demonstrating that, at least sometimes, some relationships can be different" (p. 328). Shifts in these interpersonal patterns that we have discussed form the basis of a therapeutic approach known as interpersonal therapy, which is the subject of the next section.

Interpersonal Therapy

Originally developed by Klerman and Weissman (1992), interpersonal therapy (IPT) is now an evidence-based helping approach for a variety of disorders including depression, anxiety, and eating disorders. Currently, over 200 empirical studies support the efficacy of IPT. IPT has been used in various contexts, including individual therapy, group therapy, and even telephone-assisted therapeutic interventions. IPT emphasizes that client issues do not occur in a vacuum but rather within an interpersonal context. IPT therapeutic strategies are designed to help clients respond more effectively to this interpersonal context and particularly to interpersonal issues that are associated with the onset of clinical symptoms. General goals of the ITP approach include symptom resolution, improved interpersonal functioning, and increased social support in the client's life.

IPT is considered a time-limited (three- to four-month) intervention with three distinct phases of treatment: a beginning, a middle, and an end. In the beginning phase, the helper has several tasks in particular: identifying the target diagnosis and the context in which it presents, and eliciting an interpersonal inventory that assesses the client's patterns in relationships, capacity for intimacy, and an evaluation of current relationships (Markowitz & Weissman, 2004). From this information, the helper and client collaborate to determine the extent to which the presenting symptoms reflect role or interpersonal conflicts and disputes, life changes or role transitions, or social isolation and interpersonal deficits. During the middle phase of treatment, the helper uses specific strategies to deal with these identified target areas for change: interpersonal disputes, role transitions, and interpersonal deficits (Markowitz & Weissman, 2012). In the ending phase, the helper assists the client in applying these strategies to interpersonal situations in real life. We describe the focus of the IPT change strategies in greater detail in the following three sections.

INTERPERSONAL DISPUTES These strategies help clients to identify interpersonal disputes and choose a satisfactory plan of action to address them, including modification of expectations or communication patterns. The helper works to promote client understanding of how role expectations can relate to interpersonal disputes (Weissman, Markowitz, & Klerman, 2007). Questions to help clients understand this process include the following:

- What are the issues in the disputes?
- What are the differences in the expectations and values?
- What options do I have in this dispute? (Klerman & Weissman, 1992)

In addition, the helper explores with the client whether there are also any parallels in other relationships (including the therapeutic one). For example, what is the client gaining by this interpersonal dispute? What are the unspoken assumptions behind the client's behavior, and how is the dispute perpetuated (Klerman & Weissman, 1992)?

ROLE TRANSITIONS These strategies help clients to mourn and accept any loss of an old or former role (such as spouse, employee, sibling, child, partner, etc.) as well as to regard a new role as something that can be a positive force. The helper assists clients in reviewing positive and negative aspects of both old and new life roles and in exploring feelings about what has been lost and what can be gained. The helper also attends to any appropriate expression of feelings or affect related to role change and encourages development of new social support systems and new skills (Klerman & Weissman, 1992). For example, consider the client who feels lost, abandoned, and sad after his or her last child marries and leaves home. While the primary role of parent is no longer primary, the helper helps the client explore other opportunities for new roles, with increased leisure time and fewer responsibilities for one's family. Perhaps it is a time in the client's life for some new skills training, a new job focus, or new learning that may lead to a new path or greater creativity.

INTERPERSONAL DEFICITS These strategies help clients explore issues of social isolation or deficits in social support systems. The helper assists the client to explore prior significant relationships, including both negative and positive aspects of such relationships. Additionally, the helper and client explore any repetitive patterns that crop up in the client's interpersonal relationships. For example, as we discussed above, perhaps the client withdraws socially from opportunities to meet new people. Or perhaps the client has difficulty in initiating social contacts and events, and relies on invitations and contacts only if initiated by others. This category also includes exploration about the therapeutic relationship. The helper provides the client with opportunities to discuss the client's positive and negative feelings about the helping relationship and the helper, and how these feelings may be reflections of other relationships in the client's life (Klerman & Weissman, 1992). For additional information about the IPT approach, we encourage you to consult the source guide developed by Weissman, Markowitz, and Klerman (2007). In addition, Teyber and McClure (2011) have written about an extensive, integrative approach to interpersonal therapeutic interventions. You will note some similarities between this third focus of IPT (interpersonal deficits) and the material we discuss in the following section on working with client social systems.

WORKING WITH CLIENT CULTURAL AND SOCIAL SYSTEMS

Almost all the interventions that we have presented in the preceding part of this chapter are drawn from counseling theories, such as interpersonal, self-in-relations, gestalt, rational-emotive, cognitive-behavioral, Ericksonian, and family systems. These theories have been have been critiqued by multicultural theorists as reflecting a Eurocentric bias and value system, and as being somewhat culturally irrelevant for clients who feel marginalized from the mainstream.

When issues of cultural salience—such as race, gender, religion, sexual orientation, disability, and social class—are considered, some of the classic therapeutic interventions we have described may even be culturally contraindicated. According to a classic book authored by Brown (1994), it is important to ask the following questions in selecting a helping strategy:

1. Will this strategy oppress my client even more?
2. What does my strategy need to offer in working with a "multiply oppressed" client?

For clients whose worldviews (i.e., basic perceptions and understanding of the world) do not reflect the "rugged individualism" of the Eurocentric tradition, other interventions that are more culturally appropriate are needed to address group, community, and sociopolitical causes as well as the individual causes presented by the client.

Hanna and Cardona (2013) have presented a model of multicultural counseling techniques that focus on reducing oppression and increasing freedom for clients. These authors state, "[T]he primary emphasis of multicultural counseling to date seems to be on developing and sustaining the counseling relationship with persons of differing cultures. There has been little attention devoted to how therapeutic change is to manifest among persons of differing cultures, especially within the context of oppression" (p. 350). They describe techniques designed to promote freedom for clients of oppressed groups rather than adaptation and accommodation.

Interventions to Promote Freedom from Oppression: Precursors to Change and Cognitive Challenges

Hanna and Cardona (2013) depict a model of change in which the following seven precursors are identified as necessary for clients from oppressed groups to experience liberation from oppression:

- A sense of necessity for change
- A willingness to experience discomfort
- Awareness of an issue (versus denial)
- Confrontation of the issue or situation
- Effort toward change
- Hope for change
- Social support for change

They suggest that when a client who has suffered from oppression has an adequate number of these precursors of change, then it is likely change will occur. These precursors are viewed as antecedents for other intervention strategies because when they are absent from a client, change is not likely to occur.

In addition to the precursors of change, Hanna and Cardona (2103) describe a cognitive therapy of oppression intervention strategy designed to "identify, challenge, and modify internalized, oppressive beliefs" (p. 354). As they note, in instances of oppression, these kinds of beliefs are often forced onto clients at a young age, usually to keep the person "under control;" as a result, the client becomes "victimized" by these beliefs (p. 354). Their strategy is to help the client move toward freedom by disagreeing with these oppressive beliefs, disputing these beliefs, and replacing them with beliefs that are freeing. They state, "[A]n advantage of the cognitive theory of oppression is that the source of the dysfunctional belief can be discredited and negated" (p. 354). This is an intervention that can be used both with individual clients and also with groups of oppressed clients.

The Community Genogram

Clients and their issues are connected to and affected by the cultural and social systems to which they belong. Helpers are also affected by their own cultural and social systems. The impact of communities and social groups can be positive, negative, or mixed. The concept of a genogram was originally developed as a tool used in family therapy to view the chronology of a family's life cycle—that is, the effect of family generations on the client over time and over various developmental stages (McGoldrick, Carter, & Garcia-Preto, 2011).

Ivey (1995; Ivey, Ivey, & Zalaquett, 2014) has developed the *community genogram* as a way to depict the interaction between a client and the community and cultural systems. A genogram is a tool to ensure that individual issues are seen in their full contextual background. Ivey and colleagues describe four goals of the community genogram:

1. to generate a narrative story of the client in a community context;
2. to help the client generate an understanding of how we all develop in community;
3. to understand the cultural background of the client; and
4. to focus on personal, family, and group strengths. (pp. 215–218)

Note: We agree with Ivey and colleagues that, before developing this sort of story and understanding with your clients, it is important first to develop this awareness with yourself, the helper of clients.

There are two basic processes to using the community genogram. The first process involves developing a *visual picture* of the client's culture and community. The second process involves developing a *strengths- or asset-based story or narrative of several positive images* reflected in the visual picture. When developing the visual picture with the client, the client describes his or her primary community affiliation and places the family group as well as significant other groups, such as neighborhood, religious and/or spiritual, educational, and work groups, around the community. In developing an asset-based story, the client is asked to develop an image that symbolizes a positive experience with each of these groups and then to tell a story of the assets or strengths that the image represents.

Family Genograms

The concept of the community genogram was adapted from the first use of genograms, which was with a family system rather than a community or cultural system (Bowen, 1978; McGoldrick, Carter, & Garcia-Preto, 2011). Like a community genogram, a family genogram is a visual map of a client's family, usually across several generations (three is typical) that can depict patterns of relationships that might be influencing the client's behavior and issues. A family genogram uses standardized symbols such as those depicted in Figure 9.1 to construct the genogram. Many helpers now go online to find genogram computer programs that provide a standardized family map to use with clients.

Look closely at the sample family genogram in Figure 9.1, and you will see a hypothetical genogram for a couple who sees a helper in the year 2043. This genogram tells you that Aquita had a mother and father who were married, and Maria had two lesbian mothers who were also married. Aquita's mother died at the age of 39. His father and Maria's moms are still alive. Aquita is the index person, which is the person presenting for counseling. Aquita and Maria's oldest child is a daughter, born a year after their marriage in 2040. This birth was followed by a miscarriage the next year and now, in 2043, Maria is pregnant again. As you can tell from this sample genogram, the male is placed to the left of the female in a heterosexual dyad. Children are noted oldest to youngest, left to right, in the diagram. The client or index person is marked with double lines. Names and dates of birth and death can be written above or below the symbol.

After constructing a genogram with a client, the helper uses this visual map to explore relationships and patterns across multigenerational systems within the client's family. The helper may ask questions such as the following:

• Describe your relationship with person X, Y, and Z.
• Who in this family are you closest to?
• Who in this family do you have the most conflict with?
• Describe the other relationships among the family members shown in your genogram.

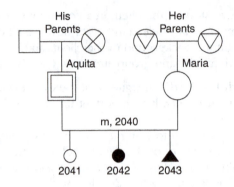

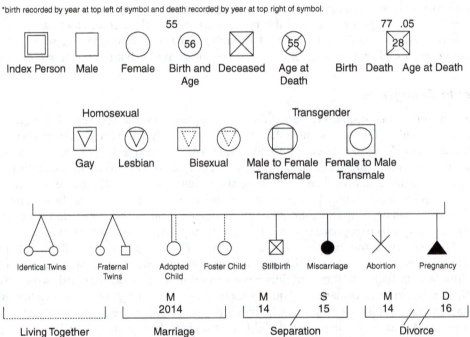

FIGURE 9.1 Sample Family Genogram

- If you had to pick someone out of this genogram who is most like you, who would it be?
- What do you detect in terms of issues and characteristics across these three (or more) generations of your family? How do you think these are affecting your life currently?

Ecomaps

Another intervention that is useful for working with client cultural and social systems is the ecomap. An *ecomap* is a visual tool used to map the ecology (hence the use of the prefix *eco*), or the client's relationship to social systems in his or her life, including relationships, resources, and systems that may be strong, stressful, or unavailable or tenu-ous (Hepworth, Rooney, Dewberry-Rooney, & Strom-Gottfried, 2013). For example, Lott (2002) described how social institutions involving education and housing distance, exclude, and discriminate against poor and low-status persons. In general, social support systems—or lack thereof—play a crucial role in the social functioning of clients. A sample ecomap for a couple (dyadic client) is shown in Figure 9.2. Note that the client—depicted in the middle of the map—is connected to various social systems by different types of lines:

1. A solid line (_____) connects the client to systems that are strong.
2. A broken line (_ _ _ _ _) connects the couple to systems that are negative or stressful.
3. A dotted line (............) connects the couple to systems that are unavailable or weak.

A helper uses an ecomap in conjunction with discussion of cultural and social sup-port systems for the client, noting areas where social support systems are positive, nega-tive, or lacking. The ecomap is a useful tool for meeting the challenge of assessing how these systems "interact, fail to interact, or are needed to interact in response to clients' needs" (Hepworth et al., 2013, p. 230).

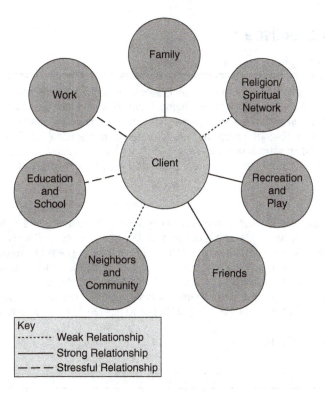

FIGURE 9.2 Sample Ecomap

Helping Roles and Indigenous Practices

In working with cultural and social client systems, a variety of roles are used to complement and extend the traditional role of helper/helpee. These additional roles are described by Atkinson and Hackett (2004) as follows:

- *Advisor:* One who provides information and guidance and who engages in problem solving with clients.
- *Advocate:* One who represents and advocates for clients to other people and organizations.
- *Change agent:* One who actively tries to have an impact on the client's social and cultural environment, especially aspects of it that are discriminatory and/or oppressive.
- *Facilitator of indigenous support systems and practices:* One who recognizes and actively uses the support people and systems indigenous or belonging to the client's culture. This may include the use of extended family or kinship; community elders; and religious and spiritual resources, such as a shamanic healer. This may also include the use of or the referral to someone trained and skilled in using healing methods indigenous or belonging to the client's culture, such as a *currandismo* (Mexican folk healer) or a tai chi instructor.

Application Exercises 9.1 to 9.3 are intended to give you opportunities to apply the concepts and skills discussed in this chapter.

APPLICATION EXERCISE 9.1

Intervention Strategies

In this application exercise, three hypothetical client cases are described. After reading each case, describe what you believe the client's probable counseling goals would be and the related intervention strategies that could be used to help each client reach these goals. Consider goals and strategies for all six areas we discussed in this chapter: feelings, beliefs, behaviors, language, interactional patterns, and cultural/social systems. We suggest doing this activity with a partner or as a small-group discussion. You may wish to exchange your responses and ideas with other helpers or share your thoughts with your instructor.

Case 1

Asani is an Asian American at a large university; she is overwhelmed by the size of the university, having lived in a small town all her life. She is concerned about her shyness and feels it is preventing her from making friends. Asani reports being uncertain about how to reach out to people and reports feeling very lonely but deeply longing for close friendships. She is also concerned about her performance on tests. Although she believes her study habits are adequate, she reports that she "blows" the tests because she gets so uptight about them. Asani believes her grades are a reflection of herself and her family. She is worried about bringing dishonor to her family if she gets low grades.

Probable Outcome Goals

1. _____

   _____

2. _____

3. _____

Possible Helping Strategies

1. _____

2. _____

3. _____

Case 2

Mr. and Mrs. Yule have been married for seven years. Both are in their sixties, and this is the second marriage for each; their previous spouses died. Mr. and Mrs. Yule are concerned that they rushed into this second relationship without adequate thought. They report that they argue constantly about everything. They feel they have forgotten how to talk to each other in a civil manner. Mrs. Yule states that she realizes her constant nagging upsets Mr. Yule; Mr. Yule discloses that his spending a lot of time with his male friends irritates Mrs. Yule. Mr. Yule calls Mrs. Yule a "nagger," and she refers to him as an "SOM—a selfish old man."

Probable Outcome Goals

1. _____

2. _____

3. _____

Possible Helping Strategies

1. _____

2. _____

3. _____

Case 3

Michael is a 13-year-old boy attending a middle school in an urban area. He is constantly starting fights and getting into trouble. He says that he finds himself suddenly punching other kids—and that he does not know how or why. Only after the fights does he realize his temper has gotten out of hand. He reports that he considers himself to be "hotheaded" and that he likes that about himself. He reports spending a lot of time on the streets, and he feels this greatly helps

(Continued)

him survive. He says that, although he is close to his mother, he rarely sees her because she works two to three jobs to support the family. He has had no contact with his father since he was a young boy.

Probable Outcome Goals

1. _____
_____
2. _____
_____
3. _____
_____

Possible Helping Strategies

1. _____
_____
2. _____
_____
3. _____
_____

APPLICATION EXERCISE 9.2

Construction of Summary Cases

This activity asks you—by yourself, with a partner, or in a small group—to create several scenarios of cases and examples. Describe each case by using the instructions below. The purpose of the activity is to help you pull together various aspects of what you have learned in this text and apply them to various helping situations.

1. Construct a helping situation that involves a client who in some way is culturally different from you—different gender, race, age, ethnicity, religion, sexual orientation, health and/or disability status, socioeconomic level, and so on.
2. Describe the cultural dimensions of the client and the cultural dimensions of the helper.
3. Describe any potential therapeutic, cultural, and ethical issues arising from this scenario.
4. Describe ways the helper should handle the situation or respond to this client, including any specific helping strategies and interventions that are needed.

APPLICATION EXERCISE 9.3

Integrative Role Plays and the Counseling Strategies Checklist

In Appendix B, we included a checklist—the Counseling Strategies Checklist—of the skills and strategies we cover in this text. This exercise gives you an opportunity to simulate some actual helping sessions, from beginning a session to forming the therapeutic relationship, implementing basic helping skills, assessing client issues, formulating change goals, selecting and using helping strategies, and terminating a session, all within a culturally relevant framework. Our suggestion is to use the three cases we describe in Application Exercise 9.1 and complete this application exercise in groups of three. There are three role plays, so each of you can assume the role once of helper, once of client, and once of skilled observer. The role-play client's task is to be the client depicted in one of the three cases. When you are the helper, your task is to conduct a one-hour helping session with the role-play client. The role play will be more effective if you can record your practice session. Familiarize yourself with the components of the Counseling Strategies Checklist in Appendix B, and strive to integrate these components in your helping session. The task of the observer is to use the Counseling Strategies Checklist to assess the helper's overall skills and to provide feedback following the role play. After you have done this once, rotate roles two more times.

You can also use the checklist to assess yourself. As you move into your field placements, you will, no doubt, have numerous opportunities to present your work via live observation, recorded reviews, case conferences, and so on. This application exercise represents a lead into some of these additional experiences as you continue your training to become a professional helper.

Summary

In working with clients—all of whom present unique concerns and circumstances—you may find the strategies described in this chapter useful. However, there are several cautions to consider in using a helping strategy effectively. The first caution in strategy implementation is to avoid oversimplification of the procedure. Although a procedure may seem relatively simple to implement, even with little experience, any therapeutic endeavor can be effective or ineffective depending on how it is administered. Second, you must practice using strategies. You will not be an expert when you first start using them, but your skills will grow as you practice. Also remember that strategies are rarely used in isolation. Several different strategies or combinations of procedures may be necessary to deal with the complexity and range of concerns presented by a single client. As an example, suppose a helper treats a client's alcoholism but ignores the anxiety for which alcohol is used as a tranquilizer. The strategies used to decrease the drinking behavior may not be too effective unless the helper and client also use strategies to deal with the client's limited coping skills, self-defeating thoughts, and environmental issues that maintain the drinking.

Remember that the effectiveness of helping strategies depends—to some degree—on the strength and trust of the helping relationship as well as on the degree to which these strategies are used in a gender- and culture-friendly way. Responding to a client's social and environmental milieu is as important in strategy implementation as responding to a client's presenting feelings, beliefs, and behaviors.

It is also important to realize the limitations of helping objectives and strategies and of helpers. One of the most frustrating experiences that helpers report is the experience of being thwarted in their attempts to help clients change and grow. Beginning helpers often approach the counseling process with a lot of zest, zeal, and unwavering idealism. Although a certain amount of this is useful, it can also lead to discouragement with oneself and with clients. Almost all clients will resist your attempts to help in some way. Some clients who see you at the request of someone else may be openly oppositional. Other clients may desire to change, but because of biochemical imbalances, they may require medication for conditions such as depression or anxiety management. Clients with addictions may also find the process of recovery especially difficult. Clients from very dysfunctional family systems may find the weight of the system working against their own individual efforts to change. So as you approach your growth and development and your own efforts in working with clients, it is important to remember that there are some limits to what happens in the counseling process and that almost all client resistance to change is about fear. As clients become more able to trust themselves and you, your efforts and theirs will be rewarded. We discuss even more of these kinds of challenges for beginning helpers in Chapter 10.

Reflective Questions

1. In this chapter, we describe a variety of interventions to work with the whole person (e.g., the client's feelings, beliefs, behaviors, language, interactional patterns, and cultural/social systems). As you have read and worked with these interventions, which ones feel most natural and comfortable for you? Which ones do you believe would cause the most trouble? Why?

2. Where in your own body do you consistently hold feelings? How do you become aware of these places in your body? What do you do to release them?

3. Can you identify situations in which your beliefs have affected the way you feel and act?

4. Which persons have you used in your life for role models? Do characters in books, television shows, or movies also serve as role models for you? Which of their characteristics appeal to you?

5. How do you apply self-management to everyday behaviors for yourself?

6. What would your life be like if you simply noticed your thoughts rather than judging them?

7. Can you identify labels you have constructed for yourself from your stories about yourself? How have these labels helped you? How have they limited you?

8. What is your characteristic interactional pattern? Can you trace it back to your family of origin? How do you think this pattern will affect the way you interact with your clients?

9. Refer again to Figure 9.1. With a partner or in a small group, construct a family genogram for yourself and your family. Discuss what you learn from this process with your partner or group members.

10. Identify ways in which the intervention strategies described in this chapter may or may not be useful for clients who present with histories of multiple oppressions. What helping strategies do you think would be most suitable for oppressed clients?

MyCounselingLab

For each exercise, log on to MyCounselingLab.

1. Select Theories of Counseling collection in the Video Library. Click on the Documents Stack and find the letter to Helen from Jim, the narrative therapist. Read the letter that Jim wrote to his client Helen. In what ways does this letter help the client restory her life and identity?

2. Next, in the Video Library, click on the Counseling Children and Adolescents collection. Locate "Constructing Letters (Stories) with/for Clients." Watch the clip and then discuss your thoughts about the use of letters with the client's siblings to address the issue of taunting. How do these letters support a narrative approach to therapy?

3. In the Video Library, choose the Family Therapy collection. Watch the clip entitled "Facilitating Insight and Emotional Experience." Discuss the ways in which the helper focused on affective interventions with the couple. How effective did these seem to you? Next, select the clip entitled "Facilitating Open Emotional Expression." What did you think of the helper's use of the affective roleplay dialogue between the mother and daughter to facilitate affective expression by the daughter?

4. Select the Counseling Children and Adolescents collection in the Video Library, and locate the clip entitled "Exploring Feelings Toward Parents." Watch this clip and comment on the helper's use of clay and play therapy as an affective kind of intervention.

5. Select the Theories of Counseling collection in the Video Library and find the clip on "Barbara: Parenting-Task Setting." Watch the clip and then discuss how Dr. Carlson seemed to use behavioral change interventions to help the client commit to behavior change in this scenario.

6. Select the Theories of Counseling collection in the Video Library. Watch two clips on cognitive therapy; the first one is called "Cognitive Session" and the second is called "Cognitive Reflections." What were the most important things you learned about doing cognitive interventions from watching these two clips?

7. Select the Family Therapy collection within the Video Library, and watch the clip "Exploring the Social Context of the Family." Describe what you saw as the major interactional patterns in this particular family.

8. In the Family Therapy collection in the Video Library, watch the video clip "Exploring Culture and Beliefs," then watch "Applying Culture and Beliefs." How did you see the two helpers use the couple's cultural background to shape effective interventions for this particular pair of clients?

Recommended Readings

Adler, J. M., Harmeling, L. H., & Walder-Biesanz, I. (2013). Narrative meaning making is associated with sudden gains in psychotherapy clients' mental health under routine clinical conditions. *Journal of Consulting and Clinical Psychology, 81,* 839–845.

Beck, J. S. (2011). *Cognitive behavior therapy* (2nd ed.). New York: Guilford.

Bitter, J. (2014). *Theories and practice of family therapy and counseling* (2nd ed.). Belmont, CA: Brooks/Cole, Cengage.

Brown, A. P., Marquis, A., & Guiffrida, D. A. (2013). Mindfulness-based interventions in counseling. *Journal of Counseling and Development, 91,* 96–104. doi: 10.1002/j.1556-6676.2013.00077.x

Cormier, S., Nurius, P., & Osborn, C. (2013). *Interviewing and change strategies for helpers: Fundamental skills and cognitive-behavioral interventions* (7th ed.). Belmont, CA: Brooks/Cole, Cengage.

Dobson, K. S. (2012). *Cognitive therapy.* Washington DC: American Psychological Association.

Dryden, W. (2009). *Skills in rational emotive behaviour counseling and psychotherapy.* Thousand Oaks, CA: Sage.

Greenberg, L. S. (2011). *Emotion-focused therapy.* Washington, DC: American Psychological Association.

Hackney, H., & Cormier, L. S. (2013). *The professional helper* (7th ed.). Upper Saddle River, NJ: Pearson.

Hanna, F. J., & Cardona, B. (2013). Multicultural counseling beyond the relationship: Expanding the repertoire with techniques. *Journal of Counseling and Development, 91,* 349–357.

Hayes, S. C., Strosahl, K. D., & Wilson, K. G. (2012). *Acceptance and commitment therapy* (2nd ed.). New York, NY: Guilford.

Hepworth, D. H., Rooney, R. H., Rooney, D. G., & Strom-Gottfried, K. (2013). *Direct social work practice. Theory and skills* (9th ed.). Belmont, CA: Brooks/Cole, Cengage.

Leach, M. M., & Aten, J. D. (Eds). (2010). *Culture and the therapeutic process: A guide for mental health professionals.* New York, NY: Routledge.

Makinson, R. A., & Young, S. (2012). Cognitive behavioral therapy and the treatment of posttraumatic stress disorder: Where counseling and neuroscience meet. *Journal of Counseling and Development, 90,* 131–140. doi:10.1111/j.1556-6676.2012.00017.x

Markowitz, J., & Weissman, M. (Eds.). (2012). *Casebook of interpersonal psychotherapy.* New York, NY: Oxford University Press.

McGoldrick, M., Carter, B., & Garcia-Preto, N. (2011). *The expanded family life cycle: Individual, family, and social perspectives* (4th ed.). Upper Saddle River, NJ: Pearson.

Prochaska, J., & Norcross, J. (2014). *Systems of psychotherapy* (8th ed.). Belmont, CA: Brooks/Cole, Cengage.

Spiegler, M. D., & Guevremont, D. C. (2010). *Contemporary behavior therapy* (5th ed.). Belmont, CA: Wadsworth/Cengage.

Sue, D. W. (2013). Race talk: The psychology of racial dialogues. *American Psychologist, 68,* 661–663.

Teyber, E., & McClure, F. (2011). *Interpersonal processes in psychotherapy* (6th ed.). Belmont, CA: Brooks/Cole, Thomson.

Watson, D. L., & Tharp, R. G. (2014). *Self-directed behavior: Self-modification for personal adjustment* (10th ed.). Belmont, CA: Wadsworth.

CHAPTER 10

Considerations and Challenges for Beginning Helpers

Beth Robinson, PhD

Whether currently a student or a recent graduate of a training program in one of the helping professions, beginning helpers are presented with a number of considerations and challenges. It can come as a surprise when new counselors discover that their anticipated success in coursework and supervised practice in their program will not represent arrival at the finish line in terms of professional preparation. Rather, the conclusion of formal studies positions counselors at the entry-to-practice threshold of a career path, and best practice throughout one's career will be marked by ongoing professional learning and development.

The hallmarks of good counselors include caring, compassion, commitment, confidence, and competence. Generally, the first two qualities are assumed to be present long before the decision is made to pursue a professional helping career. The latter three develop both during and subsequent to the course of study. As students and newly graduated students move into the field, they report experiences unique to their status as beginning helpers that influence their perceptions and demonstrations of commitment, confidence, and competence. In this chapter, we will explore early practice phenomena, experienced by beginning helpers at the student and recent-graduate stage of development. These phenomena will be examined in the context of professional identity, clinical supervision, networking, professional affiliation and credentialing, professional development, ethical and legal issues, professional resources, career rewards, and self-care.

In this chapter, terms such as *beginning helpers, new counselors,* and *novice practitioners* are understood to encompass students currently pursuing studies and supervised practice in professional helping, as well as recent graduates who are embarking on career paths as helping professionals. These career paths may be in counseling, human services, psychology, social work, or any other occupational designation in which helpers engage in counseling with clients.

PROFESSIONAL IDENTITY

As early as the point of commencing studies in the helping professions, and well into the first few years following graduation, beginning helpers are on a quest to establish a sense of identity as professional helpers. At this life stage, they will likely have established a clear sense of personal identity related to their roles and experiences as family members, friends, neighbors, community members, and secondary or postsecondary students. They may also have clarified a professional identity as colleagues or coworkers in previous and/or current employment settings.

However, no matter how stable the sense of self deriving from those life roles and experiences might have been, novice helpers typically report feeling cast adrift because the perceptions they held of themselves before entering their programs of study no longer seem to apply. It's as if they've been asked to step into a lifeboat, leave behind all belongings, and carry nothing with them that communicates their previous identity and place in the world. They've shed all reminders of who they were and the respect that they were accorded by virtue of prior accomplishments. Beginning helpers often find themselves pondering questions such as:

Who was I personally and professionally before embarking on this path to becoming a helping professional?

Does my previous sense of self still fit at the personal level? At the professional level?

How aligned do I feel with the identity of professional helper?

Questions of this nature engage nascent helping professionals in the important and expected developmental process of illuminating and reassessing attitudes, beliefs, values, priorities, and preferences as they relate to evolving professional identity. Introspection and self-monitoring are activities that are integral to this updating of self-knowledge and awareness.

Application Exercise 10.1 invites you to engage in reflective writing about your philosophy of change in a professional helping context. The intent of this application exercise is to foster professional identity and role clarification. As a helping professional, you will enrich your professional development by undertaking activities such as this while engaged in formal study and then revisiting them periodically over the course of your career to track the evolution of your perspectives.

APPLICATION EXERCISE 10.1

Reflections on a Personal Philosophy of Counseling and Change

Prepare a written reflection of two to four pages in which you articulate your philosophy of the role of counseling in supporting clients while they bring about desired changes in their lives. Note that the purpose of this activity is to encourage you to bring your own beliefs, attitudes, and values to awareness; you are not required to draw on other reference materials.

Establishing a Sense of Self as a Helping Professional

As students and recent graduates explore issues of professional identity, they begin to crystallize a sense of self not only as a *helping professional* but also as a *member of a particular helping profession*. They move beyond a generic concept of helping professional to one that is congruent with the focus of their education and training. Via a process of professional acculturation, students and graduates adopt an identity that espouses the philosophy, worldview, and values of their chosen helping profession. A developmental shift from the professional identity question of "Who shall I be?" to professional identity ownership occurs, where they can announce with conviction, "I am a counselor (or human services professional, psychologist, psychotherapist, social worker, etc.)."

These acknowledgments of self as one who is both a helping professional and a member of a particular helping profession conceivably could be represented dichotomously as either recognized or not yet recognized by beginning helpers. In this case, the question would be "Do novice helpers identify themselves as members of one of the helping professions of counseling, human services, psychology, social work, or an affiliated field?"

In contrast, there is not a clearly demarcated threshold for the establishment of a deeper sense of professional identity, which in many ways is dynamic rather than static. From the early days as a helping professional and across the career span, this more complex professional identity requires helping professionals to consider questions such as:

How do my philosophy, worldview, and values align with those of my chosen helping profession?

In which respects does my helping profession differ from and overlap with other helping professions?

What do I say and do that identifies me as a member of my particular helping profession?

The helping professions are always evolving with respect to theories embraced, bodies of knowledge accumulated, skills promoted, and practices espoused. An important developmental task for novice helpers is to establish professional identity, but the dynamism of the field calls for a certain degree of responsive flexibility. Such adaptability allows helping professionals to stay in step with developments in the field while at the same time maintaining a relatively stable core professional identity. Ultimately, this adaptability will foster a continued sense of professional belonging and congruence (or good fit), both of which contribute to career satisfaction.

Imposter Phenomenon

At about the point when beginning helpers feel that their professional identity is crystallizing, a disconcerting experience referred to as the *imposter phenomenon* may intrude on this nascent sense of professional clarity (see, for example, Clance, 1985; Harvey & Katz, 1985; McElwee & Yurak, 2010; Sakulku & Alexander, 2011). We might assume that students who are nearing the end of their studies would experience increased confidence and that recent graduates would breathe a sigh of relief at the reduced pressures now that coursework and practica are behind them, but it is not uncommon for a new form of anxiety to arise. As beginning helpers begin to embody their professional identities, they often adopt the perspective that they should be, feel, and present to others as knowledgeable and skilled at all times. However, with a greater conceptual foundation comes the awareness of the vastness of the existing knowledge base in the field, the rapid pace of new developments, and the sheer impossibility of remaining abreast of it all.

In other words, beginning helpers become painfully aware of what they don't know and the futility of aspiring to know it all. And while counselor educators and supervisors view this awareness as healthy (as long as it motivates helpers to engage in lifelong learning rather than dissuades them from doing so), it can be unnerving for beginning helpers who are plagued by the tyranny of the thought "I ought to by now." These self-expectations with respect to what they feel they should know and be able to do are what fuel the sense of being an imposter and the fear of being discovered as a fraud by clients and colleagues.

Fortunately, this anxiety tends to resolve quite quickly on its own, and its resolution can be hastened by empathic self-disclosures of supervisors and professional peers who normalize and validate this early career experience. In fact, the adage "Fake it until you make it" can be wise counsel, not unlike the therapeutic prescription to clients to act "as if." Acting as if one is realistically confident and appropriately competent for one's stage of professional development is sage advice. It opens beginning helpers to their experiences rather than channeling their energy into hiding, being invisible, or flying under the radar. This, in turn, is more likely to increase opportunities for ongoing learning and successful practice than is the case when imposter anxiety leads to so-called analysis paralysis and to fear and avoidance of reasonable professional risk taking.

A recent study (Moss, Gibson, & Dollarhide, 2014) found that novice helpers do go through a series of phases throughout their professional identity development, beginning with having idealized expectations, moving through self-doubt, gaining confidence with experience, and decreasing imposter anxiety with supervision. In this study, the importance of supervision for professional identity development was significant for helpers at all levels of experience, not just for novices. In the following section of the chapter, we discuss some important parameters of the clinical supervision process.

CLINICAL SUPERVISION

The processes of clarification of professional identity and resolution of normative developmental anxiety (such as the imposter phenomenon) can be facilitated by clinical supervision during and subsequent to the period of formal study. Clinical supervision also promotes consolidation of learning and refining of helping skills. It offers planned periods for reflection and feedback in the company of one or more helping professional colleagues, ideally in a highly supportive environment. We now recognize that engaging in clinical supervision across the career span represents best practice, with benefits accruing both to professional helpers and to their clients. The exploration and discussion of counseling-related issues in clinical supervision focuses on the well-being of clients as well as the professional growth and development of supervisees.

Professional helpers undertake rigorous education and training aimed at fostering development of conceptual knowledge, process or intervention skills, personalization skills, and professional skills. Personalization skills promote appropriate and effective use of the self of the counselor (e.g., personality, cultural background, interpersonal style) in working with clients, while professional skills include awareness of and fidelity to ethical and legal practice (see, for example, Bernard & Goodyear, 2004; Hess & Kraus, 2010; Pearson, 2004). A combination of well-honed awareness, sensitivity, knowledge, and skills serves as the foundation for caring, confident, and competent professional practice. Whether occurring during the period of formal study and/or subsequent to graduation, clinical supervision assists students and entry-level practitioners in the process of integrating and applying this foundational learning as they transition from aspiring counselors to practicing professionals.

As we explore the importance of supervision for beginning helpers, it is important to understand the distinction between the roles of *administrative* supervisors and *clinical* supervisors. Administrative supervisors oversee administrative processes in the workplace such as hiring, conducting performance appraisals for retention and promotion, and ensuring that workplace policies and procedures are followed. Thus, helping professionals who are hired to work *for* someone else at any point on their career path will become familiar with the role of an administrative supervisor. Clinical supervisors focus on the clinical skill development and practice performance of the supervisee. Students will have clinical supervisors for practicum, internship, and externship placements. They may also be required to engage in postgraduation clinical supervision for certification, registration, or licensure. In contrast to administrative supervision that may extend across the full career span, the requirement for clinical supervision for credentialing generally is time-limited to a certain number of hours or years of practice subsequent to completion of training.

During the period of formal study and for the first few years afterward, beginning helpers most likely will be on the receiving end of the clinical supervision equation. As supervisees, they will benefit from the experience of more seasoned practitioners, who will assist them in identifying their strengths and growth areas and will help them to devise a plan for meeting learning and competency goals.

As beginning helpers continue to gain knowledge and experience, they may decide that they'd like to offer service back to the field and their professional peers as administrative or clinical supervisors, consultants, or mentors. The roles of administrative supervisors, clinical supervisors, and consultants tend to entail more formal arrangements than mentorships, and supervision generally is scheduled more regularly than consultation that may be offered on an ad hoc (or as needed) basis. However, each of these roles has the potential to make valuable contributions to the conceptual and practice competencies of more junior colleagues (see, for example, Bernard & Goodyear, 2014; Campbell, 2006; Falender & Shafranske, 2008).

The field of supervision is now undergoing rather rapid growth and professionalization. The criteria for being deemed a qualified supervisor are the subject of considerable professional discussion among practitioners, researchers, faculty members in professional helping programs, and members of executive committees of professional associations and regulatory bodies. Given current prerequisites for supervisors with respect to the number of years of experience as a helping professional, and the high level of need in the field, it is conceivable that helping professionals who have been practicing for only a handful of years may find themselves in demand as supervisors for students in practicum, internship, and externship placements, and/or for certification, registration, or licensure.

Seeking Clinical Supervision

Beginning helpers face the challenge of identifying optimal practicum, internship, and/or externship opportunities during their course of study as well as finding a good supervisory match if postgraduation clinical supervision is required for certification, registration, or licensure. Training programs and regulatory bodies may have established criteria for qualified clinical supervisors with respect to educational background, number of years in practice, credentials held, and so forth. Therefore, it is important for beginning helpers to determine whether their graduation or credentialing hinges on approval of proposed supervisory arrangements and, if so, to ensure that the intended clinical supervisor meets any existing criteria.

The paradox of clinical supervision is that, while supervisees generally recognize the important contributions of supervision to their professional growth, many experience considerable anxiety about the process, at least until the clinical supervisory relationship is well established. On the one hand, clinical supervision can help to dispel any vestiges of the imposter phenomenon (as we noted earlier in the chapter); on the other hand, the prospect of supervision itself can engender intense apprehension. Recognizing that clinical supervision inherently involves some form of evaluation, beginning helpers often report great trepidation about the possibility of being discovered as unsuited to the helping profession. This angst interferes with their ability to receive and perceive clinical supervision feedback as helpful developmental guidance. Instead, some supervisees respond defensively, while others feel some shame.

To reduce the psychological and physical tension that beginning helpers may be experiencing in relation to clinical supervision, it is vital that they literally and figuratively take some deep breaths. Remember that all clinical supervisors once were novice practitioners too! The intention of clinical supervisors is to support beginning helpers in the manner in which their own supervisors supported them. Supervision is intended to be a collaborative process, not an adversarial one. For it to be an experience that optimizes growth, however, supervisees need to be open and honest. If they speak only about events that go well in helping sessions, clinical supervisors will not be able to problem-solve with them around any challenges or disappointments encountered.

Healthy and productive clinical supervisory relationships foster a mutual sense of safety, trust, control, intimacy, and esteem. Supervisees feel secure enough in the supervision sessions to share what they perceive to be failures as well as successes. They feel empowered to identify what they need from their clinical supervisors and the supervision sessions. They dare to disclose experiences that did not turn out as hoped, and they think highly enough of themselves and their clinical supervisors to trust that the learning that will come out of debriefing of such difficult situations will guide them well in the future. It is only in daring to be honest in clinical supervision that beginning helpers will move past any embarrassment, shame, or fear of letting clients, themselves, and their supervisors down.

If supervisees do not raise unsettling matters for discussion in their clinical supervision sessions, they may not be able to resolve the issues on their own, and then the imposter phenomenon will have opportunity to take root and even to grow. It takes a lot of energy to hide or pull away in supervision, with the result that supervisees leave supervision feeling drained and dreading the next supervision session. This starts a vicious cycle of supervisees concealing anything that does not cast them in a competent light, leading to further entrenchment of the sense of being an imposter or a fraud. Even more troubling is the possibility that withholding information from supervisors could place the well-being of clients in jeopardy. This in turn increases the risk for beginning helpers to engage in ethical violations or illegal actions. It also may lead to supervisors being held vicariously liable for any harm resulting from supervisee acts of commission or omission (see, for example, Falvey, 2002; Maki & Bernard, 2007; Remley & Herlihy, 2013; Saccuzzo, 2002).

In contrast, when supervisees trust their clinical supervisors and the supervision process, the professional development that is possible is quite remarkable. Beginning helpers and their clinical supervisors enter into collaborative identification of growth goals that are tailored to the unique needs of the supervisees. As supervisees share their fears and frustrations, this openness invites judicious self-disclosure on the part of clinical supervisors that normalizes and validates supervisees' experiences. Strong supervisory relationships bring out the best in beginning helpers who are able to accept positive feedback and to contemplate options for growth associated with constructive feedback. They feel free to explore possibilities and to experiment with new ideas and approaches. Application Exercise 10.2 invites you to consider a supervision metaphor that represents clinical supervision at its best.

APPLICATION EXERCISE 10.2

What's Your Supervision Metaphor?

Metaphors help to depict the meaning that we attach to experiences. For example, supervision metaphors might include a parent assisting a child in transitioning from training wheels to independent two-wheeled cycling, adult robins preparing their fledgling offspring to leave the nest, or an experienced canoeist and a novice working together to navigate challenging waters successfully. Supervision also might be envisioned as akin to orbiting the earth in a space shuttle, viewing the planet from distant perspectives in the company of a trusted co-navigator, with quiet and uninterrupted opportunity for collaborative review and reflection.

If you were to identify a metaphor that captures for you the essence of positive clinical supervision, what might it be? Why does this particular metaphor resonate with you?

Peer Supervision

Whether or not postdegree supervision is compulsory, the benefits of continued supervision throughout one's counseling career are recognized both from a professional growth and a risk management perspective. Many helping professionals transition from formal supervision (individual or group) to peer supervision once the requirements for certification, registration, or licensure have been met. In peer supervision, helping professionals engage in reciprocally supportive roles with similar-status colleagues (e.g., Borders, 1999; Hawkins & Shohet, 2012; Kassan, 2010). Peer supervision may be conducted with homogenous or heterogeneous group composition with respect to helping disciplines represented, years of professional experience, theoretical orientations, helping approaches, client population, and practice setting. For example, a peer supervision group might be comprised of school counselors from the local elementary, middle or junior high, and high schools who meet on a biweekly basis to discuss counseling issues and cases and to engage in informal professional development. Another peer supervision group might be comprised of multidisciplinary private practitioners who have been meeting monthly for over a decade to discuss professional readings, helping challenges, and self-care strategies. Peer supervision can help practitioners feel less isolated and more connected to other professionals also coping with particular practice challenges.

Offering Supervision

The demand for clinical supervision has been rising steadily around the globe. With increased regulation of professional helping practice, enhanced awareness of the career-long benefits of supervision, and heightened attunement to risk management, supervision is viewed as a preemptive approach for avoiding ethical complaints and litigation. As a result of this upsurge in demand, the reality is that early-career helpers may be approached with requests to undertake the role of supervisor only four or five years into their practice. While this possibility may be perceived as both flattering and enticing, it is also accompanied by important ethical considerations that have garnered substantial attention in the professional literature (see, for example, Barnett & Johnson, 2015; Corey, Corey, Corey, & Callanan, 2015; Maki & Bernard, 2007; Pope & Vasquez, 2011).

These ethical considerations include ensuring an adequate informed consent process for both supervisor and supervisee, clearly identifying the parameters of and limits to confidentiality (as they apply to clients, helpers, and supervisors), establishing appropriate boundaries for the supervisory relationship, clarifying any issues related to multiple professional and/or personal relationships, and acknowledging and practicing within established boundaries of competence.

Most important, beginning helpers should not undertake the role of clinical supervisor without undergoing formal training in supervision. This ethical imperative has been underscored repeatedly in the interests of safeguarding the welfare of clients, supervisees, supervisors, and the public at large (e.g., Center for Substance Abuse Treatment, 2009; Pope & Vasquez, 2011; Thomas, 2010). Recognition of clinical supervision as a practice specialty, with its own set of competencies separate and apart from counseling, is evident in the steadily increasing number of states and countries that now require aspiring supervisors to meet criteria for credentialing as an approved supervisor. Contrary to what historical traditions might imply, training as a helping professional does not automatically confer competency as a supervisor. That is, counseling knowledge and skill do not automatically confer supervisory knowledge and skill. Thus, one might be quite capable as a clinician but not optimally effective as a clinical supervisor.

NETWORKING

Networking is another professional practice that is highly recommended for helping professionals (e.g., Lairio & Nissila, 2002; Lionetti, Snyder, & Christner, 2011; Tretout, 1999). Networking refers to the processes of connecting, communicating, and interacting with professional peers in the service of reciprocally facilitating and optimizing professional growth. It cuts across professional territories and invites interdisciplinary initiatives (Bronstein, 2003). Networking subsumes a wider range of activities than clinical supervision and clinical consultation, each of which has a primary focus on issues directly related to work with clients. Networking extends opportunities for professional collaboration in research, writing, and other projects. Being able to access and call on the expertise of a network of helping professionals accelerates the process of obtaining helpful suggestions and recommendations related to all aspects of the profession, including certification, registration, and licensing; professional development; employment; referral options; and so on.

Networking also has a social component that yields notable professional benefits. Cultivating professional acquaintances reduces professional isolation. These acquaintanceships or even friendships that may emerge are particularly potent buffers against career-related stress because of the shared inside view and understanding of the risk factors for compassion fatigue, secondary traumatization, vicarious traumatization, and burnout that are inherent in the helping professions (see, for example, Figley, 2002; Kadambi & Truscott, 2004; Rainer, 2000; Skovholt & Trotter-Mathison, 2011).

The process of establishing a professional network begins when an individual enters a program of study and establishes relationships with fellow students, faculty members, and practicum and internship site supervisors. Many of these connections continue even after students graduate and embark on career paths that may take them around the globe. Today, when technology is literally at our fingertips, distance networking can be accomplished verbally and in writing via numerous phone- and Internet-based avenues, for example, e-mail, Skype, texting, listservs, online forums, blogs, and chat rooms.

A strong networking foundation is also promoted through membership and active involvement in professional associations and organizations, as well as participation in professional development activities such as workshops and conferences. These networking options will be discussed in the following chapter sections.

PROFESSIONAL AFFILIATION AND CREDENTIALING

Over the course of their formal study and training, beginning helpers are reminded of the importance of professional connections at the organizational level. Students may be apprised of affiliation, volunteerism, and credentialing considerations as early as the program admissions interview stage or in a subsequent program orientation session. They certainly will engage in related discussions with peers and professors in classes and colloquia, and with supervisors and colleagues at practica and internship sites. It is important to be acquainted with the full range of options so that informed decisions may be made about professional memberships, certification, registration, licensure, and so on. See Chapter 1 for additional information on these topics.

Membership in Professional Associations

Students in the helping professions are encouraged to consider membership in professional associations at the state, regional, national, and international levels (e.g., Dahir & Stone, 2012; Davis, 2015; Erford, 2014). In contrast to the primary mandate of regulatory bodies to protect the public via certification, registration, licensure, and ethical oversight of members, professional associations tend to invest their efforts and energies in the areas of professional advocacy, networking, and continuing education.

Often, the structure of professional associations includes divisions and chapters that focus on areas of practice in which members may wish to develop expertise and/or specialization (e.g., Erford, 2014; Leahy, 2004; Newsome & Gladding, 2014). For example, included among the American Counseling Association's (ACA's) 20 divisions are Adult Development and Aging, and Creativity and Counseling (American Counseling Association, 2014a). The American Psychological Association (APA) has 54 divisions that represent psychology subdisciplines and topic areas such as Health Psychology, Industrial and Organizational Psychology, School Psychology, and Trauma Psychology (American Psychological Association, 2014). The 11 Specialty Practice Sections of the National Association of Social Workers include Administration/Supervision, and Social and Economic Justice and Peace (National Association of Social Workers, 2014).

Student and recent graduate membership in state, regional, national, and international professional organizations promotes development of professional identity and early establishment of professional networks. Membership also offers an array of benefits that may include liability insurance; discounts on books, journals, and videos; and access to listservs, blogs, forums, members-only sections of websites, newsletters, association journals, and other information-sharing avenues that facilitate remaining abreast of developments in the field. Professional development opportunities sponsored by associations are also often accompanied by offers of reduced rates for members and even greater reductions for those of student status.

Professional Volunteerism

Even more enriching than membership alone is active engagement in the work of professional associations and other organizations (e.g., Campbell, 2006; Erford, 2014; Newsome & Gladding, 2014). This is encouraged right from the point of entry into a program of study and throughout one's career as a helping professional. There are almost limitless opportunities to assume volunteer roles at the state, regional, national, and international levels, whether as a student representative or as a recent graduate. These roles might involve membership on the board of directors or executive committee of an association; participation in task group work related to the creation or revision of brochures, manuals, ethics codes, standards of practice, and other documents; peer review of journal articles; presentations at workshops or conferences; and engagement in planning for local, state, regional, national, and international conferences and conventions.

Active participation in the work of professional organizations is another avenue for crystallizing professional identity, establishing professional connections with like-minded colleagues, and staying in tune with professional development opportunities. Volunteers enhance the visibility and credibility of helping professions in meaningful ways through advocacy and media relations, committee and task group work, and contributions to the professional development of professional peers. Documenting contributions at the local, state, regional, national, and/or international level certainly enhances the attractiveness of one's résumé or curriculum vitae!

Professional Certification and Credentialing

Depending on the particular discipline or specialty area under the helping professions umbrella, *practice* or *professional* credentialing may be offered or required at the national and state levels. As noted in Chapter 1, for example, licensure laws exist in each of the 50 states, the District of Columbia, and Puerto Rico for those in the counseling profession (American Counseling Association, 2014a; National Board for Certified Counselors, 2014a; Newsome & Gladding, 2014). This means that licensure, which is sometimes referred to as registration in Canada, is mandatory in order to practice counseling (subject to some exclusions in educational, governmental, and nonprofit settings), and the license restricts practice to the jurisdiction in which the license is granted. Counseling licensure bodies are legally entitled to decide who is qualified to practice counseling and to define the scope of practice. Currently, the titles most commonly awarded by state-level regulatory bodies include Licensed Professional Counselor (LPC), Licensed Clinical Professional Counselor (LCPC), Licensed Professional Clinical Counselor (LPCC), and Licensed Mental Health Counselor (LMHC).

The essential role of regulatory bodies that oversee licensure is to ensure the safety of the public. Meeting this mandate generally entails a series of processes aimed at ensuring that helping professionals are qualified and conduct themselves in a manner that is congruent with their profession's code of ethics and standards of practice. Thus, the first stage typically involves evaluation of the applicant's academic credentials to ensure that criteria related to formal study (e.g., coursework) and supervised practice (e.g., practicum, internship) have been met. There also may be a required period of supervised practice following completion of the program of study. During this period of supervision, the supervisee will be subject to formative and summative assessment, with supervision reports submitted to the regulatory body. The final stage commences at the point when a candidate has met all criteria for registration or licensure and now is deemed qualified to practice independently. This stage extends throughout the helping professional's career and is one during which the regulatory body provides ongoing ethical oversight and conducts investigation and intervention as warranted. Ethics committees associated with regulatory bodies are responsible for the following:

- Ethical inquiries submitted by clients or members.
- Complaints submitted by current or former clients about current or former members.
- Concerns about professional conduct arising out of information shared by other individuals or professional bodies.
- Sua sponte complaints initiated by the ethics committee itself.

In contrast to licensure, which is considered a *practice* credential because it is administered by a regulatory body that can restrict or prohibit counseling practice, certification is defined as a *professional* credential because it is not subject to statutory regulation. Although some associations and boards that issue certification also provide ethical oversight and impose sanctions for ethical noncompliance, certification is voluntary. An example of certification in the helping professions is the designation of National Certified Counselor (NCC) that may be pursued through the National Board for Certified Counselors (Bernard & Goodyear, 2014; National Board for Certified Counselors, 2014a). The National Board for Certified Counselors (NBCC) also offers Specialty Certifications as a National Certified School Counselor (NCSC), Certified Clinical Mental Health Counselor (CCMHC), and Master Addictions Counselor (MAC) (National Board for Certified Counselors, 2014a; Newsome & Gladding, 2014).

Discussions about professional certification, registration, and licensure generally commence early in a program of studies to ensure that aspiring helping professionals are fully informed of the requirements long before they begin filling out the paperwork for application. There is nothing more disheartening than learning, after the fact, of an overlooked criterion such as a required course or a minimum number of direct client contact hours. For this reason, students who are studying to become a professional helper are strongly encouraged to do all of the following:

- Visit the websites of professional organizations with which they will be seeking certification, registration, and/or licensure.
- Attend any information sessions offered by these organizations.
- Check in regularly with faculty members and supervisors about options and developments.
- Carefully document and safeguard information about the program of study that will support applications for certification, registration, and licensure, including calendar descriptions of the program, course outlines and syllabi, academic transcripts, practicum and/or internship descriptions, supervisor reports of practicum or internship performance, and client and supervision hours accrued.

Professional certification, registration, and licensure yield benefits individually to professional helpers, collectively to the profession, and to the public at large. At the level of individual helpers, these professional credentials promote employability, insurability, and eligibility for third-party payment. This is accomplished in part via the enhancement of professional credibility at the collective level of the profession through advocacy and positive public relations. Credentialing organizations educate the public about the required qualifications and competencies of their members and assure the public of ongoing over-sight by regulatory bodies that will address any ethical concerns, including incompetency or impairment. In carrying out the role of cautious gatekeeper, regulatory bodies ensure that only qualified and competent helpers are permitted to enter into and to continue to engage in independent helping practice. In this manner, the well-being of current and future clients is accorded priority. The public can trust that the profession is monitoring the comportment of its members and, by extension, attending to the safety of the public.

PROFESSIONAL DEVELOPMENT

Generally, one of the requirements for renewal of certification, registration, and licen-sure is continuing professional development. Most credentialing bodies establish a minimum threshold of number of hours devoted to continuing education that must be met within each credentialing cycle in order to remain a member in good standing (e.g., Corey, Corey, Corey, & Callanan, 2015; Erford, 2014; National Board for Certified Counselors, 2014b). Regulatory bodies vary with respect to the diversity of profes-sional learning activities that may be counted toward the requisite hours; beginning helpers are advised to become familiar with the nature of activities accepted and the manner in which these need to be documented or reported. Countable hours may include those focused on one's own learning or contributions to the learning of others (which invariably enhance one's own learning also). Regulatory bodies may require members to develop learning or continuing competency plans that are reviewed and updated at the end of every credentialing cycle. While subject to any universal require-ments of the regulatory body, these plans are tailored to the learning needs and pri-orities of the helping professional and identify specific learning goals and designated learning activities aligned with the goals. The process of designing and renewing com-petency plans ensures that members engage thoughtfully and intentionally in their professional learning and growth in a manner that is congruent with professionalism and ethical practice.

Professional Development of Self

In an era of increased emphasis on demonstration of competencies, in contrast to the his-torical focus on degree earned, beginning helpers will find that they are being asked to provide evidence of ongoing knowledge acquisition and honing and expansion of skills. This continued professional learning is essential if helping professionals are to remain abreast of developments in the field in general, and in areas of specialty practice in par-ticular. It can be a little intimidating to beginning helpers who are just embarking on a program of study to discover that, in essence, they have signed up for lifelong learning! However, the helping professions are vibrant and dynamic, with robust research and clinical communities that actively contribute to the evolution of theory and practice. There-fore, to cease the active pursuit of learning with the completion of one's training program would be a guarantee of almost immediate obsolescence. It also would contravene the codes of ethics and standards of practice of helping professions that call on practitioners to remain current and competent in their knowledge and skills.

The good news is that the opportunities for learning are as diverse as the individuals who populate the helping professions. Beyond the reading undertaken in formal coursework during and subsequent to a degree in a helping profession, helping professionals across the career span are encouraged to continue to engage in professional reading of journals, texts, newsletters, listservs, websites, and so on. Workshops, conferences, and conventions at the local, regional, state, national, and international levels afford opportunity to learn with and from professional peers who may themselves be beginning helpers or may have attained the stature of highly respected leaders in the field.

Professional Development of Peers

One manner of engaging in professional development that tends to be overlooked is that of contributing to the learning of students, supervisees, colleagues, and professional peers in the helping professions. This may be undertaken by offering presentations in one's workplace; at gatherings of local professional learning communities; via webinar or webcast; or at state, regional, national, or international workshops, conferences, and conventions. Other manners of contributing include professional writing (e.g., blogs, newsletter articles, journal articles, book chapters, texts), conducting and reporting on research, developing courses, delivering courses to aspiring helping professionals, providing consultation, and offering supervision to practicum or internship students or to postdegree candidates for certification, registration, and licensure.

Rewards accrue from devoting oneself to the learning of others. For one thing, the learning tends to be reciprocal. Whether engaged in teaching, consulting, mentoring, supervision, research, or writing, it is pretty difficult not to emerge more aware and informed oneself. Also, altruistic investment of energy and effort in the learning of others generates intrinsic fulfillment and satisfaction well beyond any tangible, extrinsic rewards of remuneration and expressed appreciation. Giving back to the profession via the sharing of one's knowledge and skills is carried forward when replicated by succeeding generations of helping professionals. This legacy of a continued pattern of ensuring the competence of those that follow is reminiscent of passing the torch to the next member of the relay team.

It bears noting that augmenting or enriching the knowledge of professional peers is not the sole domain of highly experienced helping professionals. Beginning helpers, both students and recent graduates, can make important contributions alongside their more seasoned counterparts. They should not mistakenly assume that the impact of one's involvement in the learning and growth of peers is commensurate with the number of years in the field. In fact, beginning helpers, with fresh insights and perspectives related to their reading, writing, research, and practice, can invite colleagues to step away from the tried and true or the comfort of the familiar and to consider new hypotheses, possibilities, and approaches in helping.

ETHICAL AND LEGAL ISSUES

Ongoing professional development, as discussed above, is one ethical expectation of helping professionals across the career span. In fact, helping professionals are required to demonstrate adherence at all times to the codes of ethics and standards of practice of the professional associations and/or regulatory bodies of which they are members, in addition to upholding applicable laws. For beginning helpers, this notion can be somewhat intimidating. Among their earliest learning as students in academic programs, practica, or internships is that the answer to ethical queries posed to faculty members or supervisors is often a frustrating "It depends." Ethics is typically referred to as a gray area of practice, indicating that it seldom offers a clear black-or-white answer. One might suggest, however, that ethics is more aptly associated with a rainbow of vibrant colors given the range and intensity of emotion associated with trying to address and resolve challenging ethical dilemmas.

Numerous certification, registration, and licensure bodies provide several codes of ethics (see Appendix A for a list of these ethical codes). Some address generalist practice; others focus on areas of specialist practice. For example, while members of the Association for Specialists in Group Work (ASGW) commit to upholding the Code of Ethics of the American Counseling Association (ACA) as their parent organization, they also follow Best Practice Guidelines to guide the application of the ACA Code of Ethics (American Counseling Association, 2014b) in the context of group work (Association for Specialists in Group Work, 2014; Thomas & Pender, 2008). Each ethics code embodies the philosophy and values of the profession or specialty it represents, and so each is unique. However, there are core ethical principles and standards that are common across codes of ethics. If beginning helpers demonstrate fidelity to these core elements, they definitely will be on the right track for ethically congruent practice. Among the core ethical considerations are competence; referrals; informed consent; privacy, confidentiality, and privileged communication; and appropriate boundaries (e.g., Bernard & Goodyear, 2014; Campbell, 2006; Ivey, Ivey, & Zalaquett, 2014; Newsome & Gladding, 2014). See also Chapter 7 for additional discussion of some of these ethical considerations.

Boundaries of Competence and Referrals

The recognition of boundaries of competence and practicing within those parameters is particularly salient to novice practitioners. Successful completion of most programs of study in the helping professions means that students have met general competency criteria at an entry-to-practice level. As new graduates embark on helping career paths, however, they will have to self-monitor continually and assess their competencies in light of the requests for their professional services. Developing new or specialty areas of practice beyond those that were part of their program of studies will require additional didactic and supervised training in order to ensure ethicality in practicing in these areas. For example, if beginning helpers (or in fact helpers at any point on the career trajectory) wish to work with individuals living with addictions but did not take coursework or engage in supervised practice with this clientele during their program of study, it will be important to gain appropriate and adequate training before practicing independently in this area. This ethical imperative applies to all client populations and referral issues that represent new practice ventures for helping professionals.

The ethical expectation that novice helpers will self-assess and honor boundaries of competence is intended to respect and promote the welfare of clients. It is not designed to provide helpers with an excuse for referring elsewhere those clients with whom they simply do not wish to work. Helpers are generally expected to gain competence with diverse kinds of clients (Kaplan, 2014). Boundaries of competence is an issue of knowledge and skills rather than values and biases. Helpers can't simply refer clients because they don't agree with the client's values or dislike the client (Welfel, 2013). A helper might sometimes be unable to work with a client and, if training and supervision are not immediately available, may have to refer the client to another professional. But as Kaplan (2014) observes, this is usually a last-resort option and is based on a lack of specific expertise rather than an unwillingness or discomfort with the client's lifestyle or values. Of course, legitimate referrals sometimes occur that have little to do with boundaries of competence but have implications for client welfare. If helpers become ill, find a new job, retire from practice, and so on, then options of other competent professionals are given to clients in a timely fashion.

Informed Consent

Beginning helpers should remain mindful that informed consent is most aptly conceived of as a process rather than an event. The process of ensuring that clients have the information they need to make informed decisions about counseling starts at the first point of contact with helpers and continues through termination of helping relationships. Beginning helpers who are being supervised in a practicum, internship, or externship, or as a postdegree requirement are required to notify clients of the details of the supervision as part of the informed consent process. When the charging of fees for services accompanies the transition from student to independent practitioner, beginning helpers must ensure that clients are aware of all particulars associated with those fees, again as part of the informed consent process. This information should include sliding fee schedules, penalties for missed appointments, charges for the preparation of letters and reports, and any collection policies for accounts in arrears.

Privacy, Confidentiality, and Privilege

As recommended in Chapter 7, beginning helpers should fully explore the concepts of privacy and confidentiality as part of the informed consent process with each client. The intent is to ensure that clients are never faced with unpleasant surprises. Privacy refers to the right of clients to make decisions about the disclosure of their personal information with respect to content and recipients. For example, just as helpers should not acknowledge clients out in the community unless the client has confirmed a wish to do so and has identified a greeting that will safeguard privacy, ethical practice precludes even acknowledging to third parties whether or not an individual is a current, former, or prospective client. Confidentiality refers to helping professionals' commitment to honoring the privacy of client information. Discussion of confidentiality with clients has to establish clear limits and exclusions, which can vary somewhat depending on the jurisdiction in which one practices. In both the United States and Canada, for example, practitioners are required to report child abuse and neglect to the appropriate authorities. Many jurisdictions require reporting of elder abuse. As part of the informed consent process, clients need to be informed when their helping professionals are being supervised. Supervision represents a limit to confidentiality because supervisors provide oversight of supervisees' work with clients though case discussion, record review, review of recorded sessions, and other supervisory activities. For a thorough discussion of limits and exceptions to confidentiality, we recommend two excellent ethics texts: *Ethics in Counseling and Psychotherapy* by Elizabeth Welfel (2013) and *Issues and Ethics in the Helping Professions* by Jerry Corey and colleagues (2015). Mandatory reporting and exceptions to confidentiality are one of the most challenging ethical issues for practitioners, and it is important to become familiar with the laws in your state and country surrounding this issue.

A related concept is that of privileged communication. This is a legal term that refers to the right of privilege held by clients when they disclose private information with the expectation of confidentiality. Although historically applied to the lawyer-client relationship, the right to privileged communication between a client and helping professional was upheld at the federal court level in the 1996 landmark *Jaffee v. Redmond* case (Jaffee v. Redmond 518 U.S. 1, 2014). This means that even if a helping professional is in receipt of a subpoena or court order to testify or provide counseling records, the client can choose to assert the right of privilege. If the court honors this request, the helping professional may not be required to divulge the client's private information that was shared in a counseling context. As Welfel (2013) notes, this ruling in *Jaffee v. Redmond* "applies most directly to social workers, psychologists, and psychiatrists and does not address the privilege of other kinds of mental health professionals" (p. 125). Beginning helpers are strongly encouraged to seek supervision or consultation if they become involved in any legal proceedings related to their professional helping work.

If not already familiar with the Health Insurance Portability and Accountability Act (HIPAA) of 1996 (U.S. Department of Health and Human Services [HHS], 2014), which is discussed in Chapter 7, beginning helpers are strongly encouraged to peruse summary documents and to discuss with employers, supervisors, and colleagues the implications of HIPAA for the use and safeguarding of protected health information in their practicum, internship, or work setting.

Relational Boundaries: Multiple and Nonprofessional Relationships

Another ethical (and potentially legal) consideration for beginning helpers is that of maintaining appropriate relational boundaries with clients, in both face-to-face and electronic contexts. The American Counseling Association's Code of Ethics prohibits in-person and electronic or virtual relationships of a romantic and/or sexual nature with *current* clients and their family members or romantic partners (American Counseling Association, 2014b, p. 5). The ACA Code of Ethics similarly disallows such relationships with *former* clients and their family members or romantic partners for at least five years subsequent to the last professional interaction. Even then, counselors must document a process of discernment, and if there is a risk of exploitation and/or harm, the relationship must not be pursued (American Counseling Association, 2014b, p. 5).

Counseling of former romantic and/or sexual partners is proscribed indefinitely. Furthermore, counselors should not accept friends or family members as clients when objectivity might be compromised (which we assert is always a risk with friends and family), and they should exercise thoughtful professional judgment in deciding whether to enter into counseling relationships if there have been "casual, distant, or past" personal or professional acquaintanceships (American Counseling Association, 2014b, p. 5).

Although the evolution over time of helping professions' codes of ethics and standards of practice has led to acknowledgment of the challenges in avoiding all multiple relationships, particularly in rural and/or remote areas, the prohibitions and/or time lines associated with intimate relationships are inviolable. Other nonprofessional relationships should be entered into only if the counselor's written documentation of a sound decision-making process and rationale indicates likely potential benefit and very minimal or low risk of negative consequences to the current or former client and the important persons in the client's life. If harm does result from multiple relationships or the extension of conventional counseling relationship boundaries (also known as blurred boundaries), the counselor must demonstrate and document genuine attempts at reparation (American Counseling Association, 2014b, p. 5).

The risk of blurred boundaries may be particularly salient to new practitioners who not so long ago were simply members of the general community. Now, however, these novice helpers must demonstrate fidelity to codes of ethics and standards of practice that call on them to respond thoughtfully to social invitations; business transactions outside the helping relationship; presentations of gifts by clients; and well-meaning inquiries about clients from clients' family members, friends, or employers. Beginning helpers are encouraged to refer to their profession's ethical codes and standards to clarify profession-specific directives and prohibitions related to multiple and/or nonprofessional relationships. It can also be helpful to anticipate possible situations in advance and to ponder the example questions in Application Exercise 10.3 with a supervisor and/or with colleagues.

APPLICATION EXERCISE 10.3

Ethical Challenges

Some of the following questions refer to an individual who is already a client, while others invite contemplation about whether to accept an individual as a client. We encourage you to discuss these questions with a small group of peers.

> Would I take my car to a mechanic who is or was a client?
>
> Would I get my hair cut by a current or former client?
>
> Would I accept as a client my dentist or family physician?
>
> Would I hire a former client to provide child care?
>
> Would I hire a current client to do interior or exterior painting of my home?
>
> Would I accept an offer of bartering from a client who otherwise would not be able to afford my services?
>
> Would I accept the referral of someone who is a friend of a current or former client?
>
> Would I accept the referral of someone who is a life partner of a current or former client?
>
> Would I accept the referral of a neighbor?
>
> Would I accept the referral of someone who has been a teacher or coach of my child?
>
> Would I accept an invitation to a client's wedding?
>
> Would I accept an invitation to a client's graduation?
>
> Would I attend a client's funeral?

Feedback

As you may have noticed, most if not all of these questions do not evoke a clear yes or no response, and some raise ethical issues beyond those of multiple relationships. The goal of reflection on such ethical issues is to avoid boundary crossings that might lead to boundary violations. Key considerations when uncertain about boundaries are whether objectivity can be maintained and whether there is any risk of exploitation or harm to any of the parties involved.

Discrepancies between Ethics Codes and Workplace Policies

Beyond core ethical considerations related to competence, informed consent, confidentiality, and boundaries, some additional challenges are commonly reported by beginning helpers. One relates to addressing discrepancies between professional codes of ethics and employer policies and procedures. Whether as practicum students, interns, or new employees, novice helpers can find it quite disconcerting to discover a lack of alignment between the ethical expectations of their profession and the expectations of the workplace. Perhaps the staff members of the agency or organization have not previously supervised a practicum student or intern, or at least not one in this particular helping profession. Perhaps the ethical challenges have arisen due to the multidisciplinary composition of the employment setting where myriad codes of ethics and standards of practice need to be considered. If the beginning helper is being supervised by a more senior staff member, a starting point for addressing the concern is with that individual.

Ethics and Multicultural Issues

All the major helping profession ethical codes mandate that helpers possess an awareness and knowledge of cultural issues in order to work with clients from diverse cultures and backgrounds in a competent and respectful manner. This mandate is underscored by almost all codes of ethics that incorporate multicultural and diversity issues into key areas of the code, and more recent revisions of ethical codes show much greater attention to this topic. For example, one way that ethical codes address multicultural and diversity issues relates to broadening of the definition and concept of family to include other individuals who may play critical roles in the lives of our clients (e.g., friends, ministers). Another ethical issue in the multicultural arena reflects a more thoughtful consideration of the impact that diagnosis can have on marginalized groups when cultural factors are not considered. Helpers need to understand the cultural issues involved in the giving of small gifts and in the cultural meanings of confidentiality and privacy. Houser, Wilczenski, and Ham (2006) note that the values underlying most helping professions' codes of ethics are based on Western principles and values and may not be culturally relevant for clients from different cultural backgrounds with different values and worldviews. These authors have formulated an ethical decision-making model that includes a contextual component.

Ethical Concerns about Another Helping Professional

Sometimes the ethical dilemmas encountered by practicum students, interns, or new employees do not represent ethical mismatches between professional standards and workplace practices; instead, the dilemmas concern the conduct of another individual in that setting. For example, perhaps there are legitimate concerns about breaches of confidentiality, lack of security related to recordkeeping, practicing outside boundaries of competence, or even practitioner impairment. Generally, helping professionals are encouraged to approach the other professional to discuss the issue if at all possible and appropriate. However, beginning helpers are acutely aware of the power differential between them and senior staff members and of the tenuous security of their placements as students or junior staff members.

Maybe the ethical alarm is being set off by the conduct of a clinical supervisor, administrative supervisor, friend of a supervisor, and so on. Beginning helpers may find themselves vacillating between feeling ethically compelled to broach the concern and feeling apprehensive that it may negatively affect workplace relationships, result in a poor evaluation, or preclude a positive letter of reference in the future. In such situations, it is helpful for novice practitioners to have a professional network to draw on so that they may consult in confidence and fully consider the ethical, legal, and practical implications of action versus inaction; explore options available to them; and make informed decisions about how best to proceed. At times like these, it is also beneficial to implement systematic, ethical decision-making models to guide helpers in addressing the dilemma. There are a number of models from which to choose that build on a basic problem-solving model—the kind used to tackle everyday problems in life—and tailor the steps to apply to the resolution of ethical dilemmas in the helping professions. We discuss such a model below.

Ethical Decision Making

Given the complexity of client issues in the counseling context and the fact that ethics codes tend to present considerations for best practice rather than to prescribe or prohibit, helping professionals often lament the lack of clear direction when faced with ethical dilemmas. Bear in mind, however, that ethics codes were never intended to be used like cookbooks or assembly manuals that offer step-by-step instructions in precise detail. With few exceptions, such as the inviolable prohibition of sexual relationships with current clients, codes of ethics are more likely to identify aspirational principles and general guidelines for ethical practice. Therefore, it can be helpful to have a framework to offer some structure to the ethical decision-making process (American Counseling Association, 2014b; Ametrano, 2014).

In this section, we present a generic ethical decision-making model to help you reach soundly reasoned plans for addressing ethical dilemmas that inevitably will arise during practice in the helping professions. This model represents a composite of suggestions drawn from a number of sources (e.g., Barnett & Johnson, 2015; Corey, Corey, Corey, & Callanan, 2015; Cottone & Claus, 2000; Erford, 2014; Gamino & Ritter, 2009; Hadjistavropoulos & Malloy, 2000; Hansen & Goldberg, 1999; National Association of Social Workers, 2008; Newsome & Gladding, 2014; Pope & Vasquez, 2011; Remley & Herlihy, 2013; Welfel, 2013; Wheeler & Bertram, 2012).

The steps associated with the ethical decision-making model include the following:

1. **Preparing a Problem Summary**
   Prepare a brief summary of the ethical problem, including any historical and contextual information that appears salient. Try to keep the summary to one page, and feel free to use incomplete sentences or numbered or bulleted lists. This page will serve as the repository for information that you may wish to draw on in carrying out the next steps. It also helps to clear your mind for problem solving by getting information out of your head and onto paper or a computer screen.

2. **Articulating a Problem Statement**
   Clearly identify and articulate the ethical concern. Try to do so in a problem statement of no more than one or two sentences. Aim to capture the essence of the

problem by completing this sentence stem: The crux of this ethical problem is that
_____.

3. Identifying Problem Dimensions

Identify the dimensions of the ethical problem or conflict. Are there historical dimensions? Are there relevant cultural and other diversity dimensions? What contextual dimensions are significant at the personal, familial, community, and societal levels (including sociopolitical)? What attitudes, beliefs, and values are salient?

4. Considering Problem Impact

Describe how each of the parties involved has been or potentially will be affected by the ethical problem. How does the problem create risk and for whom? What negative outcomes are anticipated if the problem is not resolved?

5. Defining the Dilemma

Based on your responses in steps 1 to 4, determine what it is that leads you to define this particular ethical problem as a dilemma. A dilemma typically is accompanied by ambiguity, perplexity, dissonance, and discomfort. This may be the case because the options for addressing the problem are unclear, are undesirable, or will create new problems.

6. Reflecting on Relevant Ethical Principles and Standards

Review and reflect on relevant codes of ethics and standards of practice. What do they say about this dilemma or this type of dilemma? How do you feel about the position that they have adopted?

7. Examining Relevant Laws and Regulations

For many ethical dilemmas, both state and federal statutes and regulations are relevant. Consider whether any of these relate to this particular dilemma. For example, what does your state say, if anything, about breaking confidentiality if a client is deemed to be a danger to self or to another? Is there alignment or disagreement between ethical and legal perspectives on this matter?

8. Investigating Workplace Policies

Does your work setting have any regulatory guidelines or policies that will affect your decision making? Is there any conflict between your professional ethics and the workplace expectations?

9. Consulting Professional Resources

Once you have gathered and reflected on the information in steps 1 to 8, consider the resources available to you to assist in ethical decision making. These resources may include the ethical board or committee of your professional association or regulatory body, legal consultants retained by your liability insurance provider, experienced colleagues who have dealt with such ethical issues before, and the professional literature on ethics. As a beginning helper, you should also consult your clinical supervisor about any and all ethical dilemmas.

10. Brainstorming Options

At this stage of ethical decision making, you essentially are engaging in a brainstorming process. The task is to generate as wide a range as possible of full or partial potential solutions. All ideas are documented, without judging or evaluating their validity (this will be undertaken in the next step). Invite your supervisor and, if appropriate, other parties to the dilemma (e.g., the client) to participate in the brainstorming of ideas.

11. **Assessing Options**

    After identifying potential solutions through brainstorming, scrutinize each one for reasonableness, feasibility, and anticipated effectiveness in resolving the ethical dilemma. Would each proposed option align with the values of the parties involved, demonstrate ethical fidelity, and be congruent with workplace policies and state and federal law? Weigh the advantages and disadvantages of each option for anyone who will be affected by the decision made. Invite the continued contributions of any parties who participated in the brainstorming step.

12. **Determining a Course of Action**

    Select and commit to the option or combination of options that seems to offer the greatest likelihood of success in resolving the ethical dilemma. Decide on a course of action that is associated with the greatest benefits and the least costs, one that prioritizes client well-being without violating ethical and legal standards. As in steps 10 and 11, it is wise to undertake this step with consultation, often involving the client and always involving your supervisor. As you finalize this plan, ask yourself:

    How would I feel if this plan were being implemented to address an ethical dilemma involving my parent, partner, or child?

    Would I recommend this course of action to a helping professional colleague?

    How would I feel if this plan were publicized in print for a national reading audience?

    Will this plan sit comfortably with my conscience and allow me to sleep well at night?

13. **Implementing the Course of Action**

    Now that a course of action has been decided upon via a comprehensive and thoughtful process of discernment, the next step is to implement it. Determine whether it would be best practice first to notify any parties to the dilemma of the details of the plan, including what will be implemented, when, how, where, and the rationale for doing so. Then proceed to carry out the plan of action.

14. **Reviewing Process and Outcomes**

    This step is often overlooked or afforded minimal attention in the process of ethical decision making. Typically, considerable time and energy is devoted to the pre-implementation phase that leads up to the formulation of a plan for action. If all goes well enough following implementation of the plan, helping professionals may not look back over steps 1 to 13, choosing instead to move as quickly as possible past the discomfort that had been associated with the dilemma. Whether or not the plan yielded desired results, however, it can be extremely valuable to reflect on both the ethical decision-making process and the final outcomes. Evaluation of the degree of success in resolving the ethical dilemma, and exploring the reasons behind it, will likely yield important information for consideration when confronted with future dilemmas.

15. **Revisiting the Model if Outcomes Are Unsatisfactory**

    If implementation of the course of action in step 13 did not result in the anticipated or hoped for outcomes, it might be productive to return to step 1 and to move through the model again. When helping professionals are able to revisit the model with a fresh mind, they may notice that they can restructure the problem statement;

consider ethical principles and standards, state or federal laws, or workplace policies in a different light; or identify new potential solutions in the brainstorming
phase. Modifications in perspective and plan may guide the ethical decision making
to more successful resolution of the dilemma on this subsequent attempt. It might
also be wise to include a wider range of perspectives in this process of revisiting the
model by inviting the input of clients, supervisors, or trusted colleagues if they were
not involved in the initial process.

16. Documenting

The final step is to ensure that you have fully documented the ethical decision-
making process and outcomes. Remember to document every step of the process,
including information gathered, actions taken, and the rationale for those actions.
Also be sure to document all consultations on this matter, including conversations
with supervisors and colleagues.

Although an ethical decision-making process does not guarantee that the decision
made will be an easy one or the "right" one, it does offer a framework that will guide you
to consider a range of informational sources and perspectives. The two key words in the
process are *consultation* and *documentation*. If you have accessed human and material
sources of input and feedback related to the dilemma, and maintained a written record of
the process, you will likely meet the criteria for a reasonable standard of professional practice and will be positioned to make the best decision possible under the circumstances.

Ethical Consultation across the Career Span

While enrolled in a program of study, aspiring helpers have a ready-made network of
ethical consultants in their course instructors and practicum and internship supervisors.
If the beginning helpers subsequently engage in postdegree supervision for licensure
purposes, those clinical supervisors will serve as consultants when ethical and legal
questions and concerns arise. As beginning helpers gradually expand their circle of
classmates, instructors, supervisors, coworkers, collaborators in research and writing
projects, and fellow participants in committee and other volunteer work, they will also
establish a network of respected colleagues. Given the inevitability of encountering ethical and legal dilemmas over the course of one's career, thoughtful identification of a
select number of those colleagues with whom to consult is highly recommended. It is
best practice to check with these professional peers about any ethical and legal uncer-
tainties and to document the discernment and decision-making process arising out of
these consultations.

RESOURCES

As students embark on programs of study in the helping professions, they begin to accumulate hard-copy and digital resources in the form of interesting and edifying books,
journal articles, theses and dissertations, websites, programs, manuals, presentations, videos, audio recordings, games, and client handouts. Depending on the nature of their
helping practice and the referral issues of their clientele, beginning helpers may also
choose to collect materials appropriate for the kinds of clients and issues they work with.
The acquisition of materials for a professional resource library is an initiative that will be
ongoing throughout the helping career.

Although the ideal would be for employers to award a budget for the purchasing of practice-enhancing resources, this typically is not the reality in an era of economic challenge. Novice helpers may already be feeling financially strapped as they seek to meet living expenses in a new employment and residence location while also repaying accumulated student debt; thus, the creative acquisition of resource supplies may become an attractive option. Some considerations for assembling materials in this manner include the following:

- Scouting for books, art supplies, and play materials at yard sales and flea markets.
- Indicating interest to professors and supervisors in helping them declutter their bookshelves by adopting their older editions of texts and other books for your library.
- Approaching retiring practitioners and academics with a request to purchase practice-related books and materials (in the hope that they might be willing to part with these at a very reasonable cost or even for free in order to support a novice practitioner).
- Sharing digital materials in the public domain with fellow students and other professional peers.
- Sharing duplicate or reproducible materials with fellow students and other colleagues.
- Identifying and following up on source options for free resources.
- Organizing a workshop to produce practice-related materials (e.g., puppets, stress balls).
- Attending conferences where there often are useful giveaways.
- Taking advantage of student discounts for books and other materials while you are still a student.
- Applying for government and other grants related to mental health and/or to your targeted client population or client referral issues.

In addition to the materials and suggestions for procuring them listed above, the development of a hard-copy or digital directory of local community, state, regional, national, and international helping profession contacts and resources can be a valuable undertaking. Such a directory might include multidisciplinary practitioners, agencies, organizations, associations, programs and services, and options for responding in crisis situations. A resource directory places contact information at helping professionals' fingertips for quick reference when needed.

REWARDS

Becoming a professional helper offers rich rewards of an intrinsic nature in addition to extrinsic rewards such as remuneration and the expressed gratitude of clients. It truly is an honor and a privilege to be invited by clients into a therapeutic alliance with them. As we step into their personal worlds, we bear witness to cognitions, affect, and behavior that they may not have explored with anyone else up to that point, including themselves. For most of us, such a deep level of trust is infrequently accorded by, or to, others in our lives. Yet it is regularly extended by clients to the helping professionals with whom they embark on journeys of healing and/or personal growth. The collaborative nature of these journeys invites helpers to share in the poignant successes of clients in overcoming obstacles in order to make desired life changes or in taking risks for opportunities for growth.

Novice practitioners commonly convey energy and enthusiasm as they embark on new career paths as helping professionals. They speak of heightened intentionality, purpose, and life meaning as they consciously dedicate their professional lives to promoting the welfare of others. In many ways, the concept of vocation or *calling* encapsulates the lived experience of successful helping professionals who embody caring, compassion, commitment, confidence, and competence.

This way of being in the world that is so often associated with helping professionals aligns quite nicely with the criterion elements of *flourishing* that have been investigated in the context of positive psychology (see, for example: Csikszentmihalyi, 1990; Fredrickson, 2006; Linley & Joseph, 2004; Sheldon & Houser-Marko, 2001). Seligman's (2011) acronym PERMA identifies the elements deemed essential for flourishing:

- **P** = positive emotions or affect
- **E** = engagement that is akin to Csikszentmihalyi's (1990) concept of flow
- **R** = relationships
- **M** = meaning or purpose in life
- **A** = accomplishment or achievement

As beginning helpers accompany clients in their pursuits of mental health and actualization goals, the helpers themselves are likely to meet the constituent criteria for flourishing. The first criterion in the PERMA acronym, the experiencing and expression of positive emotions (with a particular emphasis on compassion that correlates well with helping practice) is associated, not surprisingly, with enhanced quality of life (e.g., Fredrickson & Losada, 2005; Lilius, 2012; Rynes, Bartunek, Dutton, & Margolis, 2012). Across workplaces, positive emotions and interpersonal exchanges have been correlated with heightened motivation, creativity, performance, resilience, and overall well-being (see, for example, Amabile & Kramer, 2011; Dutton & Ragins, 2007; Fredrickson, 2001). Perhaps less expected is the finding that compassion and similar emotional states are positively correlated with physical health and longevity (e.g., Brown, Ness, Vinokur, & Smith, 2003; Harris & Thoresen, 2005; Ostir, Markides, Black, & Goodwin, 2000). Thus, meeting the criteria for flourishing through engagement with clients has the potential to yield significant physical, psychological, and performance rewards for beginning helpers and their colleagues across the career span. In fact, each of the PERMA criteria could be construed as a reward in and of itself.

SELF-CARE

As discussed above, ample research identifies the positive influence on both quality and quantity of life of meaningful engagement in relationships that promote positive affect and a sense of accomplishment. This description appears tailor-made for the helping professions, both with respect to helpers and those that they help.

However, the same qualities that promote a profound sense of career congruence and resonance for helping professionals predispose them to compassion fatigue (also referred to in the professional literature as secondary or vicarious trauma) and burnout. The daily exercising of empathy and compassion through intimate helping connections with others can be draining and, when emergent conditions of compassion fatigue and burnout are not attended to, they may worsen to the point of becoming debilitating. There is an inherent ebb and flow of energy and resilience over the course of one's helping career, reflecting the confluence of a variety of life variables. Life events such as relocation, the end of a business or intimate partnership, the addition of a child to the family, illness in a loved one, and death of a loved one place high demands on adjustment and resilience. There is a tipping point beyond which helping professionals can become overtaxed, overwhelmed, and unable to reap the rewards of their profession (see, for example, Figley, 2002; Schaufeli, Leiter, & Maslach, 2009; Skovholt & Trotter-Mathison, 2011; Zimering, Munroe, & Gulliver, 2003).

The antidote to the potential depletion of physical and psychological reserves is a commitment to regular self-care. This is particularly crucial for beginning helpers whose keen desire to get started and to demonstrate their devotion to helping others may cause them to ignore early warning signs. To ensure that novice practitioners continue to experience their new roles as fulfilling and actualizing, it is essential that they monitor their life balance and address any disequilibrium.

Not only is self-care important from the perspective of helper well-being, but it also safeguards the welfare of clients. When helping professionals develop compassion fatigue or burnout, their effectiveness as helpers is compromised. In some cases, the conduct and performance of formerly competent helping professionals deteriorates to the point of impairment.

Self-awareness is vital to knowing when to step up one's self-care plan. We know that optimal nourishment, regular physical activity, stress management, and adequate rest are important considerations in the prevention and treatment of medical conditions. They play a similar role in the primary, secondary, and tertiary prevention of compassion fatigue and burnout. Application Exercise 10.4 invites you to assess the degree to which the ingredients of good self-care practices are present in your personal and professional life spheres and to contemplate how you might make these practices a priority in your daily living.

APPLICATION EXERCISE 10.4

Self-Care

Questions that beginning helpers might revisit regularly in the service of developing and maintaining good self-care practices include the following:

Do I meet my body's needs for healthy nourishment over the course of the day?

Do I make time for physical activity at least a couple of times per week?

Do I take time to stretch and move about between clients or tasks?

Do I take time to clear my mind between clients or tasks?

Do I recognize when I am feeling stressed?

Do I implement strategies for addressing stress?

Do I meet my sleep needs most nights in terms of quantity and quality?

Do I nurture close relationships in my personal life?

Do I maintain a network of trusted colleagues with whom to consult?

Do I have one or more persons to confide in or debrief with?

Do I reach out to others when feeling anxious, worried, or stressed?

Have I made room for humor in my life?

Have I made room for play in my life?

Do I have interests and hobbies outside my professional life?

Have I allocated adequate time to engage in these leisure pursuits?

Do I derive significant fulfillment from my work?

Have I set boundaries that permit me to separate my personal and professional life spheres?

Have I made time to be totally unplugged from technology?

Have I identified short-term and long-term personal life goals?

Do I have a plan for pursuing my personal goals?

Have I identified short-term and long-term professional life goals?

Do I have a plan for pursuing my professional goals?

Do I regularly reaffirm a sense of passion and purpose across all life domains (so that there is more than a professional focus)?

Have I recognized and accepted that I cannot be masterful in all areas of knowledge and skill in my helping profession even if I devote my whole career to this endeavor?

Have I recognized and accepted that I will not be successful, to the degree that I'd like, with every client?

Have I articulated a self-care plan?

Do I review this plan periodically and revise it to reflect my current personal and professional life circumstances?

If I were to have a conversation with a client about his or her self-care, what would we be discussing?

Feedback

Beginning helpers are encouraged to reflect on and explore options for addressing not only the no responses to these questions but also the yes responses. These and additional helper-generated questions could be constructed in a manner amenable to a rating scale format that would assist in the tracking of self-care. Alternatively, the questions might serve as a pre- and postmeasure, self-administered on either end of the implementation of a self-care plan comprising a manageable number of specific self-care goals.

Summary

The journey to becoming a professional helper commences with formal education and supervised training, following which beginning helpers find themselves embarking on a path of continued, career-long learning. Contrary to what one might envision at the outset of training, completion of the program of study is not an endpoint. Rather, it positions the graduate as an entry-level practitioner, hopefully one with a solid basis of caring, compassion, commitment, confidence, and competence.

Pursuing a career as a helping professional is much like running a marathon. To run it well, one needs to get and stay in shape physically and psychologically. Commitment to learning and reflective prac-

tice is crucial. It is essential to be self-aware and to acknowledge one's strengths and limits. Appropriate pacing is of paramount importance, and this should be accompanied by devotion to self-care and life balance. Performance in the marathon will be enhanced by the support of others, in both personal and professional life spheres. The endurance required to run a marathon successfully is analogous to the energy and resilience necessary to derive reward and fulfillment over one's career span as a helping professional, and the prerequisites for success are much the same.

In this chapter, we explored a variety of considerations and challenges for beginning helpers. These individuals might recently have embarked on a program of study, could be engaged in a practicum or internship, or may be new graduates seeking or about to commence a position as a helping professional. Career issues relevant to novice helpers (and sometimes throughout the career trajectory) include crystallizing professional identity; engaging in and offering clinical supervision; networking with professional peers; establishing professional affiliations; attaining credentialing in the form of certification, registration, and/or licensure; availing oneself of professional development opportunities; identifying and addressing ethical and legal issues; building a bank of practice resources; recognizing and reaping the rewards of professional helping; and engaging in the self-care necessary to ensure effectiveness and enjoyment as a helping professional over the full duration of one's career.

The status of beginning helper is characterized by exciting potential and promise, and the expansive range of professional opportunities offers a panoramic vista. New helping professionals stand poised to set off on a path of gratifying practice and career-long learning that may include any combination of counseling, consulting, coaching, supervising, mentoring, teaching, administration, research, writing, and professional volunteerism. The settings, clientele, and issues of focus are almost unlimited. So, too, are the rewards.

Reflective Questions

1. Does the description of the *imposter phenomenon* resonate with you in any manner? How so?
2. What steps will you take to ensure that you benefit fully from clinical supervision (e.g., with respect to preparation for supervision sessions, attending and participating in a nonanxious manner, setting and pursuing growth-focused goals, and following up on feedback)?
3. Which aspects of networking hold the greatest appeal for you? What avenues for networking have you identified and/or pursued?
4. Do you anticipate developing a specialty area of practice as a helping professional? How will you pursue this goal?
5. What ethical dilemmas have you encountered most frequently as a beginning helper? How have you addressed these dilemmas?
6. What material resources do you think every beginning helper absolutely must have? If you were awarded a grant of $5,000 to purchase resources for your helping practice, what items would be at the top of your list?
7. What have been the greatest rewards for you thus far as a beginning helper? What sources of career satisfaction and fulfillment do you anticipate as you proceed further on your career path?
8. What currently are the greatest challenges for you with respect to self-care? In your ideal life, what would your self-care plan entail?

MyCounselingLab

For each exercise, log on to MyCounselingLab and click into the Video Library to locate the following clips.

1. Click the School Counseling collection and then watch the following two selections: "A Teacher Asks a Student Counselor for Help", and "Response to a Teacher Asks a Student Counselor for Help." Identify any challenges both to confidentiality and to the working relationship between the counselor and the teacher in this scenario. You may want to role-play this situation to see how you might handle a situation like this in actual practice.

2. Open the Ethical, Legal, and Professional Issues in the Counseling collection and then watch the following selections:

   - "A Sexual Attraction"
   - "A Wedding Invitation"
   - "Misinformed Consent"
   - "An Ethical Decision"

   How would you have handled these situations if you had been the helper? You could discuss this as a group, identify your approaches in writing, or even work this out in role-plays.

3. In the Ethical, Legal, and Professional Issues in Counseling collection, watch the following two videos: "A Student Faces an Ethical Challenge" and "Response to a Student Faces an Ethical Challenge."

What can you conclude about the ethical challenges in this situation? Can the ethical decision-making model described in this chapter help you identify potential responses?

Recommended Readings

Baird, B. N. (2013). *The internship practicum and field placement handbook: A guide for the helping professions* (7th ed.). Upper Saddle River, NJ: Pearson.

Barnett, J., & Johnson, W. (2015). *Ethics desk reference for counselors* (2nd ed.). Washington DC: American Counseling Association.

Bernard, J. M., & Goodyear, R. K. (2014). *Fundamentals of clinical supervision* (5th ed.). Upper Saddle River, NJ: Pearson Education, Inc.

Corey, M. S., & Corey, G. (2016). *Becoming a helper* (7th ed.). Belmont, CA: Brooks/Cole, Cengage Learning.

Corey, G., Corey, M. S., Corey, C., & Callanan, P. (2015). *Issues and ethics in the helping professions* (9th ed.). Belmont, CA: Brooks/Cole, Cengage Learning.

Corey, G., Haynes, R., Moulton, P., & Muratori, M. (2010). *Clinical supervision in the helping professions: A practical guide* (3rd ed.). Alexandria, VA: American Counseling Association.

Cormier, S., Nurius, P. S., & Osborn, C. J. (2013). *Interviewing and change strategies for helpers* (7th ed.). Belmont, CA: Brooks/Cole, Cengage Learning.

Erford, B. T. (2014). *Orientation to the counseling profession: Advocacy, ethics, and essential professional foundations* (2nd ed.). Boston, MA: Pearson/Merrill Counseling.

Kaplan, D. M. (2014). Ethical implications of a critical legal case for the counseling profession: *Ward v. Wilbanks. Journal of Counseling and Development, 92,* 142–146. doi:10.1002/j/1556-6676.2014.00140.x

Moss, J. M., Gibson, D. M., & Dollarhide, C. T. (2014). Professional identity development: A grounded theory of transformational tasks of counselors. *Journal of Counseling and Development, 92,* 3–12, doi: 10.1002/j.1556-6676.2014.00124.x

Pearson, Q. M. (2004). Getting the most out of clinical supervision: Strategies for mental health counseling students. *Journal of Mental Health Counseling, 26*(4), 361–373.

Pope, K. S., & Vasquez, M. J. T. (2011). *Ethics in psychotherapy and counseling: A practical guide* (4th ed.). Hoboken, NJ: John Wiley & Sons.

Shohet, R. (2011). *Supervision as transformation: A passion for learning.* London: Jessica Kingsley Publishers Ltd.

Skovholt, T. M., & Trotter-Mathison, M. J. (2011). *The resilient practitioner: Burnout prevention and self-care strategies for counselors, therapists, teachers, and health professionals* (2nd ed.). New York, NY: Routledge.

Sweitzer, H. F. (2014). *The successful internship: Personal, professional, and civic development in experiential learning* (4th ed.). Belmont, CA: Brooks/Cole, Cengage Learning.

Welfel, E. R. (2013). *Ethics in counseling & psychotherapy: Standards, research, and emerging issues* (5th ed.). Belmont, CA: Brooks/Cole, Cengage Learning.

APPENDIX A

Websites for the Ethical Codes and Related Standards of Professional Organizations for the Helping Professions

American Association of Marriage and Family Therapy:
aamft.org

American Association of Pastoral Counselors:
aapc.org

American Counseling Association:
counseling.org

American Group Psychotherapy Association:
agpa.org

American Mental Health Counselors Association:
amhca.org

American Psychological Association:
apa.org

American School Counselor Association:
schoolcounselor.org

Association for Multicultural Counseling and Development:
amcdaca.org

Association for Specialists in Group Work:
asgw.org

Canadian Association of Social Workers:
casw-acts.ca

Canadian Counselling and Psychotherapy Association:
ccpa-accp.ca

Canadian Psychological Association:
cpa.ca

Code of Professional Ethics for Rehabilitation Counselors:
crccertification.com

International Association of Marriage and Family Counselors:
iamfc.com

International Society for Mental Health Online:
ismho.org

National Association of Social Workers:
naswdc.org

National Board for Certified Counselors:
nbcc.org

National Organization for Human Services:
nationalhumanservices.org

APPENDIX B

Counseling Strategies Checklist

Most trainees view the opportunity for supervision as a mixed blessing. They know that their performance has weaknesses that are more easily identified by an observer. On the other hand, they feel vulnerable at the prospect of having someone view and assess their interview behavior, particularly when they cannot see that person. There are no easy solutions to this problem. Learning to feel comfortable is uniquely a function of your own goals and the observer's awareness of your discomfort. Therefore, you must identify the implications of your helping goals in terms of your own risk-taking, and you must be prepared to communicate your fears.

The Counseling Strategies Checklist (CSC) is suggested as one means of assessing your performance. It is divided into categories, with content headings that make it easy to choose a section; the categories also conform to the chapters in this text. The instructor or supervisor may want to use parts of the checklist for each interview rather than attempt to complete the entire checklist each time you are observed. The checklist provides a point of departure for you and your supervisor to discuss the progress of the interview as well as your input and its effect on your client.

HOW TO USE THE COUNSELING STRATEGIES CHECKLIST

Each item in the CSC is scored by circling the most appropriate response. The items are worded so that desirable responses are yes. No is an undesirable response. Following each section of the CSC, there is space for observer comments. Your supervisor can use this to record general impressions and specific observations. One way we like to use the CSC is to note to what degree the student helper's responses are culturally appropriate for each client. Specific assessment of multicultural competencies can be found in Part X of the checklist.

After the instructor or supervisor has observed and rated the interview, the two of you can plan to sit down and review the ratings. Where noticeable limitations exist, you and the supervisor can identify a goal or goals that will remedy the problem. Beyond this, you should list two or three action steps that permit you to achieve the goal. After three or four more interviews, the observer should evaluate you again and then compare the two sets of ratings to determine whether progress was evident.

Part I: Opening the Interview

1. In the first part of the interview, the counselor used several different nonverbal gestures (smiling, head nodding, hand movement, etc.) to help put the client at ease.   Yes   No

2. In starting the interview, the counselor remained silent or invited the client to talk about whatever he or she wanted, thus leaving the selection of an initial topic up to the client.   Yes   No

3. After the first five minutes of the interview, the counselor refrained from encouraging social conversation.   Yes   No

4. After the first topic of discussion was exhausted, the counselor remained silent until the client identified a new topic.   Yes   No

5. The counselor provided structure (information about the nature and purposes of counseling, time limits, etc.) when the client indicated uncertainty about the interview.   Yes   No

6. In beginning the *initial* interview, the counselor used at least one of the following structuring procedures:

  a. Provided information about recording the interview for evaluation purposes or observation by a supervising helper.   Yes   No

  b. Commented on confidentiality and privacy; stated limits of confidentiality.   Yes   No

  c. Made remarks about the counselor's role and purpose of the interview.   Yes   No

  d. Discussed with the client his or her expectations about counseling.   Yes   No

Comments: _____

Part II: Counselor Attending Behavior (Nonverbal)

1. The counselor maintained eye contact with the client.   Yes   No

2. The counselor displayed several different facial expressions during the interview.   Yes   No

3. The counselor's facial expressions reflected the mood of the client.   Yes   No

4. The counselor often responded to the client with facial animation and alertness.   Yes   No

5. The counselor displayed intermittent head movements (up and down; side to side).   Yes   No

6. The counselor refrained from head nodding when the client did not pursue goal-directed topics.   Yes   No

7. The counselor demonstrated a relaxed body position.   Yes   No

8. The counselor leaned forward as a means of encouraging the client to engage in some goal-directed behavior.   Yes   No

9. The counselor demonstrated some variation in voice pitch when talking.   Yes   No

10. The counselor's voice was heard easily by the client.   Yes   No

11. The counselor used intermittent vocalizations ("uh-huh") to reinforce the client's demonstration of goal-directed topics or behaviors.   Yes   No

Comments: _____

Part III: Counselor Attending Behavior (Verbal)

1. The counselor usually spoke slowly enough so that each word was easily understood.   Yes   No
2. A majority (60 percent or more) of the counselor's responses could be categorized as complete sentences rather than monosyllabic phrases.   Yes   No
3. The counselor's verbal statements were concise and to the point.   Yes   No
4. The counselor refrained from repetition in verbal statements.   Yes   No
5. The counselor made verbal comments that pursued the topic introduced by the client.   Yes   No
6. The subject of the counselor's verbal statements usually referred to the client, either by name or the second-person pronoun *you*.   Yes   No
7. A clear and sensible progression of topics was evident in the counselor's verbal behavior; the counselor avoided rambling.   Yes   No

Comments: _____

Part IV: Verbal Following: Listening and Action Skills

1. The counselor's responses were usually directed toward the most important component of *each* of the client's communications.   Yes   No
2. The counselor followed client topic changes by responding to the primary idea communicated by the client.   Yes   No
3. The counselor reflected the feelings of the client.   Yes   No
4. The counselor reflected the meaning of the client's communications.   Yes   No
5. The counselor verbally acknowledged several (at least two) nonverbal affect cues.   Yes   No
6. The counselor encouraged the client to talk about his or her feelings.   Yes   No
7. The counselor challenged incongruent or discrepant client messages.   Yes   No
8. The counselor asked questions that the client could not answer in a yes or no fashion (typically beginning with words such as *how, what, when, where, who*, etc.).   Yes   No
9. Several times (at least two) the counselor used responses that supported or reinforced something the client said or did.   Yes   No
10. The counselor sometimes restated or clarified the client's previous communication.   Yes   No
11. The counselor used several (at least two) responses that summarized client messages.   Yes   No

Comments: _____

Part V: The Process of Relating

1. The counselor made statements that reflected the client's feelings.	Yes	No
2. The counselor responded to the core of a long and ambivalent client statement.	Yes	No
3. The counselor verbally stated his or her desire and/or intent to understand.	Yes	No
4. The counselor made verbal statements that the client reaffirmed without qualifying or changing the counselor's previous response.	Yes	No
5. The counselor made attempts to communicate verbally his or her understanding of the client that elicited an affirmative client response ("Yes, that's exactly right," and so forth).	Yes	No
6. The counselor reflected the client's feelings at the same or at a greater level of intensity than originally expressed by the client.	Yes	No
7. In communicating understanding of the client's feelings, the counselor verbalized the anticipation present in the client's communication (i.e., what the client would like to do or how the client would like to be).	Yes	No
8. When the counselor's nonverbal behavior suggested that he or she was uncertain or disagreeing, the counselor verbally acknowledged this to the client.	Yes	No
9. The counselor answered directly when the client asked about his or her opinion or reaction.	Yes	No
10. The counselor encouraged discussion of statements made by the client that challenged the *counselor's* knowledge and beliefs.	Yes	No
11. Several times (at least two) the counselor shared his or her own feelings with the client.	Yes	No
12. The counselor encouraged the client to identify and discuss his or her feelings concerning the counselor and the interview.	Yes	No
13. The counselor voluntarily shared his or her feelings about the client and the counseling relationship.	Yes	No
14. The counselor expressed reactions about the client's strengths and/or potential.	Yes	No

Comments: _____

_____

Part VI: Assessment

1. The counselor asked the client to provide basic demographic   Yes   No
   information about him- or herself.

2. The counselor asked the client to describe his or her current   Yes   No
   concerns and to provide some background information about
   these concerns.

3. The counselor asked the client to list and prioritize problems.   Yes   No

4. For each identified problem, the helper explored the:

   a. Affective dimensions.   Yes   No

   b. Cognitive dimensions.   Yes   No

   c. Behavioral dimensions.   Yes   No

   d. Interpersonal dimensions.   Yes   No

   e. Contextual/Cultural dimensions.   Yes   No

5. The counselor asked the client to identify possible strengths,   Yes   No
   resources, and coping skills the client could use to help solve
   the problem.

Comments:_____

_____

Part VII: Goal Setting

1. The counselor asked the client to identify some of the   Yes   No
   conditions surrounding the occurrence of the client's problem
   ("When do you feel _____?").

2. The counselor asked the client to identify some of the   Yes   No
   consequences resulting from the client's behavior ("What
   happens when you _____?").

3. The counselor asked the client to state how he or she would   Yes   No
   like to change his or her behavior ("How would you like things
   to be different?").

4. The counselor and client decided *together* on counseling goals.   Yes   No

5. The goals set in the interview were specific and observable.   Yes   No

6. The counselor asked the client to state orally a commitment to   Yes   No
   work for goal achievement.

7. If the client appeared resistant or unconcerned about achieving   Yes   No
   change, the counselor discussed this with the client.

8. The counselor asked the client to specify at least one action step   Yes   No
   he or she might take toward his or her goal.

9. The counselor suggested alternatives available to the client.   Yes   No

10. The counselor helped the client to develop action steps for goal   Yes   No
    attainment.

11. Action steps designated by the counselor and client were specific and realistic in scope.	Yes	No
12. The counselor provided an opportunity within the interview for the client to practice or rehearse the action step.	Yes	No
13. The counselor provided feedback to the client concerning the execution of the action step.	Yes	No
14. The counselor encouraged the client to observe and evaluate the progress and outcomes of action steps taken outside the interview.	Yes	No

Comments:_____

_____

Part VIII: Strategy Identification

1. The counselor suggested some possible strategies to the client based on the client's stated goals.	Yes	No
2. The counselor selected strategies related to the assessment results that reflected integration of affect, cognition, behaviors, language, and interpersonal and cultural dimensions.	Yes	No
3. The counselor involved the client in the choice of strategies to be used.	Yes	No
4. The counselor suggested a possible sequence of strategies to be used when more than one strategy was selected.	Yes	No
5. The counselor provided a rationale about each strategy.	Yes	No
6. The counselor provided instructions about how the strategy would be used.	Yes	No
7. The counselor assessed for client understanding of the strategies and interventions to be used.	Yes	No

List the strategies and interventions suggested by the counselor:

_____

_____

Comments: _____

_____

Part IX: Termination of the Interview

1. The counselor informed the client before terminating that the interview was almost over.	Yes	No
2. The counselor refrained from introducing new material (a different topic) at the termination phase of the interview.	Yes	No

3. The counselor discouraged the client from pursuing new topics   Yes   No
within the last five minutes of the interview by not asking for
further information about it.

4. Only one attempt to terminate the interview was made before   Yes   No
the termination was actually completed.

5. The counselor initiated the termination of the interview through   Yes   No
use of some closing strategy, such as an acknowledgment of
time limits and/or summarization (by self or client).

6. At the end of the interview, the counselor offered the client an   Yes   No
opportunity to return for another interview.

Comments: ————————————————————————————

Part X: Multicultural Competencies*

1. The counselor displayed an awareness of his or her own racial   Yes   No
and cultural identity development and its impact on the
counseling process.

2. The counselor was aware of his or her own values and biases   Yes   No
about other racial and cultural groups and did not let these biases
and assumptions impede the counseling process.

3. The counselor exhibited a respect for cultural differences among   Yes   No
clients.

4. The counselor was sensitive to nonverbal and paralanguage   Yes   No
cross-cultural communication clues.

5. The counselor demonstrated the ability to assess the client's   Yes   No
level of acculturation and to use this information in working
with the client to implement culturally sensitive counseling.

6. The counselor displayed an understanding of how race,   Yes   No
ethnicity, and culture influence the treatment, status, and life
chances of clients.

7. The counselor was able to demonstrate awareness of the   Yes   No
client's worldview.

8. The counselor was able to recognize and work with the client   Yes   No
dealing with multiple oppressions.

9. The counselor and client *worked together* to determine   Yes   No
mutually acceptable and culturally sensitive goals.

10. The counselor was able to identify and utilize culturally   Yes   No
appropriate intervention strategies.

Comments: ————————————————————————————

*Part X Adapted from Robinson and Howard-Hamilton (2000); Sue and Sue (2008); and Wehrly (1995).

REFERENCES

Adler, A. (1958). *What life should mean to you*. New York, NY: Capricorn.

Adler, J. M. (2012). Clients' and therapists' stories about psychotherapy. *Journal of Personality, 81*, 595–605.

Adler, J. M., Harmeling, L. H., & Walder-Biesanz, I. (2013). Narrative meaning making is associated with sudden gains in psychotherapy clients' mental health under routine clinical conditions. *Journal of Consulting and Clinical Psychology, 81*, 839–845.

Amabile, T. M., & Kramer, S. J. (2011). *The progress principle: Using small wins to ignite joy, engagement, and creativity at work*. Boston, MA: Harvard Business School Press.

American Association for Marriage and Family Therapy. (2012). *Code of ethical principles for marriage and family therapists*. Washington, DC: Author.

American Counseling Association (ACA). (2014a). *About ACA*. Retrieved from http://www.counseling.org/about-us/about-aca

American Counseling Association. 2014b. *Code of ethics* (rev. ed.). Alexandria, VA: Author.

American Psychiatric Association. (2002). *Documentation of psychotherapy by psychiatrists* (data file). Retrieved from http://www.psych.org

American Psychological Association. (2009). *Insufficient evidence that sexual orientation change efforts work*. Retrieved from http://www.apa.org/news/press/releases/2009/08/therapeutic.aspx

American Psychological Association. (2010). *Ethical principles of psychologists and code of conduct*. Retrieved from www.apa.org/ethics/code/index.aspx

American Psychological Association. (2012a). Guidelines for assessment of and intervention with persons with disabilities. *American Psychologist, 67*, 43–62.

American Psychological Association. (2012b). (Division 44/Committee on Lesbian, Gay, and Bisexual Concerns Joint Task Force on Guidelines for Psychotherapy with Lesbian, Gay, and Bisexual Clients). Guidelines for psychotherapy with lesbian, gay, and bisexual clients. *American Psychologist, 67*, 10–42.

American Psychological Association. (2013). *Enhancing your interactions with persons with disabilities*. Washington, DC: Author.

American Psychological Association. (2014). *About APA*. Retrieved from http://www.apa.org/about/index.aspx

American School Counselor Association. (2012). *The ASCA National Model: A framework for school counseling programs* (3rd ed.). Alexandria, VA: American Counseling Association.

Ametrano, I. (2014). Teaching ethical decision making: Helping students reconcile personal and professional values. *Journal of Counseling and Development, 92*, 154–161. doi:10.1002/j.1556-6676.2014.00143.x

Antony, M. M., & Roemer, L. (2011). *Behavior therapy*. Washington DC: American Psychological Association.

Arredondo, P., & Perez, P. (2006). Historical perspectives on multicultural guidelines and contemporary applications. *Journal of Counseling Psychology, 37*, 1–5.

Artman, L., & Daniels, J. (2010). Disability and psychotherapeutic practice: Cultural competence and practical tips. *Professional Psychology, 41*, 442–448. doi:10.1037/a0020864

Association for Lesbian, Gay, Bisexual, and Transgender Issues in Counseling. (2008). *Competencies for counseling gay, lesbian, bisexual, and transgendered (GLBT) clients*. Retrieved from www.algbtic.org/resources/competencies.html

Association for Specialists in Group Work. (2014). *Welcome to ASGW*. Retrieved from http://www.asgw.org/index.htm

Atkinson, D. R., & Hackett, G. (2004). *Counseling diverse populations* (3rd ed.). New York, NY: McGraw-Hill.

Baker, S. B. (2000). *School counseling for the twenty-first century*. Upper Saddle River, NJ: Prentice Hall.

Baker, S. B. (2012. December). A new view of evidence-based practice. *Counseling Today*, 42–43.

Bandura, A. (1969). *Principles of behavior modification*. New York, NY: Holt, Rinehart & Winston.

Banikiotes, P. G., Kubinski, J. A., & Pursell, S. A. (1981). Sex role orientation, self-disclosure, and gender-related perceptions. *Journal of Counseling Psychology, 28*, 140–146.

Barnett, J., & Johnson, W. (2015). *Ethics desk reference for counselors* (2nd ed.). Washington, DC: American Counseling Association.

Bartholomew, C. G. (2003). *Gender-sensitive therapy: Principles and practices.* Prospect Heights, IL: Waveland Press.

Beck, A. T. (1976). *Cognitive therapy and the emotional disorders.* New York, NY: International Universities Press.

Beck, A. T. (2005). The current state of cognitive therapy: A 40-year retrospective. *Archives of General Psychiatry, 62,* 953–959.

Beck, A. T., & Alford, B. A. (2009). *Depression: Causes and treatment* (4th ed.). Philadelphia, PA: University of Pennsylvania Press.

Beck, J. S. (2011). *Cognitive behavior therapy* (2nd ed.). New York, NY: Guilford.

Bedi, R. P., Davis, M., & Williams, M. (2005). Critical incidents in the formation of the therapeutic alliance from the client's perspective. *Psychotherapy: Theory, Research, Practice, Training, 42,* 311–323.

Bein, A. (2008). *The Zen of helping: Spiritual principles for mindful and open-hearted practice.* Hoboken, NJ: John Wiley & Sons.

Bemak, F., & Chung, R. C.-Y. (2008). New professional roles and advocacy strategies for school counselors: A multicultural/social justice perspective to move beyond the nice counselor syndrome. *Journal of Counseling and Development, 86,* 372–381.

Bernard, J. M., & Goodyear, R. K. (2004). *Fundamentals of clinical supervision* (3rd ed.). Boston, MA: Allyn & Bacon.

Bernard, J. M., & Goodyear, R. K. (2014). *Fundamentals of clinical supervision* (5th ed.). Upper Saddle River, NJ: Pearson Education, Inc.

Birman, D., Simon, C., Yi Chan, W., & Tran, N. (2014). A life domains perspective on acculturation and psychological adjustment: A study of refugees from the former Soviet Union. *American Journal of Community Psychology, 53,* 60–72.

Bitter, J. (2014). *Theory and practice of family therapy and counseling* (2nd ed.). Belmont, CA: Brooks/Cole, Cengage.

Bohart, A., & Greenberg, L. (1997). Empathy and psychotherapy: An introductory overview. In A. Bohart & L. Greenberg (Eds.), *Empathy reconsidered* (pp. 3–32). Washington, DC: American Psychological Association.

Borders, L. D. (1999). A systematic approach to peer group supervision. *Journal of Counseling & Development, 69*(3), 248–252.

Bowen, M. (1978). *Family therapy in clinical practice.* New York, NY: Jason Aronson, Inc.

Boyd, V., Hattauer, E., Spivack, J., Deakin, S., Hurley, G., Buckles, N., Erskine, C., Piorkowski, G., Brandel, I., Simono, R. B., Locher, L., Steel, C., & Davidshofer, C. (2003). Accreditation standards for university and college counseling centers. *Journal of Counseling and Development, 81,* 168–177.

Bozarth, J. (1997). Empathy from the framework of client-centered theory and the Rogerian hypothesis. In A. Bohart & L. Greenberg (Eds.), *Empathy reconsidered* (pp. 81–102). Washington, DC: American Psychological Association.

Bradley, L., Sexton, T., & Smith, H. (2005). The American Counseling Association Practice Research Network (ACA-PRN): A new research tool. *Journal of Counseling and Development, 83,* 488–491.

Brammer, L. M., Abrego, P. J., & Shostrom, E. L. (1993). *Therapeutic counseling and psychotherapy: Fundamentals of counseling and psychotherapy* (6th ed.). Englewood Cliffs, NJ: Prentice Hall.

Branden, N. (1971). *The disowned self.* Los Angeles, CA: Nash.

Bronstein, L. (2003). A model for interdisciplinary collaboration. *Social Work, 48*(3), 297–306.

Brooks-Harris, J. (2008). *Integrative multitheoretical psychotherapy.* Boston, MA: Houghton Mifflin, Lahaska Press.

Brown, A. P., Marquis, A., & Guiffrida, D. A. (2013). Mindfulness-based interventions in counseling. *Journal of Counseling and Development, 91,* 96–104. doi:10.1002/j.1556-6676.2013.00077.x

Brown L. (1994). *Subversive dialogues: Theory in feminist therapy.* New York, NY: Basic Books.

Brown, L. (2010). *Feminist therapy.* Washington DC: American Psychological Association.

Brown, S. L., Ness, R. M., Vinokur, A. D., & Smith, D. M. (2003). Providing social support may be more beneficial than receiving it: Results from a prospective study of mortality. *Psychological Science, 14,* 320–327.

Buie, D. (1981). Empathy: Its nature and limitations. *Journal of the American Psychoanalytic Association, 29,* 281–307.

Burdick, D. (2013). *Mindfulness skills workbook for clinicians and clients.* Eau Claire, WI: PESI Publishing.

Campbell, J. M. (2006). *Essentials of clinical supervision.* Hoboken, NJ: John Wiley & Sons.

Canadian Association of Social Workers. (1994). *Code of ethics.* Ottawa: Author.

Canadian Counselling and Psychotherapy Association. (2007). *Code of ethics.* Ottawa: Author.

Canadian Psychological Association. (2007). *Canadian code of ethics for psychologists* (3rd ed.). Ottawa: Author.

Casas, J. M. (2005). Race and racism: The efforts of counseling psychology to understand and address these terms. *The Counseling Psychologist, 33,* 501–512.

Castillo, R. J. (1997). *Culture and mental illness.* Pacific Grove, CA: Brooks/Cole.

Center for Substance Abuse Treatment. (2009). *Clinical supervision and professional development of the substance abuse counselor.* Treatment Improvement Protocol (TIP) Series 52. DHHS Publication No. (SMA) 09-4435. Rockville, MD: Substance Abuse and Mental Health Services Administration.

Chung, R. C.-Y., & Bemak, F. (2002). The relationship of culture and empathy in cross-cultural counseling. *Journal of Counseling and Development, 80,* 154–159.

Chung, R. C.-Y., Bemak, F., Ortiz, D. P., & Sandoval-Perez, P. A. (2008). Promoting the mental health of immigrants: A multicultural/social justice perspective. *Journal of Counseling and Development, 86,* 310–317.

Ciarrochi, J., & Bailey, A. (2008). *A CBT practitioner's guide to ACT.* Oakland, CA: New Harbinger Publications.

Claiborn, C. D., Goodyear, R. K., & Horner, P. A. (2002). Feedback. In J. C. Norcross (Ed.), *Psychotherapy relationships that work* (pp. 217–234). New York, NY: Oxford University Press.

Clance, P. R. (1985). *The impostor phenomenon: When success makes you feel like a fake.* New York, NY: Bantam Books.

Clark, A. J. (2007). *Empathy in counseling and psychotherapy.* New York, NY: Erlbaum.

Clark, D. A., & Beck, A. T. (2010). *Cognitive therapy of anxiety disorders.* New York, NY: Guilford.

Clark, M. A., & Breman, J. C. (2009). School counselor inclusion: A collaborative model to provide academic and social-emotional support in the classroom setting. *Journal of Counseling and Development, 87,* 6–11.

Colbert, R. D., Vernon-Jones, R., & Pransky, K. (2006). The school change feedback process: Creating a new role for counselors in education reform. *Journal of Counseling and Development, 84,* 72–82.

Cook, E. (2012). *Understanding people in context: The ecological perspective in counseling.* Washington DC: American Counseling Association.

Corey, G. (2013). *Theory and practice of counseling and psychotherapy* (9th ed.). Belmont, CA: Brooks/Cole, Cengage.

Corey, G., Corey, M. S., & Callanan, P. (2010). *Issues and ethics in the helping professions* (8th ed.). Belmont, CA: Brooks/Cole, Cengage.

Corey, G., Corey, M. S., Corey, C., & Callanan, P. (2015). *Issues and ethics in the helping professions* (9th ed.). Belmont, CA: Brooks/Cole, Cengage.

Corey, G., Haynes, R., Moulton, P., & Muratori, M. (2010). *Clinical supervision in the helping professions: A practical guide* (2nd ed.). Alexandria, VA: American Counseling Association.

Cormier, S., Nurius, P. S., & Osborn, C. J. (2013). *Interviewing and change strategies for helpers* (7th ed.). Belmont, CA: Brooks/Cole, Cengage.

Cottone, R. R., & Claus, R. E. (2000). Ethical decision-making models: A review of the literature. *Journal of Counseling & Development, 78,* 275–283.

Cowan, E. W., Presbury, J., & Echterling, L. G. (February, 2013). The paradox of empathy: When empathy hurts. *Counseling Today,* 56–61.

Crethar, H. C., Rivera, E. T., & Nash, S. (2008). In search of common threads: Linking multicultural, feminist, and social justice counseling paradigms. *Journal of Counseling and Development, 86,* 269–278.

Csikszentmihalyi, M. (1990). *Flow: The psychology of optimal experience.* New York, NY: Harper & Row.

Dahir, C. A., & Stone, C. B. (2012). *The transformed school counselor* (2nd ed.). Belmont, CA: Brooks/Cole, Cengage.

Daughtry, D., Gibson, J., & Abels, A. (2009). Mentoring students and professionals with disabilities. *Professional Psychology, 40,* 201–205.

Davidson, R. (2012, September). In Winerman, L., Changing our brains, changing ourselves. *Monitor on Psychology,* 30–33.

Davis, T. E. (2015). *Exploring school counseling: Professional practices and perspectives* (2nd ed.). Stamford, CT: Cengage.

Day-Vines, N. L., Wood, S. M., Grothaus, T., Craigen, L., Holman, A., Dotson-Blake, K., & Douglas, M. J. (2007). Broaching the subjects of race, ethnicity, and culture during the counseling process. *Journal of Counseling and Development, 85,* 401–409.

De Jong, P., & Berg, I. K. (2013). *Interviewing for solutions* (4th ed.). Belmont, CA: Brooks/Cole, Cengage.

Dermer, S. B., Smith, S. D., & Barto, K. K. (2010). Identifying and correctly labeling sexual prejudice, discrimination, and oppression. *Journal of Counseling and Development, 88,* 325–331.

Dobson, K. S. (2012). *Cognitive therapy.* Washington DC: American Psychological Association.

Doran, G. T. (1981). There's a SMART way to write management's goals and objectives. *Management Review, 70*(11), pp. 35–36.

Dryden, W. (2009). *Skills in rational emotive behaviour counselling and psychotherapy.* Thousand Oaks, CA: Sage.

Dutton, J. E., & Ragins, B. R. (Eds.). (2007). *Exploring positive relationships at work: Building a theoretical and research foundation.* Mahwah, NJ: Lawrence Erlbaum Associates.

Edwards, C., & Murdock, N. (1994). Characteristics of therapist self-disclosure in the counseling process. *Journal of Counseling and Development, 72,* 384–389.

Efthim, P. W., Kenny, M. E., & Mahalik, J. R. (2001). Gender role stress in relation to shame, guilt, and externalization. *Journal of Counseling and Development, 79,* 430–437.

Egan, G. (1975). *The skilled helper.* Pacific Grove, CA: Brooks/Cole.

Egan, G. (2014). *The skilled helper: A problem-management and opportunity-development approach to helping* (10th ed.). Belmont, CA: Brooks/Cole, Cengage.

Elliott, R., Bohart, A. C., Watson, J. C., & Greenberg, L. S. (2011). Empathy. In J. C. Norcross (Ed.), *Psychotherapy relationships that work: Evidence-based responsiveness* (2nd ed., pp. 132–152). New York, NY: Guilford.

Enns, C. (2000). Gender issues in counseling. In S. D. Brown & R. W. Lent (Eds.), *Handbook of counseling psychology* (pp. 601–638). New York, NY: John Wiley & Sons.

Erford, B. T. (2014). *Orientation to the counseling profession: Advocacy, ethics, and essential professional foundations* (2nd ed.). Boston, MA: Pearson/Merrill Counseling.

Falender, C. A., & Shafranske, E. P. (Eds.). (2008). *Casebook for clinical supervision: A competency-based approach.* Washington, DC: American Psychological Association.

Falvey, J. E. (2002). *Managing clinical supervision: Ethical practice and legal risk management.* Pacific Grove, CA: Brooks/Cole.

Faqrrell, E. F. (2005, December 16). Need therapy? Check your inbox. *The Chronicle of Higher Education, 52,* 17.

Farber, B. A., & Doolin, J. S. (2011). Positive regard and affirmation. In J. C. Norcross (Ed.), *Psychotherapy relationships that work* (pp. 168–186). New York, NY: Oxford University Press.

Festinger, J. (1957). *A theory of cognitive dissonance.* Stanford, CA: Stanford University Press.

Figley, C. R. (Ed.) (2002). *Treating compassion fatigue.* New York, NY: Brunner-Routledge.

Foa, E. B., Keane, T. M., & Friedman, M. J. (Eds.). (2009). *Effective treatment for PTSD: Practice guidelines from the International Society for Traumatic Stress Studies* (2nd ed.). New York, NY: Guilford.

Fosha, D. (2000). *The transforming power of affect.* New York, NY: Basic Books.

Fosha, D. (2002). The activation of affective change processes in AEDP (Accelerated Experiential-Dynamic Psychotherapy). In J. J. Magnavita (Ed.), *Comprehensive handbook of psychotherapy. Vol. 1: Psychodynamic and object relations psychotherapies* (pp. 309–344). New York, NY: John Wiley & Sons.

Fosha, D. (2005). Emotion, true self, true other, core state: Toward a clinical theory of affective change process. *Psychoanalytic Review, 92,* 513–552.

Fredrickson, B. L. (2001). The role of positive emotions in positive psychology: The broaden-and-build theory of positive emotions. *American Psychologist, 56,* 218–226.

Fredrickson, B. L. (2006). Unpacking positive emotions: Investigating the seeds of human flourishing. *The Journal of Positive Psychology, 1*(2), 57–59.

Fredrickson, B. L., & Losada, M. F. (2005). Positive emotions and the complex dynamics of human flourishing. *American Psychologist, 60,* 678–686.

Gale, A. U., & Austin, B. D. (2003). Professionalism's challenges to professional counselors' collective identity. *Journal of Counseling and Development, 81,* 3–10.

Gamino, L. A., & Ritter, R. H., Jr. (2009). *Ethical practice in grief counseling.* New York, NY: Springer Publishing.

Gilligan, S. (1997). *The courage to love: Principles and practices of self-relations psychotherapy.* New York, NY: Norton.

Gottman, J., Gottman, J. S., & DeClaire, J. (2007). *Ten lessons to transform your marriage.* New York, NY: Three Rivers Press.

Greenberg, L. (2002). *Emotion-focused therapy: Coaching clients to work through their feelings.* Washington, DC: American Psychological Association.

Greenberg, L. (2011). *Emotion-focused therapy.* Washington DC: American Psychological Association.

Greenberg, L. (2012). Emotions, the great captains of our lives: Their role in the process of change in psychotherapy. *American Psychologist, 67,* 697–707.

Grepmair, L., Metterlehner, F., Lowe, T., Bachler, E., Rother, W., & Nickel, M. (2007). Promoting mindfulness in psychotherapists in training influences the treatment results of their patients: A randomized, double-blind, controlled study. *Psychotherapy and Psychosomatics, 76,* 332–338.

Gysbers, N., & Henderson, P. (2012). *Developing and managing your school guidance and counseling program* (5 ed.), Alexandria, VA: American Counseling Association.

Hackney, H., & Cormier, L. S. (1973). *Counseling strategies and objectives.* Englewood Cliffs, NJ: Prentice Hall.

Hackney, H., & Cormier, L. S. (2013). *The professional counselor* (7th ed.). Upper Saddle River, NJ: Pearson.

Hadjistavropoulos, H., & Malloy, D. C. (2000). Making ethical choices: A comprehensive decision-making model for Canadian psychologists. *Canadian Psychology, 41,* 104–115.

Haeffel, G. (2010). When self-help is no help: Traditional cognitive skills training does not prevent depressive symptoms in people who ruminate. *Behaviour Research and Therapy, 48,* 152–157.

Haley, J. (1997). *Leaving home* (2nd ed.). New York, NY: Brunner-Mazel.

Halpern, J., & Tramontin, M. (2007). *Disaster mental health.* Belmont, CA: Brooks/Cole, Thomson.

Hanna, F. J., & Cardona, B. (2013). Multicultural counseling beyond the relationship: Expanding the repertoire with techniques. *Journal of Counseling and Development, 91,* 349–357.

Hansen, N. D., & Goldberg, S. G. (1999). Navigating the nuances: A matrix of considerations for ethical-legal dilemmas. *Professional Psychology: Research and Practice 30,* 495–503.

Hansen, N. D., Randazzo, K. V., Schwartz, A., Marshall, M., Kalis, D., Frazier, R., Burke, C., Kershner-Rice, K., & Norvig, G. (2006). Do we practice what we preach? An exploratory study of multicultural psychotherapy competencies. *Journal of Counseling Psychology, 37,* 66–74.

Hardy, K. V., & Laszloffy, T. (1995). The cultural genogram: Key to training culturally competent family therapists. *Journal of Marital and Family Therapy, 21,* 227–237.

Harris, A. H. S. (2009). Carl Thoresen: The evolving pioneer. *The Counseling Psychologist, 37,* 275–295.

Harris, A. H. S., & Thoresen, C. E. (2005). Volunteering is associated with delayed mortality in older people: Analysis of the longitudinal study of aging. *Journal of Health Psychology, 10*(6), 739–752.

Harris, R. (2006). Embracing your demons: An overview of acceptance and commitment therapy. *Psychotherapy in Australia, 12,* 2–8.

Harvey, J. C., & Katz, C. (1985). *If I'm so successful, why do I feel like a fake?* New York, NY: St. Martin's Press.

Hawkins, P., & Shohet, R. (2012). *Supervision in the helping professions* (4th ed.). London: McGraw-Hill Education/Open University Press.

Hayes, S. C. (2004). Acceptance and commitment therapy, relational frame theory, and the third-wave of behavioral and cognitive therapies. *Behavior Therapy, 35,* 639–665.

Hayes, S. C., Luoma, J., Bond, F., Masuda, A., & Lillis, J. (2006). Acceptance and commitment therapy: Model, processes, and outcomes. *Behaviour Research and Therapy, 44,* 1–25.

Hayes, S. C., & Smith, S. (2005). *Get out of your mind and into your life*. Oakland, CA: New Harbinger.

Hayes, S. C., Strosahl, K., & Wilson, K. G. (2012). *Acceptance and commitment therapy: An experiential approach to behavior change* (2nd ed.). New York, NY: Guilford Press.

Hays, P. A., & Iwamasa, G. (2006). *Culturally responsive cognitive-behavioral therapy*. Washington, DC: American Psychological Association.

Helms, J., & Cook, D. (1999). *Using race and culture in counseling and psychotherapy*. Boston, MA: Allyn & Bacon.

Hepworth, D. H., Rooney, R. H., Dewberry-Rooney, G., & Strom-Gottfried, K. (2013). *Direct social work practice: Theory and skills* (9th ed.). Belmont, CA: Brooks/Cole, Cengage.

Hess, S. A., & Kraus, K. L. (2010). Supervision-based integrative models of counselor supervision: Interpersonal models. In N. Ladany & L. J. Bradley (Eds.), *Counselor supervision* (4th ed., pp. 125–144). New York, NY: Routledge.

Hewlett, K. (2001). Can low self-esteem and self-blame on the job make you sick? *Monitor on Psychology, 32*(7), 58.

Hill, C., & Knox, S. (2002). Self-disclosure. In J. C. Norcross (Ed.), *Psychotherapy relationships that work* (pp. 255–266). New York, NY: Oxford University Press.

Hoffman, R. M. (2001). The measurement of masculinity and femininity: Historical perspective and implications for counseling. *Journal of Counseling and Development, 79*, 472–485.

Horney, K. (1970). *Neurosis and human growth*. New York, NY: Norton.

Houser, R., Wilczenski, F., & Ham, M. (2006). *Culturally relevant ethical decision-making in counseling*. Thousand Oaks, CA: Sage.

Hurley, E. J., & Gerstein, L. H. (2013). The multiculturally and internationally competent mental health professional. In R. L. Lowman (Ed.), *Internationalizing multiculturalism* (pp. 227–254). Washington DC: American Psychological Association.

Hutchins, D., & Cole-Vaught, C. (1997). *Helping relationships and strategies* (3rd ed.). Pacific Grove, CA: Brooks/Cole.

Ivey, A. (1971). *Microtraining: Innovations in interviewing training*. Springfield, IL: Thomas.

Ivey, A. E. (1995, April). *The community genogram: A strategy to assess culture and community resources*. The annual meeting of the American Counseling Association, Denver, CO.

Ivey, A. E., D'Andrea, M., & Ivey, M. B. (2012). *Theories of counseling and psychotherapy: A multicultural perspective* (7th ed.). Thousand Oaks, CA: Sage.

Ivey, A. E., Gluckstern, N., & Ivey, M. B. (1997). *Basic influencing skills* (3rd ed.). North Amherst, MA: Microtraining Associates.

Ivey, A. E., Gluckstern-Packard, N., & Ivey, M. B. (2006). *Basic attending skills* (4th ed.). North Amherst, MA: Microtraining Associates.

Ivey, A. E., Ivey, M. B., & Zalaquett, C. P. (2014). *Intentional interviewing and counseling: Facilitating client development in a multicultural society* (8th ed.). Belmont, CA: Brooks/Cole, Cengage.

Ivy, D. K. (2012). *GenderSpeak* (5th ed.). Upper Saddle River, NJ: Pearson.

Jaffee v. Redmond 518 U.S. 1. (2014). *The psychotherapist-patient privilege*. Retrieved from http://www.jaffee-redmond.org/

Jenkins, A. H. (1997). The empathic context in psychotherapy with people of color. In A. Bohart & L. Greenberg (Eds.), *Empathy reconsidered* (pp. 321–342). Washington, DC: American Psychological Association.

Johnson, D. W. (2014). *Reaching out: Interpersonal effectiveness and self-actualization* (11th ed.). Upper Saddle River, NJ: Pearson.

Joormann, J., & Gotlib, I. (2008). Updating the contents of working memory in depression: Interference from irrelevant negative material. *Journal of Abnormal Psychology, 117*, 182–192.

Jordan, J. (1997). Relational development through mutual empathy. In A. Bohart & L. Greenberg (Eds.), *Empathy reconsidered* (pp. 343–352). Washington, DC: American Psychological Association.

Jourard, S. M. (1963). *Personal adjustment*. New York, NY: Macmillan.

Joyce, P., & Sills, C. (2010). *Skills in gestalt counselling and psychotherapy* (2nd ed.). Thousand Oaks, CA: Sage.

Kabat-Zinn, J. (2012). *Mindfulness for beginners*. Boulder, CO: Sounds True Publishing.

Kadambi, M. A., & Truscott, D. (2004). Vicarious trauma among therapists working with sexual violence, cancer, and general practice. *Canadian Journal of Counselling, 38*, 260–276.

Kaplan, D. (2011, July). Changing distorted thinking: An interview with Judith S. Beck about cognitive-behavioral therapy. *Counseling Today,* 36–38.

Kaplan, D. (2014). Ethical implications of a critical legal case for the counseling profession: *Ward v. Wilbanks. Journal of Counseling and Development,* 92: 142–146. doi:10.1002/j.1556-6676.2014.00140.x

Karasu, T. B. (1992). *Wisdom in the practice of psychotherapy.* New York, NY: Basic Books.

Karen, R. (1992). Shame. *Atlantic Monthly, 269,* 40–70.

Kassan, L. D. (2010). *Peer supervision groups: How they work and why you need one.* New York, NY: Jason Aronson.

Kelley, C. R. (1979). Freeing blocked anger. *The Radix Journal, 1,* 19–33.

Kennedy, A. (2004, September). College counseling center extends reach through technology. *Counseling Today,* 10–11.

Kleist, D., & Bitter, J. (2014). Virtue, ethics, and legality in family practice. In J. Bitter, *Theories and practice of family therapy* (pp. 71–93). Belmont, CA: Brooks/Cole, Cengage.

Klerman, G., & Weissman, M. (1992). Interpersonal psychotherapy: Efficacy and adaptations. In E. S. Paykel (Ed.), *Handbook of affective disorders* (pp. 501–510). Edinburgh: Churchill Livingstone.

Knapp, M. L., Hall, J., & Horgan, T. G. (2014). *Nonverbal communication in human interaction* (8th ed.). Boston, MA: Wadsworth.

Koerner, K. (2012). *Doing DBT: A practical guide.* New York, NY: Guilford.

Kolden, G., Klein, M., Wang, C.-C., & Austin, S. (2011). Congruence/genuineness. In J. C. Norcross (Ed.), *Psychotherapy relationships that work: Evidence-based responsiveness* (2nd ed., pp.187–202). New York, NY: Oxford.

Kottler, J. (1991). *The compleat therapist.* San Francisco, CA: Jossey-Bass.

Kramer, P. D. (1993). *Listening to Prozac.* New York, NY: Viking.

Kuyken, W., Weare, K., Ukoumunne, R., Motton, N., Burnett, R., Cullen, D., Hennelly, S., & Huppert, F. (2013). Effectiveness of the mindfulness in schools programme: Non-randomised controlled feasibility study. *The British Journal of Psychiatry.* Advance online publication: doi:10.1192/bjp.bp.113.126649

Lairio, M., & Nissila, P. (2002). Towards networking in counselling: A follow-up study of Finnish school counselling. *British Journal of Guidance & Counselling, 30*(2), 159–72.

Leahy, M. J. (2004). Qualified providers. In T. F. Riggar & D. R. Maki (Eds.), *The handbook of rehabilitation counseling* (pp. 142–158). New York, NY: Springer Publishing.

Lee, J. H., Nam, S. K., Kim, A.-R., Kim, B., Lee, M. Y., & Lee, S. M. (2013). Resilience: A meta-analytic approach. *Journal of Counseling and Development, 91,* 269–279.

Lewis, J. B. (1971). *Shame and guilt in neurosis.* Lido Beach, NY: International Universities Press.

Lilius, J. M. (2012). Recovery at work: Understanding the restorative side of "depleting" client interactions. *Academy of Management Review, 37,* 569–588.

Lilliengren, P., & Werbart, A. J. (2005). A model of therapeutic action grounded in the patients' view of curative and hindering factors in psychoanalytic psychotherapy. *Psychotherapy: Theory, Research, Training, Practice, 42,* 32–39.

Linehan, M. (1993). *Cognitive-behavioral treatment of borderline personality disorder.* New York, NY: Guilford Press.

Linehan, M., & Dexter-Mazza, E. (2008). Dialectical behavior therapy for borderline personality disorder. In D. H. Barlow (Ed.). *Clinical handbook of psychological disorders* (4th ed., pp. 365–420). New York, NY: Guilford.

Linley, P. A., & Joseph, S. (Eds.). (2004). *Positive psychology in practice.* Hoboken, NJ: John Wiley & Sons.

Lionetti, T. M., Snyder, E. P., & Christner, R. W. (2011). *A practical guide to building professional competencies in school psychology.* New York, NY: Springer.

Lott, B. (2002). Cognitive and behavioral distancing from the poor. *American Psychologist, 57,* 100–110.

Lowen, A. (1965). *Breathing, movement, and feeling.* New York, NY: Institute for Bioenergetic Analysis.

Lowman, R. L. (2013). Multicultural and international: Why and how both should matter in professional practice. In R. L. Lowman (Ed.), *Internationalizing multiculturalism* (pp. 3–31). Washington DC: American Psychological Association.

Maki, D. R., & Bernard, J. M. (2007). The ethics of clinical supervision. In R. R. Cottone & V. M. Tarvydas (Eds.), *Ethical and professional issues in counseling* (3rd ed., pp. 347–368). Upper Saddle River, NJ: Merrill.

Makinson, R. A., & Young, J. S. (2012). Cognitive behavioral therapy and the treatment of posttraumatic stress disorder: Where counseling and neuroscience meet. *Journal of Counseling and Development, 90,* 131–140. doi:10, 1111/j/1556-6676.2012.00017.x

Markowitz, J. C., & Weissman, M. M. (2004). Interpersonal psychotherapy: Principles and applications. *World Psychiatry, 3,* 136–139.

Markowitz, J. C., & Weissman, M. M. (Eds.). (2012). *Casebook of interpersonal psychotherapy.* New York, NY: Oxford University Press.

McElwee, R. O., & Yurak, T. J. (2010). The phenomenology of the impostor phenomenon. *Individual Differences Research, 8*(3), 184–197.

McGoldrick, M., Carter, B., & Garcia-Preto, N. (2011). *The expanded family life cycle: Individual, family, and social perspectives* (4th ed.). Upper Saddle River, NJ: Pearson.

McMullin, R. E. (2000). *The new handbook of cognitive therapy techniques.* New York, NY: Norton.

McNeil, D. W., Kyle, B. N., & Nurius, P. S. (2013). Exposure therapy strategies: Imaginal, in vitro, in vivo, and intensive. In S. Cormier, P. S. Nurius, & C. J. Osborn, *Interviewing and change strategies for helpers* (7th ed., pp. 475–512). Belmont, CA: Brooks/Cole, Cengage.

Meichenbaum, D. (2007). Stress inoculation training: A preventive and treatment approach. In P. M. Lehrer, R. L. Woolfork, & W. Sime (Eds.), *Principles and practice of stress management* (3rd ed., pp. 497–518). New York, NY: Guilford.

Mellin, E. A., Hunt, B., & Nichols, L. M. (2011). Counselor professional identity: Findings and implications for counseling and interprofessional collaboration. *Journal of Counseling and Development, 89,* 140–147.

Mellody, P. (1989). *Facing codependence.* New York, NY: Harper and Row.

Mesquita, B., & Frijda, N. (1992). Cultural variations in emotions: A review. *Psychological Bulletin, 112,* 179–204.

Miller, A. (1981). *The drama of the gifted child.* New York, NY: Basic Books.

Miller, B. (2011). Narrative gerontology: A post reading later stage of life: A conversation with William Randal. *Journal of Systems Therapies, 30,* 64–75.

Miller, G. (2006, May 12). Probing the social brain. *Science, 312* (5775), 838–839.

Miller, R. (2010). *Yoga nidra: A meditative practice for deep relaxation and healing.* Boulder, CO: Sounds True Publishing.

Miller, S. (1985). *The shame experience.* Haberford, PA: Analytic Press.

Miller, W. R., & Rollnick, S. (2012). *Motivational interviewing* (3rd ed.). New York, NY: Guilford.

Minuchin, S. (1974). *Families and family therapy.* Cambridge, MA: Harvard University Press.

Morrison, J. (2014). *The first interview: A guide for clinicians* (4th ed.). New York, NY: Guilford.

Moss, J. M., Gibson, D. M., & Dollarhide, C. T. (2014). Professional identity development: A grounded theory of transformational tasks of counselors. *Journal of Counseling and Development, 92,* 3–12. doi:10.1002/j.1556-6676.2014.00124.x

Murdin, L. (2000). *How much is enough? Endings in psychotherapy and counseling.* London: Routledge.

Myers, J. E., Sweeney, T. J., & White, V. E. (2002). Advocacy for counseling and counselors: A professional imperative. *Journal of Counseling and Development, 80,* 394–402.

Myers, K. (2013, August). Effective treatment of military clients. *Counseling Today,* 62–64.

Nadal, K. L., Griffin, K. E., Wong, Y., Hamit, S., & Rasmus, M. (2014). The impact of racial microaggressions on mental health: Counseling implications for clients of color. *Journal of Counseling and Development, 92,* 57–66. doi:10.1002/j.1556-6676.2014.00130.x

National Association of Social Workers (NASW). (2008). *Code of ethics of the National Association of Social Workers* (rev. ed.). Washington, DC: Author. Retrieved from http://www.socialworkers.org /pubs/code/code.asp

National Association of Social Workers (NASW). (2014). *About NASW.* Retrieved from http://www .socialworkers.org/nasw/default.asp

National Board for Certified Counselors (NBCC). (2014a). *About NBCC.* Retrieved from http://www .nbcc.org/

National Board for Certified Counselors (NBCC). (2014b). *Continuing education requirements for*

NBCC recertification. Retrieved from http://www.nbcc.org/Recertification/CEReqs

National Organization for Human Services. (2000). Ethical standards of human service professionals. *Human Service Education, 20*(1), 61–68.

Neimeyer, R. A. (2012). *Techniques of grief therapy: Creative practices for counseling the bereaved*. New York, NY: Routledge.

Nepo, M. (2012). *Seven thousand ways to listen*. New York, NY: Free Press.

Newman, C. F. (2003). Cognitive restructuring: Identifying and modifying maladaptive schemas. In W. O'Donohue, J. E. Fisher, & S. C. Hayes (Eds.), *Cognitive-behavior therapy: Applying empirically supported techniques in your practice* (pp. 89–95). New York, NY: John Wiley & Sons.

Newsome, D. W., & Gladding, S. T. (2014). *Clinical mental health counseling in community and agency settings* (4th ed.). Boston, MA: Pearson/Merrill Counseling.

Nichols, M. P. (2009). *The lost art of listening* (2nd ed.). New York, NY: Guilford.

Nissen-Lie, H., Havik, O. E., Hoglend, P. A., Monsen, J. T., & Ronnestad, M. H. (2013). The contribution of the quality of therapists' personal lives to the development of the working alliance. *Journal of Counseling Psychology, 60*, 483–495. doi:10.1037/a0033643

Norcross, J. C. (2001). Empirically supported therapy relationships: Summary report of the Division 29 Task Force. *Psychotherapy, 38*(4), 495–497.

Norcross, J. C. (Ed.). (2011). *Psychotherapy relationships that work* (2nd ed.). New York, NY: Oxford University Press.

Norcross, J. C. (2012). *Changeology: 5 steps to realizing your goals and resolutions*. New York, NY: Simon & Schuster.

Norcross, J. C., Pfund, R. A., & Prochaska, J. O. (2013). Psychotherapy in 2022: A Delphi poll on its future. *Professional Psychology, 44*, 363–370.

Ogrodniczuk, J. S., Joyce, A. S., & Piper, W. E. (2005). Strategies for reducing patient-initiated premature termination of psychotherapy. *Harvard Review of Psychiatry, 13*, 57–70.

O'Neil, J. M. (2013). Gender-role conflict research 30 years later: An evidence-based diagnostic schema to assess boys and men in counseling. *Journal of Counseling and Development, 91*, 490–498.

O'Neill, T. D. (1993). "Feeling worthless": An ethnographic investigation of depression and problem drinking at the Flathead Reservation. *Culture, Medicine, and Psychiatry, 16*, 447–469.

Osborn, C. J. (2004). Seven salutary suggestions for counselor stamina. *Journal of Counseling and Development, 82*, 319–328.

Ostir, G. V., Markides, K. S., Black, S. A., & Goodwin, J. S. (2000). Emotional well-being predicts subsequent functional independence and survival. *Journal of the American Geriatrics Society, 48*, 473–478.

Pearson, Q. M. (2004). Getting the most out of clinical supervision: Strategies for mental health counseling students. *Journal of Mental Health Counseling, 26*(4), 361–373.

Pedersen, P., Crethar, H. C., & Carlson, J. (2008). *Inclusive cultural empathy*. Washington DC: American Psychological Association.

Pedersen, P., & Ivey, A. (1993). *Culture-centered counseling and interviewing skills*. Westport, CT: Praeger.

Pennebaker, J. W. (1990). *Opening up: The healing power of confiding in others*. New York, NY: Morrow.

Perls, F. (1969). *Ego, hunger, and aggression*. New York, NY: Vintage.

Perls, F. (1973). *The gestalt approach and eyewitness to therapy*. Palo Alto, CA: Science and Behavior Books.

Pittman, F. (1985). Gender myths: When does gender become pathology? *Family Therapy Networker, 9*, 25–33.

Ponton, R. F., & Duba, J. D. (2009). The ACA *Code of Ethics*: Articulating counseling's professional covenant. *Journal of Counseling and Development, 87*, 117–121.

Pope, K. S., & Vasquez, M. J. T. (2011). *Ethics in psychotherapy and counseling: A practical guide* (4th ed.). Hoboken, NJ: John Wiley & Sons.

Power, S. J., & Rothausen, T. J. (2003). The work-oriented midcareer development model: An extension of Super's maintenance stage. *The Counseling Psychologist, 31*, 157–197.

Prochaska, J. O., DiClemente, C., & Norcross, J. C. (1992). In search of how people change. *American Psychologist, 47*, 1102–1114.

Prochaska, J. O., & Norcross, J. C. (2014). *Systems of psychotherapy: A transtheoretical analysis* (8th ed.). Stamford, CT: Cengage.

Rainer, J. P. (2000). Compassion fatigue: When caregiving begins to hurt. In L. Vandecreek & T. L. Jackson (Eds.), *Innovations in clinical practice: A source book* (pp. 441–453). Sarasota, FL: Professional Resource Press.

Reiser, M. (2008, September). Five tips for mindful living. *Counseling Today,* 14–15.

Remley, T. P., Jr., & Herlihy, B. (2013). *Ethical, legal, and professional issues in counseling* (4th ed.). Upper Saddle River, NJ: Merrill/Prentice-Hall.

Rifkin, J. (2009). *The empathic civilization.* New York: Penguin.

Robinson, T. (1997). Insurmountable opportunities. *Journal of Counseling and Development, 76,* 6–7.

Robinson, T., & Howard-Hamilton, M. (2000). *The convergence of race, ethnicity, and gender.* Upper Saddle River, NJ: Prentice Hall.

Rogers, C. (1951). *Client-centered therapy.* Boston, MA: Houghton Mifflin.

Rogers, C. (1957). The necessary and sufficient conditions of therapeutic personality change. *Journal of Counseling Psychology, 21,* 95–103.

Rollins, J. (2005, September). The need to reach across campus: Strategies for engaging special student populations. *Counseling Today,* 10–13.

Roysircar, G., Arredondo, P., Fuertes, J., Ponterotto, J., Coleman, H., Israel, T., & Toporek, R. (2002). *Updated operationalization of the multicultural competencies.* Alexandria, VA: American Counseling Association.

Roysircar, G., Sandju, D. S., & Bibbins, V. (2002). *Multicultural competencies: A guidebook of practices.* Alexandria, VA: American Counseling Association.

Rynes, S. L., Bartunek, J. M., Dutton, J. E., & Margolis, J. D. (2012). Care and compassion through an organizational lens: Opening up new possibilities. *Academy of Management Review, 37*(4), 503–523.

Saccuzzo, D. (2002). *The Psychologist's Legal Update # 13: Liability for failure to supervise adequately: Let the master beware (Part 1).* National Register of Health Service Providers in Psychology. *The Psychologist's Legal Update, 13,* 1–14.

Sakulku, J., & Alexander, J. (2011). The impostor phenomenon. *International Journal of Behavioral Science, 6*(1), 73–92.

Sanchez-Hucles, J., & Jones, N. (2005). Breaking the silence around race in training, practice, and research. *The Counseling Psychologist, 33,* 547–558.

Schaufeli, W. B., Leiter, M. P., & Maslach, C. (2009). Burnout: 35 years of research and practice. *Career Development International, 14*(3), 204–220.

Schulte, R. (2013, June). Think this, not that. *Counseling Today,* 53–54.

Segal, U. A., & Mayadas, N. S. (2005). Assessment of issues facing immigrant and refugee families. *Child Welfare, LXXIV,* 563–583.

Segal, Z. V., Williams, J. M., Jr., & Teasdale, J. D. (2013). *Mindfulness-based cognitive therapy for depression* (2nd ed.). New York, NY: Guilford Press.

Seligman, M. (2011). *Flourish: A visionary new understanding of happiness and well-being.* New York, NY: Free Press.

Shallcross, L. (2013a, February). Bully pulpit. *Counseling Today,* 31–39.

Shallcross, L. (2013b, April). Building a more complete client picture. *Counseling Today,* 31–39.

Shallcross, L. (2013c, August). Claiming their rightful place at the table. *Counseling Today,* 35–43.

Sharf, R. S. (2012). *Theories of psychotherapy and counseling: Concepts and cases* (5th ed.). Belmont, CA: Wadsworth.

Sharpley, C. F., Munro, D. M., & Elly, M. J. (2005). Silence and rapport during initial interviews. *Counseling Psychology Quarterly, 18,* 149–159.

Shaw, H. E., & Shaw, S. F. (2006). Critical ethical issues in online counseling: Assessing current practices with an ethical intent checklist. *Journal of Counseling and Development, 84,* 41–53.

Shelton, K., & Delgado-Romero, F. A. (2011). Sexual orientation microaggressions: The experience of lesbian, gay, bisexual, and queer clients in psychotherapy. *Journal of Counseling Psychology, 58,* 210–221.

Sheldon, K. M., & Houser-Marko, L. (2001). Self-concordance, goal-attainment, and the pursuit of happiness: Can there be an upward spiral? *Journal of Personality and Social Psychology, 80,* 152–165.

Siegel, D. (1999). *The developing mind: Toward a neurobiology of interpersonal experience.* New York, NY: Guilford.

Siegel, D. (2006). An interpersonal neurobiology approach to psychotherapy: Awareness, mirror neurons, and neural plasticity in the development of well-being. *Psychiatric Annals, 36,* 248–256.

Siegel, D. (2007). *The mindful brain.* New York, NY: Norton.

Siegel, D. (2010). *The mindful therapist*. New York, NY: Norton.

Siegel, D., & Hartzell, M. (2003). *Parenting from the inside out*. New York, NY: Tarcher Penguin.

Siegle, G., Carter, C., & Thase, M. (2006). Use of fMRI to predict recovery from unipolar depression with cognitive behavior therapy. *American Journal of Psychiatry, 163*, 735–738.

Singer, R. R., & Tummala-Narra, P. (2013). White clinicians' perspectives on working with racial minority immigrant clients. *Professional Psychology, 44*, 290–298.

Skovholt, T. M., & Trotter-Mathison, M. J. (2011). *The resilient practitioner: Burnout prevention and self-care strategies for counselors, therapists, teachers, and health professionals* (2nd ed.). New York, NY: Routledge.

Smith, E. (1985). *The body in psychotherapy*. Jefferson, NC: McFarland.

Smith, E. (2006). The strength-based counseling model. *The Counseling Psychologist, 34*, 13–79.

Smith, T. B., Rodriguez, M. D., & Bernal, G. (2011). Culture. In J. C. Norcross (Ed.), *Psychotherapy relationships that work: Evidence-based responsiveness* (2nd ed., pp. 316–335). New York, NY: Oxford University Press.

Smyth, L. (1999). *Overcoming post-traumatic stress disorder: A cognitive-behavioral exposure-based protocol for the treatment of PTSD and the other anxiety disorders*. Oakland, CA: New Harbinger.

Sommers-Flanagan, J., & Sommers-Flanagan, R. (2012). *Counseling and psychotherapy theories in context and practice*. Hoboken, NJ: Wiley.

Sommers-Flanagan, J., & Sommers-Flanagan, R. (2014). *Clinical interviewing* (5th ed.). Hoboken, NJ: John Wiley & Sons.

Sperry, L., Carlson, J., & Kjos, D. (2003). *Becoming an effective therapist*. Boston, MA: Allyn & Bacon.

Spiegler, M. D., & Guevremont, D. C. (2010). *Contemporary behavior therapy* (5th ed.). Belmont, CA: Wadsworth, Cengage.

Stanard, R. P. (2013). International registry of counselor education programs: CACREP's contribution to the development of counseling as a global profession. *Journal of Counseling and Development, 91*, 55–60.

Steinem, G. (1992). *Revolution from within: A book of self-esteem*. Boston, MA: Little, Brown.

St. John, W. (2009). *Outcasts united*. New York, NY: Spiegel and Grau.

Sue, D. W. (2010). *Microaggressions in everyday life: Race, gender, and sexual orientation*. Hoboken, NJ: John Wiley & Sons.

Sue, D. W. (2013). Race talk: The psychology of racial dialogues. *American Psychologist, 68*, 661–663.

Sue, D. W., Arredondo, P., & McDavis, R. J. (1992). Multicultural competencies/standards: A call to the profession. *Journal of Counseling and Development, 70*, 477–486.

Sue, D. W., Capodilupo, C. M., Torino, G. C., Bucceri, J. M., Holder, M. B., Nadal, K. L., & Esquilin, M. (2007). Racial microaggressions in everyday life: Implications for clinical practice. *The American Psychologist, 62*, 271–286.

Sue, D. W., & Sue, D. (2008). *Counseling the culturally diverse*. New York, NY: John Wiley and Sons.

Sue, D. W., & Sue, D. (2013). *Counseling the culturally diverse* (6th ed.). Hoboken, NJ: John Wiley & Sons.

Sue, S., & Lam, A. (2002). Cultural and demographic diversity. In J. C. Norcross (Ed.), *Psychotherapy relationships that work* (pp. 401–422). New York, NY: Oxford University Press.

Sullivan, J. G. (2004). *Living large: Transformative work at the intersection of ethics and spirituality*. Laurel, MD: Tai Sophia Press.

Sweeney, T. J. (1995). Accreditation, credentialing, professionalization: The role of specialties. *Journal of Counseling and Development, 74*, 117–125.

Teyber, E., & McClure, F. (2011). *Interpersonal processes in psychotherapy* (6th ed.). Belmont, CA: Brooks/Cole, Cengage.

Thomas, J. T. (2010). *The ethics of supervision and consultation*. Washington, DC: American Psychological Association.

Thomas, R. V., & Pender, D. A. (2008). Association for Specialists in Group Work: Best practice guidelines 2007 revisions. *The Journal for Specialists in Group Work, 33*(2), 111–117.

Tretout, P. (1999). *Choosing a career in the helping professions*. New York, NY: Rosen Publishing Group.

Urofsky, R. I. (2013). The council for accreditation of counseling and related educational programs: Promoting quality in counselor education. *Journal of Counseling and Development, 91*, 6–14.

U.S. Department of Health and Human Services (HHS). (2014). *Health information privacy.* Retrieved from http://www.hhs.gov/ocr/privacy/

Vacc, N. A., & Loesch, L. C. (2000). *Professional orientation to counseling* (3rd ed.). Philadelphia, PA: Brunner-Routledge.

Vailant, G. (2000). The mature defenses: Antecedents of joy. *American Psychologist, 55,* 89–98.

Vasquez, M. (2005, November/December). How to terminate psychotherapy. *The National Psychologist, 21.*

Vogel, D. L., Epting, F., & Wester, S. B. (2003). Counselors' perceptions of female and male clients. *Journal of Counseling and Development, 81,* 131–140.

Walen, S. R., DiGiuseppe, R., & Wessler, R. L. (1992). *A practitioner's guide to rational-emotive therapy* (2nd ed.). New York, NY: Oxford University Press.

Walinski, A., & Kirschner, J. (2013). Joining forces: Counselors collaborating to serve military families. *Journal of Military and Government Counseling, 1,* 19–25.

Watson, D., & Tharp, R. (2014). *Self-directed behavior* (9th ed.). Belmont, CA: Wadsworth, Cengage.

Watson, O. M. (1970). *Proxemic behavior: A cross-cultural study.* The Hague: Mouton.

Watts-Jones, D. (2004, March–April). Social justice or political correctness? *Psychotherapy Networker,* 27–28.

Watzlawick, P., Beavin, J. H., & Jackson, D. D. (1967). *Pragmatics of human communication.* New York, NY: Norton.

Wedding, D. (2013). Improving international multicultural competence by working and studying abroad. In R. L. Lowman (Ed.). *Internationalizing multiculturalism* (pp. 289–300). Washington DC: American Psychological Association.

Wedding, D., & Corsini, R. (Eds.). (2014). *Current psychotherapies* (10th ed.). Belmont, CA: Brooks/Cole, Cengage.

Wehrly, B. (1995). *Pathways to multicultural counseling competence.* Pacific Grove, CA: Brooks/Cole.

Weissman, M., Markowitz, J., & Klerman, G. (2007). *Clinician's quick guide to interpersonal psychotherapy.* New York, NY: Oxford University Press.

Welfel, E. R. (2013). *Ethics in counseling and psychotherapy: Standards, research, and emerging issues* (5th ed.). Belmont, CA: Brooks/Cole.

Wheeler, A. M., & Bertram, B. (2012). *The counselor and the law: A guide to legal and ethical practice* (6th ed.). Alexandria, VA: American Counseling Association.

Whiston, S. C., Tai, W. L., Rahardja, D., & Eder, K. (2011). School counseling outcome: A meta-analytic examination of interventions. *Journal of Counseling and Development, 89,* 37–55.

White, M. (2007). *Maps of narrative practice.* New York, NY: Norton.

White, M. (2011). *Narrative practice: Continuing the conversations.* New York, NY: Norton.

White, M., & Epston, D. (1990). *Narrative means to therapeutic ends.* New York, NY: Norton.

Whyte, A. K., Aubrecht, A. L., McCullough, C. A., Lewis, J. W., & Thompson-Ochoa, D. (2013, October). Understanding deaf people in counseling contexts. *Counseling Today,* 39–45.

Wicks, R. (2008). *The resilient clinician.* New York, NY: Oxford University Press.

Williams, L. E., & Bargh, J. A. (2008). Experiencing physical warmth promotes interpersonal warmth. *Science, 322*(5901), 606–607.

Wilson, G. T. (2010). Behavior therapy. In R. J. Corsini & D. Wedding (Eds.), *Current psychotherapies* (8th ed., pp. 235–275). Belmont, CA: Brooks/Cole, Cengage.

Wolpe, J. (1958). *Psychotherapy by reciprocal inhibition.* Stanford, CA: Stanford University Press.

Wood, J. T. (2013). *Gendered lives: Communication, gender, and culture* (10th ed.). Boston, MA: Wadsworth.

Woolams, S., & Brown, M. (1979). *TA: The total handbook of transactional analysis.* Englewood Cliffs, NJ: Prentice Hall.

Young, M. E. (2013). *Learning the art of helping* (5th ed.). Upper Saddle River, NJ: Pearson.

Younggren, J. N., & Gottlieb, M. C. (2008). Termination and abandonment: History, risk, and risk management. *Professional Psychology, 39,* 498–504.

Zimering, R., Munroe, J., & Gulliver, S. B. (2003). Secondary traumatization in mental health providers. *Psychiatric Times, 20*(4), 43–47.

Zur, O., Williams, M., Lehavot, K., & Knapp, S. (2009). Psychotherapist self-disclosure and transparency in the Internet age. *Professional Psychology, 40,* 22–30.

INDEX

Note: Entries for tables are followed by "*t*".